Mid-South

Garden Guide

The Essential Reference Tool For Every Gardener

FOR THE BEAUTY OF THE EARTH

BY

Dr. Carolyn M. Kittle
Memphis Garden Club

7TH EDITION

PUBLISHED BY MEMPHIS GARDEN CLUB
MEMBER OF THE GARDEN CLUB OF AMERICA
MEMPHIS, TENNESSEE
2007

MEMPHIS GARDEN CLUB

ORGANIZED 1921

THE GARDEN CLUB OF AMERICA MEMBER SINCE 1925

Since its establishment, Memphis Garden Club has adhered closely to its purpose which is: to advance and encourage the knowledge and practice of horticulture; to promote an active interest in flower arranging and in the design and development of gardens; to aid in conservation of trees, native plants and wildflowers; to aid and carry on scientific and educational activities in these areas; to cooperate in civic improvements; and to further the projects of The Garden Club of America.

MEMPHIS GARDEN CLUB
C/O THE DIXON GALLERY AND GARDENS
4339 PARK AVENUE
MEMPHIS, TENNESSEE 38117
WWW.MEMPHISGARDENCLUB.ORG
901-312-1259

Memphis Garden Club is a non-profit organization. Proceeds from the sale of this book are used to support community gardening projects. **Additional copies may be ordered at www.memphisgardenclub.org.**

MEMPHIS GARDEN CLUB

DEDICATES

THE SEVENTH EDITION OF
MID-SOUTH GARDEN GUIDE TO

DR. CAROLYN M. KITTLE

In acknowledgement of her vast and profound knowledge of horticulture, gardening, science, and computer skills, and in appreciation of her countless hours researching, writing, revising, editing, indexing, and preparing for publication this reference compendium of Mid-South plants and gardening.

AND APPRECIATES

BUFF ADAMS (MRS. THOMAS C., JR.)
MS. DABNEY COORS
GWIN ERB (MRS. FARGASON)
PEGGY PETERS (MRS. HAGEN H.)
CAROLYN ROGERS (MRS. ROBERT M.)

WHOSE SUPPORT AND COMMITMENT NEVER WITHERED.

ISBN 978-0-9792271-0-3

First Edition	1954
Second Edition	1958
Revised Edition	1968
Revised Fourth Edition	1972
Fifth Edition	1975
Sixth Edition Completely Revised	
First Printing	1984
Second Printing	1986
Third Printing	1988
Fourth Printing	1992
Fifth Printing	1996
Seventh Edition Completely Revised	
First Printing	2007

Front cover photo features a Magnolia hybrid blossom (M. liliiflora x M. stellata). Photograph by Newton Reed at The Dixon Gallery and Gardens, Memphis, TN.

Back cover photo features Memphis Garden Club member. Photograph by Barbara Prest (Mrs. William M.).

TOOF COMMERCIAL PRINTING
670 South Cooper Street
Memphis, Tennessee 38104

ACKNOWLEDGEMENTS

GARDEN GUIDE COMMITTEE

Editor... Dr. Carolyn M. Kittle

Assistant Editor .... Peggy Peters (Mrs. Hagen H.)

Assistant Editor .... Buff Adams (Mrs. Thomas C., Jr.)

Assistant Editor .... Ms. Dabney Coors

Business Manager .... Carolyn Rogers (Mrs. Robert M.)

Assistant Editor .... Gwin Erb (Mrs. Fargason)

Executive Board.................................... Judith Mitchener (Mrs. Frank M., Jr.)

Joy Doggett (Mrs. John H., Jr.)

CONTRIBUTORS

Jeanne Arthur (Mrs. William T., Jr.)	Julia Hussey (Mrs. Edwin C.)	Rick Pudwell
Ginger Austin (Mrs. Albert M., III)	Veazey Krausnick (Mrs. E. Carl, Jr.)	Diane Reed (Mrs. Newton)
Cary Brown (Mrs. Keith W.)	Len Lawhon	Ms. Alice Rhodes
Ms. Ginny Bush	Susan Lawhon (Mrs. Len)	Ms. Kathy Shannon
Mike Chambers	Ellen LeBlond (Mrs. Daniel)	Tim Sykes
Jim Crowder	Booker T. Leigh	Plato Touliatos
Nancy Erb (Mrs. Guy T.)	Paul Little	Larry Tucker
Ms. Angie Gastel	Margaret Mallory (Mrs. W. B., III)	Dabney Turley
Ferd Heckle	Kenneth Mabry	Ms. Vador Vance
Edwin Hussey	Ms. Jill Maybry	Ms. Mary Wade

The *Mid-South Garden Guide*, 7th Edition would not be possible without the inspiration and expertise provided by the authors of the original volume. This committee wishes to thank those who led the way and in whose footsteps we follow.

Mrs. G. Blair Macdonald	Mrs. R. Dale Woodall
Mr. Edwin J. Toth	Mrs. Wm. Fitzgerald Fay
Mrs. Albert M. Austin, III	Mrs. E. Alan Catmur
Mrs. Richard D. Harwood	Mr. Elvin McDonald
Mrs. Helen Norfleet Panton	Mrs. Robert E. Norcross
Mrs. G. Carroll Todd	Mrs. James W. Moore
Mrs. Harry W. Wellford	Mrs. Ross M. Lynn
Mrs. Sidney Farnsworth, Jr.	Mrs. John A. Austin, Jr.
Mrs. Herbert Humphreys	

TABLE OF CONTENTS

XII

CONSIDERATIONS FOR LANDSCAPING

Nothing speaks to the heart as directly as a lovely garden. And nothing improves basic architecture as effectively as beautiful landscaping. A garden is a "work in progress", changing daily, seasonally, yearly, always evolving as plants mature, as we add new ones, and remove others.

It is a great pleasure to find, for example, that the unfamiliar plant you bought "just to see what it will do" blooms more beautifully than you had ever imagined. In time you may have enough of this treasure to pass along to other gardeners. Exchanging plants, experience, and growing tips with others is part of the fun.

Your own concepts of "beauty" change and evolve over time as well, and can be creatively expressed in your garden. Like Picasso, you too can have a "blue period".

The goal of the *Mid-South Garden Guide* is to present the reader with a selection of good plants that will definitely grow and thrive in this area, as well as practical gardening advice for keeping them beautiful and healthy. While this book is written for the Mid-South, the gardening advice is applicable to most other parts of the country; some adjustment might be necessary in plant selections. Before you begin your garden, you should understand a little about the climate of the Mid-South.

MID-SOUTH CLIMATE

The entire Mid-South, meaning West- and parts of Middle Tennessee, Northern Mississippi, and Eastern Arkansas, was a clay-soil-based, "old growth", hickory-oak forest a couple of hundred years ago when European explorers first

1

arrived. The Mid-South has a silt layer on the soil that originated upstream in the Mississippi, Arkansas, and Missouri Rivers, and has been carried downstream or wind-blown across the country. This top few inches of alluvial silt is called *loess*, and is rich in nutrients and easily amended in texture to create very good garden soil.

The Mid-South is fairly flat with elevations above sea level ranging from 180' to 450'. Elevation is an important factor in determining which plants are naturally adapted to an area, that is, which plants are "native".

We are located between 33½°N and 36½°N latitude, and it is latitude which determines the number of daylight hours and the duration of seasons, and consequently our growing conditions. We have short winters and long, hot, humid summers. While the climate in the Mid-South is mild, we face some challenges.

First, our winter temperatures range from 20°– 60°F, often with daily 20 – 35 degree fluctuations, and occasional dips to 0°F. Our first freeze is around the middle of November. Winters are fairly rainy. There is usually no snow cover, but there are occasional, very destructive ice storms. The ground doesn't freeze more than an inch or so, and doesn't stay frozen all winter, but it is enough to heave perennials out of their holes. Wide temperature fluctuations and continual freeze-thaw cycles, especially with winter wind, are hard on a plant. If you inspect your garden in late winter, you might find bare roots needing cover and heaved-up plants needing resetting. Mulch is a huge help in controlling this heaving.

Our spring starts coming in February in the sense that there is the occasional 60°– 65°F day. Plants begin to stir out of dormancy and get badly bitten by a 15°F night. It is usually safe to start planting on Good Friday and thereafter. Early spring bulbs, and many woodland perennials, shrubs, and under-story trees flower before the tall trees leaf out, so for a few weeks they enjoy full sun and ideal 50°– 70°F weather. As the heat intensifies in May, these plants need shade. Some woodland perennials, the "spring ephemerals", die back when it gets hot, to reappear next year.

It is not unusual in the summer for temperatures to remain in the 90°s with 70%–85% humidity and a heat index of 110° for weeks on end. Summers always include torrential thunderstorms and periods of drought. In mid-summer, ferns and foliage plants, hydrangeas and lilies, dominate the woodland. Many annuals, and a few perennials and vines, provide all-summer color in sunny sites.

September and October have cooler evening temperatures and many flowers get a second wind and re-bloom. Late-season bulbs and perennials, and fall-blooming camellias are at their peak now. Trees and shrubs start changing color in mid- to late-October. It is possible to have something blooming twelve months of the year in a Mid-South garden.

PLANT CHOICES

We tend to think of plant hardiness in terms of tolerating cold weather. The United States Department of Agriculture Plant Hardiness Zones, which range from 1 – 10, reflect the average minimum winter temperatures in 10° increments across

North America, and are the industry standard for discussing cold-hardiness. The Mid-South is in Zones 7a, 7b, and 8, which correspond to lows ranging from 0°F – 20°F. See color photos for the USDA Cold Hardiness Map. Winters in the Mid-South are cold enough to satisfy plants which require a chill period, and mild enough to leave hardy tropicals in the ground. So why are there so many plants, like most of those pictured in English cottage gardens, that don't do well here?

The real killers are the *high humidity* and *high night time temperatures,* often remaining above 80% humidity, with temperatures in the high 80°s to low 90°s even at night. The average year-round humidity in the Mid-South is 70%, but summer afternoon readings can be almost 90%, while spring and fall humidity is a more comfortable 50% – 60%.

Botanists know that heat is as hard on plants as cold, and that above 86°F plant tissues become stressed and cellular damage can occur. Even when well-watered, there are clear differences in the ability of plants to tolerate hot weather.

The American Horticulture Society collated temperature data and developed Heat Zones ranging from 1 – 10, which are based on the number of days a year that temperatures exceed 86°F. The Mid-South is in Heat Zones 7 & 8 which corresponds to 90 – 120 days that are hotter than 86°F. See color photos for A.H.S. Heat Zone Map.

Hot and humid conditions are also ideal for fungus, bacteria, and virus growth, and many plants either succumb to disease or look too shabby to merit garden space. The good news is that hybridizers have produced wonderful new disease- and pest-resistant cultivars of garden favorites that, in the past, could only be grown with lots of toxic sprays.

Most woodland plants are adapted to the Mid-South climate. Some prairie plants can adapt, but few alpine ones are able to. At low elevations, there is not a natural cooling-off at night like you find in mountainous areas (7°F cooler for every 1000' rise in elevation). Alpine plants (and many others) require cool evening temperatures to allow their metabolisms to slow down and "rest"; these plants burn up or "melt out" in the Mid-South. Nothing you can do will ever make delphinium, campanula, or mountain laurel (*Kalmia*) as happy here as they are in the Smoky Mountains or the Pacific Northwest. East Tennessee has much different growing conditions and is not properly considered the Mid-South.

Mid-South climate conditions *do* exist in some parts of the world such as Japan, Korea, Viet Nam, parts of China, Argentina, Mexico, and New Zealand, and plants from these similar regions do very well here. In fact some species that we think of as Southern, like azaleas (*Rhododendron*), peonies (*Paeonia*), and camellias, are originally from the Orient. Many exciting new garden plants, which are currently being commercially propagated through tissue culture, are the "finds" of plant explorers who visited these, and other, countries. While these plants may be unfamiliar, they are worth experimenting with; many are as easy to grow as nandina or hosta. A number are included in the *Flowers* and *Shrubs* chapters. The many reputable mail order and internet nurseries offer new and unusual plants if you can't find them locally.

A number of plants considered marginally hardy in Zone 7 can be grown successfully with careful placement. Examples include gardenia, japonica and sasanqua camellias, daphne, andromeda (*Pieris*), primrose (*Primula*), and ginger lilies (*Hedychium*). The heat reflected off a western wall, for example, may be just enough to create a Zone 8 microclimate for the few plants in that area. Backed by a fence and flanked by other shrubs, a semi-hardy plant might thrive, while it wouldn't if planted as an exposed "specimen". The plant hybridizers are steadily improving the cold-hardiness of many species, and the improved cultivars are mentioned in the main tables in *Shrubs* and *Flowers*.

TYPES OF SHADE DEFINED

"Shade" can vary from deep shade to mostly sun with many gradations. Before getting too far along in your garden design you should study the sun/ shade patterns in your yard. Watch at different times of day and different times of year to see which sun/ shade category describes your beds.

The following definitions provide some help. However, areas of "morning sun with afternoon shade" can be more forgiving to plants that prefer partial shade than "morning shade with afternoon sun". To expand the point further, "morning shade with afternoon sun" in more northern areas is less damaging than in deep southern areas where the afternoon sun is very hot. Many plants that require full sun in more northerly zones prefer some degree of shade here. Your own experience with particular plants will be the deciding factor.

Deep shade: Beneath evergreen trees and decks. This is usually also **dry shade**, as rain does not penetrate dense cover very well. This is the most difficult site to grow other plants.

Full shade: Beneath mature deciduous trees such as oaks and maples. This can also be **dry shade**, especially under maples, as their roots absorb most available water.

High, open shade: The shade beneath trees that have been limbed up. This is a very desirable type of shade.

Dappled or filtered shade: A continuous shifting pattern of shade, ideal for growing shade plants.

Light or part shade: Full shade for 2 – 3 hours during mid-day. Full sun plants may still do well in such a situation since they get about 5 – 6 hours of sun during the day.

Half shade: Shade for 4 – 5 hours with periods of full sun and periods of full shade. It is more sun than most shade plants can tolerate.

Northern exposure: Sites on the north side of walls, fences, or a solid row of trees. It is open to the sky, but gets no direct sun.

Morning sun: provides light without the hot baking of the afternoon sun. Both shade- and sun-loving plants may do well, depending on the total hours of sun.

Full sun: would be five or more hours of direct sun.

Effect of latitude: The length of the growing season, the number of daylight hours, and seasonal temperature fluctuations are all related to latitude. Plants that need sun in the north will need more shade in the south.

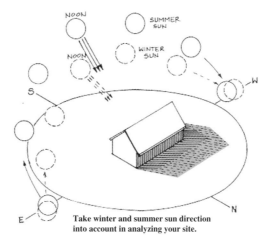

Take winter and summer sun direction into account in analyzing your site.

As you plan your garden, study the sun's movement and notice which beds get sun or shade at what time of day. The sun clocks across your yard from east to west in the southern sky. Using the above descriptions, and the cultivation needs of the plants under consideration, you should be able to site your plants successfully. Young plants are easily moved if your first spot was not to their liking.

NOMENCLATURE

The first word of a scientific name is the *Genus,* always written in capitalized italics. The second word is the *species*, in lowercase italics. 'Cultivar' names are written in capitalized plain text within apostrophes; common names are lowercase plain text. A cultivar is a "cultivated variety" of a particular species; by way of example, *Hydrangea macrophylla* 'All Summer Beauty' is a particular bigleaf hydrangea cultivar. 'Mr. Lincoln' is a particular hybrid tea rose cultivar.

The nomenclature for hybrid crosses between species of the same genus, which are man-made and not found in the wild, includes an "x" between the *Genus* and *species*. *Viburnum x pragense* (the Prague viburnum) is an inter-species cross between two other naturally occurring viburnums, *V. utile* and *V. rhytidophyllum*. By further example, crinum lilies have been crossed with amaryllis to produce

5

X Amarcrinum, which is a new inter-genus (or bigeneric) hybrid, written *X Genus.* The "x" is written but not pronounced.

Consulting the *Glossary* for botanical terms, and harkening back to your junior-high Latin, you can infer something about a plant from its name. *Japonica* means it is native to Japan; *hydra-* means it likes water; *microphylla* means "little leaf", and *henryii* means it was discovered in the wild and introduced to the Western world by a botanist named Henry. Although natives might have known the plant for centuries, Henry got to name it for the rest of the world, following the guidelines given in the "International Code of Botanical Nomenclature". He could also apply his name to a new cultivar he created.

When dealing with your nurseryman, you would be well advised to order by scientific name, as common names can be confusing. We have, for example, sweetflag, sweetshrub, sweetspire, sweetleaf, sweet box, sweet olive, summersweet, wintersweet, bittersweet, sweetbells, and Sweet William, all of which are very different plants and you may not get what you had in mind. [These are *Acorus, Calycanthus, Itea, Symplocos, Sarcococca, Osmanthus, Clethra, Chimonanthus, Celastrus, Leucothoe* and *Phlox,* respectively.]

Throughout this book, the main Tables of Plants for the Mid-South are arranged by "scientific name / common name" as is customary, while the various categorical lists are usually arranged by "common name/ scientific name". When plants are mentioned in the text, the scientific name is given in parentheses if it is different from the common name, to facilitate using the tables. When the common and scientific name is the same, it is given once.

BEGINNING YOUR GARDEN PLAN

The creation of a garden is an act of love, and you want to surround yourself with plants that give you pleasure in return for your care. As you design your garden, take photographs, consult libraries, and go on house and garden tours. This will help you decide what garden styles and plants you like best, and what you think will most enhance your architecture. You may want to enlist the help of a landscape architect or garden planner to create an overall long-range design, which may be executed over five to ten years, as budget permits. Be careful with those lush gardening catalogs, as you will want everything pictured.

The following points should be considered as you plan:

• Whether creating a new garden or renovating an old one, a *topographical survey* is extremely helpful. It is a way of determining the drainage of the entire property, which will affect any and all garden plans.

• Depending on your lot size, enthusiasm for gardening, and budget, the *plans* could include a garage and utility area, a terrace, deck or outdoor living area, grill area, formal beds, informal beds or cutting garden, lawn, play area for children, a water feature, potting shed, vegetable patch, compost bin, storage shed for equipment, or dog kennel.

6

- *Future plans* should be incorporated for eventual family and entertaining needs (i.e., swimming pool and bath house, tennis court, and greenhouse). Most of us do not have estates to landscape, and our plans may be much less ambitious.

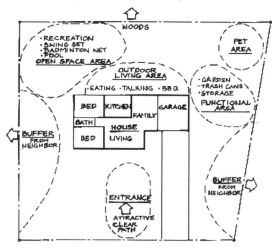

Plan showing location of the various
public, private, and utility areas.

- *Fencing* will determine the bounds of the property and will protect children and dogs. Plant shrubs in front of the fencing to define the background of your garden, offer privacy, serve as a windbreak, diminish street noise, and control erosion. See *Hedges* in the *Shrubs* chapter.

- Plan an *inviting entrance/ driveway* with proper off-street parking and car turnaround area. Design some entrance with handicapped accessibility in mind, as you or your parents may need it someday.

- Provide *access* to the terrace, deck, and back yard which does not go through the garage or kitchen. The day may come when you need a tree crane in your backyard after a storm, so plan for access if possible.

- An *automatic sprinkler system* is now a fairly affordable luxury and is much more convenient than manual irrigation. Have water faucets (hose bibs) installed in exterior walls and out in the yard; even if you do have a sprinkler system.

- *Foundation planting*: The front of the house foundation planting is often more restrained and formal to create nice curb appeal. Favorites for the front include evergreens like boxwood (*Buxus*), azaleas (*Rhododendron*), hollies (*Ilex*), laurels (*Prunus*), and arborvitae (*Thuja, Thujopsis*). Plant at least 3' away from the house to allow for dripline, pruning, and painting. In selecting foundation plants, do not use many deciduous plants which will be bare in winter, or shrubs which will grow too large for the space and dwarf your house or require constant pruning. See the Shrubs chapter for a table of *Shrubs by Size and Sun/ Shade Requirements*.

- Pay special attention to define the *entryway* and consider the *scale of your house*. Low or medium shrubs at the doorway make it inviting, and larger ones anchor the far corners of the house. If your home is one storey, you will probably want plants in the two to six foot range. If it is two stories, you could have ten foot or larger plants against big blank walls.

- Do not blot out *windows*, and make sure there is a pleasing view from each. Keep shrubs under windows in the 3' range. Some people plant a "sticker bush", such as holly (*Ilex*), mahonia, or barberry (*Berberis*), under the windows to thwart burglars. Others plant fragrant flowering shrubs near windows. Put a bird-feeding area near a window that is used frequently.

- There should be *trees shading outdoor living areas*, especially from the Western sun. Do not plant trees too close to the house; roots can damage the foundation and limbs can damage the roof.

- *Laying out beds*: To make a bed with straight edges, stretch a string between stakes and dig along the string. Lay a hose on the ground to outline curved beds. See *Flowers* for more on planning beds.

- Create *"garden rooms"* for interest. Have curves and bays in your shrub/ flower border, a vine-covered trellis behind a bench, a hedge wall to hide the tool shed, an artistic gate, a tall clump of non-invasive bamboo by the fishpond waterfall, a hot tub discreetly tucked among tall ginger lilies, a focal point statue or birdbath, etc. You create different areas by use of visual breaks or barriers that draw the visitor to see what's around the corner. Some area should evoke "secret garden" if possible. Trellises and hedge walls can be used to create shade where you want it. These "rooms", ironically, make a small space seem larger if it's done correctly.

- Have an open *lawn* for a look of spaciousness.

- *Low hedges* are quite useful for outlining a flower border or defining a walkway. French Parterre gardens are low hedges planted and pruned into formal geometric patterns.

- Make main *walkways* wide with comfortable steps and risers. A 4" – 7" riser to a 12" – 16" tread is considered typical. Use brick or concrete paving instead of gravel where high heels might be worn. Be sure you will be able to get a wheelbarrow around the paths.

- Consider your brick or siding when selecting vividly colored azaleas and crape myrtles so you don't create clashing *color combinations*.

- *Provide textural contrast*. While masses of one shrub are very attractive, you want to avoid the monotony of small oval leaves by having a variety of leaf sizes, shapes, and shades of green in the landscape plan. A garden of azalea (*Rhododendron*), boxwood (*Buxus*), and privet (*Ligustrum*), for example, would be more interesting with the addition of hydrangea, arborvitae (*Thuja*), anise (*Illicium*), mahonia, spiny holly (*Ilex*), or buckeye (*Aesculus*) to provide textural contrast.

- Provide *night lighting* for entertaining areas and pathways. There are many options in low-voltage or solar-powered lighting in addition to regular 110V fixtures. "Moonlighting" in trees is very lovely, but requires an electrician with a "cherry picker" lift to change light bulbs. Have outdoor "ground-fault interrupt circuit" (or GFIC) outlets installed to run power tools, lights, or fountains. Variegated plants and fragrant, light-colored flowers are most effective at night when strategically lit.

- *Remember that in 10 – 15 years everything will be different.* All plants will be larger, and there will be more shade. If the plants are well-chosen for their spot, the garden will be rather low maintenance.

- *Have fun with it.* There are no hard and fast rules and gardening can be a very creative artistic pursuit. Play with it on paper first. Make notes of what blooms when and in what color. You can select only plants with white flowers, or go for a rainbow palette, or have no (noticeable) flowers at all. In creating your garden you are free to express your particular vision of natural beauty. Move things around to create different compositions if you wish. You're bound to make a few mistakes, whether in meeting sun/ shade requirements or general aesthetics, and that's how we all learn what works in our garden.

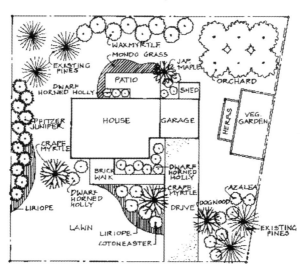

9

TYPES OF GARDENS

To begin your design plan, decide on the general type of garden, choose a color palette, and find plants that are suited to your sun exposure. Get the "bones" in first, meaning major trees, shrubs, and walkways. Then fill out the design with perennials, vines, bulbs, and annuals, using a variety of plant forms and foliage characteristics, as well as bloom times.

FORMAL GARDEN

Formal gardens have been popular for centuries. They beautifully enhance architecture, create a serene mood, and perfectly showcase statuary or fountains. Geometric shapes and straight lines are used to define the formal space in a garden, and this area is usually close to the house or created as a focal point to be viewed from the living areas. The pathways and bed-edging may be any combination of brick, limestone, bluestone, slate, pea gravel, and so on.

Plants used in formal gardens are usually evergreens that lend themselves to shearing or closely controlled shapes; topiary and espalier are right at home in this setting. Perennials are usually low-growing, shrubby, and handsome with or without flowers. Clipped germander, thyme, and lavender are frequently used to create a French parterre garden. Seasonal, long-blooming annuals are usually planted *en masse* in one color.

PLANTS FOR THE FORMAL GARDEN

SHRUBS FOR FORMAL GARDEN	
Arborvitae (*Thuja*)	Japanese Plum Yew (*Cephalotaxus*)
Box-leaf Euonymus (*Euonymus japonica* 'Microphylla')	Juniper (*Juniperus*)
Boxwood (*Buxus*)	Leyland Cypress (X *Cupressocyparis leylandii*)
Dwarf Conifers (many)	Soft-Touch Holly (*Ilex*)
Japanese & Korean Holly (*Ilex crenata*)	Yew (*Taxus*)
PERENNIALS FOR FORMAL GARDENS	
Germander (*Teucrium*)	Rosemary (*Rosmarinus*)
Lavender (*Lavandula*)	Thyme (*Thymus*)
VINES FOR FORMAL GARDENS	
Fig Vine (*Ficus pumila*)	Virginia Creeper (*Parthenocissus*)
Ivy (*Hedera*)	

ANNUALS FOR FORMAL GARDENS	
Begonia, fibrous (*Begonia*)	Impatiens (*Impatiens*)
Caladium (*Caladium*)	Fan Flower (*Scaveola*)

FRAGRANCE GARDEN

A fragrance garden can be enchanting, especially at night. The best fragrance flowers are listed below. While insignificant in size, the flowers on sweet box, sweet olive, and cleyera are pleasantly scented as well. Many white flowers are fragrant.

FRAGRANT FLOWERS

Clematis	Narcissus
Cleyera	Phlox
Daphne	Rose
Gardenia	Rosemary
Ginger Lily (*Hedychium*)	Sweet Box (*Sarcococca*)
Honeysuckle (*Lonicera*)	Sweet Olive (*Osmanthus*)
Jasmine	Sweet Peas
Lavender	Viburnum
Lily	Witch-hazel (*Hamamelis*)
Mock orange (*Philadelphus*)	

NATIVE PLANTS GARDEN

Native plants are obviously adapted to Mid-South growing conditions, but some have specific culture requirements, and are not adaptable to all gardens. For example, pitcher plant (*Sarracenia*) likes a sunny swamp, and lady's slipper orchid (*Cypripedium*) requires a certain soil fungus to grow happily.

In growing wildflowers it is important to create their native habitat, so attention must be paid to soil pH, leafmold, moisture, amount of sun, and so on. Some wildflowers will not bloom as handsomely in a rich, fertile soil, for they will go to foliage at the expense of flowers. Others adapt to good garden care and increase in size and beauty. Below are listed good native plants for shade and sun.

Improved hybrids of these wildflowers are now available which have longer bloom periods, better disease resistance, and so on. Some purists believe in retaining

11

these species in their original form, and there are unimproved wildflowers available as well, often as seeds.

NATIVES FOR THE SHADY GARDEN

Bloodroot (*Sanguinaria*)	Mayapple (*Podophyllum*)
Celandine poppy, Wood Poppy (*Stylophorum*)	Merrybells (*Uvularia*)
Columbine (*Aquilegia*)	Trillium
Foamflower (*Tiarella*)	Variegated Solomon's-seal (*Polygonatum*)
Indian Pink (*Spigelia*)	Virginia Bluebells (*Mertensia*)
Jack-in-the-pulpit (*Arisaema*)	Wild Blue Phlox (*Phlox divaricata*)
Louisiana Iris (*Iris*)	Wild Ginger (*Asarum*)

NATIVES FOR THE SUNNY GARDEN

Beard-tongue (*Penstemon*)	Joe-Pye weed (*Eupatorium maculatum*)
Bee Balm (*Monarda*)	Maiden Grass (*Miscanthus*)
Black-eyed Susan (*Rudbeckia*)	Rose (*Rosa*)
Blue Sage (*Salvia*)	Rose Verbena (*Glandularia canadensis*)
Bluestar (*Amsonia tabernaemontana*)	Salvia – many
Butterfly Weed (*Asclepias*)	Sedum
Coneflower (*Echinacea*)	Spiderflower (*Cleome*)
Coralbells (*Heuchera*)	Spiderwort (*Tradescantia*)
Evening Primrose (*Oenothera*)	Sunflower (*Helianthus*)
False Indigo (*Baptisia*)	Swamp Lily (*Crinum americanum*)
Fountain Grass (*Pennisetum*)	Swamp Rose Mallow (*Hibiscus moscheutos*)
Garden Phlox (*Phlox paniculata*)	Sweetflag (*Acorus americanus*)
Gayfeather (*Liatris*)	Virgin's Bower (*Clematis virginiana*)
Geranium, Cranesbill (*Geranium*)	Yarrow (*Achillea*)
Hardy Ageratum (*Eupatorium coelestinum*)	

SHADY OR WOODLAND GARDEN

The lowest-maintenance gardens are the ones closest to the natural habitat, and in the Mid-South this is usually *"shady woodland"*. There is a high canopy of shade trees under-planted with smaller trees, shrubs, ferns, perennials, bulbs, vines, and annuals.

Some of the most charming inhabitants of the shady garden are the "spring ephemerals" [mayapple (*Podophyllum*), bloodroot (*Sanguinaria*), toothwort (*Dentaria*), Virginia bluebells (*Mertensia*), dog-tooth violet (*Erythronium*), wake robin trillium (*Trillium*), bleeding-heart (*Dicentra*), etc.], which bloom early and die back in the heat of early summer. Later-emerging ferns and perennials are used to fill in the bare spots left by the ephemerals.

Ground cover plants can be used to prevent excessive evaporation and to cover bare areas in deeply shady spots. It is often a problem to keep fallen leaves from smothering ground covers. The ideal thing to do is remove fallen leaves from beds with a blower, shred them with a mower, and re-apply the shredded leaves as mulch, but this takes some effort. The natural mulch layer enriches the soil and keeps weeds from being a problem.

Most shade-loving plants need well-amended soil, rich in humus, leaf mold, and pine bark, with coarse sand added for drainage. (See *Garden Care–Soil Basics* and *–Amending the Soil* for more on shade gardening. See the *Ferns* chapter for hardy and tender, or houseplant, varieties. The main tables in the *Trees, Shrubs, Vines,* and *Flowers* chapters give many additional shade plants. See the Special Articles on hostas in *Flowers* and on azaleas, boxwood, camellias, and hydrangeas in *Shrubs. Container Plants* offers suggestions for shady outdoor pots.)

The list below is a good starting point for reliable shade plants.

TABLE 1. PLANTS FOR PARTIAL SHADE

ORNAMENTAL TREES FOR PARTIAL SHADE	
Dogwood (*Cornus*)	Redbud (*Cercis*)
Fringetree (*Chionanthus*)	Serviceberry (*Amelanchier*)
Silver-bell (*Halesia*)	Sourwood (*Oxydendrum*)
Japanese Maple (*Acer*)	Snowbell (*Styrax*)
Magnolia (Several spp.)	Tupelo (*Nyssa*, non-blooming)
Red Buckeye (*Aesculus*)	
BLOOMING BROAD-LEAVED EVERGREENS FOR PARTIAL SHADE	
Abelia	Laurel, English & 'Otto Luyken'

13

	(Prunus)
Agarista	Leucothoe
Andromeda *(Pieris)*	Loropetalum
Azaleas *(Rhododendron)*	Rhododendron (heat tolerant)
Camellias	Viburnum
Indian Hawthorn *(Rhaphiolepis)*	

FOLIAGE BROAD-LEAVED EVERGREENS FOR PARTIAL SHADE	
Anise *(Illicium)*	Holly *(Ilex)*
Aucuba	Japanese Plum Yew *(Cephalotaxus)*
Bamboo *(Bambusa, Fargesia, and Phyllostachys)*	Mahonia
Boxwood *(Buxus)*	Nandina
Cherry Laurel *(Prunus)*	Sweet Olive *(Osmanthus)*
Cleyera	Pittosporum
Euonymus (Shrub)	Poet's Laurel *(Danae)*
Fatsia	Sweet Box *(Sarcococca)*

DECIDUOUS BLOOMING SHRUBS FOR PARTIAL SHADE	
Chinese Indigo *(Indigofera kirilowii)*	*Magnolia stellata*
Deutzia	Mock orange *(Philadelphus)*
Forsythia	St.-John's-wort *(Hypericum)*
Fothergilla	Spirea *(Spiraea)*
Hydrangea	Sweetshrub *(Clethra)*
Kerria (Single and double)	Viburnum
Leatherwood *(Cyrilla)*	Wintersweet *(Chimonanthus)*

GROUND COVERS FOR PARTIAL SHADE	
Ajuga	Mondo grass *(Ophiopogon)*
Arborvitae Fern *(Selaginella)*	Pachysandra
Archangel, Spotted Nettle *(Lamium)*	Peacock Moss *(Selaginella)*
Cyclamen, hardy	Sedum stonecrop (many)

14

Epimedium	Strawberry begonia (*Saxifraga*)
Euonymus (creeping vine)	Sweet William (*Phlox*)
Ferns - many	Vinca Major
Foamflower (*Tiarella*)	Vinca Minor
Goutweed (*Aegopodium*)	Violets
Ivy (*Hedera*)	Wild Ginger (*Asarum*)
Lily-of-the-valley (*Convallaria*)	Yellow Archangel (*Lamiastrum*)
Liriope	

PERENNIALS FOR INTEREST AND COLOR FOR PARTIAL SHADE

Astilbe	Indian Pink (*Spigelia*)
Bear's Breeches (*Acanthus*)	Jack-in-the-Pulpit (*Arisaema*)
Bee Balm (*Monarda*)	Jacob's-ladder (*Polemonium*)
Begonia, Hardy	Leopard plant (*Ligularia*)
Bleeding-heart (*Dicentra*)	Lilies (*Lilium*)
Bletilla Orchids	Liriope
Bugloss (*Anchusa*)	Lungwort (*Pulmonaria*)
Calla lily 'Crowborough' (*Zantedeschia*)	Merrybells (*Uvularia*)
Columbine (*Aquilegia*)	Oxalis
Coralbells (*Heuchera*)	Phlox
Daylilies (*Hemerocallis*)	Saruma
Elephant's-ear (*Colocasia*)	Solomon's-seal (*Polygonatum*)
Ferns (many)	Taro
Foamflower (*Tiarella*)	Toad lily (*Tricyrtis*)
Forget-me-not (*Myosotis*)	Trillium
Helleborus	Virginia Bluebells (*Mertensia*)
Horsetail Reed (*Equisetum*)	Wood Poppy (*Stylophorum*)
Hosta	Yellow wax bells (*Kirengeshoma*)

15

ANNUALS FOR PARTIAL SHADE	
Begonias, fibrous	Fuchsia, heat-tolerant
Browallia	Impatiens
Caladium	Pansy (*Viola*)
Flowering Tobacco (*Nicotiana*)	Wishbone Flower (*Torenia*)

One example of a shade garden design could include the following:

A WHITE AND SILVER BORDER FOR PARTIAL SHADE
WITH ALL-YEAR BLOOM

[*ornamental trees*] dogwood (*Cornus*), fringetree (*Chionanthus*), serviceberry (*Amelanchier*)

[*spring-blooming shrubs*] oakleaf hydrangea, 'Glacier' azalea, Dodd's pieris, leatherwood (*Cyrilla*)

[*evergreen ground covers, ferns, perennials*] variegated pachysandra, autumn fern, tassel fern, helleborus, acanthus

[*spring perennials*] lily-of-the-valley, variegated Solomon's-seal, 'Niveum' epimedium, star-of-Bethlehem, deciduous ferns, 'Panda Face' wild ginger (*Asarum*), trillium, 'Beacon Silver' lamium, strawberry begonia

[*summer-blooming shrubs*] 'Sister Therese' mophead hydrangea, 'Fuji Waterfall' lacecap hydrangea, 'Hummingbird' clethra

[*early – mid-summer perennials*] white astilbe, 'Sum and Substance', 'Royal Standard', and 'Albomarginata' hostas, white Asiatic lily, 'Crowborough' calla lily

[*fall-blooming shrubs*] 'Snow Flurry' (and other white) camellias

[*fall perennials*] white martagon lily, white toad lily (*Tricyrtis hirta* 'Alba')

[*winter-blooming shrubs*] white japonica camellias, winter honeysuckle

[*annuals*] white caladiums, white fibrous begonias, or white impatiens

SUNNY GARDEN

A sunny border might be against the south or west side of the house, or be in an open area without a canopy of tall trees. It could include small trees, shrubs, perennials, bulbs, vines, and annuals. In time the trees and shrubs could turn this into a shade garden, at which point some plants might need to be rearranged and resited.

A COTTAGE GARDEN is a sunny border that contains no trees or large shrubs and therefore remains sunny. Sun-loving flowers vary in their growing requirements, so combine ones with similar soil fertility and water needs. Below are listed a few sun-loving plants for the Mid-South.

TABLE 2. PLANTS FOR SUN

ORNAMENTAL TREES FOR SUN	
Cherry and other fruit trees (*Prunus*)	Magnolia (*Magnolia*)
Crape myrtle (*Lagerstroemia*)	Maple (*Acer*)
Juniper (*Juniperus*)	Paulownia (*Paulownia*)
Leyland Cypress (*Cupressocyparis*)	Snowbell (*Styrax*)
Plum (*Prunus*)	Cryptomeria
BLOOMING BROAD-LEAVED EVERGREENS FOR SUN	
Abelia (*Abelia*)	Loropetalum (*Loropetalum*)
Azalea (*Rhododendron*)	Viburnum (*Viburnum*)
FOLIAGE BROAD-LEAVED EVERGREENS FOR SUN	
Arborvitae (*Thuja*)	Euonymus
Barberry (*Berberis*)	Holly (*Ilex*)
Cherry Laurel (*Prunus*)	Juniper (*Juniperus*)
Cleyera (*Cleyera*)	Privet (*Ligustrum*)
Eleagnus	Pyracantha
DECIDUOUS BLOOMING SHRUBS FOR SUN	
Beauty Berry (*Callicarpa*)	Forsythia (*Forsythia*)
Buckeye (*Aesculus*)	St.-John's-wort (*Hypericum*)
Bluebeard (*Caryopteris*)	Rose (*Rosa*) [some are evergreen]
Butterfly Bush (*Buddleia*)	Spirea (*Spiraea*)
Chaste Tree (*Vitex*)	Sweetshrub (*Calycanthus*)
Deutzia (*Deutzia*)	Weigela (*Weigela*)
GROUND COVERS FOR SUN	
Creeping juniper (*Juniperus*)	Plumbago, Leadwort (*Ceratostigma*)
Geranium, hardy	Sedum, stonecrop

Mondo grass (*Ophiopogon*)	Vinca minor (*Vinca*)
Phlox subulata	
PERENNIALS FOR INTEREST AND COLOR IN SUN	
Black-eyed Susan (*Rudbeckia*)	Lily (*Lilium*)
Coneflower (*Echinacea*)	Phlox
Coreopsis 'Zagreb' (*Coreopsis*)	Rosemary, 'Arp'
Daisy, 'Becky' (*Chrysanthemum*)	Sage (*Salvia*)
Daylily (*Hemerocallis*)	Salvia (*Salvia*)
Gaura (*Gaura*)	Sedum
Germander (*Teucrium*)	Thyme (*Thymus*)
Gladiolus	Verbena x 'Homestead Purple'
Iris	Veronica 'Georgia Blue'
ANNUALS FOR SUN	
Ageratum	Mexican Sage (*Salvia*)
Fan Flower (*Scaveola*)	Million Bells (*Calibrachoa*)
Mexican Heather (*Cuphea*)	Pentas
Geranium (*Pergolarium*)	Petunia
Hollyhock (*Alcea*)	Portulaca
Lantana (*Lantana*)	Salvia
Marigold	Zinnia

A sunny bed in two colors could be devised from these plants:

A YELLOW AND BLUE BORDER for SUN WITH ALL-YEAR BLOOM:

[*early-spring shrubs*]   forsythia, spicebush (*Lindera benzoin*)

[*evergreen groundcovers, herbs*]   germander, 'Arp' rosemary, thyme, vinca minor

[*early-spring perennials*]   crocus, Daffodil, scilla, tulip

[*mid- to late-spring perennials*]   blue hyacinth, mazus, amsonia, iris, yellow or blue baptisia

[*summer-blooming shrubs*]   buddleia, St.-John's-wort, yellow rose

18

[*summer perennials*] yellow lily, agapanthus, yellow canna, achillea, 'Goldsturm' black-eyed Susan (*Rudbeckia*), 'Zagreb' coreopsis, 'Indigo Spires' salvia, 'Blue on Blue' velvet sage, clematis vine

[*fall-blooming shrubs*] buddleia, bluebeard, chaste tree

[*late-summer to fall perennials*] aster, chrysanthemum, verbascum, veronica

[*annuals*] pansies, ageratum, 'Line' coleus, snapdragon, marigold

[*winter-blooming shrubs*] witch-hazel, yellow fragrant wintersweet (*Chimonanthus*)

[*winter-blooming bulbs*] winter aconite

While you would not want to use them all, you can see what a variety of plant sizes, shades of green, leaf textures, and bloom times you have to choose from using only this partial list of blue and yellow flowers for sun.

TROPICAL GARDEN

The Mid-South climate is suitable for growing quite a few hardy tropicals in the ground. Hybridizers have improved the cold-hardiness of some formerly Zone 10 species, to now be reliable in Zone 7 and even 6. Hardy tropicals from around the world are now commercially available, thanks to intrepid plant hunters and tissue culture. Browse the specialty catalogs for the latest cultivars. (See the articles in *Container Plants – Orchids* and *–Palms*; and also *Ferns* and *Flowers*)

The wonderful foliage gives you many design possibilities; they are especially nice around a swimming pool or water feature. Pots of tropical houseplants, like croton and zebra plant, can be summered outside in a shady spot.

Needle palm, with its fan-shaped foliage, is hardy to a surprising –10°F. *Bletilla* and *Calanthe* orchids are native to Japan and quite hardy in a woodland garden, despite their elfin delicacy.

A single *Hedychium* ginger lily looks a little like corn, but a stand of them is gorgeous. The rhizome produces strong 4' – 7' canes, topped with spectacular, (usually) fragrant flowers, late summer through fall. One plant will become 4' wide in a couple of seasons, so begin with about 4 or 5 plants to have a nice stand. Plant the rhizome horizontally, just below the surface, and fertilize several times during the growing season. *Hedychium* prefers part sun and loam, but tolerates heavy clay soil. Leave the dead brown foliage over winter to protect the rhizome from rotting.

The old-fashioned, common canna was a garish thing relegated to the back of the border, and subject to leaf-roller. Canna has been extensively hybridized, however, and is available in a wonderful variety of heights, flower colors, and foliage patterns; they are long-blooming, designer-friendly, and eye-catching. The flowers range from soft pastels to screaming-orange, and the foliage runs the gamut from solid gray to candy-striped magenta. Both cannas and callas can be grown in the ground or in a water garden.

19

Listed below are a few tropical-looking plants. Some are quite at home in temperate climates, and some are barely hardy, so site them accordingly.

HARDY TROPICALS FOR THE MID-SOUTH

Lily-of-the-Nile (*Agapanthus*) (Z 8)	Dwarf Palmetto (*Sabal minor*)
Angel's-trumpet (*Brugmansia* and *Datura*) (Z 8)	Elephant's-ear (*Colocasia, Alocasia, Taro*)
Aralia	Fatsia
Bamboo non-invasive (*Bambusa, Fargesia, Pleioblastus* and *Phyllostachys*)	Hardy Hibiscus
Banana Tree (*Musa basjoo*)	Ginger Lily (*Hedychium*)
Banana Shrub (*Michellia figo*)	Needle Palm (*Rhapidophyllum hystrix*)
Bletilla Orchid	*Petasites*
Calanthe Orchid	Purple Heart, Wandering Jew (*Setcresea pallida*)
Calla Lily	Saw Palmetto (*Serenoa repens*)
Canna	Split-leaf Philodendron (*Philodendron selloum*)
Chinese Windmill Palm (*Trachycarpus fortunei*)	Zingiber Ginger
Curcuma Ginger	

The bold foliage of tropicals does not blend well with every plant in the garden. A dramatically variegated elephant's-ear might look out of place with azalea or holly, but look great with fatsia or aucuba. Good companions for tropicals could include:

GOOD COMPANIONS FOR HARDY TROPICALS

Acanthus	Horsetail Reed (*Equisetum*)
Aspidistra	Leopard Plant (*Ligularia*)
Aucuba	Mimosa
Autumn Clematis	Nandina
Ferns	Toad Lily (*Tricyrtis*)

Hardy Begonia	Trumpet Vine
Honeysuckle (*Lonicera*)	Umbrella Magnolia

WATER GARDEN

Water features have become very popular in the last few years and can range from a birdbath to an elaborate, multi-level, waterfall lagoon. Water lends a Zen-like peacefulness and attracts wildlife to the garden. An expert can help with the design and installation; you are limited only by your imagination and budget.

OVERVIEW OF POND DESIGN

A reflecting pool or birdbath can be formed of concrete and painted with black epoxy paint to waterproof the interior. A pond or creekbed is usually formed using black polybutylene sheeting, which is cut to size and fit into an excavated hole. It is especially amenable to free-form, naturalistic shapes. Field stone or river rock coping around the edge helps secure the pond liner and gives a lovely natural backdrop for water plants.

As you are forming the pond, using either polybutylene sheeting or concrete, create a "shoulder" at the edge of the excavated hole to act as a shelf on which to set the submerged pots of water plants. Make it about a foot wide, and a foot below the anticipated water level. If your water feature is large, you may want two or three shoulders at different depths to allow "tiering" of your pots.

Circulate the water to re-oxygenate it, and prevent stagnation, by running a fountain or waterfall. Re-circulating water pumps, available at home centers, are designed to pump a certain number of gallons in a certain period of time. Calculate the number of gallons to be circulated as follows:

Measure (in feet) the length, width, and depth of your pond, and multiply these three numbers, L x W x $D = V$, to find the pond volume, V, in cubic feet. If your water feature is circular, find the volume by multiplying the area of the circle, (πr^2), by the depth, measured in feet. That is, πr^2 x $D = V$, where the value of π is 3.14, and r^2 is the radius squared, or half the diameter multiplied by itself.

Then, multiply your pond volume, V, in cubic feet, by 7.481 (or round to 7.5) gallons of water per cubic foot, which is a physical property of water, and which serves as a "unit conversion constant" that allows us to find the pond volume in units of gallons instead of cubic feet. That is, $V (ft^3)$ x 7.5 $(gal/ft^3) = V (gal)$. Units cancel, and you arrive at the number of gallons of water in the pond, which is what you need to know to purchase the correct pump.

Filter assemblies are also available, and should be incorporated in-line with the pump to strain out debris and silt particles. Some filters are designed to promote the growth of beneficial pond bacteria, which play a vital role in maintaining the

21

oxygen balance. Operate your pump on a ground-fault-interrupt circuit, so your fish are not injured in the event of an electrical short caused by a frayed wire, for example.

There is one caution regarding the polybutylene liners, and that is, *hard-to-find leaks.* Be very careful not to puncture the liner. When installing, seams should be glue-welded, and not merely overlapped. Set the re-circulating pump and tubing to the fountain-head on the surface of the rubber liner; never install tubing beneath the liner with the intention of bringing it up through a puncture hole. Dog toenails can create punctures. If your water level drops by a few inches in a day or two, you probably have a leak and should do some investigating.

FISH AND PLANTS

Have a few goldfish or minnows to eat mosquito larvae, but do not allow too much "fruitful multiplying" or your eco-system will get out of kilter. The rule of thumb is often quoted as "an inch of fish per gallon of water", but it is more correctly "an inch of fish per cubic foot of water, or per 7.5 gallons". Fish are happiest with a little room to move, even the "schoolers". Also, fish diseases are more common with over-crowding, and it's very sad to watch pond fish die.

With over-crowding, the water will not be able to provide enough oxygen for the fish to breathe, and the excrement-load that is not absorbed by water-plant roots, can lead to algal bloom. In the presence of sunlight, this excess "fertilizer" supports the growth of long strands of hair-like green algae, which spoils the look of your water garden. Add "oxygenator" plants and "root-filtering" plants, and remove a few fish, to restore the oxygen balance in your water. Occasional algal bloom is natural, but if the water is well-oxygenated, the pond will be clear and clean, as the balance of nature between water, plant, fish, air, and sun is established.

Hornwort and anachyris are "oxygenator" plants that tangle like seaweed just below the surface, and can either float freely or be rooted in pots. You need a few "oxygenators" if you plan to have fish, because these plants slowly bubble oxygen into the water through their leaves. Small fry and tadpoles find safety in the tangle of anachyris. Azolla and duckweed are tiny little plants that float on the surface, and are eaten by the fish.

Water hyacinth and water lettuce are free-floating, "root-filtering" plants. Water hyacinth is used in waste-water treatment facilities because its roots are so efficient at absorbing organic substances from water. It, therefore, helps keep your water clear. Japanese iris roots are also very good water purifiers.

Larger plants, referred to as "marginals", are used around the perimeter of the pond, usually in submerged plastic pots. *Always use unimproved clay,* and not woodland loam, for potting soil, as loam introduces additional organic matter which will consume pond oxygen as it decomposes. Your fish need this oxygen.

Some "marginals" can be planted directly in the muck at the bottom of the pond, but be aware that if the plant grows out-of-bounds, you will have to wade into the water to divide or remove it, working underwater. On the other hand, growing

22

"marginals" in pots controls their spread, and makes it easier to divide or re-pot them. This is where those "shoulders" come in handy, as it is relatively easy to remove a pot from the water to work on it, although it will be very heavy to lift.

The depth to set the pot depends on the nature of the particular water plant. Pitcher plant, pickerel weed, and marsh marigold want to be planted at, or just below, the water's surface. Lotus and water lilies have long leaf stems, and prefer their soil line be at least a foot below the water line.

Be careful about adding "city" water to the pond if you have fish, as it contains chlorine which can be harmful. The chlorine will dissipate in a few hours upon exposure to air, but drastic changes in aqueous environment can shock or kill your fish. They are especially sensitive to sudden changes in water temperature. Avoid total water changes, but rather, drain and re-add about one-third of the water at a time. If the water seems muddy, a handful of rock salt will help settle the silt.

The following is a list of water garden and pond plants. A few can be grown equally well in either garden soil or a bog.

WATER PLANTS

PLANT	USDA ZONE	PLANT	USDA ZONE
Arrow Arum (*Peltandra*)	4 – 9	Parrotfeather (*Myriophyllum*)	5 – 11
Arrowhead (*Sagittaria*)	5 – 11	Pitcher Plant (*Sarracenia*)	4 – 9
Arum (*Arum*)	4 – 8	Rush (*Juncus*)	4 – 9
Bitter Cress (*Cardamine*)	4 – 8	Rush (*Scirpus*)	3 – 9
Calla Lily (*Zantedeschia*)	7 – 10	Sedges (*Carex*)	3 – 9
Canadian Elodea (*Elodea*)	8 – 11	Sweetflag (*Acorus*)	4 – 11
Canna Lily(*Canna*)	7 – 11	Taro (*Colocasia*)	9 – 11
Cardinal Flower (*Lobelia*)	3 – 9	Water Celery, Water Parsley (*Oenanthe*)	5 – 11
Cattail (*Typha*)	3 – 11	Water Clover (*Marsilea*)	6 – 11
Fairy Moss (*Azolla*)	5 – 11	Water Hibiscus (*Hibiscus*)	5 – 11
Floating Heart (*Nymphoides*)	6 – 11	Water Hyacinth (*Eichhornia*)	8 – 11
Frogbit (*Hydrocharis*)	6 – 11	Water Lettuce (*Pistia*)	9 – 11
Garden Cress (*Lepidium*)	4 – 9	Water Lily – Hardy (*Nuphar*)	Varies
Horsetail Reed (*Equisetum*)	5 – 11	Water Lily – Tropical (*Nymphaea*)	10 – 11
Iris (*Iris*)	3 – 9	Water Lotus – hardy	4 – 11

PLANT	USDA ZONE	PLANT	USDA ZONE
		(*Nelumbo*)	
Marsh Marigold (*Caltha*)	6 – 11	Water Pennywort (*Hydrocotyle*)	7 – 11
Papyrus (*Cyperus*)	8 – 11	Watercress (*Nasturtium*)	4 – 8

VARIEGATED PLANTS – ACCENTS FOR THE GARDEN

Variegate literally means to diversify the appearance with various colors. Green foliage can be variegated with streaks, stripes, or spots of other colors or the foliage can be altogether non-green. White, gray, silver, yellow, chartreuse, gold, amber, pink, red, purple, bronze, maroon, black, and blue are all in the palette. This is an area in which the plant hybridizers have hit their stride. There are many gorgeous variegated plants available now ranging from ground covers to shade trees. Hundreds are available through catalogs, but local nurseries carry some of the best offerings.

White and green caladiums and variegated hydrangeas brighten up shady areas. The bright chartreuse of sweet potato vine stands out nicely against the deeper greens of the garden. Red-backed foliage, like hardy begonia, catches the light in a wonderful way. Yellow spots on aucuba and leopard plant give the effect of dappled sunlight. The bold vertical stroke of purple-black elephant's-ear will stop them in their tracks.

Variegated foliage adds color and interest with or without flowers, but there are a few cautions. Low-growing purple or bronze foliage, of heuchera or 'Gin' begonia for example, is quite beautiful, but it can "disappear" against a mulch background. Consider putting silver companion plants with the purple to help them stand out, or plant in containers.

In some instances, all-over veining in gray or yellow can give the appearance in the garden that the plant is ailing. While it is a hybridizer's triumph, "anemia" may not wear well over time. However, with the proper companions, all-over yellow or gray veining can be extremely pretty. It's all in how you put things together with variegation.

The garden can easily become chaotic if you use too many bold and diverse plants. But well-chosen touches of color and pattern give welcome relief from the monotony of medium green. Further, many excellent variegated plants are very subtle and quite easy to work into your design. The following list gives a few good choices in variegated plants.

VARIEGATED PLANTS

Artemisia	Japanese Silver Grass (*Miscanthus*)
Arum	Leopard Plant (*Ligularia*)
Aucuba	Liriope
Beauty berry (*Callicarpa*)	Lungwort (*Pulmonaria*)
Begonia (all types)	'Mariesii' Variegated Hydrangea
Caladium	Pachysandra
Canna	Painter's Palette (*Tovara*)
Coleus	Persian shield (*Strobilanthes*)
Coralbells (*Heuchera*)	Trillium
Croton (*Codiaeum*)	Pittosporum
Daphne	Sedum
Dusty-miller (*Centaurea*)	Spirea (*Spiraea*)
Euonymus	Strawberry Begonia (*Saxifraga*)
Five-leaf Aralia (*Acanthopanax or Eleutherococcus*)	Sweet Potato Vine (*Ipomoea*)
Ginger, Wild (*Asarum*)	Kousa Dogwood (*Cornus*)
Ginger Lily (*Hedychium*)	Toad Lily (*Tricyrtis*)
Hosta	Wandering Jew (*Zebrina or Tradescantia*)
Ivy (*Hedera*)	Zebra Grass (*Miscanthus*)
Japanese Privet (*Ligustrum*)	Japanese Painted Fern (*Athyrium*)

Garden design begins with an overall plan taking into consideration the architecture, climate, and soil that one has to work with. The real fun is that there are few hard and fast rules, there are hundreds of good plants for the Mid-South, and you are free to create what's beautiful to you. In order to make anything grow well, however, you must have "good" soil.

GARDEN CARE

SOIL BASICS

SOIL ANALYSIS

The soil in this section of the country is mostly neutral *red clay* with a few inches of wind-borne delta silt, or *loess,* on the surface. It can easily be amended with humus, organic matter, and fertilizers to be highly productive.

Soil test kits may be purchased at most seed and garden stores, or information regarding soil testing may be obtained from agricultural extension services. If you have your soil analyzed, you will know your soil pH and which nutrients are deficient or in excess, and will be able to amend your beds accordingly. It is not essential that you do this testing, but it is a good idea.

DRAINAGE

Good drainage is essential for the long term success of a garden. While many plants like moist soil, very few will tolerate their feet staying wet all the time, especially in winter. Root growth will not penetrate into waterlogged areas (aquatic, marsh, and river bottom plants are exceptions). Therefore, if the fundamental drainage is not properly handled, waterlogged soil will cause the demise of many garden plants.

It is wise to get expert advice to find out what type of drainage is necessary for each individual garden, for there is no way for the average gardener to know whether or not all or any part of the land needs drainage. Be careful to consider the drainage around the house foundation in order to prevent rotting substructure. Many gardeners think that a sloping land is a guarantee of effective drainage and thus enjoy a false sense of security. A severe drainage problem may require the underground installation of agricultural tile or perforated black pipe (drainage pipes) to carry off

27

the excess water. Do not plant anything with a large root system (i.e., willows) near the tiling, as roots will clog drains.

What is Good Garden Soil?

It is a lesson born of harsh experience that without good soil, gardening will be a constant struggle. So it is important to do the front-end drudgery of bed preparation in order to have years of enjoyment from thriving, self-sufficient plants. Soil is generally evaluated on both *fertility* and *texture*. Fertility is a combination of essential nutrients and a pH that makes these nutrients available to the plants. Organic gardening methods have proven that if the soil is "good", plants will require very little spraying for pests and diseases, and we encourage this approach to gardening.

Plant Nutrients from the Soil

Plants are made of proteins, carbohydrates such as sugar, cellulose, and starch, and many other things. They make these complex molecules from a few simple starting materials. Through the wonderful planet-sustaining process called photosynthesis, the plant absorbs carbon dioxide from the air through its leaves, and water through its roots, and converts them into carbohydrates. Oxygen gas is given off through the leaves as a waste by-product of this reaction. The oxygen produced by forests world-wide is what makes earth habitable.

What we as gardeners need to concern ourselves with are the nutrients which *don't* come from air and rain, and which must be supplied by the soil. The three primary plant nutrients absorbed from the soil are nitrogen (N), phosphorus (P), and potassium (K). These are, not surprisingly, the main ingredients in fertilizers. See the *Fertilizer* section in this chapter for adding nutrients.

Nitrogen is largely responsible for healthy leaf and stem growth, and for the production of chlorophyll which imparts a deep green color. It is for plants what protein is for people. Atmospheric nitrogen is made available to plants by nitrogen-fixing bacteria in the soil which convert nitrogen gas into nitrates, a form plants can use. Thus, plants are able to partially satisfy their need for nitrate from the atmosphere. In order to look their best, however, they need a little more nitrate as provided by fertilizer. Interestingly, a few plants like legumes and clover are able to "fix" atmospheric nitrogen in their root systems, independent of the soil bacteria, and do not require additional nitrate from fertilizers.

Nitrates do not remain in the soil for long. They get used up by plants and by decaying matter in the soil. They are also water soluble and can wash out of the soil rather quickly. Even so, an excess of nitrogen will cause a lot of foliage growth at the expense of flowers and fruit, and can burn leaf tips and grass blades, turning them brown.

Phosphorus is very important for root growth, bloom, and fruit. Flowering bulbs and root crops can always use some phosphorous. That's why bone meal is often recommended as a soil amendment when planting bulbs. It also is crucial for producing flowers and you will sometimes see fertilizers with a high phosphorus content advertised as flower boosters. It is difficult to maintain phosphorus in soil balance, however, and, therefore, must be supplemented occasionally.

Potassium is needed for overall plant health, rather like vitamins in humans. It keeps the plants growing, promotes strong stems and roots, and aids their immune systems in warding off disease. Like nitrogen, potassium is water soluble and needs to be replenished from time to time.

Besides the three primary nutrients, a number of other soil elements are essential as *secondary and trace nutrients*: calcium, magnesium, sulfur, iron, zinc, molybdenum, copper, manganese, aluminum, selenium, etc. The secondary and trace nutrients are required in the life processes of the plant, much in the way we need iron for our blood, calcium for our bones, and copper for our joints. For the most part, these elements occur in the soil naturally in sufficient quantity to satisfy a plant's need for trace amounts. However, over the years a plant uses up the trace elements in its root zone and requires more. This is why you see very small amounts of odd metal salts on the label of a complete fertilizer.

A number of plant ailments that look like disease can actually be caused by trace metal deficiency (or toxicity). The experienced nurseryman you trade with is often willing to look at a sprig of a poorly performing plant and recommend the correct "food". Iron deficiency in evergreens (called "chlorosis"), for example, is manifested by anemic-looking, sickly yellow foliage, and is corrected by applying iron sulfate; soil acidification may also be necessary to insure that the available iron is in the chemical form a plant can use. Magnesium deficiency also results in yellowing leaves, and may be corrected with either Epsom Salt (magnesium sulfate) or dolomitic lime (magnesium carbonate/ calcium carbonate). See *Pests and Diseases–Identifying Problems of Garden Plants* for more.

As an off-beat aside, there is a weedy meadow plant called tansy which happens to absorb selenium from the soil in much larger than average quantities (for reasons known only to the plant). A little selenium is essential for both plant and animal health, but in any quantity, it is toxic to animals. Well, it seems that General Custer's horses were grazing in a tansy field in South Dakota, and took ill from "blind staggers", a debilitating livestock disease attributed to selenium poisoning. Perhaps the Sioux knew some herbal medicine and maneuvered Custer's cavalry to that field. While history often overlooks this detail, stating only that Custer was out-gunned and out-manned, the outcome of the Battle of Little Bighorn was possibly affected by a plant!

SOIL PH

A lot is made of soil pH. In layman's terms, pH is a measure of the soil acidity or alkalinity. The scale goes from 1.0 to 14.0, with 7.0 being neutral. The lower the numbers go from 7.0, the more acidic the soil. The higher they go above 7.0, the more alkaline. Tap water has a neutral pH of about 6.8. Soils in the Mid-

South might range from 5.3 to about 7.3, covering the whole acidic-to-alkaline range.

The reason we care about soil pH is that nutrients in the soil are only available to plants if the soil acidity is within a certain range. Outside of that pH range, the nutrients will still be present but will be in a chemical form the plant cannot assimilate. For many garden trees, shrubs, and flowers the soil should be slightly acidic to neutral; with a target pH of around 6.8. But that's not true for all plants. Azaleas, camellias, hollies, hydrangeas, blueberries, and pyracantha favor more acidic soils (pH 5.4 – 6.5), while clematis, peonies, and iris will thrive in more alkaline or even chalky soil (pH 6.7 – 7.2). The presence of moss usually suggests that the soil is acidic (pH lower than 6.8) and rather low in nutrients. (See below *Altering the Soil pH*)

Plant nutrition and soil chemistry are very complex subjects, but luckily you don't have to understand all that much to be a good gardener. Follow the simple soil amendment and fertilizing recommendations and watch your garden grow.

SOIL TEXTURE

Soil is composed of varying amounts of clay, sand, silt, and organic matter. Texture refers to the size of the soil particles and their tendency to stick together or cohesiveness. Sandy soils have very large particles which allow easy penetration of water, air, and plant roots. At the other end of the spectrum is clay. Clay particles are so small they pack together tightly and leave little room for water, air, roots, or a shovel blade. It can be very difficult to dig unimproved clay soil without a pickaxe!

An easy test for soil texture is to make a ball of damp garden soil. If it falls apart when you tap it, it's sandy. If it feels slippery and you can press it between your thumb and finger and make a ribbon, it's clay. Most soils are somewhere in-between.

What you are ideally going for is called a sandy loam. It should be almost black, easily workable with a trowel, porous enough to allow for air and water movement, and have a fine bread crumb like texture, or tilth, which usually occurs when there is plenty of organic matter in the soil. It is like a heavy version of houseplant potting soil.

Don't try to change your soil texture by adding sand to clay or vice versa. That is a recipe for cement. Some amendment recommendations for clay do include a portion of coarse sand to improve drainage, but always with the addition of much more organic matter. Although cinders, gravel or sand will lighten heavy clay, they have no water-holding capacity and little food value.

As you read the various plant culture requirements, you will see "ordinary soil" or "woodland" or "rich, moist, well-drained" or "sandy loam" or "rock garden". These are descriptions of the soil texture and fertility preferred by the plant. Plain clay is red and, while it has nutrients, it is too dense in texture for your garden and must be amended.

Ordinary or garden soil is red clay-loess with some sand and organic amendment, but is still rather heavy and water-retentive. It is grayish- or reddish-brown in color and has not been treated with much fertilizer. This soil packs hard in hot sun and requires light cultivation with a hoe so water can penetrate. If garden soil is very dry, a pickaxe may be required! Mulch eventually improves this type of soil by adding organic matter. Most prairie-type flowers, some vegetables, some shrubs, and most trees do well in ordinary soil.

Woodland soil is ordinary soil that has years' worth of decayed leaves on top, and is consequently referred to as "rich", "humusy", and "high in organic matter". The leaf mold, or humus, that forms is rich in microorganisms and greatly improves soil texture. When you till humus, leaf mold, pine bark chips, compost, dehydrated manure, or rotted sawdust into your ordinary soil, you are creating "woodland" soil. It will be very dark with an easier-to-work, small-clod texture, and yet be moisture retentive and a bit heavy. Woodland shrubs and trees, spring ephemerals, many shade perennials, and ferns like this type of soil.

This woodland soil with a little more sand or pine bark chips added for lightness and drainage is called sandy loam. It is rich, moist, well-drained soil and is excellent for many plants, in both sun and shade. It is dark, crumbly, full of worms, and a joy to work in.

Rock garden soil would be the sandy side of ordinary soil, with pebbles and rather low fertility and excellent drainage. You could also create a sandier version of loam for plants that like a "rich" but sandy soil.

SAND

Always use coarse builder's sand (or red sand) in the garden to lighten the soil and improve drainage. Children's play-box sand does not provide the coarse particle size you are looking for. Sand can provide some trace metal nutrients as well; see the *Nutrients* section below. Buy sand in bags or take empty garbage cans to a gravel company and buy it in bulk. Use several small containers as they get heavy very fast.

Perhaps even better than sand, is *granite grit* which provides coarse particles for improved drainage, and also supplements the soil with some trace minerals.

Some people omit sand altogether and rely on pine bark chips to lighten and aerate the soil, especially for woodland gardens.

ORGANIC MATTER

Organic matter is simply dead plant or animal material. There is always some in your soil but usually not enough for a plant's needs. Organic matter improves soil structure, aids in necessary microbial activity, attracts earthworms which are very beneficial for soil aeration, suppresses several soil-born diseases and holds its nutrients in slow-release form, allowing for availability throughout the growing season. It helps sandy soil by retaining water that would otherwise wash

31

away and it corrects clay soil by making it looser, so that air, water and roots can penetrate. Humus is nature's way of feeding the circle of life. There are many types of bulk organic matter which you can incorporate into your garden dirt as *soil amendments*. If you spread the bulk matter on the surface it is considered a *mulch or top dressing*.

- **Compost or humus** is the end product of the decomposition of organic matter, which includes such things as leaves, grass clippings, garden waste, kitchen scraps, hair, manure, and straw. [While kitchen scraps make fine compost, they can attract raccoons and rats.] Compost is not particularly high in essential nutrients, (N–P–K), and is considered a soil conditioner rather than a fertilizer. It lightens and aerates the soil, and stimulates microorganisms and healthy bacteria which are necessary for plant growth. You can never add too much compost to your soil. Use one spadeful to each square yard of surface; spread on the surface of an established bed and work in with a hoe. Rain and snow will help humus penetrate. If the soil is in particular need, humus can be spaded in between the plants with a sharpshooter. Humus decomposes further as it nourishes the plant, and consequently must be replaced every year or two. There are many methods of composting and many styles of composting bins, but all organic matter will eventually decompose, with or without our help, so there is not one best method. See the section to follow on *Making Compost*.

- **"Hu-More"**® and other alfalfa-based soil conditioners are similar to compost. May be purchased in bags from the nursery.

- **Dehydrated composted manure** may be purchased in bags from your nursery. Fresh manure can often be obtained from local farms and stables. Manure should be composted and decomposed until it turns dark, crumbly, and odorless. Fresh manure has too much ammonia in it and can burn your plants and offend your neighbors.

- **Peat moss** is cheap and works well to loosen the soil. It is also very dusty, so wet it first to make it easier to work with. Incorporate thoroughly into existing soil to prevent it "floating" to the top. It tends to crust over and repel water, so don't use as mulch. Peat moss decomposes to become acidic and is good for azalea soil amendment. Not as popular as it once was for amending.

- **Pine Bark Chips** are useful as both a mulch and soil amendment. The coarse particle size aids in aeration and drainage, and it decomposes to make the soil more acidic. An excellent and increasingly popular amendment. Available in several chip and nugget sizes; the small chips are best for amendment.

- **Grass clippings** and other debris may be worked directly into the garden bed to decompose slowly. During the grass clippings' decomposition process, soil nitrate will be consumed, and therefore your plants may be deprived of that nutrient. Once the decomposition is complete, the nitrate again becomes available as fertilizer. Be sure whatever you put down is free of weed seed and toxic chemical sprays.

- **Leaf mold**, a highly desirable amendment, may already be in your possession if you have an area which doesn't get raked in the fall. Leaf mold is the rich, dark, layer of old, decomposed, leaf matter beneath the loose, fallen leaves, and is very good to till into your beds. Avoid using the whole leaves; use the decayed ones instead. A mower works well to shred leaves.

MULCH

As mentioned, mulch is organic matter spread around plants on the soil surface. The purpose of mulching is to conserve moisture, insulate roots from heat and cold, discourage weeds, feed the soil, and improve general appearance of the beds. **A 1" – 2" layer of mulch should remain on all beds at all times**.

Shredded or chipped pine bark, shredded or chipped aged hardwood bark, leaf mold, pine needles, or shredded oak leaves make the best mulch. Bark mulches are available as nuggets of various sizes, chips, or shredded, and come in several earthy colors. Cypress mulch is gray and long-lasting. Cedar and Eucalyptus mulches both repel insects. While purely a matter of aesthetics, try to avoid the lurid orange "redwood" mulch seen in shopping mall landscapes.

The smaller nuggets decompose or wash away faster than the larger chunks, but they have the look of a natural woodland floor. Pine needles and shredded leaves also have a nice woodland feeling. Camellias and azaleas like pine needles or shredded oak leaf mulch; run your lawn mower back and forth over a pile of leaves and, voila!

Peat moss is not a good mulch as it will crust over, tending to smother the roots, and it sheds water. Never use woody materials or sticks as mulch. Avoid cotton boll hulls; they carry nut grass and weed seeds. Do not use fresh wood-chip mulches as they rob the soil of nitrogen as they are decomposing. The mulch should be fine to use if aged six months or longer. Beware of mulch from areas that are known for heavy termite infestations, especially the Formosan termite. This sort of "tainted" mulch is usually offered at a bargain price, probably in bulk, and can cause you a world of trouble.

Organic mulches gradually decompose and improve the soil's texture and food value, and are washed away in heavy rains. Consequently they must be replenished twice yearly. Apply mulch about an inch or so deep to the entire garden around April 1st and October 1st. Mulch is even more necessary in the summer to protect plants from the scorching heat than it is in the winter months. If only one mulching is used, the April mulch is the more important one.

If you wish, you may sprinkle a little manure, compost, bone meal or lime lightly around some or all of the plants for extra nourishment before mulching. Remove some of the old mulch before feeding and then replace with fresh mulch.

If you have a large area to mulch, it is convenient to have a truckload delivered and dumped in your driveway on a sheet of plastic. Use a wheelbarrow to carry mulch to various beds, and toss handfuls of it between the plants. Spread around evenly with your hand or rake, being sure to shake any off the foliage. For smaller areas it is more convenient to purchase bags of bark mulch at your nursery.

Don't let mulch build up too deeply around any tree or shrub, as it can smother the roots. A collar or ring of mulch can be formed about a foot out from the trunk at planting time to help hold water near the root ball, but don't let this layer get too deep.

Never let mulch pile up too deeply around your house foundation as it will hold moisture and rot your substructure. (See the *Winter Protection* section below)

MAKING COMPOST

Compost is odorless vegetable manure made by the decomposition of organic matter. It is an essential element in good gardening for it returns to the soil the same material used to feed the growing plants the previous year. If you haven't the space or energy to make compost, buy a good, bagged soil conditioner like Hu-More® instead.

Any organic material is a candidate for the compost heap. Leaves make up the main body of the compost, but grass clippings and faded blossoms are also good, as long as they are not diseased. Table scraps, eggshells, coffee grounds, anything, in fact, that goes in the disposal goes into compost, but be aware that food may attract raccoons and rats. Fireplace ashes, along with dog and human hair, are a welcome addition. Twigs and branches should not be used since it takes hard woody material too long to break down; do not use pressure-treated wood shavings or chips.

The simplest way to go about composting is to pile leaves in an out-of-the-way spot, give them an occasional turn to aerate them, and wait for them to decompose and turn into a rich, brown organic fertilizer known as "compost", or in this case "leaf mold". This method is no trouble and will require one or more years to complete the breakdown.

It is possible to speed up the process by the addition of other organic or chemical materials, such as a complete granular fertilizer like 6–10–10, cottonseed meal, blood meal, Milorganite®, and the most treasured of all, dehydrated or composted manure. The ideal way to do this is to sprinkle some or all of these additives alternately between layers of leaves and compost materials. For example, make a layer of compost material about 6" deep, sprinkle with dolomitic or calcitic lime and the additives, make another layer of leaves, and continue with another sprinkling of the various additives. Lime reduces acidity, but do not use slaked lime. Commercial additives can be bought at garden centers.

Turning the pile from time to time also speeds up the breakdown. Keep the pile damp. By layering as suggested above and turning a few times, the compost will be ready in three to four months. The use of a grinding machine still further advances the decaying time because the material is reduced to smaller particles.

To build a compost bin, set 4 posts firmly in the ground in a 5' square. The posts should stand 5' above ground. Stretch strong chicken wire or hardware cloth around three sides. The wire on the fourth side should be movable to allow leaves

34

and other material to be put in, and compost to be shoveled out. In the center of the square sink an iron pipe which has holes drilled in it. The pipe allows one to water the center of the pile and allows oxygen to penetrate the heart of the compost, partially eliminating the need for turning.

If building a bin is not feasible, there are many ready-made compost bins on the market that are satisfactory. For large gardens, a pair of bins made of loose concrete blocks is suggested. More compost can be made at a faster rate. Refer to the diagram for the process.

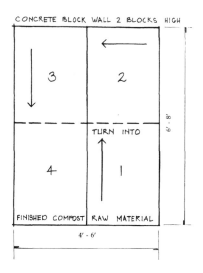

PLANTING AND MAINTAINING

AMENDING THE SOIL

The addition of organic matter and sand may be accomplished in several ways. If you are **starting from scratch** and creating a good-sized flower bed or shrub border in an open area, rent a tiller and make three full passes over the area to turn the dirt to a depth of about 10" – 12". Break up the big clods and chop out roots (if you are sure you won't be killing something you want to keep). Then add dehydrated manure by shaking out of the bag to cover the area about 1" deep. Shake coarse builder's sand (red sand) or granite grit evenly over the area to a depth of about 1". Do the same with Hu-More®, or compost, or pine bark chips to a depth of 1½" – 2". Sprinkle an even dusting of dolomitic lime (5 lbs. per 100 square feet) and

35

some bone meal over the area. Re-till to mix in the amendments and create a loose, clump-free, well-drained soil.

This is what we would call "*ordinary garden soil*" at this stage; you've added some organic matter and sand but in relatively conservative proportions, and the soil is probably a nice reddish gray-brown color but not black. This "ordinary garden soil" would be suitable for most trees, and plants such as forsythia, viburnum, spirea, althea, fothergilla, coreopsis, black-eyed Susan, coneflower, daisies, liatris, phlox, marigolds, zinnias, portulaca, and so on. It seems that many "prairie-type" full-sun plants like ordinary soil.

Depending on what you are growing, you may need a richer soil, so add more manure, cottonseed meal, pine bark chips, compost or Hu-More® and maybe more sand or granite grit and mix again. Evaluate to see if you have created "*sandy loam*"; take a bit of the soil and pinch it between your fingers. It should have a cake-crumb-like texture, and both stick together and fall apart like a heavy houseplant potting soil, and should be a dark blackish-brown color.

"*Loam*" or rich, moist, humusy, well-drained soil has a light, porous texture. "*Woodland*" soil contains as much organic matter as loam, but less sand so is heavier and a little more water-retentive. Loam is preferred by azaleas, camellias, hollies, hydrangeas, boxwood, roses, all bulbs and woodland plants, hostas, hellebores, foxgloves, epimediums, ferns, impatiens, begonias, anemones, and ground covers

If you are creating a new bed, consider making a **raised bed**. Almost all perennials and bulbs perform best with good drainage, especially in winter, and there is no easier way to insure this than with raised beds. Use railroad ties, 6" x 6" pressure treated beams, bricks, rocks, or cinderblocks as the retainer wall material; the design and construction may be as simple or complex as you desire. Fill the bed about 2/3 full of purchased "topsoil", which can be conveniently delivered to your home and dumped onto a plastic sheet as close to your new bed as possible. Then amend that lumpy topsoil with manure, pine bark chips, compost, sand, lime, and bone meal, as above, using a garden rake and shovel to mix and move. Turn the dirt thoroughly to blend, and break up clods. Leave several inches at the top of the bed to allow for mulch to be added over the years without spilling out.

If you are adding plants to an established garden under mature trees, which is often the case, then you simply **amend the planting hole**. This is very easy. You will need a trowel, conveniently sized bags of the above amendments, and a wheelbarrow to move this gear around the garden.

An invaluable tool is called *The Claw*®. It is a blessing for those who have bad backs or knees, or are not strong enough to be effective with a sharp-shooter shovel. The Claw® is also good for pulling out weed clumps and for aeration/ cultivation around existing plants. It is a lightweight, four-foot-long metal pole with a T-bar type handle in the shape of an "S" at the top, and five 6" long, curved tines at the bottom.

While standing over the desired spot, hold the S-handle and twist or rotate the claw back and forth in the dirt a few times and with very little effort you have a finely turned planting hole. You may need to trowel out the loosened dirt in order to claw deeper. Then add the various additives in the above-described proportions to your planting hole and claw it all together. If you do not have The Claw®, use a sharp-shooter shovel to turn the soil and a garden fork to chop in the additives. Make the amended hole wide and deep enough to accommodate the mature root system of the plant.

Soil amendment is rather like cooking, and you can vary the proportions of the few basic ingredients to create the growing environment your plant likes best. That is, you add a little more pine bark chips or sand if the plant wants really good drainage. In some cases you may want to put a ½" layer of sand or bark chips in the planting hole right under the roots to insure sharp drainage, or plant in a raised bed. You can add more manure, cottonseed meal, and compost if the plant likes rich soil or is a "heavy feeder". Rock garden plants require very sharp drainage and fairly low fertility, so you would use less manure and more sand, bark chips, and pebbles. If the results of your soil pH test indicate the need for alteration, you may acidify by adding garden sulfur or ammonium sulfate, in the package-prescribed amount, at the same time as the other soil amendments. The addition of lime to the planting hole was not so much for the purpose of neutralizing acidity as it was to add calcium and magnesium and improve soil condition.

PLANTING

The following applies to annuals, perennials, trees, and shrubs. Bulbs are covered in their own section in *Flowers,* and roses are covered in the *Shrubs – Roses* special article, as they have a few special requirements. Planting grass is discussed in *Lawns*.

When to Plant: In the spring, plant after the last frost date, usually around early- to mid-April. The old Southern tradition holds that anything planted on Good Friday is sure to grow. All annuals, summer- and fall-blooming bulbs, many perennials, and some shrubs are planted in spring.

For fall planting, wait until late September or October when the extreme heat is over. Most trees, many shrubs and perennials, and all spring-flowering bulbs are planted in fall.

ANNUALS AND PERENNIALS

Planting: When you are satisfied with the color and texture of the soil, you are ready to plant. Scoop out a hole a little larger than your plant's root ball. Carefully invert the plant, and tap or push it gently out of its pot or 6-pack, trying to retain as much of the potting soil as possible. Loosen the roots if they appear matted and pot-bound so they will be able to penetrate outward into the soil. This does not hurt the plant if you are gentle with the delicate roots. Make a little mound of soil in the center of your hole to support the roots, and allow the plant to be seated at the

37

same depth it was in the pot. Maybe allow the plant to sit a little higher than the surrounding ground in order to improve drainage and allow for settling. Spread the roots evenly over the mound and carefully backfill with good soil, tamping it down gently with your palm. Water thoroughly, and top with a light dressing of pine bark or shredded hardwood mulch. If you wish, you can sprinkle a little Osmocote® over the mulch, or stick a time-released fertilizer tablet in the ground near, but not touching, the plant roots.

Spacing: The spacing of the plants depends on their ultimate size, and is usually given on the plant tag. Allow room for the plants to breathe; densely packed foliage can foster diseases. You are trying to strike a balance between lush and full, versus overcrowded. When you plant a perennial that you know is going to get big in time, plant annuals or easily-transplanted perennials around it for a few years to cover the ground until it matures.

Transplanting: You may need to dig up and move flowers or shrubs for various reasons. One would be for artistic composition; that you want purple flowers in one bed, for example. Another reason might be the sun/ shade conditions are not right for the plant. Or maybe you want to divide for increase; spring bloomers are divided in fall, and summer or fall bloomers are divided in spring. (See *Propagation*, in this chapter, for details)

In any case, do not jab the shovel in at a sharp angle right at its stem. Imagine the root ball underground and try to dig out a big enough hunk of dirt that you disturb the roots as little as possible. Some bulbs and tap-root plants, like balloon flower, are difficult to transplant because they are so deep. Hellebores and peonies resent disturbance but will usually survive. When you replant, be sure to water well and often until the roots become re-established in their new soil. It is best to transplant shrubs during their dormant winter period.

TREES AND SHRUBS

Trees and shrubs which are bare-rooted or balled-in-burlap should be purchased and planted when they are dormant, from about October 15th to March 15th. It is too hot to plant anything from July through September. Be sure to water very often until the roots are established.

Never pick up trees by the trunk only; always support the ball. Depending on the size of the tree, you may want to have your nurseryman plant it for you as you probably don't own a tree dolly, and the root ball can weigh hundreds of pounds. Between purchasing and planting a tree it is very important to keep it moist and cool.

Planting: All trees and shrubs should be planted in a large hole with loose soil around the ball. Dig a hole a little deeper than the root ball and at least twice as wide. Mix the soil that has been removed with a few shovelfuls of ground pine bark, compost or soil conditioner, and sand (a little manure is optional); this mixture is called *backfill soil*. Trees usually do fine in ordinary garden soil and don't require rich loam. Some shrubs are also fine in ordinary soil such as the tough, cold-hardy, full-sun shrubs and many native species. Woodland or shade-loving shrubs

38

generally prefer a good humusy loam. Make your backfill soil according to what you are planting.

It used to be thought necessary to dig an enormous hole for a tree, two or three times the depth and width of the root ball, but that thinking has changed and our backs are grateful. Interestingly, many American gardening practices have been adopted from the British, who are trying to plant on a limestone island. As we have clay soil in the Mid-South, some of the learned practices, such as "double-digging", are not necessary.

Never plant a tree or shrub too deep. If planting in heavy clay, set the root ball in a shallower hole, and mound amended soil and mulch around the partially raised root ball. In gauging the depth, be sure to allow for settling of loose dirt. If the tree is a graft, be sure the graft union is at least 2" above soil level. If you "plant high", you need to check periodically that mulch and soil have not washed away leaving exposed roots; when this happens, simply pack some dirt and mulch back around the root ball. Dogwoods, azaleas, boxwoods, hydrangeas, and camellias like to be "planted high" with their crown elevated a couple of inches above surrounding grade and covered with mulch.

For *bare-rooted trees and shrubs*, mound backfill soil into a cone within the hole, and adjust the plant to the correct height. Carefully spread the roots around the cone, and fill with backfill dirt. Tamp the soil with your shovel or foot, being careful not to injure the roots. Then water well and mulch. Do not mix chemical fertilizer with backfill in the planting hole as this can injure the roots. Most trees and shrubs will grow well the first season without additional fertilizer.

For *balled and burlap trees and shrubs*, shovel enough soil mixture into the hole to raise the top of the ball at least 2" above the level of surrounding ground. Place the tree or shrub in the hole and pull burlap away from trunk, rolling it down below the soil level. It is not necessary to remove the burlap since it will rot within a year. Make a few slices in the sides and bottom to allow for easy root penetration. Add the backfill soil and pack it firmly; water the plant thoroughly, and mulch.

Container-grown trees and shrubs: Remove the plant from the container and inspect the roots. Some plants grown in containers, especially azaleas, become root bound very quickly, and if planted in this condition, will die within a year. Slice firmly through the ball in 3 to 5 places vertically with a sharp knife to loosen any roots that may be matted around the ball. Set the plant in the hole so it will be at the same level or a little higher than the surrounding ground, fill in with backfill soil, pack firmly, water thoroughly, and mulch.

If the tree is planted in an open area, make a 4" high rim or saucer with extra dirt at the perimeter of the hole. Fill with 1" or 2" of mulch to retain moisture and discourage weeds. A small barrier of wood or wire is also a protection from lawn mowers. Trees planted in woodland gardens need no levee as the leaves, mulch, and ground cover hold the moisture.

Staking: Do not stake the young tree unless it will not stand up without it. A young tree standing alone with its top free to move usually becomes a stronger tree and better able to withstand the elements. Large trees may need to be staked for support.

WATERING

You should water thoroughly at least once a week during the summer months, and also during dry spells in fall and winter. Ideally you would water 4" – 6" down to the root zone once a week, and then let the top inch of soil dry out before watering again. This develops more drought-tolerant roots. As soil fungus diseases are more concentrated on the soil surface, letting the soil dry out a bit helps kill them.

It is amazing how long the hose has to stay in one place for the water to permeate the soil. Make this test just once: water one area for thirty minutes, then dig down next to the bottom of the root of a plant and see whether or not the soil is moist at that level.

Your watering plan should result in evenly moist soil; not wet and soggy, not dry and compacted. And, definitely, not dry one week and wet the next. Shallow watering merely brings the roots to the surface and cakes the ground on top, which cuts off air from the roots. Flooding washes away plant food and mulch. Proper watering dissolves the elements in the soil and makes them available to the plants. Plants absorb their food in liquid form only. Mulch helps conserve moisture in the soil.

It is best to *water in the early morning* so foliage will dry in the morning sun. Do not water in the evening because fungus diseases thrive in the dark, hot, humid conditions of our summer nights. Contrary to belief, most plants do not suffer from being watered with the sun on them. There are some exceptions. In very hot weather, water must not touch the leaves of dogwood, boxwood, or ferns while the sun is on them or they will curl and dry up.

WATERING METHODS:

- **An automatic sprinkler system** is a tremendous convenience and has become fairly affordable. The whole garden will be irrigated on a regular basis according to your programmed zones, and you have only to be sure that all plants are being adequately covered. Your sprinkler service can add pipe extensions or change spray heads to keep pace with the growth of your plants. You can create "micro-climates" like boggy areas or very dry areas by altering your programmed times. The down side to automatic sprinkler systems is that they provide a mist of water and can encourage shallow root growth. They must be turned off in winter and restarted in spring.

- **Drip irrigation systems:** Require an initial investment of time and money, but once installed, are convenient and conserve water. You can set up a drip system to meet the needs of individual plants precisely and then alter it throughout the growing season as watering needs change. Caution in use of soil soakers or drip irrigation – some plants in the bed may get skipped entirely because water finds

40

little paths along which to run off. You must have adequate water pressure if you plan to have long runs of hose.

- **Manual irrigation:** Let hose run slowly for a long time. Hand watering delivers water directly to the plants, thus eliminating waste, but it takes time. Spot check to make sure you are delivering enough water, and be careful to give all areas of the garden adequate coverage. To soak ground, place nozzle of hose in empty flower pot on its side. Water will flow in and out and not make a hole in the ground.

- **Hose-End Sprinklers:** If you use oscillating sprinklers, elevate them above the tallest plants so the water streams are not blocked. A tall, tripod-mounted sprinkler called the Rain Bird® can throw water 30' and thereby cover a 60' diameter circle; adjustment clips allow you to cover a smaller arc of the circle for more localized watering. Small hose-end oscillating sprinklers are convenient as you can adjust the angle of spray to cover the area you want. Move the sprinkler every few hours to another location until you have watered everything in your garden; place sprinklers so their patterns overlap. Runoff indicates you need to water at a slower rate. Sprinklers have the disadvantage of wasting water by watering paths and other open spots in the garden. They also lose water to evaporation and wind drift. Because they wet the foliage, sprinklers also can promote the development of leaf diseases.

MONITOR YOUR GARDEN

Don't stick rigidly to a once a week schedule, but monitor your garden and consider recent weather and your particular plants. Hot, windy weather dries out the soil. And different plants in your garden will have different water requirements.

Larger plants consume more water than seedlings, but seedlings need more frequent watering. Germinating seeds and seedlings need to be kept uniformly moist without being washed away, so water them with a gentle spray every day or two.

Developing plants need to be watered deeply, but less often, to encourage deep root growth. Water to a depth of at least 6 inches and then let the surface inch or two dry out completely before watering again.

A newly planted tree must have water every ten days during the first two summers, especially during drought. Let the hose trickle slowly for an hour or two. Frequent shallow watering, such as from a sprinkler system, is not as helpful to new trees as occasional deep watering which promotes deep root growth. Maple trees are greedy and anything planted under one will need extra water.

For azaleas, a good watering once a week should be sufficient through June unless it is exceptionally hot and dry. In July and August more water is needed, as that is the period when the buds are developing, and it takes water to produce buds. During September and October, if dry weather prevails, water only enough to keep azaleas from wilting, so as not to promote new growth which might be damaged by an early freeze.

CAUTIONS IN WATERING

- Except when washing off foliage, do not stand and hold the hose to water. This does the plant more harm than good, as it promotes shallow root growth.

- Many plants are lost during warm, dry autumns because of watering neglect. They need to go into and through cold or freezing weather well watered. Check and water if needed during dry spells in winter.

- Be careful how you point your sprinkler at your house, because you can easily rot your window sills, doors, and wood siding. If wet mulch is allowed to get too deep against the foundation, it can cause rotten wood under the house which is very difficult to repair, so keep the mulch layer thin there.

- Be sure, however, that you have good drainage because root rot will kill any plant. Use good judgment in watering, as you certainly don't want to drown your plant, or waterlog the soil so that no air is able to reach the roots.

- The high concentration of chlorine in your pool water can have an adverse effect on your plants. Do not use back-flush water on your plants, especially not on fruits and vegetables.

CULTIVATION

Even after proper preparation, soil, overtime, packs again and needs some cultivation for aeration and proper penetration of water. A sharp shooter shovel is excellent for this, for it can be driven into the ground in the area between plants without damaging the roots. The Claw® may be used to stab the ground and create air holes, or a small hoe may be used to chop slits into the bed surface without damaging the roots. Doing this assures not only better aeration, but also a deeper penetration of humus and plant food.

This time-honored tradition of "turning the soil" in the spring has more merit in the sunny border where earth gets baked. In a shady woodland area, however, if you have lots of earthworms for aeration, your mulch layer always in place, and your garden evenly watered, then your dirt won't crust over or require turning. And turning the dirt brings us around to weeds.

WEEDS

Ralph Waldo Emerson said, "a weed is a plant whose virtues have not yet been discovered". Some invasive weeds, like wild violets, admittedly have some charm.

Thousands of weed seeds lie dormant in the soil and spring to life when we disturb the dirt. Weed seeds are also brought in by wind, rain, birds, and certain mulches. They are an undeniable fact of gardening life.

Most weeds have to be hand pulled, and they do need to be removed as they compete for both space and nutrients. "Methodically" is the best approach; take a bed at a time and weed it thoroughly. Next week do another. Take a plastic trash bag or empty bucket with you and clean up as you go. Use a Claw® or a garden fork to remove tough weeds. There can be a certain Zen-like peacefulness in pulling weeds, and this is the mantra you can repeat to yourself.

When you create a brand new bed, having done all the soil amending described above, you may (or may not) notice a great many weeds showing up. This is why some people prepare a bed in the fall to plant in the spring. The weed seeds have a chance to sprout and be pulled before you put in your flowers.

There are systemic herbicides that can be sprayed on walkways and hard-scape, but they kill earthworms and you do not want to do that, so don't use them in your beds.

Some people advocate laying a **sheet of black plastic** over the soil with holes cut out for the plants, and then mulching over the plastic. This may be a useful strategy for small areas or vegetable gardens. It is effective against weeds, but it deprives the soil of life; landscape cloth is a better choice. See *Vegetables* for a discussion of the planting method.

If plastic is used to pre-kill weeds in a bed you want to plant later, there is still a good chance new weed seeds will be awakened when you dig. If you spray a systemic herbicide and put down plastic, you have really done a number on your beneficial soil microorganisms and worms.

Some schools of thought hold that you want to disturb the soil and its weed seeds as little as possible when planting, and recommend digging individual planting holes instead of turning the entire bed.

If you are trying to create a meadow of naturalized wildflowers in an open, sunny, well-drained area, you especially want to avoid unearthing weed seeds. In such an effort, scrape off the existing grass and vegetation and discard. Disturb the soil no more than 1" deep, but chop the surface lightly with a hoe to accept seeds. Mix the wildflower seeds with sand to better broadcast over the area. Tamp in gently with the flat of the hoeblade, but do not really cover with dirt, and then water well with a light spray. Weeds are the bane of a wildflower meadow (feuding cousins), and this method gives your flowers a shot at choking out the weeds.

DEADHEADING

Deadheading refers to the practice of cutting off faded flowers before they go to seed. Many flowers will re-bloom if spent blossoms are removed, extending the flowering period considerably. The following table gives practical information about many garden perennials.

TABLE 3. DEADHEADING FOR RE-BLOOM

SCIENTIFIC NAME/ COMMON NAME	RE-BLOOM	SPECIAL INSTRUCTIONS
Alcea rosea **Hollyhock**	Yes	Pinch off spent flowers along the stem as they wilt; leave a few flowers to reseed; cut stem to basal foliage once all the flowers

43

SCIENTIFIC NAME/ COMMON NAME	RE-BLOOM	SPECIAL INSTRUCTIONS
		have finished; may re-bloom on short stems.
Aquilegia **Columbine**	Yes	Snip off spent flowers to side stems to keep columbines blooming; cut entire stem to the ground when finished; allow some seed heads to ripen to ensure replacement plants.
Astilbe spp. **Astilbe**	No	Deadheading won't stimulate more flowers so leave seed heads standing for late-season interest; when they look ratty, cut them to the ground.
Chelone lyonii **Turtlehead**	No	No need to deadhead because this late-blooming plant has seed pods that add winter interest; if seed heads are objectionable cut them back to healthy foliage.
Coreopsis verticillata **Threadleaf Coreopsis**	Yes	Use scissors or hedge clippers to shear plants to the ground in August to stimulate September and October re-bloom; deadheading also prevents reseeding.
Dianthus gratianopolitanus **Dianthus**	No	Some cultivars reseed, so deadhead as soon as the flowers fade unless you want it to spread. Remove spent stems but leave the clump of foliage.
Dicentra eximia **Bleeding-heart, Fringed**	Yes	Keep up with removing spent flower stems down to the foliage and this perennial can continue to bloom into fall; does not die back like *D. spectabilis*.
Digitalis spp. **Foxglove**	Yes	Pinch off individual flowers along the stem; remove stems to the basal rosette of leaves when most of the flowers are finished; may re-bloom later with smaller flowers. May reseed if not deadheaded.
Echinacea purpurea **Coneflower, Purple**	Yes	Re-blooms fine even without deadheading; cutting off early blooms to a side shoot keeps later flowers larger; leave a few seed heads for bird food unless reseeding is a problem.
Echinops ritro **Globe Thistle**	Yes	Cut spent flowers to a side branch to keep the plant flowering as long as possible; cut entire stems to basal foliage when finished;

SCIENTIFIC NAME/ COMMON NAME	RE-BLOOM	SPECIAL INSTRUCTIONS
		late re-bloom with smaller flowers.
Eupatorium spp. **Joe-Pye weed**	No	Will not re-flower if deadheaded; can reseed; leave spent flowers standing for later season and winter interest if you want; cut the stems to the ground in spring with pruning shears.
Gaillardia grandiflora **Blanket Flower**	Yes	Snip off the individual flowers a few inches below the seed head to prolong bloom; later cut stems to within 6" of the ground; stop deadheading in August.
Gaura lindheimeri **Gaura**	Yes	Flowers much of the summer without deadheading on stems that just keep branching; cut out stems that have bloomed to reduce reseeding; cutting encourages more branching.
Geranium spp. **Geranium, Hardy**	Yes	Hard to deadhead individual flowers, so cut tall cultivars to 2" – 3" after most of the flowers have finished; cut low spreaders back to 4" – 6"; some species re-bloom.
Geum hybrids **Geum**	No	Can flower much longer with deadheading; cut spent flowers back to budded side branches; later remove the entire stem to the low mound of foliage.
Helenium autumnale **Sneezeweed**	Yes	Snip spent flower heads only down to foliage to force side branches to develop and bloom; will continue to bloom until freezing weather if deadheaded.
Heliopsis helianthoides **Heliopsis Sunflower**	No	Don't cut off all the spent flowers – goldfinches are fond of the seeds; or tie a paper bag around stalk to catch seeds, and add them to bird feeder. Reseeds, so you might want to remove some of the seed heads. Will not re-bloom after deadheading.
Helleborus orientalis **Helleborus**	No	Pinch off spent flowers with fingers or small scissors to prevent reseeding; deadheading will not cause the plant to re-flower. Flower bracts are decorative for up to 6 months.
Hemerocallis hybrids **Daylily**	Yes	Snap off spent flowers as they wilt to keep the later flowers as large as possible; once

45

SCIENTIFIC NAME/ COMMON NAME	RE-BLOOM	SPECIAL INSTRUCTIONS
		the stem is finished, cut it to the ground. Some cultivars re-bloom, others do not.
Heuchera hybrids **Coralbells**	Yes	Cut flowering stems below the low mound of foliage as they finish; deadheading will extend the flowering and sometimes promote a smaller second bloom.
Hibiscus coccinia **Hibiscus, Hardy**	No	Pluck off spent flowers daily to keep the plant looking tidy and keep it flowering as large and as long as possible; this prevents re-seeding; cut dead stems down in spring.
Iris Hybrids **Iris, Bearded**	No	Pinch off spent flowers before they form seedpods; cut entire stem to the foliage fan after all flowers have faded to keep the plant looking neat and tidy.
Iris sibirica **Iris, Siberian**	No	Pinch or cut off flowers as they wither to keep the plant looking tidy and prevent seed formation; remove entire stem down into foliage when all flowers are finished.
Lavandula spp. **Lavender**	Yes	Harvest flowers with stems; cut entire plant back to healthy foliage to promote a second flowering; re-bloom is shorter than first; harvest late flowers, leaving foliage.
Liatris spicata **Spike Blazing-star**	Yes	Cut stems back to the top of the foliage after the flowers fade; smaller second flowers may sprout from the stem or near the ground; if not deadheaded, birds will eat the seeds.
Lilium hybrids **Lily**	No	Pinch or cut individual flowers as they fade; leave foliage until it yellows to supply food for the bulb; always try to leave as many leaves as possible. If not deadheaded, may naturalize. Will not re-bloom.
Lobelia cardinalis **Cardinal Flower**	yes	Cutting down spent spikes 2" – 3" from the ground will sometimes promote a small re-bloom. Short-lived, so allow a few seeds to ripen, or ground layer a stem or two.
Leucanthemum x superbum	Yes	Deadhead spent blooms to side shoots to keep this perennial blooming almost all

SCIENTIFIC NAME/ COMMON NAME	RE-BLOOM	SPECIAL INSTRUCTIONS
Shasta Daisy		summer; cut the spent stems down to 2" – 3" for smaller re-bloom.
Monarda didyma **Bee Balm**	No	Cut spent blooms back to side buds to prolong blooming; after it has finished flowering, cut stems down to 4" – 5" to promote mounds of clean, healthy foliage; rarely re-blooms.
Nepeta spp. **Catmint**	Yes	Cut stems down to 2" – 3" after flowering to keep plant looking neat; may or may not re-flower after deadheading, but will not reseed.
Paeonia spp. and hybrids **Peony**	No	Snip off spent flowers back to the first leaf to keep the plant looking tidy; leave as much foliage as possible to feed the plant.
Penstemon spp. **Penstemon**	No	Deadhead to side buds or branches to prolong flowering; cut stems down to the ground when finished blooming; usually will not re-bloom.
Phlox paniculata **Garden Phlox**	No	Snip off spent flower clusters; flowering side branches develop; deadhead to the ground when it's finished blooming; seedlings will revert to less desirable colors.
Platycodon grandiflorus **Balloon Flower**	Yes	Prolong bloom and keep the plants fresh by removing individual spent flowers; stems are tough – use small scissors and dip them in alcohol to clean the sticky sap. Reseeds.
Pulmonaria spp. **Lungwort**	No	Cut away flowering stems to tidy up the plant after they fall to the side, exposing the new mound of foliage in the center; will not re-bloom; can reseed; prickly stems – wear gloves.
Salvia spp. **Salvia**	Yes	Deadheading promotes a long bloom period; snip off spikes to side branches; cut stems back to the basal foliage to encourage a late-summer re-bloom.
Sedum spectabile **Sedum**	No	No need to deadhead; leave seed heads standing for winter interest and wildlife, or harvest them for dried arrangements; cut

SCIENTIFIC NAME/ COMMON NAME	RE-BLOOM	SPECIAL INSTRUCTIONS
		stems down in spring as new growth starts.
Solidago spp. **Goldenrod**	Yes	Deadhead first and largest flowering back to healthy foliage to promote smaller second flowering from side buds; cut all seed heads to prevent reseeding.
Tiarella spp. and hybrids **Foamflower**	Yes	Some will re-bloom after deadheading. Cut or pinch off entire stem down into the low mound of foliage to improve appearance.
Tradescantia **Spiderwort**	Yes	After all the buds in a cluster have finished, cut the stems back to a side shoot or leaf axil for more flowers; if the plant looks ratty, cut it back by half to encourage re-bloom.
Veronica spicata **Speedwell, Veronica**	Yes	To prolong the bloom, cut the spent flower spike back to side branches; once finished, cut entire stem down to the ground; may produce a small re-bloom later.

HYGIENE

Help prevent the spread of over-wintering diseases by disposing of infected foliage and stems in a sealed plastic garbage bag. Never put anything diseased in a mulch or compost pile. See *Pests and Diseases* for more information.

Many plants are through blooming long before frost and their flower stalks dry up naturally by late summer. Examples include foxglove, hosta, and helleborus. Feel free to remove these stems for a tidier garden and to prevent certain species from re-seeding excessively. If the plant material is healthy it may be added to the compost pile.

Perennial flowers "die back" for the year when the first freeze hits. Any perennials still blooming when the freeze comes, seem to survive winter better if the spent stems and foliage are left intact until spring. Some plants, like salvia, have hollow stems and it is best if winter rain is not allowed to freeze in the open stem. Similarly, semi-hardy rhizomes survive much better if their dried, brown, protective foliage is allowed to remain through the winter, as with hedychium ginger lilies. If this looks messy to you, keep in mind that birds relish the seeds in dried flower-heads and will appreciate your laziness.

WINTER PROTECTION

If the garden has adequate trees, let some of the fallen leaves stay on the beds, and they will be splendid winter mulch. Ideally, you will run the mower over a pile of leaves and use chopped leaves. The April mulch can be put directly over the leaves in shrub borders but not the flower borders. Shrubs are a bit tougher than flowers and are not as easily smothered. In spring, rake out excess leaves from flower borders and add them to your compost pile, or discard, and replace with pine bark mulch.

What about protecting the small evergreen perennials? Many perennials form a small green rosette of foliage for the winter, and some, like hellebores and autumn fern, are truly evergreen. The rosettes need just a few leaves lightly around because you don't want to rot the crown; at the same time, you want to protect the plant from dry, cold wind and drastic temperature fluctuations. Keep leaves close to the sides of evergreen perennials without covering them. Perennials which disappear completely, like hostas, may be loosely covered with a few leaves.

The problem is that in a wet winter, a thick layer of leaves traps and holds too much water around the crown of the plant, and the root zone may stay saturated with water if drainage is not adequate. Waterlogged soil excludes air and prevents oxygen from reaching the roots. The lack of air in the soil leads to rotting. This is responsible for killing more perennials than almost anything else, and is a good reason for using raised beds. Perennials may "heave" out of frozen ground and should be replanted and re-mulched as soon as you notice this.

At the same time, all plants, from trees to ground covers, like to go into winter well-watered. The roots of a plant can become dried out after a prolonged hot summer and dry fall, and a plant can better protect itself from the rigors of winter if it is properly hydrated. Clay soil stays moist for a long time in cold weather, so any watering would be infrequent.

This is really about all you have to do. With the soil prepared and enriched and mulched on a regular basis, plants have the necessary nutrients to grow and thrive without further intervention from you except for watering, weeding, and occasional applications of fertilizers. Earthworms will take up in your soil to further improve it. Birds will help with the insects. When the balance of nature is established in your garden, your plants' own immune system will fight off most diseases, and you will find that you don't have to work very hard to maintain your beds in good condition.

FERTILIZERS

METHODS OF USING FERTILIZER

When you want to add nutrients to your soil, you'll have a wide selection. A so-called *"complete" fertilizer* may be of either organic or inorganic origin, and contains the three primary plant nutrients (nitrogen, phosphorus, and potassium) as well as secondary and trace nutrients. There are three distinct approaches to fertilizing. *Organic Gardening* and *Combined Organic and Chemical* are the generally accepted methods.

- *Organic Gardening*: Only natural materials are used. It is a sure, safe, and long-lasting system.

- *Combined Organic and Chemical*: This method always includes the abundant use of humus, which is combined either with measured quantities of chemical fertilizers or with chemical and organic fertilizers.

- *The Dead End*: This is the use of inorganic chemical fertilizers only. Although it will seemingly work for a number of years, it leads to a salt build-up in the soil and does not replenish the organic matter necessary for beneficial soil microorganisms to thrive. *Never use chemical fertilizers over a period of time without the addition of humus and mulch.*

INORGANIC FERTILIZERS

Inorganic fertilizers are made in chemical plants from earth's mineral deposits, synthesized salts, and certain waste materials. It is usually cheaper than organic fertilizer and it acts more quickly. Inorganic fertilizers don't "amend" the soil, in the sense of improving its texture or stimulating beneficial microorganisms; they simply feed the plant. Some manufacturers change their fertilizer formulas to meet the needs of different areas.

Formulas always contain nitrogen (N), phosphorus (P), potassium (K), and may or may not contain secondary and trace elements [calcium (Ca), magnesium (Mg), sulfur (S), iron (Fe), copper (Cu), molybdenum (Mo), zinc (Zn), aluminum (Al), manganese (Mn), selenium (Se), etc.]. The proportions of the three major elements in fertilizers are always written on the package in the order N–P–K; for example, (6–10–4) contains 6 units of nitrogen by weight, 10 of phosphorus, and 4 of potassium. This would be considered a "flower-booster" fertilizer due to the large proportion of phosphorus, but would also be considered rather mild because the numbers are relatively small. (14–14–14) is a good all-purpose fertilizer for maintaining an established garden as it provides even amounts of the three major nutrients. (19–6–12) would be good for fertilizing young plants as the high nitrogen promotes foliage growth and the high potassium promotes root growth. All of them, except (0–20–20), contain nitrogen which can burn, and should never be put directly on the stalk or foliage, and should be watered in after applying.

Chemical fertilizers in ready-to-use liquid form, or as a powder to be dissolved in water, or as granules to be sprinkled and watered in, are sold under trade names such as Miracle-Gro®, Mir-Acid®, Rapid-Gro®, Ortho-Gro®, Vigoro®, Hi-Yield®, and many others. Most contain the trace elements. The nitrogen in these preparations is in a chemical form which makes them non-burning and, therefore, safe to dilute and spray directly on the plant. Foliar feeding, as this is called, reaches both the leaf and root. Time-released inorganic fertilizer pellets like Osmocote® (14–14–14) or (19–6–12), or Osmocote Plus® (15–9–12 plus trace elements) are very convenient to broadcast in beds and last about six months.

LIME

Lime is an inorganic additive which benefits all flowers, lawns, shrubs, and trees. No other amendment can influence the chemical, physical, and microbiological properties of the soil as much as lime.

It is used to neutralize soil acidity or raise the pH or "sweeten the soil" or make the soil more alkaline, all of which mean the same thing. Although certain plants require an acidic environment (a pH lower than 7), they still need calcium and magnesium for optimum growth. Dolomitic lime supplies these essential nutrients.

Lime also promotes soil microbial activity. Microbes help breakdown organic matter and certain types of slow-release fertilizers, and convert them into nutrients the plant can use. Additionally, lime improves the soil texture by reducing the cohesiveness of tightly-packed clay particles which improves air, water and root movement throughout the soil.

Lime is insoluble and reacts over time in moist soil to effect the changes in pH, textural improvement, microbe stimulation, and calcium and magnesium amendment. Apply any time of the year, but don't overdo it in any one application. Of the various kinds of lime on the market, *ground lime* and *hydrated lime* are used in gardening.

Ground lime is slow-acting, taking up to 6 months to work its magic, but is safe for use around existing plants. Ground lime is pulverized limestone bedrock, and the proportion of calcium and magnesium carbonates varies by quarry. The two primary types of ground lime are *calcitic* and *dolomitic*; both are pale gray powders and are also known as agricultural lime or "aglime". Calcitic lime is 70% – 100% calcium carbonate and no more than 3% magnesium carbonate. Dolomitic lime, on the other hand, is approximately 50% calcium carbonate and 46% magnesium carbonate. Dolomitic lime is generally easier to find, and adds both calcium and magnesium to your soil. Ground dolomitic lime is available in a convenient pellet form which is quite easy to broadcast, and not dusty like bagged lime. If you have been applying heavy doses of Epsom Salt (magnesium sulfate) to your beds, you might want to use calcitic lime to prevent excess soil magnesium build-up.

Hydrated lime or *slaked lime* or *builder's lime* is calcium hydroxide, and it is a white powder. It will act faster, changing the pH within 2 to 3 months, but can burn roots of existing plants. It is also caustic, so handle with gloves. Hydrated lime would be useful in building a new flower or vegetable bed in the fall that won't be planted until spring. This allows time for reaction to occur and creates a better environment for plants to grow.

Do not use burned lime or unslaked lime or quicklime (all are common names for calcium oxide); they will fry your plants.

SULFUR

Sulfur is an inorganic element from the earth, a yellow powder that is available in two forms for gardeners. *Garden sulfur* or *flowers of sulfur* is used to lower soil pH, and helps the plant make structural proteins. *Dusting sulfur* is a slightly different formulation that also has insecticidal/ fungicidal properties; it is useful for control of black spot and powdery mildew. It is low in toxicity and therefore safe to use. Dusting sulfur can burn the tender new foliage and buds of fruit trees, so use a different disease control for these trees.

ORGANIC FERTILIZERS

Organic fertilizers are made from once-living matter, plant or animal. They include bulk materials like compost, dehydrated manure, and pine bark mulch, as well as factory-made potions to be diluted and sprayed or sprinkled around the plants, such as fish emulsion, Milorganite®, and Green-Up®. As organic fertilizers are derived from once-living things, they contain all the non-volatile macronutrients and micronutrients, in varying states of decomposition, that the source vegetation/ animal had, and are therefore chemically complex and variable substances. Plants make an astonishing variety of interesting and medically useful compounds, and a given alkaloid, enzyme, steroid, or ester molecule might require a zinc or selenium atom, for example, in its structure. Generally speaking, organic fertilizers are more effective at supplying these esoteric nutrients than are inorganic ones.

Many organic fertilizers have become available in recent years. The fact that organic fertilizers are slower acting is actually a good thing, as they release their nutrients over a period of time. For an all-purpose fertilizer, start perhaps with the Espoma® or Nitron® mixtures, dehydrated manure, Milorganite®, or cottonseed meal. If you want to add specific nutrients, use products like fish emulsion or urea for nitrogen, bone meal for phosphorus, and wood ashes for potassium, or potash. Look at labels to see the relative proportion of nutrients. Table 4 gives a list of organic fertilizers and soil amendments. The percentage of N–P–K and rate of availability is given in brackets for a number of these additives.

TABLE 4. ORGANIC FERTILIZERS AND SOIL AMENDMENTS

A-35®: An enzyme soil conditioner and detoxification agent. Helps leach chemical toxins from the soil. It makes fertilizers more efficient. A-35® has the capacity to revitalize poor soils and make good soils better.

Alfalfa Meal: Contains a substance identified as "Triacontanol", a powerful plant growth regulator. Contains 11 vitamins, 6 minerals, plus 16 amino acids, co-enzymes, sugars, starches, proteins, and fiber.

Blood Meal: Provides a slow steady feeding of nitrogen. Blood meal is a great supplement for annuals and perennials. This product is also a great additive for compost piles and lawns. Said to deter rabbits, but can attract voles and dogs. [12–1.5–0.5, rapid]

Bone Meal: Use steamed product. It is an organic source of calcium and phosphorus, the elements that produce fruit and bloom. Bone meal can be safely used since if not needed by the plant, it merely remains in the soil. [1–11–0, slow]

BTN, Cotton Burr Compost: Cotton burr compost is natural fertilizer with a protein content of approximately 35%, making it an excellent food source for the beneficial microorganisms that help make soil nutrients available to plants, aerate the soil, and keep harmful organisms and diseases in check. Can have weed seeds in it.

Cottonseed Meal: Provides a slow steady feeding of phosphorus and nitrogen. Helps develop sturdy root systems and stimulates plant growth. After compost, this is the number one fertilizer. In addition to testing high in food value, it is safe to use on any plant. Buy cottonseed meal that has been processed mechanically, not chemically.

Compost: Already discussed under *Soil Basics – Organic Matter* and *Making Compost*. [1.5–0.5–1, slow]

Dehydrated Manure: Manure in which weed seeds have been killed. An excellent fertilizer. Can be bought in bags at garden stores under various trade names. Can be used as is.

Earthworm Castings: Rich in nitrogen, calcium, magnesium, potassium, and phosphorus, as well as many beneficial enzymes and bacteria. Worm castings will not burn; they improve aeration of the soil, and have great water-retention capabilities. This is the purest form of fertilizer or top-dressing, and is good for all plants in the garden.

Epsom Salts: A good source of magnesium ($MgSO_4$). Acid-loving plants can become deficient in magnesium or iron. Symptoms of both deficiencies are similar (yellowing leaves).

Espoma® Products: Mixture of all above. When you don't have time to pre-mix your own fertilizers or you would like to be sure you're getting everything your plant needs, try the products created by Espoma® or Nitron®.

Fish Emulsion: (5–1–1) An excellent nitrogen-rich, non-burning fertilizer for garden and houseplants. Fish meal is also good. [10–4–0, slow]

Green Sense® Lava Sand: Smaller material left from lava gravel manufacturing. Loosens clay soils, holds and releases moisture and makes it available to the plant when needed. Lava sand is a highly paramagnetic soil-amending material.

Greensand: An ocean mineral that has the analysis of 5% potash and 1% phosphorous and contains traces of 30 or more elements. Greensand can absorb and hold large quantities of water in the root feeding zone as well as stimulate microbes and loosen clay soil.

Green-up®: Contains 6.1% iron, 13% copper, 13% manganese, 13% zinc. Prevents yellowing, encourages vigorous, green growth.

Humate: Leonardite Shale, a mined deposit. It contains the richest of natural organic matter, composted over the millennia. Any thing that grows will benefit from applications of humate. It helps produce thicker greener and healthier foliage.

Hu-More®: Hu-more® also feeds the soil microbes and improves the texture, or tilth, of the dirt. Hu-more® is similar to alfalfa meal.

Leaf Mold: Surface soil of the forest; rich, crumbly, desirable, but expensive and scarce. Acid in reaction.

Manure – Chicken, Cow, Horse, Pig, or Sheep: Even more than for its importance as plant food and humus, herbivore manure is valued as the greatest possible source of beneficial soil bacteria. CAUTION: Fresh manure will burn plants. Because manure contains weed and grass seed, keep separate until well rotted and then add to the compost pile. Do not use with bulbs except as top dressing as it causes fungus and rot. Keep well away from plant stems. [Cow: 0.25–0.15–0.25, medium] [Horse: 0.3–0.15–0.5, medium] [Sheep: 0.6–0.33–0.75, medium] [Pig: 0.3–0.3–0.3, medium] [Chicken: 2–2–2, rapid]

Maxicrop® Seaweed: Improves germination, increases chlorophyll production, pre-conditions plants for stress. [1–0.5–9, rapid]

Michigan Peat: A domestic soil conditioner, dark brown and rich-looking made from sedge grass and reeds. Acid reaction in soil. [1.5–0.25–0.5, slow]

Milorganite®: A superb, non-burning product. It is sterilized sediment made from a waste-disposal plant. Do not use on vegetables. [5–(2 – 5)–2, medium]

Sea-grow Plus®: This is a blend of seaweed and fish emulsion. Sea-grow Plus® provides a balance between nitrogen, phosphorus, and potash. Sea-grow Plus® also provides plant hormones and micronutrients which accelerate growth, increase fruit and flower production, and intensify color. [2–1–2, medium]

Soft Rock Phosphate: Supplies phosphorus and calcium, and many trace elements. Phosphate is essential for photosynthesis and also works with nitrogen to increase the metabolism rate of the plant. [0–25–0, slow]

Soil Soup®: Soil Soup® will enhance the performance of chemical or organic fertilizers. This is because the beneficial microbes, bacteria, and protozoa in Soil Soup® make nutrients more available to the plant. Soil Soup® can remediate sterile and chemically-damaged soil. It repopulates the soil with microbes which aid in the uptake of nutrients by roots, and helps break down

55

thatch in the lawn. It is like Geritol® for microorganisms.

Sul-po-mag®: Contains 22% Sulfur, 22% Potash, and 11% Magnesium. Sulfur is required for the formation of certain amino acids. Potash (potassium) stimulates and promotes root growth, and increases plant vigor, stem strength, and resistance to many diseases. Magnesium is necessary in the formation of chlorophyll, and is essential for plant utilization of nitrogen and sulfur. This product does not increase the acidity of the soil.

Urea: Urea is derived from mammal urine and contains the highest concentration of nitrogen of any fertilizers. It is widely used in commercial farming operations. In granular form, it is broadcast and worked into the soil, rather than used as surface topdressing. Very soluble. When first applied, it increases soil alkalinity, but as the ammonia is converted to ammonium ions, the long-range effect is to acidify soil. Do not let urea come in contact with germinating seeds; keep it several inches away. [45–0–0, rapid]

Wood Ashes: Fireplace ashes are a good source of potassium, phosphorus, and calcium. They are alkaline in reaction and can cause salt build-up, so don't overuse. Best worked into the soil, but can be used as top-dressing if kept a few inches away from stems. [0–(1 – 2)–(3 – 7), rapid]

Suggested Schedule for Fertilizing the Garden

In using any fertilizer, be sure to follow directions. Beginners are inclined to apply plant food in astonishing proportions, and sometimes with disastrous results. This is true of both organic and inorganic materials. If you've had your soil tested, you'll know more precisely what nutrients your soil is lacking.

Be mindful of growing requirements of certain plants; you may apply soil-Ph-altering compounds at the same time as fertilizer if necessary. Grow bearded iris, maidenhair fern, peonies, lilacs, and clematis in a slightly alkaline soil, while Siberian and Japanese iris, azaleas, camellias, hollies, blueberries, and most woodland perennials like an acidic loam. Refer to the following section, *Altering the pH of Soil,* for details.

Azaleas and Camellias

Feed these shrubs twice a year with prepared azalea-camellia fertilizer available at garden stores; it is acidic in reaction and may be used on all *acid-loving plants.* If a dry form is used, scatter it on the surface of the ground, but do not scratch it in or the shallow roots may be damaged; water in well after applying. Fertilize azaleas immediately after blooming in the spring and again four to six weeks later. Fertilize camellias once in March and again in early June.

MOST OF THE GARDEN

Fertilize first in late winter, preferably February. Use a bulk top-dressing of compost, or well-rotted, dehydrated manure, or use a commercial organic fertilizer, such as cottonseed meal or Milorganite®. Or, a time-released, granular fertilizer such as Osmocote® may be sprinkled lightly over all the beds. Follow directions. *Fertilize again very lightly about July 1st* with a complete fertilizer and water in well after applying.

It is highly recommended that the entire garden be given a top-dressing of (0–20–20) in November to enter winter dormancy in good condition. *Never use a nitrogen-containing fertilizer this late in the year*, because you do not want to stimulate new foliage growth which will be damaged in a freeze.

Ambitious gardeners may supplement these main feedings with small amounts of an all-purpose fertilizer, or any of the above listed organic fertilizers, at monthly intervals during the entire growing season. Some experts advise very light fertilization every two weeks from spring until fall in order to maintain a constant supply of nutrients. These supplementary applications are optional.

Never fertilize when soil is dry or plant is in bad shape. Too much fertilizer will burn leaf tips. Also, the resultant buildup of salts from overuse of inorganic fertilizers can damage plant roots. If time or temperature prevents such careful attention to detail, then March and November are good times to fertilize.

TREES

Trees should be fed regularly. Fertilize during January, February, or March. There are many ways to fertilize. Spread the fertilizer directly on the ground or use a crowbar to form holes 8" deep, making a circle below the tips of the branches, and fill with fertilizer.

Cottonseed meal and Milorganite® are excellent because they release nutrients slowly and will not burn the roots. A good chemical fertilizer is 10–8–6. Slow release lawn fertilizers are also effective. Spread it in a circle at the drip line or on the outer edge of the hole in which the tree was planted. There are special fertilizer sticks that can be hammered into the ground. Nutrients can also be squirted into the soil with an injector, called a needle probe or root feeder, which is attached to a garden hose. Foliar feeding (spraying nutrients on the leaves) works quickly and often produces dramatic results. This method is highly recommended in combination with punch-hole or injector feeding for trees that are seriously undernourished and for trees whose roots spread under paving and cannot be reached otherwise.

57

ALTERING THE PH OF SOIL

A quick estimate of your soil's health can be made by looking at your plants. If they are thriving, don't fix what isn't broken. If your plants are languishing, yellowing or otherwise looking sickly or you feel like you are forever feeding them, it would be worth testing your soil. Your Agricultural Extension Service probably provides this service for a nominal fee. Many nurseries also test soil. Garden centers sell inexpensive pH kits which allow you to test your own soil. Keep in mind that it takes time to alter soil pH and your soil will tend to revert to its old pH over time, necessitating repeated treatment.

WHAT EFFECT DO THE VARIOUS SOIL AMENDMENTS HAVE ON PH?

Organic matter will lower the pH slightly. Compost is fairly neutral, but peat moss, sawdust, conifer needles, and bark chips will lower the pH more noticeably.

Sulfate salts will generally lower soil pH, but they are used sparingly to correct nutrient deficiencies when plants develop chlorosis and other ailments, rather than being applied in great quantity to the whole bed. Ammonium sulfate is a common source of nitrogen in fertilizer mixes, and is acidic in reaction. Iron sulfate (Ironite®) and chelated iron both lower soil pH, and also improve color and vigor in plants showing iron deficiency (yellowing leaves with dark green veins). Follow directions – too much will burn. "Chelated" simply means that the iron atom is "caged" inside an organic molecule, and this strategy assures delivery of iron in the chemical form a plant can use. Aluminum sulfate works quickly to reduce pH, but overuse can cause soil toxicity; it is useful for turning hydrangeas from pink to blue. Magnesium sulfate (Epsom Salt) will reduce pH, and improves the green color of leaves. Potassium sulfate is neutral.

Garden sulfur is the most economical and widely used product for reducing a high pH. Garden sulfur has the added benefit of helping build plant proteins. It is available in either powdered or granular form, and is also known as *flowers of sulfur*.

As you can see, many products we add to our soils as nutrients have the added effect of reducing pH. This, plus the naturally acidic nature of our local soils, is why we rarely have a problem with too-high pH, other than in the immediate vicinity of masonry foundations and walls.

LOWERING PH – INCREASING SOIL ACIDITY:

Plants preferring *acidic* soil include azaleas, camellias, gardenias, hollies, blueberries, and pyracantha. Broad-leaved evergreens, most ground covers, some ferns, and small perennials of the woodland garden prefer a soil somewhat on the acidic side. To make the soil more acidic (lower the pH) use garden sulfur according to package directions. The following chart gives the number of pounds of sulfur needed to lower the pH to 6.5 in 100 sq. ft. (10' x 10' area) of various types of soil.

TO LOWER PH – MAKE SOIL MORE ACIDIC

Pounds of Garden Sulfur per 100 sq. ft. to lower pH to 6.5 in various types of soil			
Current pH	Sandy	Woodland or Loam	Ordinary or Clay
7.0	0.5	1.0	1.4
7.5	1.0	2.0	2.7
8.0	1.7	3.4	4.7
8.5	3.0	5.0	6.0

RAISING PH – INCREASING SOIL ALKALINITY:

Plants preferring an *alkaline* soil are bluegrass, all members of the bean and pea family (this includes sweet peas), bearded iris (but not all iris varieties – see *Iris* article in *Flowers – Bulbs*), peony, clematis, lilac, fruit trees, and maidenhair (and a few other) ferns. Lawns benefit greatly from application of lime yearly.

Dolomitic, and sometimes calcitic, lime is used to make the soil more alkaline (raise the pH), and may be added to the garden any time of year. Raising pH is not a fast process as lime is insoluble and requires time to react with moist soil. The chart indicates how much lime should be added to different types of soil to bring the pH up to 6.5. A pound of lime is one cup. Follow package directions and do not overdo an application. Use no more than 5 pounds per 100 square feet per application, and repeat again several weeks later if a larger amount is required.

TO RAISE PH – MAKE MORE ALKALINE

Pounds of Lime per 100 sq. ft. to raise pH to 6.5 in various types of soil			
Current pH	Sandy	Woodland or Loam	Ordinary or Clay
4.5	12.6	25.3	34.8
5.0	10.6	21.1	29.0

59

| 5.5 | 4.2 | 8.4 | 11.6 |
| 6.0 | 1.7 | 3.3 | 4.5 |

BENEFICIAL WILDLIFE AND INSECTS

The idea that "the only good bug is a dead bug" needs rethinking. While termites, ticks, and mosquitoes certainly need to be controlled, many insects either help the garden or do no harm. Pesticides are indiscriminate in killing, so use them as a last resort, and sparingly.

- **Bees, butterflies, ants**, and other insects are necessary for pollination, and flowers evolve shapes and colors that attract these pollinators. For example, bees have ultra-violet vision, and certain flowers have developed an ultra-violet "target" near their centers to help bees find the pollen. Butterflies have long tongues suitable for reaching nectar in trumpet-shaped flowers that bees can't reach. See Table 5. below for a list of butterfly-attracting plants. A few plants require very specific pollinators and have developed symbiotic (mutually beneficial) relationships with them, such as the yucca and yucca moth and the fig and fig wasp.

- **Ants** have long been observed around peonies. The peony flower bud secretes a honeydew sap which ants love and they do no harm by dining on this nectar. It is very probable that if the honeydew remained on the peony bud it would attract "sooty mold" which would disfigure the blossom. In fact, "old wives" claim peonies bloom better if tended by ants, but this may not be true. In this instance ants are not a "pest".

  Interestingly, ants have learned to "farm" aphids for the honeydew they produce, and in this case, the plant *is being harmed* by the aphids sucking the juice out of it. The aphid then secretes honeydew as a waste product, and the ants collect and store this nectar. If you notice a lot of ant activity around a plant, see if there are small green aphids on the stems and leaves. If so, a strong spray of water or an insecticidal soap will disrupt this farming operation.

- **Ladybugs** eat aphids, fruit worms, mites, and whiteflies. If you purchase ladybugs, it helps keep them in your yard if you release them in the evening, as they don't fly at night. Release them into an aphid-infested plant if possible. You can also paint a sugar-water solution on twigs and leaves in the release area to give them a ready food source. Ladybugs are territorial, and if they are born in your yard they will usually stay there, so the trick is to keep the "introduced" ladybugs around long enough to lay eggs.

- **Green Lacewings** eat aphids, leafminers, mites, and whiteflies.

- **Praying Mantis** is a general insect predator.

60

- **Beneficial Nematodes** control root weevil, European crane fly, grubs, ants, fleas, cutworms and other soil pests. Beneficial nematodes are microscopic worms that live below the soil line in a moist environment. They do not harm earthworms, birds, plants, or the environment, and are naturally occurring in soils the world over. Beneficial nematodes are sold on sponges that may be stored in the refrigerator for several weeks. Dissolve the sponge in water and spray the nematode solution around the plants with a hose-end sprayer or watering can.

- **Toads:** If you are lucky enough to have toads in your yard, they eat slugs and insects. Please do not let your children and pets torture toads. They do not cause warts and do absolutely no damage. You may want to invert several clay flowerpots, with an "entrance door" chipped out of the rim, in a nice shady bed to serve as toad houses.

  If you have a fish pond or water feature, toads will appear on rainy spring evenings when the mating instinct stirs, and serenade you endlessly. The next morning long translucent spaghetti strands filled with tiny black eggs will be entwined in your water plants and before you know it, there will be thousands of tadpoles. Fish do not seem to eat the tadpoles. Eventually they will climb, with rudimentary legs, up onto a lily pad and transform themselves into tiny toads the size of a lady pea. At this point in their development, they are tasty morsels for the fish and birds. Of all the tadpoles, perhaps five baby toads will survive to maturity and live in your garden, such is the attrition rate planned by nature.

  Toads have very sensitive skin and any caustic chemicals used in the yard will very likely injure or kill them. Biologists are especially interested in toads and frogs as indicators of water pollution and ecological danger.

- **Bats** are a special blessing and eat their body weight in insects every day. Bat houses are available and should be installed about 15 feet high in an out of the way spot. Healthy bats will not attack you, and the vast majority of bats do not carry disease. They have developed marvelously accurate sonar which allows them to fly and hunt insects in the dark. If you have ever seen a bat "buzz" across your patio or swimming pool at night, this is what he was doing. Bats, like toads, deserve more compassion.

- **Snakes** are important components of natural ecosystems as both predators and prey. Common in many types of habitat, all snakes are predators, whether venomous or not.

  The most commonly encountered *non-poisonous* snakes in the Southeast are common garter, Eastern ribbon, coachwhip, ringneck, rat, Eastern hognose, racer, milk, Southeastern crown, common kingsnake, corn, scarlet, mud, rainbow, prairie kingsnake, and plain-bellied water. Try to resist the urge to kill them, because they are harmless.

  Depending on size and species, they may feed on invertebrates such as slugs, worms and insects, or on fish, amphibians, snakes, birds, bird eggs, and small mammals. Species such as the milk snake and black rat snake consume great

61

numbers of rodents; they enter burrows and consume young mice and rats right in the nests. Garter snakes frequently consume garden pests such as slugs and certain soft-bodied insects.

Snakes and their eggs are in turn eaten by fish, amphibians, other snakes, birds, and predatory mammals such as skunks, raccoons, and opossums. Birds are their most serious predators - and not just hawks and owls. Songbirds consume great numbers of small snakes and it is not unusual to see the tail of a young garter snake dangling from the overstuffed gullet of a nestling robin!

Venomous snakes of the southeast include copperheads, cottonmouth (water moccasin), and rattlesnakes. They are not usually found in the urban garden, but can pose a threat to children and pets if they are harassed.

- Finally, **fruit- and insect-eating birds** such as robins, mockingbirds, wrens, purple martins, warblers, hummingbirds, nuthatches, woodpeckers, and so on, eat many insect pests. Even seed-eaters will relish the occasional beetle or caterpillar added to the feeder.

ATTRACTING BIRDS TO YOUR GARDEN

Growing the following plants will ensure a productive crop of berries from summer through winter, and provide a bounty for your feathered friends. (Refer to Table 17 in *Shrubs* for a more extensive list)

Late spring through summer: cherry (*Prunus*), chokecherry (*Prunus virginiana*), serviceberry (*Amelanchier*), elderberry (*Sambucus canadensis*).

Late summer through fall: blueberry (*Vaccinium),* dogwood (*Cornus*), inkberry (*Ilex glabra*), juniper (*Juniperus*), holly (*Ilex*), viburnum (*Viburnum*).

Winter through early spring: black chokeberry (*Aronia melanocarpa*), common snowberry (*Symphoricarpos albus*), American highbush cranberry (*Viburnum trilobum*), deciduous and evergreen holly (*Ilex*), coralberry *(Symphoricarpos orbiculatus)*, sumac (*Rhus*), crabapple (*Prunus malus*).

Many berries do not soften enough to be palatable to birds until they have been through several freeze-thaw cycles, so you will have berries on some shrubs for winter color well into January or February. Robins, mockingbirds, warblers, and many other small birds prefer insects, berries, and fruit to birdseed mix, and will be very appreciative of your thoughtfulness.

Birds help control insects, in addition to providing beauty and entertainment. Provide feeding stations and birdbaths and keep filled daily. Fresh water is especially important in icy weather. Birds like wild birdseed mixture, crumbs, suet, apples, and sunflower seed. In heavy snowfall, put a piece of black plastic out and throw seeds on top.

For an easy homemade treat, mix two tablespoons of peanut butter with two tablespoons of vegetable/animal shortening and enough cornmeal or oatmeal (about one cup) to make a stiff "cookie dough". Spread this on tree bark or in the crevices of pinecones or in a suet basket for a treat that woodpeckers, wrens, nuthatches, robins, titmice, and cardinals, as well as squirrels will love.

You may want to hang a hummingbird feeder out at the end of March to help migrants flying northward, and again in September for their return trip to Mexico and Central America. Some hummers stay in the Mid-South all summer if there is a ready food supply. Trumpet vines, red buckeye, honeysuckle, bee balm (*Monarda*), shrimp plant, and many other flowers are highly attractive to them. You may buy Hummingbird nectar and dilute it according to the package directions, or you may put a quarter cup of white sugar in two cups of water and microwave until the sugar dissolves, and fill the feeder with this solution. Change the sugar water every three of four days to prevent bacteria.

ATTRACTING BUTTERFLIES TO YOUR GARDEN

If you want butterflies in your garden, plant the following types of "nectar" perennials and annuals in masses to attract their attention. Also grow the "host" plants where adult butterflies lay their eggs, and on which the larvae feed. You may want to plant these "sacrificial" host plants in a remote area as they are liable to become unsightly. Keep in mind when using pesticides that caterpillars become butterflies.

TABLE 5. BUTTERFLY-ATTRACTING FLOWERS

NECTAR FLOWERS	
Bee balm (*Monarda*)	Lantana (annual & perennial *Lantana*)
Black-eyed Susan (*Rudbeckia*)	Liatris (*Liatris*)
Cardinal flower (*Lobelia*)	Mexican sunflower (*Tithonia*)
Coreopsis (*Coreopsis*)	Moss verbena (annual *Verbena*)
Cosmos (*Cosmos*)	Pentas (*Pentas*)
Daylilies (*Hemerocallis*)	Purple coneflower (*Echinacea*)
French marigold (*Tagetes*)	Red valerian (*Centranthus*)
Goldenrods (*Solidago*)	Sages (*Salvia*)
Gomphrena (*Gomphrena*)	Showy sedum (*Sedum*)
Hardy ageratum (*Eupatorium*)	Swamp sunflower (*Helianthus*)
Heliotrope (*Heliotropium*)	Verbena (*Verbena*)

63

Impatiens (*Impatiens*)	Yarrow (*Achillea*)
Joe-Pye weed (*Eupatorium*)	Zinnia (*Zinnia*)
HOST FLOWERS	
Butterfly weed (*Asclepias*)	Rabbit's tobacco (*Gnaphalium*)
Common fennel (*Foeniculum*)	Rue (*Ruta*)
Dill (*Anethem*)	Spicebush (*Lindera*)
Milkweed (*Asclepias*)	Swamp hibiscus (*Hibiscus*)
Parsley (*Petroselinum*)	Sweet violet (*Viola*)
Queen-Anne's-lace (*Daucus*)	Wormwood (*Artemisia*)

PESTS AND DISEASES

THE RISK OF USING PESTICIDES

The use of pesticides should be undertaken with caution. Long-range effects on the food chain and water table are better understood, and a great many pesticides that were recommended in earlier editions of the *Mid-South Garden Guide* have been taken off the market.

Pesticides are designed to affect the central nervous system or the reproductive system of the target insect. It is worth understanding that certain pesticide molecules are very similar in size and shape to sex hormones like testosterone and estrogen, and they will substitute, lock-and-key fashion, into sex hormone receptor sites and interfere with fertility and reproduction.

Some pesticides that are designed to disrupt an insect's reproductive cycle, unfortunately work just about as well on frogs, birds, and humans! A great many grossly deformed frogs were discovered in the Great Lakes region some years ago, and the cause was traced to pesticide run-off. The well-known case of DDT practically eliminating the Bald Eagle was due to reproduction interference; the eggshell produced by contaminated birds was too thin and would crack long before the baby was ready to hatch. Among humans, doctors are seeing more cases of infertility and miscarriage despite good nutrition and health care, and this is thought to be possibly correlated with pesticides in the food chain.

You can create a perfectly beautiful garden without spraying anything. If you have good soil, select disease-resistant plants, allow for air circulation around plants, and use proper irrigation, you will minimize trouble from diseases. There are many good plants that soldier on without attack by either disease or insect, and these should be your mainstays. Roses are the exception, and almost all growers agree that some spraying is necessary. See *Roses* in the *Shrubs* Chapter.

In any event, use the least toxic chemicals available for the pest problem at hand, and consult your nurseryman for recommendations if the problem is not described below.

DESTRUCTIVE INSECTS AND WILDLIFE

Some destructive insects like beetles and termites are a vital part of the decay and recycling processes in nature, but we do not particularly want them in our gardens. Rotting wood attracts a procession of "decay" bugs that are apt to move on to your tender perennials, so keep your yard clear of dead trees, limbs, and stumps.

- **Ants, Beetles, Army Worms, and Diseases in Lawn:** Use an insecticide, such as Sevin® dust, or introduce beneficial nematodes. For mildew or rust that appears on lawn grasses, spray with a fungicide, such as neem oil, or consult a professional.

- **Aphids on tender new shoots of chrysanthemum, roses, etc.:** Spray with an insecticidal soap or a strong spray of water. Introduce ladybugs.

- **Bagworm on arborvitae and junipers:** Watch for bagworms in May. Picking off "bags" may be sufficient control. If infestation is very bad, spray with an insecticidal soap or with an insecticide containing either spinosad or pyrethrin.

- **Blight on perennials, peonies, lilies, clematis:** Healthy plants need no spray. If they had disease last season, spray with a fungicide such as neem oil, potassium bicarbonate or dusting sulfur as soon as plants come up in spring. Repeat twice at intervals of two weeks.

- **Caterpillars:** can do an amazing amount of damage to foliage. They may be handpicked (maybe using gloves or a tissue) and added to the birdfeeder, or discarded. Some caterpillars have developed poisonous or stinging spines; an adaptation which makes them unpalatable to birds and helps ensure their survival.

  Serious infestation by hundreds of tent caterpillars or gypsy moths can quickly defoliate large trees, and requires treatment by a professional. Prevent infestation by scraping the tan egg casings off the tree bark and destroying them in soapy water if you notice any. New pheromone-scented (hormone-like substances which stimulate sexual response in others of the species) molasses traps are becoming available as an organic way to trap the gypsy moth and prevent caterpillar infestations.

  Natural parasitism by certain wasps and flies also helps control caterpillar populations. The eggs of these parasitic insects are injected through the skin of the caterpillar, and the caterpillar is consumed as the wasps and flies grow to maturity.

Keep in mind that some caterpillars become desirable butterflies, so you may want to familiarize yourself with the various butterfly larvae by consulting an insect reference book. Some people plant milkweed vine, spicebush, or other "sacrificial" plants in a remote corner to feed the voracious caterpillars. (See *Beneficial Insects and Wildlife – Attracting Butterflies to Your Garden*)

- **Holly Leafminer:** Apply dormant spray in February then use spinosad to control leafminer (follow directions and handle with care). Always dispose of all fallen holly leaves as they may harbor pests.

- **Fire ants:** are very different than ordinary ants and can sting you or your pets. Consult a professional exterminator if you have large underground colonies of fire ants.

- **Japanese beetles** are large enough to see easily, and can be picked off by gloved-hand and added to the bird feeder before they decimate your favorite plants. You may have to spray with pyrethrin.

- **Lacebug on azaleas and pyracantha:** Spray with pesticidal oil or insecticidal soap three times: after blooming, in summer as a preventative measure, and in early fall (worst period of infestation). If problem arises, use two or three applications spaced a week or ten days apart.

- **Leaf Roller on photinia:** Use an insecticide such as pyrethrin or Sevin®. Apply first spray about June 1st. Follow with two more applications at ten day intervals.

- **Leaf Spot on lilac, ivy, chrysanthemum, vinca minor, and ajuga:** Use a fungicide, such as neem oil, potassium bicarbonate, copper, or dusting sulfur for brownish splotched or spotted leaves. Apply spray at first sign of leaf spot. Repeat twice at ten day intervals.

- **Mealybugs on house plants, etc.:** Remove with cotton swabs dipped in alcohol and rinse with water, or spray with an insecticidal soap.

- **Mildew on plants:** Use a fungicide such as dusting sulfur, copper, neem oil, or potassium bicarbonate.

- **Moles** eat underground insects, like grubs, and not plant roots, but their tunnels are still unwelcome. Their relative, the **vole**, is another matter entirely and will decimate your perennials, especially hostas and bulbs. You can buy "hardware cloth", a rigid ½"-square-grid wire screen, and plant your perennials and bulbs in cages of this wire. Another strategy is to grow the at-risk perennial in a pot, and "plant" the pot in the ground. If this is not practical, use a rodent poison and consult an exterminator. Do not to let your children or pets near the bait.

- **Nematode on chrysanthemum, peony, boxwood, and azaleas:** When plants look wilted or sick with no trouble visible above ground, dig into roots. If there are small pea-like knots along roots, the trouble is nematode. Consult local County Agent. Much research is still needed on nematode control, but these are not the same as the beneficial nematodes recommended above as organic pest control.

66

- **Poison ivy and poison oak:** Hand-pull wearing protective clothing and gloves. Disposable latex gloves and a plastic garbage bag will help minimize skin contact with the toxic leaves. Change clothes after weeding, and launder your work clothes separately.

- **Red Spider and Chewing Insects on pyracantha, etc.:** Use an insecticide such as neem oil, pyrethrin, or insecticidal soap.

- **Scale on evergreens and euonymus:** In February use a dormant oil spray. During the growing season, if needed, use an insecticide such as pyrethrin or potassium bicarbonate, or a summer pesticidal oil spray.

- **Snails and Slugs:** Use product containing the chemical iron phosphate such as Slug-go®; follow directions. Wood ashes put on ground around plants, especially hostas, kill snails and slugs by dissolving them as they crawl over ashes. Diatomaceous earth is gritty and discourages slugs from crawling through it. Saucers of beer also are effective.

- **Spider Mite on boxwood, camellia, and juniper:** Use a miticide such as neem oil or pyrethrin. One application may be enough, but check to be sure.

- **Thrips on gladiolus:** Before planting, soak corms for 3 hours in a disinfectant such as a solution of 1 to 1½ tablespoons Lysol® to 1 gallon of water. Spray bi-weekly after plants come up and until buds show color with pyrethrin or spinosad.

- **Whitefly on azaleas, gardenia, lantana, and house plants:** Spray with an insecticidal soap. Introduce ladybugs.

- **Worms on mimosa:** Use an insecticide such as Sevin® or pyrethrin. Apply first spray the end of May. Watch for later crops of worms which hatch at three week intervals.

DOGS AND YELLOW SPOTS ON LAWNS

It's hard to live and be happy without the company of dogs, but they can do a little damage in the yard. Yellow spots in lawns, which are caused by dog or cat urine, is a frequent pet owner complaint. The yellow spots are from excess nitrogen, in the form of urea, burning the grass.

The chemical makeup of urine depends, of course, on diet, but in all mammals, waste-product nitrogen is excreted as urea or one of its derivatives. While logic suggests that urea should fertilize the lawn, and it does, if you are already feeding your lawn, then this additional nitrogen load becomes toxic.

Old wives tales attribute the yellow stains to the acidity of dog urine, and recommend feeding tomato juice to the animal to "sweeten" his urine. This is nonsense. The problem is not pH related.

The problem is the concentration of urine in one spot. The female dog usually empties her bladder completely in one spot, whereas a male "marks" many spots. The male or female may mark the same few plants or lawn areas every day, however, and in time the concentration of nitrogen in the urine will damage the

67

chosen plants. Cows, by contrast, don't cause yellow spots in their pastures because they urinate randomly around the whole field.

It turns out that diluting the urine with water will completely prevent yellow spots in lawns. As long as you water the lawn or shrub sometime within the first 3 – 5 hours after the urine is deposited, there will be no problem. Hardly anyone is willing to follow their animal around with a watering can, but there you have it.

It may be possible to train pets to "go" in one particular out-of-the-way area, but not necessarily easy. You could consider "hard-scaping" an area for dogs to use, where nothing is planted; concrete or brick paving, a gravel bed, or sand box are possibilities.

If this is an unappealing solution, there is another option. There are no more urine-resistant grasses than Bermuda and fescue, which are probably already in your yard. You could have an unconventional lawn, however, and plant *clover* which is discussed in the *Lawns* chapter. It has many virtues as a ground cover; among them is resistance to dog urine. Otherwise, dilution with water is the best bet.

Dog urine kills boxwood, turning the leaves tan, and dogs seem to favor boxwood above all other bushes. Some people use small-leaved hollies or box-leaf euonymus for the look of boxwood but with better tolerance to urine.

COMPANION GARDENING

A time-honored pest control method is *companion gardening* which is based on the ability of some plants to attract or repel insects and to improve the growth of certain nearby plants. Companion gardening offers an alternate approach to today's over-reliance on chemicals.

Allium – Member of the onion family; repels voles and insects.

Basil – Companion to tomatoes; improves growth and flavor; repels flies and mosquitoes.

Bee balm – Companion to tomatoes; improves growth and flavor.

Borage – Companion to tomatoes, squash, and strawberries; deters tomato worm; improves flavor and growth.

Chives – Companion to carrots; improves growth and flavor; repels aphids.

Coriander – Contains an oil which will repel spider mites and aphids.

Fritillaria – repels voles and other rodents, and is a very showy and unusual bulb.

Garlic – Plant near roses and raspberries; improves growth and health; deters Japanese beetles and aphids.

Horseradish – Plant at corners of potato patch to deter potato bug.

Marigolds – The workhorse of pest deterrents. Plant throughout the garden. It discourages Mexican bean beetles and nematodes. Companion to tomatoes. Deters asparagus beetle, tomato worm, and general garden pests.

Mint – Repels ants.

Nasturtium – Companion to radishes, cabbage, and cucumber; plant under fruit trees. Deters aphids, squash bugs, striped pumpkin beetles.

Petunia – Protects beans.

Peppermint – Planted among cabbages, it repels the white cabbage butterfly.

Rosemary – Companion to cabbage, bean, carrots, and sage; deters cabbage moth, bean beetles, and carrot flies

Sage – Discourages troublesome insects.

IDENTIFYING PROBLEMS OF GARDEN PLANTS

To identify the cause of the plant's problem, it is usually necessary to look at the plant closely; examine the flowers, leaves, stem, and (sometimes) the roots; and do some detective work to determine possible causes. Often the process of elimination will lead to the identification of the problem. Once the cause is identified, measures can be taken to correct the problem.

The following tables from the University of Tennessee Agricultural Extension Service (http://www.utextension.utk.edu) are checklists for diagnosing garden problems. The symptoms are divided into 1) problems mainly on flowers; 2) problems confined to the leaves; and 3) problems that affect the entire plant.

Under each of these three categories there are symptom descriptions with a list of possible causes and corrective measures that can be taken. Because there are a large number of similar pesticides under various brand names that can be used for control, no specific pesticides are listed in the chart.

TABLE 6. PROBLEM OCCURS MAINLY ON THE FLOWERS

TABLE 6. SYMPTOMS ON FLOWERS	POSSIBLE CAUSES	CONTROLS/ COMMENTS
Plants fail to flower; foliage looks healthy	Wrong season	Some plants have specific day-length requirements for flowering
	Low temperatures, freeze injury	Low temperature injury may damage flower buds
	Insufficient light	Do not plant sun-loving plants in the shade
	Too much nitrogen	Do not over-fertilize as too much nitrogen stimulates foliage, not flower, production; follow soil test recommendations

TABLE 6. SYMPTOMS ON FLOWERS	POSSIBLE CAUSES	CONTROLS/ COMMENTS
	Overcrowded plants	Divide perennials at recommended time of year
	Immature plants	Biennials and perennials often do not flower the first year; peony may not flower for several years
	Undersized bulbs	
Too many small flowers	Plants not debudded	Some flowers, e.g. chrysanthemum, need to have some buds removed to produce large flowers
Flowers wilt or fail to open; grayish mold appears on flowers and leaves in moist weather conditions	Botrytis gray mold (fungal disease)	Pick off and destroy affected flowers to remove a source of disease; Keep water off foliage or water early in morning; use a registered fungicide
Flowers distorted and abnormally colored	Thrips; small tannish-yellow or brown wedge-shaped insects mainly found inside flower petals	Use registered insecticide
Rosetting of florets; ring pattern on leaves; yellow and light green mosaic or mottle	Virus disease (any of several)	Destroy affected plants; insect control may reduce virus spread to non-infected plants
Light green, yellow or white flecks on leaves	Spider mites; tiny 8-legged 'spiders' with webbing on underside of leaves	Hard blast of water on underside of leaves; use insecticidal soap or horticultural oil or a registered miticide (insecticide for spider mites) on underside of leaves

TABLE 7. PROBLEMS MOSTLY CONFINED TO LEAVES

TABLE 7. SYMPTOMS ON LEAVES	POSSIBLE CAUSES	CONTROLS/ COMMENTS
Corky, raised spots on lower leaf surfaces	Edema, a physiological problem usually associated with excess humidity	Do not over-water; space plants to increase air movement around plants, esp. geranium; thinning foliage may help reduce humidity
Brown, dead areas on outside margins of leaves and/or between leaf veins	Scorch, due to hot, dry weather conditions or newly transplanted plants	Supply water by soaker hose; mulch plants; can also occur on plants divided and moved at wrong time of year
	Severe nutritional deficiency	Soil test and follow fertilizer recommendations
	Chemical injury	Check for pesticides used in area of affected plants; follow pesticide label directions
	Salt injury	Do not salt iced sidewalks where water will run off into plant beds
	Anthracnose leaf blight (fungal disease)	Cut and remove diseased foliage in late fall or early spring to remove source of disease. Avoid overhead watering or water so that leaves dry before nightfall. Use recommended fungicide sprays for leaf spots
	Sun scald & winter sunburn as foliage dries when roots cannot take up enough water to keep foliage alive	Mainly occurs on evergreen plants such as magnolia and rhododendron during the winter. New foliage will be fine. Can use an anti-desiccant on foliage to help retain moisture
Bleached leaves	Sunburn	Move plant under shade;

71

TABLE 7. SYMPTOMS ON LEAVES	POSSIBLE CAUSES	CONTROLS/ COMMENTS
		use only sun loving plants in areas with fun sun; moving plants from shade (or from inside house) immediately to intense sunlight will cause sunburn; move plants gradually from one light intensity level to another to acclimate them slowly
Brown, purple or black circular or irregular spots on dead leaves	Fungal, bacterial or leaf nematode disease (any of several)	Submit leaf sample for laboratory diagnosis
Grayish-white powdery growth on leaves, stems, and flowers	Powdery mildew (fungal disease)	Use registered fungicide; buy resistant varieties of plants
Pustules containing orange, yellow or brown powdery substance on leaves	Rust (fungal disease)	Use registered fungicide; destroy infected plants
Leaves wilt, turn yellow, and/or drop; roots decayed	Root rot (any of several)	Many perennials will not tolerate poorly drained soils; check cultural conditions; submit sample with roots and soil for laboratory diagnosis
Yellow and green mottle or mosaic pattern on leaves	Virus disease (any of several)	Remove affected plants; do not touch healthy plants after diseased ones; avoid use of tobacco products (which can harbor plant viruses) before handling plants; wash hands in milk to neutralize virus particles before handling plants; control insects that can spread virus to other plants
	Nutrient deficiency	Soil test and follow fertilizer recommendations
Twisted, stunted or	Herbicide injury	Check for use of phenoxy-

TABLE 7. SYMPTOMS ON LEAVES	POSSIBLE CAUSES	CONTROLS/ COMMENTS
puckered leaves, often mottled or abnormally colored		type herbicides, e.g. Dicamba® and/or 2, 4-D used in area. May be taken up by root zone (granular herbicide) or drifted on wind up to ½ mile.
Tiny white flecks or white interveinal areas on leaves	Ozone injury	Some plant varieties are more susceptible to ozone injury (air pollution damage) than others
	Spider mites; tiny 8-legged 'spiders' with webbing on underside of leaves	Hard blast of water on underside of leaves; use insecticidal soap or horticultural oil or a registered miticide on underside of leaves
	Thrips; small tannish yellow or brown wedge-shaped insects mainly found inside flower petals	Use registered insecticide
Light colored tunnels, blisters, or blotches in leaves	Leafminers	Use registered insecticide; remove affected leaves if only a few are infected
Leaves chewed with ragged holes or may be completely eaten	Various insects – usually caterpillars or beetles	Submit insect for identification
Leaves chewed with ragged holes; slime trails	Slugs	Use beer bait or commercial slug bait; check plants at night for actively feeding slugs
Only leaf veins or clear areas left on leaf; no green in these sections	Sawfly caterpillars or leaf skeletonizer beetle	Submit insect for identification
Leaves with smooth holes or only slightly ragged areas with yellow halo	Bacterial shot hole	Cut and remove diseased foliage in late fall or early spring to remove source of disease. Avoid overhead watering or water so that

73

TABLE 7. SYMPTOMS ON LEAVES	POSSIBLE CAUSES	CONTROLS/ COMMENTS
		leaves dry before nightfall
Black soot on surface of leaf or stem; scrapes off surface easily; may peel off in sheets	Sooty mold	Secondary fungus growing on surface of honeydew sap left by insects (aphids, scale or whiteflies) as they feed on plant; control insects with registered insecticide
Clusters of insects on stems or underside of leaves; leaves may be curled or distorted; may have sooty mold	Aphids; soft bodied round insects with two small 'stalks' on rear end, may be green, red, or tan depending on sap	Use registered insecticide or insecticidal soap
Leaves and stems covered with small, soft-bodied or crusty insects that can easily be removed	Scale (various)	Use registered insecticide
Tiny white winged insects on underside of leaves	Whiteflies	Use registered insecticide
White, cottony masses on leaves or stems	Mealybugs	Use registered insecticide
Irregular bronze or brown spotting on leaves	Four-lined plant bug; adults are yellowish-green with four black stripes down wing covers; immature insects are orange to red with black spots and yellow stripes	Use registered insecticide
Grayish mold appears on flowers, stems, and leaves in moist weather conditions	Botrytis gray mold (fungal disease)	Pick off and destroy affected flowers to remove a source of disease; Keep water off foliage or water early in morning; use a registered fungicide

TABLE 8. PROBLEM AFFECTS ENTIRE PLANT

TABLE 8. SYMPTOMS ON PLANT	POSSIBLE CAUSES	CONTROLS/ COMMENTS
Plants wilt; flowers may drop and leaves may turn yellow; check roots and stems for possible rot disease	Dry soil	Supply water
	Waterlogged soil may drown plants due to lack of oxygen in soil	Improve drainage; do not allow plant roots to sit in water or in waterlogged soil; some perennials will not tolerate poorly drained soils
	Transplant shock	Do not transplant in heat of day; water regularly after transplanting; divide and transplant perennials in fall or spring
	Root or stem or corm rot; may be fungal or bacterial disease	Plant in well-drained soil; destroy affected plants; do not purchase plants with brown or black rotted roots
Seedlings wilt; stems turn brown and soft and may be constricted at the soil line	Damping-off (fungal disease)	Plant in well-drained, disease-free soil; plants should be planted in sterile potting soil
Tall, "leggy" plant; stem and foliage are pale and yellow	Insufficient light	Pay attention to light requirements of plants (putting a sun-loving plant in shade will result in weak, leggy plants)
General yellowing of leaves; yellowing may be interveinal; plant may be stunted; but no wilting	Nutrient deficiency	Perform soil test and follow fertilization recommendations
	Virus disease	Submit sample for laboratory diagnosis; may need to destroy affected plants as virus may be

TABLE 8. SYMPTOMS ON PLANT	POSSIBLE CAUSES	CONTROLS/ COMMENTS
		spread further by insects or through handling plants
Plants stunted and yellow; small galls or swellings on roots	Root knot nematodes (Note: galls are normal on leguminous plants)	Use resistant species of plants in these locations; replant susceptible varieties in another area
General browning of foliage; on tender, new foliage can look bronze or red; occurs after a cold spell	Frost injury	New growth should occur below damaged area; do not plant annuals until danger of frost is passed
Small, gnat-like flies around potted plants; small ¼" white maggots (larvae) with black heads in soil around plant roots	Fungus gnats	Use registered insecticide; avoid over watering plants; clean up and remove all plant debris in area; if planting in pots or planters, use sterile potting soil
Plants cut off at ground level	Cutworms	Worms hide during day in soil or in debris close to base of plants. Spray soil & base of plant with labeled insecticide or uncover and kill cutworms around base of plants. Beneficial nematodes may be used

SPRAYS

Pesticidal, fungicidal, and miticidal sprays should be used in moderation or not used at all. Spraying is not recommended as a substitute for good gardening practices, but as a helping hand when problem conditions make it necessary. Take the diseased branch, leaf, or plant to a garden center for diagnosis before spraying if you are unsure of the problem.

DORMANT OIL SPRAY

If insects and scale are a particular problem in your yard, you might consider applying a *dormant oil spray* in late winter or early spring. Such a spray at this time will greatly cut down later trouble by killing the eggs and spores of many pests and diseases, such as scale, whiteflies, aphids, spider mites, and so on.

Practically everything in the garden will be benefited by this spraying: trees, shrubs, evergreens, roses, and perennial border.

The oil acts to suffocate the insect eggs and disease spores, and therefore the leaves and stems must be thoroughly covered with spray to be effective. Pick a calm day when the temperature is above 40° and below 80°, as treated plants are more susceptible to freeze damage and sunburn. Spray plants before the leaf buds open to avoid burning them.

Examples of currently available horticultural oils include: Hi-Yield Dormant Spray®, Bonide All-Seasons Horticultural & Dormant Spray Oil®, Monterey Saf-T-Side®, Fertilome Scalecide®, Fertilome Dormant Spray & Summer Oil Spray®, and Ortho's Volck Oil®. Some are gentle enough to spray in the summer when plants are in foliage, but most are for use in winter. Follow directions and dilute appropriately to avoid damaging plants.

Note: Do not use oil spray on sugar or Japanese maple, walnut, beech, or magnolia trees.

The following table gives several organic pesticides and the pests they affect. The term "organic" only means they are from natural sources, and does not mean that they are not toxic. Use with care according to package directions.

TABLE 9. ORGANIC PESTICIDES AND AFFECTED INSECTS AND DISEASES

ACTIVE INGREDIENT	COMMON BRAND NAMES	AFFECTED INSECTS AND DISEASES	NOTES
Copper	Copper	Alternia Blight, Bacterial Blight, Black Spot, Botrytis Blight, Leaf or Fruit Spots, Rhizoctania	Fungicidal properties. Follow package directions.
Carbaryl	Sevin	Ants, Bagworm, Grubs, Japanese beetles, Whiteflies, Most insects	A broad-spectrum control for most insects. Not as toxic as many pesticides. Comes as powder, granules, or liquid.
Sulfur	Dusting Sulfur	Black Spot, Powdery Mildew, Rust	Good control for many funguses. Also acidifies the soil and helps plant build proteins.

Active Ingredient	Common Brand Names	Affected Insects and Diseases	Notes
Jojoba Oil	E-Rase	Powdery Mildew	
Pyrethrin and Canola Oil	Take Down Garden Spray	Aphids, Caterpillars, Colorado Potato Beetle, Flu Beetle, Leaf Hoppers, Leaf Rollers, Mealy Bugs, Mites, Scale, Thrips, and others	On all products, possible Allergies – Read the label carefully before use. Pyrethrin is derived from daisies.
Spinosad	Monterrey Garden Insect Spray, Ferti-lome Borer and Bagworm Killer	Army Worms, Bagworms, Borers, Cat Fleas, Colorado Potato Beetle, Fire Ants, Fruit Flies, Katydids, Leafminers, Leaf Rollers, Sod Webworms, Tent Caterpillars, Thrips, Worms	Remember – insects and diseases only become a problem when your plant is stressed.
Neem oil	Rx 3-in-1 Neem	Aphids, Black Spot, Mites, Powder Rust, Whiteflies, and others	Frequently used fungicide, insecticide, miticide.
Potassium Bicarbonate	Remedy	Alternaria Blight, Anthracnose, Black Spot, Botrytis Blight,	

ACTIVE INGREDIENT	COMMON BRAND NAMES	AFFECTED INSECTS AND DISEASES	NOTES
		Downy Mildew, Fusarium Leaf Spot, Gray Mold, Helminthosparin Leaf Spot, Scale, Septoria Leaf Spot	
Rotenone Pyrethrin	Bonide Rotenone and Pyrethrin	Cucumber Beetles, European Corn Borer, Fruit Worm, Japanese Beetles, Leaf Hoppers, Mites, Rose Chafers, Squash Bug, Squash Vine Borer, Thrips, Tortoise Beetles, Web Worm	
Pesticidal Oil	Ultra-Fine Sun Spray	Aphids, Lacebug, Mealy Worms, Mites, Scale, Web Worms, Whitefly	
Bacillus Thuringiensis	Thuricide, BT, or Dipel	All Worms	Note – The effects of the BT may not be instantly visible. Rather the BT introduces a natural predator into the soil, and eliminates all worms, both pest and beneficial ones, without the use of chemicals. Consider using beneficial nematodes, as you do not want to kill earthworms.

ACTIVE INGREDIENT	COMMON BRAND NAMES	AFFECTED INSECTS AND DISEASES	NOTES
Diatomaceous Earth	D/E	Numerous Insects, Slugs	
Iron Phosphate	Sluggo	Snails and Slugs	Note – This product can be used safely around dogs, cats, and other wildlife.
Potassium Salts of Fatty Acids	Safer Soap	Aphids, Grasshoppers, Scale, Spider Mites, Tent Caterpillars, and others	Insecticidal soap is good to try first, as it is less toxic than other substances.

ATTENTION: When a range of rates and application intervals are recommended, use the lower rate and longer interval for mild-moderate infestations and the higher rate and shorter interval for moderate-severe infestations.

EMERGENCY POISON CONTROL PHONE NUMBERS

Human Pesticide Emergency
Poison Control Center Hotline   **(800) 222-1222**

General Questions on Pesticides
EPA Pesticide Telecommunications   **(800) 858-7378**

Pesticide Emergency
Nat'l Pesticide Safety Network   **(800) 424-9300**

Animal Pesticide Emergency:
Nat'l Animal Pesticide Control Center   **(800) 548-2423**

Try to encourage beneficial insects and wildlife to live in your garden. Avoid spraying any toxic chemicals unless there is no other choice. A garden is a big financial investment over time and it is heartbreaking to have favorite plants destroyed, so exercise caution and moderation in spraying poisons.

PRUNING

Pruning woody shrubs is both art and science. The science is based upon plant growth habits, while the art is in creating an aesthetically pleasing form and shape. Try to shape your plant according to its natural growth pattern or habit; a well pruned plant shows no sign of pruning. Espalier and topiary are special techniques of creating stylized forms, and are exceptions to this general rule.

Pruning should ideally begin when the plant is young as its future beauty is determined then. How often mature shrubs require pruning depends on how vigorous and fast-growing the plant is, as well as the growing conditions (soil fertility and texture, sunlight, and water). Some shrubs need attention every year, others every four or five years. It's not logical or practical to fertilize and water to encourage fast growth in a plant and then prune away the new growth. Moderation in amounts of fertilizer and minimal pruning will achieve good results with less effort and expense.

For years it was thought that any cut should be sealed with black pruning paint, but that has been found unnecessary if the cut is properly made. Roses, however, should have cuts sealed with white glue to prevent disease and borers.

Always prune with clean sharp tools that are appropriate for the type of pruning being done. You will need hand pruners for small accessible branches, and loppers, a small tree saw, and/or pole pruner for large shrubs and small trees. Electric hedge clippers are used for formal sheared hedges.

WHY DO WE PRUNE?

- *To remove unsightly, diseased, and dead branches*, those that are misshapen, crossed, or rubbing together. This may be done at any time of year.

- *To rejuvenate an old plant*. With no pruning at all, or when only the tips of branches are pruned, the shrubs become overgrown. Overgrown shrubs will have leaves on only the outer branch tips, bare branches in the center, and bare lower branches. *Renewal pruning* is often drastic cutting-back, and involves *thinning* about 1/3 of the oldest branches back to the ground, and *heading back* lateral branches to allow sunlight and air into the interior of the plant. It is sometimes done in stages over a two or three year period. This will allow for new branches to grow from the base and allow leaves to grow throughout the entire plant. A few plants are best cut back to about 8" – 12" high and allowed to re-grow.

- *To stimulate new growth on a plant*. *Heading back* and *pinching* are used to create a bushier, fuller plant. Usually the cut is made above a leaf bud or a twig turning outward.

- *To control growth and maintain a desirable size and shape of the plant*. If you select plants whose natural habits and sizes at maturity are appropriate for their places in your landscape, you can greatly minimize the need to prune for size

81

control, which is a real plus. (Refer to the *Shrubs* chapter, Table 14, for shrubs sorted by size and sun requirements to help make your selections) You may need to do some *heading* and *thinning* for the health of the plant and to keep the interior full of foliage.

TECHNIQUES FOR PRUNING

Five basic techniques are used for pruning shrubs: *pinching, heading, thinning, renewal pruning,* and *shearing.* Some plants require more of one method than another, but good pruning is usually a combination of *thinning* and *heading.* The basic techniques are:

PINCHING - is the removal of the terminal portion of a succulent, green shoot before it becomes woody and firm. Strategic *pinching* can greatly reduce the need for more dramatic pruning later on. Whenever (except late summer or fall) you see a shoot becoming excessively long, simply *pinch* off the stem tip, or cut the shoot to reduce its length, to promote side branching. Long, vigorous shoots should be cut back into the canopy instead of cut at the outer limits of the existing foliage.

Pinching is also the method used with perennials and annuals to induce branching, fuller growth, and more flowers. When flowers fade, they are removed by *deadheading.* (See the *Garden Care – Deadheading* for more details, as some plants will re-bloom)

HEADING - involves removing part of a shoot or branch, but *not at a branch point.* The branch point is the point of attachment of a branch to the trunk or another limb. *Heading* increases the number of new shoots formed from lateral buds. *Heading* stimulates branching and makes plants shorter and denser. Avoid making all heading cuts at the surface of the shrub (this is, however, the desired effect when shearing), as you will most likely destroy the graceful natural habit of the plant. Instead, cut branches randomly and at varying lengths to create a beautiful, natural, yet tidy, appearance.

The drawing below indicates where to make the *heading cuts* (on the left), and how the shrub will re-grow (on the right). Repeated *heading back* with no *thinning* cuts results in a top heavy plant. Dense top growth reduces sunlight and results in the loss of foliage inside the plant canopy.

The shape of the plant will be influenced by where you make the cut on the stem. The new terminal bud should be located on the side of the branch that faces the direction new growth is desired. The flow of sap past the cut into the shoot or new leaf bud will cause the wound to heal and prevent die-back. Make your cut above a leaf bud, flower bud, or a twig turning outward to maximize healthy outward-facing growth; if the cut is made above an inward-turning twig or bud, the new growth will be weak and spindly as it will be deprived of light.

Some plants will have two buds opposite each other on the stem. When such stems are cut, remove one of the buds if you need to control the direction of new growth. If both are allowed to grow, a forked and often weak stem may develop.

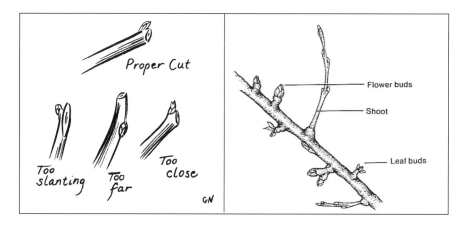

Always use clean, sharp tools, and prune on a slant. When heading, make the cut at a slight angle ¼" above the leaf bud, flower bud, or shoot turning outward. The angle will allow moisture to flow off the cut. Avoid making the cut at a sharp angle because it will produce a larger wound. A cut too far from the bud results in a dead stub that will not re-grow.

THINNING - is the least conspicuous method of pruning and results in a more open plant without stimulating excessive new growth. With *thinning,* an entire shoot or limb is removed back to a branch point, to the main trunk, or to the ground. Thinning reduces the number of new shoots from lateral buds; it inhibits branching and lets limbs grow longer. Never leave a stub when cutting off a branch, as the wound is slow to heal. If the branch is cut back to the trunk on a slant parallel with the trunk, the cut will heal and bark will grow over it.

The drawing below shows where to make the thinning cuts (on the left) and how the plant will re-grow (on the right).

A good rule-of-thumb is to thin out the oldest and tallest stems first, allowing vigorous side branch development. This method of pruning is best done with hand pruners, loppers, or a saw --- not hedge shears. Repeated *thinning* with no *heading* results in plants with long spindly branches; the entire plant may take on a straggly look.

Before   **After**

By using a combination of *thinning out* and *heading back*, as shown above, a shrub may be maintained at the same height and width for years.

RENEWAL PRUNING (REJUVENATION) - involves removing the oldest branches of a shrub by pruning them at, or slightly above, ground level leaving only the younger, more vigorous branches. Side shoots and twigs on these remaining stems may need to be *headed* or *thinned* as well if the framework has become too congested. On some shrubs, such as 'Annabelle' hydrangea and beauty berry (*Callicarpa*), all woody branches are cut back to a predetermined height each year, and foliage and flowers grow on new wood.

Before   **After**

To *rejuvenate* an old, overgrown, *multi-stemmed* shrub, 1/3 of the oldest, tallest branches can be removed at, or slightly above, ground level before new growth starts. This should be repeated over a two or three year period for complete renewal without damaging the plant. *Rejuvenation* pruning should be done during winter dormancy regardless of when the shrub flowers (on old wood or new, evergreen or deciduous), as you are trying to regain control over the shape and size of your plant and to force maximum new growth in the spring. Mid-January to early March is probably the best time for most shrubs.

If a *single-trunk* shrub has been neglected or has gotten too tall, it may not be possible to successfully rejuvenate it by this method. In such a case, *"tree up"* the shrub by cutting off lower branches and letting the top go. Alternatively, the shrub may be cut back to about 8" – 12" and let grow anew.

SHEARING – is a specialized form of *heading,* and involves cutting the terminus of most shoots with shearing or hedge clippers. This method should not be used on foundation plants but should be restricted to creating formal hedges. *Shearing* destroys the natural shape of the plant. It causes a thick profusion of growth on the exterior of the plant that precludes light from entering the center. Foliage on the interior of the plant dies and does not re-grow. *Shearing* is used in creating topiary, and over time, the result is often a veneer of green leaves over a bare woody framework. This may be acceptable for topiary, but it is not desirable for hedges.

If you want a sheared hedge, choose a small-leaved evergreen which responds well to shearing. The *Shrubs* chapter lists several good choices for this application. Spacing depends on the ultimate size of the particular plants; in general, plant the hedge material slightly closer together than the identification tag recommends. When the shrubs are a season or two old, begin to shape and prune them carefully to insure a lush, full hedge in the future. Allow the hedge to make new growth in the spring. Then prune when growth slows down or "hardens off" in May.

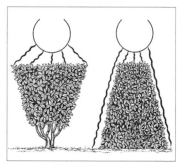

As mentioned above, a combination of pruning methods is often best, and in this case, *shearing* should be accompanied by some *thinning* to create holes for light and air to reach the interior of the hedge. Equally important is how you wield the hedge clippers. Always shape sheared hedges so they are wider at the bottom than at the top, as shown here. This allows sunlight to reach lower branches and encourages full healthy growth to ground level.

Avoid pruning shrubs into round mounds or meatballs, but rather, let the shrubs grow together on the sides. Clip along the front and back sides but not between the plants.

The subsequent frequency of shearing depends on the rate of growth of the plants since neatness and precision are essential to the beauty of a clipped hedge. Many formal hedges require shearing three or four times a year to look their best. If you are a lazy gardener, this is another good reason to let plants grow in their natural habits.

ROOT PRUNING – is used extensively in bonsai horticulture. See *Container Plants – Bonsai* for a description of the method.

Trees and shrubs, such as boxwood, which are difficult to transplant, should be root pruned two to six months before relocating in order to encourage new feeding roots to develop. Use a sharpshooter to slice all the way around the plant, either at the drip line (outer tip of the branches), or a little closer in towards the trunk. Make the cut the depth and width of the sharpshooter blade. The plant can be moved two to six months later.

Root pruning is a clever was to increase plants like *Acanthus,* which is known to re-sprout from root fragments. Circumscribe the plant with a sharpshooter as described above and new plants will soon appear near the cut line. They may be transplanted or left to create a denser stand of *Acanthus.*

FACTORS THAT DETERMINE WHEN AND HOW TO PRUNE

Knowing when and how to prune shrubs is very important, as they are not all treated the same. The major consideration when pruning *flowering shrubs*, both deciduous and evergreen, is whether they bloom on old wood (last season's growth) or new wood (current season's growth). If you prune at the wrong time of year, you will not have flowers.

The major consideration when pruning *non-flowering shrubs* (and those with inconspicuous flowers that are grown primarily for foliage), both broad-leaved and needle-leaved evergreens, is to maintain a pleasing, natural shape. Needle evergreens are generally slow-growing and should not be cut back severely. If pruned incorrectly, you may create dead stubs that never re-sprout, thereby spoiling the appearance of the plant.

PRUNING FLOWERING SHRUBS – DECIDUOUS AND EVERGREEN

SPRING BLOOMERS ARE PRUNED AFTER FLOWERING (THEY BLOOM ON OLD WOOD)

Shrubs that flower in the spring are blooming on "old wood" that was formed the previous season. They are pruned soon after flowering. This allows for vigorous growth during the summer, to provide flower buds for the following year.

The techniques of *pinching, heading,* and *thinning* are used for routine maintenance; *renewal pruning* may be necessary if the plant has been neglected.

Table 10 gives tips for pruning *spring-flowering* deciduous and evergreen shrubs and small ornamental trees. If no Special Instructions are given, prune very soon after flowering is finished.

TABLE 10. SPRING BLOOMERS – PRUNE SOON AFTER FLOWERING

SPRING BLOOM ON OLD WOOD – PRUNE AFTER FLOWERING	SPECIAL INSTRUCTIONS
Buddleia alternifolia **Butterfly Bush**	Cut back lightly after bloom.
Cercis chinensis **Chinese Redbud**	
Chaenomeles japonica **Japanese Quince**	
Chionanthus virginicus **Fringetree**	
Cornus florida **Dogwood**	
Cornus sericea **Red-Osier Dogwood, Red Twig Dogwood**	Cut back severely, almost to the ground in late Feb. – early March for more colorful stems next winter.
Deutzia species **Deutzia**	Use renewal pruning and thinning techniques.
Exochorda racemosa **Pearlbush**	
Forsythia species **Forsythia**	Flowers only on wood from previous season. After bloom, prune branches that have bloomed last two seasons by cutting to center of bush. Prune young plants lightly; old ones severely. Retain vase-like arching habit for best appearance.
Fothergilla **Fothergilla**	
Hamamelis species **Witch-hazel**	Requires little pruning.
Hydrangea macrophylla	Prune while dormant only for renewal; otherwise

SPRING BLOOM ON OLD WOOD – PRUNE AFTER FLOWERING	SPECIAL INSTRUCTIONS
Bigleaf Hydrangea	prune lightly after flowering and leave some dead flower heads over winter.
Hydrangea quercifolia **Oakleaf Hydrangea**	Prune while dormant only for renewal; otherwise prune lightly after flowering and leave some dead flower heads over winter.
Itea virginica **Virginia Sweetspire**	Prune after flowering with both thinning and heading cuts.
Kerria japonica **Kerria**	Thin all 2-year-old canes to ground level after flowers fade. New canes from base may reach height of shrub and bloom the next season. Cut off root suckers to limit spread.
Kolkwitzia amabilis **Beautybush**	Withstands, but does not require heavy pruning. Thin some of the oldest canes to ground level each spring. Head after bloom if necessary.
Leucothoe species **Leucothoe, Agarista**	Slow growing and requires little pruning. Cut older stems back to ground by thinning if desired. Some are deciduous and some evergreen.
Lonicera species **Honeysuckle**	All species grow strongly after heavy pruning. Thin all unwanted branches and head remaining branches.
Loropetalum chinense **Loropetalum**	Prune by thinning after flowering. Retain vase-like arching habit for best appearance.
Magnolia soulangiana **Saucer Magnolia**	Prune by thinning, as head cuts make for unsightly branching.
Magnolia stellata **Star Magnolia**	Prune by thinning, as head cuts make for unsightly branching.
Mahonia bealei **Mahonia**	Head old bare stems to ground after flowering (in late spring). Pinch new growth after flowering to encourage bushiness. Do not trim along top of plant.
Malus species **Crabapple**	Train to central leader 10'-12', then head leader to encourage branching. Thin lower wood to lighten branch ends each year. Prune lightly and remove suckers after bloom. Avoid severe pruning.
Philadelphus species **Mock Orange**	Use renewal pruning technique. Thin after blooming. When a branch is 4-5 years old, thin back to ground

SPRING BLOOM ON OLD WOOD – PRUNE AFTER FLOWERING	SPECIAL INSTRUCTIONS
	level. On very vigorous specimens, half of stems may be cut to ground.
Pieris species **Pieris,** **Andromeda** **Lily-of-the-valley Shrub**	
Prunus species **Cherry, Peach, Plum,** **Apricot, Almond**	
Pyracantha **Pyracantha**	Can be espaliered. Can be grown as specimen in natural landscape, which requires little pruning. For maximum berry production, remove wood that has fruited by thinning to well-placed shoots. Pinch shoots just outside outermost flower clusters to control growth.
Pyrus species **Pear**	
Rhododendron species **Azalea, Rhododendron**	Prune lightly after flowering, retaining natural habit. Open interior to light by minor thinning and heading cuts.
Rosa species **Climbing Rose,** **Rambling Rose**	See article in *Shrubs – Roses*. Climbers require little pruning; train new canes horizontally for increased flowering.
Salix discolor **Pussy Willow**	Prune by thinning.
Spiraea prunifolia **Bridal Wreath Spirea**	Prune by thinning, as head cuts make for unsightly branching. Use renewal pruning technique.
Spiraea species other spring bloomers	Prune by thinning, as head cuts make for unsightly branching. Use renewal pruning technique.
Spiraea thunbergii **Thunberg Spirea**	Prune by thinning, as head cuts make for unsightly branching. Use renewal pruning technique.
Syringa cultivars **Lilac (heat tolerant** **species)**	Prune by thinning, as head cuts make for unsightly branching.
Vaccinium ashei	Slow-growing woody shrub that flowers in early spring and fruits in mid-summer. Requires little

89

Spring Bloom on Old Wood – Prune After Flowering	Special Instructions
Blueberry, Rabbiteye	pruning. Remove oldest, weakest stems in winter or early spring. Remove weak side shoots in top of plant. Increase fruit size by heading back shoots that have an abundance of flower buds, taking care not to remove all buds.
Viburnum species **spring blooming Viburnum**	Prune by thinning, as head cuts make for unsightly branching. Prune fruit-bearers in late winter before new growth starts
Weigela florida **Weigela**	Use renewal pruning technique
Wisteria species **Wisteria**	Can be severely cut back after blooming. It can get away from you and become invasive

Summer/ Fall Bloomers are Pruned while Dormant (They Bloom on New Wood)

Shrubs that flower after June 1ˢᵗ are blooming on "new wood" that is formed in the current season. They should be pruned while dormant in late winter to promote vigorous new growth in the spring. The techniques of *pinching, heading, and thinning* are again used for routine maintenance; *renewal pruning* may be used as needed.

Table 11 gives tips for pruning *summer/fall-flowering* deciduous and evergreen shrubs and small trees. If no Special Instructions are given, prune while dormant in late winter (late January – early March is best in the Mid-South).

TABLE 11. SUMMER / FALL BLOOMERS – PRUNE WHILE DORMANT

Summer/Fall Bloom on New Wood – Prune while Dormant	Special Instructions
Abelia x grandiflora **Glossy Abelia**	Blooms on both old and new wood. Thin some old stems to ground annually in dormant season. Prune for containment in spring. Retain arching habit.
Albizia julibrissin **Mimosa**	

SUMMER/FALL BLOOM ON NEW WOOD – PRUNE WHILE DORMANT	SPECIAL INSTRUCTIONS
Berberis **Barberry**	Prune fruit-bearers in late winter before new growth starts.
Buddleia davidii, globosa **Butterfly Bush**	Prune all branches back to the second set of leaves (8" – 12" from ground) or to a low woody framework while dormant and let re-grow annually.
Callicarpa japonica **Japanese Beauty berry**	Severely cut back almost to the ground each year in late winter to promote more berries.
Calycanthus floridus **Sweetshrub**	Thin old branches in early spring. Pinch during growing season to increase bushiness.
Camellia **Camellia**	Slow growing; only requires light heading and thinning every few years after flowering. Wait to prune fall-bloomers until late winter so new growth is not stimulated in fall.
Caryopteris **Bluebeard, Blue-mist Shrub**	
Clethra alnifolia **Summersweet, Clethra**	Prune by thinning.
Gardenia **Gardenia**	Prune by heading back to promote bushiness.
Hibiscus syriacus **Shrub Althea**	
Hydrangea arborescens **'Annabelle', 'Hills of Snow' Hydrangea**	Prune to first pair of buds above the ground before new growth starts.
Hydrangea paniculata **'Pee Gee', 'Tardiva' Hydrangea**	Prune to first pair of buds above the ground before new growth starts for 'Pee Gee'. Prune 'Tardiva' less drastically.
Hypericum species **St.-Johns-wort**	

SUMMER/FALL BLOOM ON NEW WOOD – PRUNE WHILE DORMANT	SPECIAL INSTRUCTIONS
Lagerstroemia indica **Crape Myrtle**	Prune by thinning and head cuts; do not massacre. Remove suckers and old flowers. See illustration below for proper pruning technique. "Pollarding" crape myrtles is not as popular as it once was.
Nandina **Nandina**	Gradually becomes too tall with bare lower stems. Head back half of stems at 6" – 12" to refurbish lower stems. In spring peel off old leaf sheaths on the lower part of leggy nandina canes to promote fullness at the bottom. Thin some stems to ground when older leaves have turned from red to green in spring. Thin remainder of stems the following year.
Osmanthus heterophyllus or *O. x fortunei* **Holly Tea Olive, Holly Osmanthus, Fortune's Osmanthus**	Slow-growing. Pinch branch tips in spring to direct growth. Can be sheared into hedge. Thin long growth of shrub to inside laterals in April. Rejuvenation should be done in March. Will withstand heavy pruning.
Rosa species – **Floribunda Rose, GrandifloraRose**	See *Rose* article in *Shrubs* chapter
Spirea bumalda – **'Anthony Waterer' Spirea**	Prune to first pair of buds above the ground before new growth starts. Spreads by suckering.
Spiraea japonica – **Japanese Spirea**	Flowers best on young branches, so cut stems to first pair of buds before new growth starts in spring.
Symphoricarpos – **Snowberry**	
Vitex agnus-castus – **Chaste Tree**	

Many people are unsure how to prune a young crape myrtle (*Lagerstroemia*) shrub so that it will become a graceful, multi-trunked tree. The illustration below demonstrates the proper *thinning* technique, and the incorrect *heading* cuts.

**PROPER METHOD OF
PRUNING CRAPE MYRTLE**

This plant, pictured before
pruning, needs to have all weak
and dead stems removed.

Same shrub after removal of
weak and interfering wood
and base sucker growth.

Results of proper pruning are
graceful, vigorous growth with
distinctive shape.

**IMPROPER METHOD OF
PRUNING CRAPE MYRTLE**

Cutting at the dotted line is
the usual course taken by
those who prune shrubs.

The same plant after bad pruning,
as indicated above. The sucker
growth remains.

Results: the lovely natural shape
of the shrub is lost, and bloom
will be sparse.

PRUNING BROAD-LEAVED EVERGREENS GROWN FOR FOLIAGE

These shrubs normally need less pruning than deciduous shrubs because they are slower growing and usually have a more restrained growth habit. Some evergreens grow so slowly they need almost no pruning.

Begin size and shape control when plants are young. Do not wait until they are old and woody. Branches in center get shaded out. First cut out all the dead wood and the branches that turn in and overlap in the center. This opens up the plant to light. The plant will thicken where it is cut.

For most broad-leaved evergreens, *thinning* and judicious *heading* is the most desirable procedure. Some evergreens, like boxwood, holly, and box-leaf

93

euonymus, can be *sheared* when a stiff, formal appearance is desired; however, they will still need to be thinned occasionally to prevent bare interior branches.

Evergreen shrubs grown for foliage, listed in Table 12, should be pruned in late winter before new growth starts; late January to early March is best. Minor corrective pruning can be done at any time.

Coniferous, needle-leaved evergreens, while also pruned in late winter, are treated somewhat differently and will be discussed separately below.

TABLE 12. BROAD-LEAVED EVERGREENS FOR FOLIAGE – PRUNE WHILE DORMANT

BROAD-LEAVED EVERGREENS FOR FOLIAGE – PRUNE WHILE DORMANT	SPECIAL INSTRUCTIONS
Aucuba japonica **Aucuba**	Slow growing and requires little pruning. Thin whole branches close to the ground to retain natural shape and to induce new low growth if old plant becomes leggy and tall.
Buxus species **Boxwood**	See special article on boxwood in Shrubs. Important to open center to light and air by thinning. Does not respond well to severe pruning, and may not survive it.
Cleyera japonica (or *Ternstroemia*) **Cleyera**	Produces fragrant, inconspicuous flowers in late spring. Shape lightly by heading and thinning after blooming or anytime in growing season. Good 4' – 6' shrub.
Cotoneaster species **Cotoneaster**	Prune these berried shrubs in late winter for control of tangled growth, even though it is a spring bloomer.
Danae racemosa **Alexandrian Laurel,** **Poet's Laurel**	Slow-growing elegant 3' shrub has inconspicuous flowers in late spring and berries in the fall, but is grown for foliage. Prune by thinning after flowering if necessary.
Elaeagnus pungens **Thorny Eleagnus**	Insignificant flowers in fall on this fast-growing unruly evergreen. Prune by thinning and heading the longest stray shoots in late winter, or as needed through the growing season.

BROAD-LEAVED EVERGREENS FOR FOLIAGE – PRUNE WHILE DORMANT	SPECIAL INSTRUCTIONS
Euonymus japonica **Evergreen Euonymus**	Some are variegated; all subject to scale and have inconspicuous flowers. Prune by thinning and heading in late winter.
Fatsia japonica **Japanese Fatsia**	Requires little pruning. Can grow to 20'. To control size remove largest stems at ground level in spring. For bigger leaves, remove little golf-ball bloom.
Ilex cornuta and other spiny hollies **Chinese Holly**	Very important to select correct size holly for your site; then it requires little pruning. May be treed-up if too overgrown. Prune by thinning and heading in winter; cut berried branches for Christmas decorations if desired. Refer to the hollies article in Shrubs for more.
Ilex crenata **Japanese Holly**	Requires little pruning as it is slow-growing. May be sheared for formal hedges or topiary; can be pruned like boxwood so inside branches have light and air and don't become bare.
Ilex vomitoria **Yaupon**	Weeping varieties require little pruning. Shrub types may be sheared into clipped hedge. Prune lightly in late winter if desired.
Illicium species **Anise**	The white or maroon flowers in spring are not very showy; anise is grown for beautiful foliage and neat rounded habit. Requires little pruning other than thinning and heading occasionally for best appearance.
Ligustrum japonicum **Japanese Privet, Wax-leaf privet**	Used for hedges. Shearing 3 – 4 times a year produces dense growth.
Ligustrum lucidum **Glossy Privet**	Tree growing to 40'; can be trained as shrub, hedge, or tree. Leave young shoots rising from spreading laterals to fill in center.
Osmanthus fragrans **Osmanthus, Fragrant Tea Olive**	Produces tiny, fragrant flowers sporadically from fall through spring. Pinch branch tips in late spring to direct and control growth. Hedges can be sheared in early spring. Thin long growth of shrub to inside laterals in May. Heavy pruning of overgrown specimens should be done in April.

BROAD-LEAVED EVERGREENS FOR FOLIAGE – PRUNE WHILE DORMANT	SPECIAL INSTRUCTIONS
Photinia **Photinia**	Grown primarily for evergreen habit and bright red new foliage. Fast growing, it sprouts from old wood if pruned hard for containment or renewal. Attractive when sheared several times a season as it produces new red foliage. Can be grown as tree or shrub.
Prunus laurocerasus **Laurel**	Some of these evergreens have inconspicuous flowers, others are showier, but all have good dark foliage. Fast-growing, dense, large-leafed. Black berries are spread by birds. Used as hedge or screen. Overgrown specimens respond to renewal pruning in late winter. Otherwise, prune during growing season.
Sarcococca confusa **Sarcococca,** **Sweet Box**	Produces fragrant, inconspicuous flowers in late spring. Shape lightly by heading and thinning after blooming.

PRUNING NEEDLE-LEAVED EVERGREENS – CONIFERS

Coniferous, or cone-bearing, evergreen trees and shrubs require little or no pruning if sited where they have plenty of room to grow. One of the characteristics of coniferous, needle-leaved evergreens, like pine (*Pinus*), Japanese cedar (*Cryptomeria*), white cedar (or false cypress) (*Chamaecyparis*), China fir (*Cunninghamia*), and hemlock (*Tsuga*), is that they develop a pyramidal or columnar growth habit from a "central leader" or central main stem. Hemlock, spruce, and fir do not generally perform as well in the heat of the South as do pine, Leyland cypress, Japanese cedar, arborvitae, juniper, and white cedar.

They branch once a year, when new growth starts, and produce a *whorl* or circular growth of branches at the growing tips, which is referred to as a "candle". When the candle has extended almost to its full length, but before the needles are fully developed, remove about half the length of the candle. The central leader, however, may not be shortened by more than a couple of inches or it will not re-grow as these conifers lack latent buds on old wood. When pruning is necessary, it is done in early summer with the removal of half of the terminal candle, as shown.

For extra bushiness, terminals of lateral branches may be removed as shown below on the left. New growth on lateral (side) branches may be cut slightly shorter than that on the leader.

Terminal buds of evergreen trees are easily damaged. When the entire terminal dies or is removed, a new leader can be developed by tying up a lateral branch where the original terminal had been, as indicated in the drawing above on the right. Evergreen trees will not recover well if cut back severely.

 Japanese cedar (*Cryptomeria*)**, deodar cedar** (*Cedrus*)**,** and **white cedar (or false cypress)** (*Chamaecyparis*)**,** all medium-to-fast growing *cone-bearers*, are usually not pruned much, if at all, because the natural form is so lovely when they have space to grow. They may be *thinned* and *headed back* lightly if desired.

 Another cone-bearer, the **Leyland cypress** (*X Cupressocyparis*) grows very quickly to 60'; a tree with pyramidal habit and fine, feathery foliage. By contrast, it may be pruned almost indefinitely to maintain a certain shape. Owing to its fast growth rate, it is very popular for quick hedges, screens, or groupings. S*hearing, thinning, and heading* are used anytime in the growing season.

 Juniper (*Juniperus*)**, arborvitae** (*Thuja*)**,** and **Japanese plum yew** (*Cephalotaxus*) are the most commonly planted *narrow-leaved, "berry-forming" evergreens*. The berries are technically cones, but they do not look it. Although

97

some dwarf forms are available, most cultivars require some annual pruning to control size, shape, and density. This type of evergreen branches as growth proceeds through the season and will produce new shoots at the point of pruning. *Thinning* and *shearing* are the best techniques for juniper and arborvitae; Japanese plum yew responds best to *heading* and *thinning* cuts but not *shearing*.

Soon after a period of new growth, thin to side shoots near the plant's center to give a natural appearance, especially for shrubs that branch irregularly. Start thinning in the top of the shrub and work downward. Prune less severely as you proceed. More compact plants result when long branches are pruned back to their junction at a lateral branch during early spring.

Cuts should be made "back in" so that new growth will soon cover exposed stubs as shown at right. Green foliage must remain on any branches of junipers, plum yew, and arborvitae that are cut back. They are seldom able to develop new growth from bare stubs.

Arborvitae and juniper develop a *dead zone* in the center of the plant. When pruning is done either on the top or the sides, cuts should not be made into the dead zone. A new leader cannot develop on plants that have been cut back too far. Overgrown arborvitae and pyramidal juniper cannot be pruned back more than 20 percent, and it is best done in March or April.

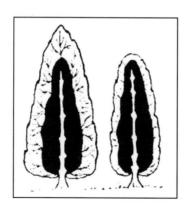

For many years, shearing needle-leaved evergreen shrubs was popular. Sheared plants, however, suggest a formality that is somewhat incompatible with today's more natural landscapes. Once a plant has been sheared, it is almost impossible to restore its natural form. It is therefore best to reserve shearing for broad-leaved hedge plants.

Yews can be cut back more severely and are often able to survive a 40 percent size reduction, but as they are slow-growing it is hard to imagine why you would do this. Major pruning should be done in April if needed, although light shaping may be done at any time of year.

Japanese plum yew (*Cephalotaxus*) does not respond well to shearing. English Yew (*Taxus*) and Juniper (*Juniperus*) are well-suited to shearing, but both are equally beautiful left in their natural shape. Remember to create some thinning "holes" for light to penetrate to interior branches and keep them green.

If a needle-leaved evergreen has become overgrown, past the point that it can be successfully pruned back to size, the best option is to dig it up and replace it with a more appropriately-sized plant.

SPECIALTY PRUNING – ESPALIER, TOPIARY

ESPALIER

Espalier (pronounced ess–*pall*–iyea) is the training and pruning of a plant against walls, fences, trellises, or wire frames. Skillful shaping of shrubs, vines, and trees can make them conform to any number of formal or informal designs. An espaliered plant is grown flat in one plane and only one branch thick so all other growth must be pruned off. This is done after new growth has matured in the spring and again in late August.

Choose a northern or eastern location where the plant does not receive full, hot summer sun. If possible, a wooden or metal trellis, latticework, or wires should stand about 6" away from the house or wall so air can circulate. This allows plants

99

to be conveniently sprayed and wood structures to be painted. However, plants may be espaliered directly on a brick surface using masonry nails.

Start with a young one- or two-year-old plant with lateral branches which will conform to the planned design. Plant the bush or tree just like any other. Do not overfeed because rampant growth is undesirable. A nursery plant which is already growing on a trellis may be quicker.

Gently bend the lateral branches into position, and attach them to the support with a soft material (leather or rubber strips, raffia) which will not cut the bark as wire does. As with any pruning, speed vertical growth by removing side shoots or turn one stem into many by cutting back to force branching. Slow growth by turning shoots down or stimulate growth by turning shoots up.

The plants best adapted to espalier produce many side branches and tolerate constant pruning. They are ivy, sasanqua camellia, eleagnus, fig vine, dwarf fruit trees, holly, juniper, photinia, pyracantha, loropetalum, flowering quince, Japanese plum yew, and wisteria.

TOPIARY

Topiary is the art of sculpting a plant into a three dimensional shape, usually geometric, but also whimsical figures of animals, etc. Topiary must be continually clipped and pruned so use a very hardy plant species. Two or three plants are needed for some large designs. Elaborate figures usually require a metal frame. It takes four to five years to produce a conventional topiary.

It is much quicker to shape a frame from aluminum wire tied at the joints. Mount the frame securely in a pot. Small-leafed ivy, creeping fig, or other healthy, small-leaved vines will grow up and over it. Keep clipped and use hairpins to tie any loose vine in place.

Another method is to fill a frame with sphagnum moss. Wrap the sphagnum moss with nylon fishing line to hold it in place. Plant the vine in the moss. It will quickly cover the surface. Keep the potted topiary moist by misting and occasionally add fertilizer to the water. Never allow the moss to dry out.

PROPAGATION

Increasing the number of plants from existing ones is known as plant propagation. Plants are propagated from seeds or by vegetative methods (cuttings, etc.). Nearly all annuals, some perennials, and most vegetables are easily grown from seeds. It is usually best to purchase new seeds rather than to plant saved seeds, because few seeds remain viable long enough. Most seedlings do not "breed true" or duplicate their parents. Because the seeds of some flowers and vegetables are difficult to germinate, it is best to start those from bedding plants purchased from a garden store or catalog. Propagation is fun, economical, and rewarding.

SEED PLANTING

Most garden plants can be grown at home from seeds, and this may be the best route for hard-to-find flowers, wildflowers, or for very easy ones like zinnias. A few can be planted directly into the flower bed, but in general they should be started indoors or in a cold frame about six weeks before outdoor planting time. (See *Sheltered Gardening – Cold Frames*)

In a cold frame, seeds can be planted either in flats or boxes or directly in the soil in the frame. Here they can be protected by glass from frost and beating rains. A miniature cold frame can be improvised with a box and a piece of window glass. When the weather gets warm, the glass can be removed and the box or frame shaded with slats or burlap.

COLD FRAME – Take any good garden loam, pulverize, and mix with compost or peat moss for humus, and builder's sand for drainage. Firm the soil by tamping with hand or tool.

- Make shallow furrows with finger or pencil, drop seed in furrows.
- Cover seed lightly with soil, firm with fingers. Small seeds, like petunia, should be barely covered. Check package for planting depth. Plant seeds deeper in sandy soil, and shallower in heavy clay soil.
- Level off by firming overall again with board or brick.
- Water thoroughly with fine spray.
- Cover with two thicknesses of damp newspaper which must be weighted down. This keeps the soil moist and prevents seed from washing away.
- Water daily through newspaper.
- At first sign of seedlings breaking through ground, remove paper and shade frame with slats or burlap.
- As soon as the second set of leaves appears, thin seedlings or transplant into rows 2" apart. Lift seedling by leaves rather than stems to avoid injuring stem.
- Remove to the garden when root system has developed and after the danger of frost is past.

OPEN GROUND – Use the same system with sturdy seeds like zinnias and marigolds. Too much stress cannot be put upon the importance of firming the seed in the ground. If the soil is loose on top, the seed will wash or float away with the first watering.

101

STARTING SEED INDOORS – Seeds may be started in a sunny southern window in large flower pots or shallow pans. Put broken flower pot shards in the bottom for drainage and fill to 1" from the top of the pot with a commercial seed starter mix or a sifted mixture of half garden loam and half sand. Sow seed as above, water gently, and shade with newspaper. Keep moist and warm (60° – 70°). A miniature greenhouse can be made by enclosing the container with a plastic bag or covering it with glass or plastic. Uncover as soon as sprouts appear. When the second set of leaves appears (in two to three weeks) transplant into flats containing a sifted mixture of 1/3 soil, 1/3 sand, and 1/3 humus. Do not crowd. Give the seedlings warmth, full sun, and daily watering until ready to move into the garden. Garden centers have a variety of seed starting materials (sterile soil, peat pots, flats, etc.)

VEGETATIVE PROPAGATION

Many shrubs and perennials and most house plants are easy to reproduce *vegetatively*. Small pieces of a plant can be rooted and grown into exact duplicates of the parent plant. This offspring is known as a clone. This type of propagation makes it possible to increase one's stock of plants very inexpensively. Only the simplest methods will be described here: divisions, softwood cuttings, leaf cuttings, runners, layering, and air layering. Tissue culture is mentioned only because it has had such a huge impact on the nursery world.

DIVISIONS: Many house plants and perennials can be increased by the division of old plants. Dig up the plant with a large enough dirtball that the roots aren't damaged. A machete or spade may be used to slice the clump into two or three sections for replanting.

Divide plants with multiple crowns or roots and grow the divisions as separate plants. Carefully cut or pull apart the crown or root mass, plant each one individually, and water thoroughly. Keep shaded for a week or so and water sparingly until new plants have begun to grow.

The best time to separate house plants such as African violet or Boston fern is when new growth starts. Spring and summer flowering perennials (iris, phlox, columbine, Shasta daisy, etc.) should be lifted with a spading fork and divided in September. Divide fall flowering perennials in the spring. Some perennials, such as helleborus, bleeding-heart, and peony, can be left undisturbed for years.

CUTTINGS: A cutting is a piece of a plant which, when severed from the parent plant, will form new roots and grow into an exact replica of the parent plant.

SOFTWOOD CUTTINGS: Softwood or stem tip cuttings are used to propagate almost all houseplants (begonia, fuchsia, geranium, and philodendron), many perennials (phlox and pinks), and shrubs (azalea, boxwood, euonymus, and quince).

Cuttings from houseplants may be taken at any time of the year so long as the plant is in active growth and not dormant. Cuttings taken from dormant plants root very slowly. Cut perennials in early summer when the season's growth is well advanced. Take cuttings of shrubs from the current season's growth in late spring or early summer as soon as the new growth begins to become firm.

The rooting medium should hold moisture, but drain well, and remain well aerated. The best mediums are perlite; clean, sharp sand; or a mixture of equal parts of sand, vermiculite, and peat moss, or you can buy Pro-Mix®. Some plants root easily in water though the root system will be a bit fragile and the cuttings a little more difficult to plant. Put the rooting medium in flower pots, any household container with drainage holes punched in the bottom, flats, cold frames, or beds in shady outdoor spots. Have the medium well moistened before inserting the cuttings.

To make the cuttings, choose the tips of short healthy stems, trying to avoid a flowering stem. With a clean, sharp knife or razor blade make a diagonal cut just below a node or place where the stem and leaf come together. The cuttings should be from 2" – 6" long, depending upon the size of the plant from which they are taken. Remove all flower buds and the leaves on the lower one-third of the cutting. Large-leaved plants such as hydrangea or fig must have one-half of each leaf snipped off. This allows all energy to be channeled to root growth.

Dip the bottom of the cutting in a commercial root hormone powder and shake off excess. With a pencil or sharp stick make a hole for the cutting in the rooting medium. Insert the cutting and firm the medium around it to hold it upright. Space the cuttings about 3" apart. Keep shaded. Keep moist but not wet. This is easier if the container is enclosed in a plastic bag or covered with glass or plastic for a greenhouse effect. The humidity stays high and the soil moist with little watering. It may be necessary to raise the cover daily and wipe off excess moisture to prevent fungus, mildew, or decay. Rooting time varies from a few weeks to months, depending on the type of plant.

As roots begin to grow well, gradually remove the covering to harden the new plants. Houseplants should be planted in small pots just large enough to hold them. When the roots are 1" long, move to progressively larger pots as needed. Increase only one size at a time. Plant perennials and shrubs in the ground as soon as their root systems are nicely formed. Water new plantings well and shade for 7 – 10 days. Pinch out the tiny growing tips to make bushy plants. Do not fertilize until plants are well established. If new growth has not appeared on cuttings of slow-growing shrubs by fall, leave them in the rooting medium and keep protected in a cold frame until spring.

LEAF CUTTINGS: Leaf cuttings are used to propagate houseplants with thick fleshy leaves, such as African violets, gloxinias and other gesneriads, begonias, peperomias, and many succulents. Cut a healthy mature leaf with about 2" of leaf stalk. Set into moist rooting medium so that the leaf just touches the medium. Cover with plastic or glass to create a greenhouse effect. Give plenty of light. Roots will form and eventually small shoots will appear at the base of the parent leaf. When the plantlets are one-third the size of the parent, gently pull the new shoots away from the parent and pot separately.

Many plants, such as Rex begonias and African violets, are propagated by *vein leaf cuttings*. Slit the large veins on the underside of the leaf with a razor blade. Lay the leaf, right side up, on wet sand or other rooting medium. Push the leaf stem down into the rooting medium. Secure the cuts by hair pins or weight the leaf with sand or a pebble. Cover and treat as above. New plants will grow at each incision.

RUNNERS: It is a simple matter to propagate plants which produce runners (Boston fern, pick-a-back, spider plant). Runners are prostrate shoots which appear at the base of the plant and root at the joints, forming plantlets. Simply fasten down a runner into a pot filled with potting soil and keep moist. When a good root system is established and new leaves appear, sever the new plant from its parent.

LAYERING: Layering is a good method for increasing plants like azalea, boxwood, and forsythia. Bend a flexible branch to the ground, a foot from the tip. Dig a shallow trench and mix in sharp sand and peat. Scrape away about 2" of the bark on the underside of the branch. Dust with hormone powder and bury the branch 3" deep. Secure it with wire or a brick. The buried stem will have roots by spring. At this time cut the plant from its parent and transplant.

AIR LAYERING: Air layering is recommended for woody plants such as camellia, hibiscus, and magnolia which are difficult to root. Use this method with house plants which have grown too tall or leggy or those which are hard to root (croton, corn plant, dieffenbachia, rubber plant, and schefflera). Any time of the year is satisfactory, but spring is most successful. Make a slanting cut one-half way through a stem or branch 8" – 14" below the growing tip. Do not detach from the parent plant. Treat the cut with hormone powder and place wet sphagnum moss over it and wedge it into the cut. Wrap the moss with plastic and tie it with string at each end. Do not allow the moss to dry out. When new roots are plentiful, sever the stem below the ball of moss, remove plastic, and plant without disturbing the roots. Cover with a plastic bag until the new plant is well established. Be sure to allow air circulation on hot days.

TISSUE CULTURE: This is the propagation method that has revolutionized the nursery trade in the last decade. It is possible but not easy for the home gardener to do, because everything must be sterilized at every step; test tubes, growing medium, forceps, pipettes, and Petri dishes. Basically you sterilize a section of plant root, stem, meristem, or leaf in a bleach solution, and cut it into small pieces and place these pieces in test tubes with a gel growing medium. As the cells divide and the plantlets get larger, they are eventually transferred to sterile potting soil and allowed to grow. The new plant is genetically identical to the parent, so there is no variability as you sometimes get with seeds.

When "plant explorers" and the nurseries they are associated with, find wonderful plants in Korea, China, Syria, Argentina, and so on, they are able to propagate them by tissue culture and have enough to sell in a couple of years, instead of the five to ten years it takes to get a new species to market if grown from seeds. This has made it economically feasible for nurseries to offer many more interesting species than ever before.

Tissue culture is also used to create improved hybrids of almost anything. The hybridizers can introduce or alter such characteristics as variegation, disease-resistance, flower color, duration of bloom, growth habit, cold-hardiness, and so on. The improved garden-worthiness and disease resistance of so many new plants greatly decreases the need for pesticides.

SHELTERED GARDENING

COLD FRAME

A cold frame is a bottomless box with a transparent cover which is used to extend the growing season. Cold frames can be bought or built, and are generally about 6' x 3'. They may be made of wood, brick, or concrete. If wood is used, it should be painted or treated to prevent rot. The lid on the cold frame may be either window-pane glass or clear acrylic plastic. While not as transparent as glass, plastic has the advantages of being lighter and non-breakable.

The top should be hinged either at the back of the frame or from a central bar in the middle to allow ventilation. A cold frame gets hot even on cold days and ventilation is a must. In this area there are very few days cold enough to keep the glass down tight. Most of the time, the glass should be kept open a crack at the low end by inserting a notched stick or other device. On warm days, when the temperature gets to 70°F or above, ventilation should be provided on the high side as well.

Ideally the frame should face south so that it gets full benefit of winter sun. The rear of the frame should be 18" high, sloping to 12" in the front. This sloping toward the front allows more sunlight in the frame.

The frame can be placed directly on the ground or can be secured to a foundation of brick or concrete. The soil must be well drained. This may be achieved by digging down 12", adding a 4" layer of sand or pea gravel, and replacing the dirt. The soil inside a cold frame should be a rich mixture of equal parts soil, humus, and sand. The soil needs to be revitalized each year with the addition of humus.

105

Cold frames have many uses. They can be used to start seedlings in advance of the outdoor season. In the cold frame, seeds may be sown directly in the ground or started in peat pots or flats. Cold frames are also useful in hardening off seedlings and other small plants that have been grown in the greenhouse and are not ready for full exposure to outdoors. They can be used to carry less hardy patio plants over the winter and to propagate plants from cuttings taken in early-to-mid summer.

Bulbs for the house may be forced in cold frames. Put the pots in the frame, fill the frame with wet leaves, and cover with the glass top; two months later the pots should be filled with vigorous roots. After moving the bulb pots into a lighter area, there is still plenty of time to start seedlings for spring planting.

Cold frames can be converted to hot frames by the addition of electric heating cables placed 6" under the soil. These cables (with instructions) are available from garden supply stores or catalogs.

BAY WINDOW GREENHOUSE

Some successful indoor gardeners have had amazing results by the use of a "bay window greenhouse". Southern exposure is most preferable; an eastern exposure is second best. Build or place a copper-lined plant box (copper prevents rust) across the entire window space. Length and breadth depend on individual requirements, but the depth should be 6 to 12 inches. Fill the bottom of the box with sand or pebbles to retain moisture. Set the flower pots on this base and water them when the surface of the soil begins to dry out. The constant evaporation from the wet sand or pebbles will furnish the necessary humidity for the plants. In this manner the three indoor gardening essentials – good drainage, moisture, and sunlight – are provided. It is also desirable to keep the room temperature as cool as possible. Using this method, one can successfully grow a wider variety of tender plants than would be possible otherwise.

MONTH BY MONTH GUIDE

The calendar of garden activities which follows is the culmination of years of gardening experience in the Mid-South. Many gardeners today are less ambitious about growing plants from seed or starting their own truck patch, but the advice is retained for those who are interested.

Many garden plants today have improved insect- and disease-resistance and do not require constant spraying. Use your judgment when consulting this calendar. If your plants are insect-free, do not spray them. The calendar is meant to acknowledge the fact, for example, that whiteflies are worse in summer than other times of the year, and you would be more likely to find infestations then.

As for the fertilizing schedule, you do not want to overdo it. The minimum recommendations are to top-dress the entire garden in early spring with compost, dehydrated manure, and pine bark mulch. In July, you could broadcast a little slow-release fertilizer on all the beds. In November, top-dress all beds with 0–20–20 and fresh mulch. This should be adequate for keeping your beds in good condition.

Some excellent gardeners go way beyond the minimum, however, and many of their secrets have been incorporated into this calendar over the years. Use this Month by Month Guide as a reference for timing garden activities, but do not feel compelled to bug spray or over-fertilize plants which are thriving merely because this guide says to.

JANUARY

January is usually a quiet month in the garden and is a good time to prepare for spring. Order annual seeds and perennials from catalogs; experiment with some new and unusual plants.

107

Photograph your winter garden to reveal the bones. It is easier to see how and where to create garden rooms, or where you might need more evergreen material, taller plants, and other aesthetic concerns.

PLANTING

- Perennials, trees, and shrubs – may be moved while they are winter dormant as long as the ground is not frozen and the soil is workable.

- Sweet peas – the latter part of this month is the ideal time for planting.

- Seeds – start your vegetable seeds such as broccoli, cabbage, cauliflower, onions, Bibb lettuce, and annual flower seeds indoors in plastic cell packs. Write the name of seeds and date on plastic plant stakes to avoid confusion. Use a light soil mixture such as metro mix. After planting the seeds, mist soil until thoroughly damp and cover with plastic wrap. Check soil weekly to make sure it is damp. Put seed trays in a sunny window to keep warm. (See *Garden Care – Propagation* for more details)

- Plant asparagus, horseradish, and Jerusalem artichoke in the ground now. Remove the dead tops of old asparagus plants now to prevent damage to any new growth shoots.

- Pansy seedlings may still be moved into border if you didn't do this in late fall.

FREEZE PROTECTION

- Always water plants well before a severe freeze to insulate the roots; they should still be covered with their fall mulch. When perennials come out of the frozen ground, or "heave", push them back into the ground as soon as possible and cover with mulch. Watch pansies and roses carefully for heaving problems.

- To protect evergreens during extreme cold, use old sheets to loosely cover plants. Pile extra leaves or straw around the trunk of young evergreens to help them preserve moisture.

FERTILIZE

- Trees and some shrubs – the period of January, February, and March is the proper time to fertilize. Fertilize winter-blooming camellias after they flower. (See *Garden Care – Suggested Schedule for Fertilizing Garden*) Apply Osmocote®, or Milorganite® and cottonseed meal fertilizer, to both newly-planted and well-established trees and bushes.

- Lawns – apply lime if needed, and if not done in December. Spread sand in low areas.

SPRAY

- Spraying dormant oil is one of the most important activities during January or February to protect holly, boxwood, camellia, photinia, and euonymus (broad-leaved evergreens) from scale, spider mites, aphids, and so on. Roses, most perennials, trees, and shrubs benefit from this dormant oil spraying as it helps curtail insect problems later in the season. (See *Garden Care – Pests and Diseases* for more on the use of dormant oil)

- Kill winter weeds with an herbicide. Spray only the green clumps and not the dormant lawn.

MULCH

- Turn compost piles to encourage decomposition.

PRUNE

- Prune summer-flowering shrubs, needle-leaved evergreens, and broad-leaved evergreens grown for foliage anytime from mid-January to early March. Refer to *Garden Care – Pruning* for techniques and a table of plants to prune while dormant.

- Boxwood – most cultivars do not require much pruning and look best in their natural shape. Clean up boxwood by removing all the dead leaves from the interior branches. Shake out dead foliage and rake up debris. Major pruning is also done at this time if necessary. Thin boxwood foliage by cutting small branches about 6" – 8" in length; this is discussed in detail in *Shrubs – Boxwood*. Varieties such as 'Green Pillow', 'Compacta', 'Morris Dwarf', 'Morris Midget', 'Curly Locks', and 'Kingsville Dwarf' have dense foliage that benefits from thinning. Thin boxwood in December if you want greenery for Christmas decorations. Do not shear for formal hedges until June.

- Do not prune spring-blooming trees or shrubs until after they bloom. Do not prune roses until late February or March.

- Helleborus and epimedium – trim off weather-beaten evergreen leaves to allow February flowers to show their best and stimulate production of new foliage. Do not be alarmed if helleborus leaves lie flat on the ground; they often do this before sending up new foliage and flowers in January and February.

- Remove dead, diseased, or crossed branches anytime. Be on the look out for insects and disease.

WINTER GREENERY FOR HOUSE DECORATIONS

- Aucuba will root in water; as light is required, use a glass container.
- Mahonia will bloom and last a long time.
- A tablespoon of sugar added to the water will help hold berries on holly.

HOUSE PLANTS

- Poinsettias and Christmas cactus make great house plants if you keep them watered and in good light.

- After holiday-blooming, paperwhite narcissus have finished flowering, plant in the yard, fertilize, and allow foliage to die back naturally. To try and save forced hyacinth, cut off the flower stalk, keep watered, fertilized, and located in a sunny window until danger of frost has passed, and then plant in the garden in a sunny spot. They may produce flowers again.

- Wash and dust off leaves. Water only when soil surface is dry; mist often. Do not mist geraniums or *Gesneriads* (African violets, gloxinia, etc.). Increase house plant fertilizer applications to full strength as days are getting longer which means house plants begin to grow.

- Inspect for insects and disease. To keep your house plants free of red spider mites, scale, whitefly, and other indoor pests, spray with insecticidal soap or other organic products.

MISCELLANEOUS

- See that birds are provided with crumbs, wild bird seed, and suet (either store-bought or a homemade mixture of peanut butter, cornmeal or oatmeal, and shortening). Peanut butter alone will choke birds. Water is essential.

- Get lawn mowers, hedge clippers, and pruning tools cleaned, repaired, sharpened, and lubricated with WD–40®.

- Place catalog orders for summer-fall-blooming bulbs such as lily, gladiolus, dahlia, calla, oxalis, hedychium, and so on, to be delivered in spring for March – April planting time.

JANUARY BLOOM

Perennials – galanthus, fetid helleborus, hardy cyclamen

Shrubs – camellia, forsythia, winter honeysuckle, quince, vernal witch-hazel, winter jasmine, wintersweet, and Persian ironwood or parrotia

Berries – aucuba, deciduous holly, winterberry, most hollies, nandina, juniper, yaupon, viburnum

FEBRUARY

The weather in February is highly variable with days as warm as 65° and as cold as 10°. Many planting, pruning, and garden maintenance tasks may be done during a warm period in February when the ground is workable.

PLANT

- Get dormant trees and shrubs planted or moved by the end of this month. Planting as early as practicable will give the root system a chance to establish before the onset of hot summer weather. If you are planting dogwoods or broad-leaved evergreens like boxwood, holly, or photinia, remember that they like to be "planted high" and have good drainage. Consult *Trees* and *Shrubs* chapters for culture of specific plants.

- Seed – sow seed outdoors of cornflowers (*Centaurea*), larkspur (*Consolida*), and *Phlox drummondi*. Start annual, perennial, and vegetable seeds indoors, as described in January, if you haven't already done so. Start tomatoes, peppers, and eggplants in mid-February.

- Seedlings that were started in January need to be toughened up now by moving them outside to a cold frame.

- Most perennials may be divided and transplanted at the end of this month.

- Roses – plant roses anytime between February 15th and April 15th. This applies to planting of new roses and moving old ones. (See *Shrubs – Roses*)

- Clematis, lilac, and peony should be planted now in soil that has a pH of 6.5 or higher; add dolomitic lime if necessary. Make sure that the clematis roots will be shaded and that the vine will be in the sun. Peonies and lilacs prefer an eastern exposure that protects them from our hot afternoon sun.

- If plants heave, add more soil and mulch around the ball of the plant and then soak with water.

LAWNS

- Apply post-emergent weed control on your lawn if weeds were not killed in January. Do not use herbicide on Saint Augustine grass.

- Apply pre-emergent weed control on lawns about the time forsythia blooms.

- Apply lime to lawn if needed and not done in December or January.

- De-thatch lawns.

FERTILIZE

- Any time from mid-February to late-March, top-dress flower and shrub borders with amendments (manure, compost, lime, bone meal, etc.) and/or mulch (pine bark chips, pine needles, etc.) as needed. When forsythia blooms, the soil temperature will be around 50°F. Plants are stirring out of dormancy and their roots will absorb fertilizer.

- Roses – apply top-dressing of cottonseed meal or Milorganite® under generous layer of compost or rotted manure. Keep manure away from stems. (See *Shrubs – Roses*)

- Fertilize fruit trees and summer-flowering shrubs with a 5–10–15 or 10–10–10 fertilizer. Measure the circumference of the tree that needs to be fertilized at about knee height. As a rule of thumb, use a pound of 10–10–10 or 5–10–15 per inch of circumference. Scatter the fertilizer at the "drip line", or the outer tip of the furthest branch.
- Fertilize pecan trees with a zinc-type fertilizer.
- Fertilize boxwood now. Several recipes are suggested in the *Shrubs – Boxwood* chapter. Fertilize once yearly, anytime in February or March.
- Lightly sprinkle all blueberry bushes with a camellia-azalea type fertilizer. Be careful of their shallow roots.

PRUNE

- The latter part of the month, it is important to get evergreens pruned for size and shape control before new growth comes out. Prune trees and shrubs that bloom after June 1st now, while they are dormant. (Prune trees and shrubs that bloom before June 1st after they flower.) Read the *Garden Care – Pruning* section carefully before getting started. Also refer to the special articles in *Shrubs* for specifics on several bushes. After pruning shrubs, fertilize with a slow release fertilizer.
- Prune shade trees now. Hire a professional to "limb up" big trees to create high shade which most plants love.
- Cut out dead wood on any trees or shrubs.
- Prune crape myrtles now. Do not cut them back to the trunk.
- Prune any orange bronzing off of boxwood to prepare for new growth.
- Prune off old holly berries to promote blooming for new berries, if you didn't cut them for Christmas decorations.
- Renewal-prune overgrown mophead, lacecap, and oakleaf hydrangeas the last week in the month; otherwise, prune after flowering, or leave old flower-heads on the stems. 'Annabelle', 'Tardiva', and 'Pee Gee' hydrangeas should be cut back to 12" – 24" tall now.
- Some roses are pruned now, but not all. Refer to *Shrubs – Roses* for details. Climbers are not pruned as severely as floribundas, polyanthas, and hybrid teas.
- Prune summer-flowering clematis hybrids, which bloom on new growth, to about 18". (See *Vines – Clematis* for a full discussion)

SPRAY

- The first big job of the month is to get a dormant spray on the garden if you did not do so in January.
- Yellow, raised blisters on boxwood indicate leafminer infestation. Take a small branch to your nursery for an insecticide recommendation.

112

- Spray peonies with a fungicide, such as Copper or potassium bicarbonate, to protect them from botrytis which damages the peony blooms, turning the petals brown.

- Watch for hosta shoots coming up in late February, and apply the first treatment of slug bait.

COLD FRAME

- Flower seeds of perennials and annuals – for early bloom, plant seeds of blue salvia, feverfew (*Tanacetum*), lupine, nicotiana, scabiosa, snapdragon (*Antirrhinum*), verbena, and so on. See *Garden Care – Seed Planting* and – *Shelter Gardening* for details on constructing and using a cold frame.

- Cuttings – plant cuttings of shrubs (clippings from pruning). Make cuttings about 8" long, strip lower leaves, dip in rooting hormone. Put at least two buds underground. Use 1/3 perlite, 1/3 sand, and 1/3 soil.

- Vegetables – plant seeds of Brussels sprouts, spring cabbage plants, kale, lettuce, onion sets, English and snap peas, radishes, spring spinach in a cold frame if you didn't start them in trays indoors in January. Plant asparagus in already-prepared beds.

MISCELLANEOUS

- Indoor blooming branches – as soon as buds begin to swell, sprays of forsythia, fruit trees, Japanese quince, or Oriental magnolia may be cut and forced into bloom in water. Place in sunny window.

- Watch for early spring ephemerals to appear. Wake robin trillium, dog-tooth violet (*Erythronium*), bloodroot (*Sanguinaria*), toothwort (*Dentaria*), winter aconite, *Anemone nemorosa,* Spanish hyacinth, crocus, *Ipheion, Chionodoxa,* and *Scilla* are all early harbingers.

FEBRUARY BLOOM

Spring Bulbs & Perennials – crocus, early daffodils, epimedium, winter aconite, helleborus, hyacinth, pansy, scilla, snowdrop (*Galanthus*), snowflake (*Leucojum*), wake robin trillium, violet

Shrubs – camellia, flowering quince (*Chaenomeles*), fragrant honeysuckle (*Lonicera*), forsythia, pussy willow (*Salix*), vernal witch-hazel (*Hamamelis*), Chinese witch-hazel (*Hamamelis*), *Mahonia bealei*, corneliancherry dogwood (*Cornus mas*), sweet box (*Sarcococca*)

Trees – saucer magnolia, star magnolia, almond (*Prunus*)

Berries – aucuba, deciduous holly, winterberry, most spiny hollies, nandina, juniper, yaupon, viburnum

MARCH

March, with its lavish display of daffodils, azaleas, and flowering trees, is one of the most beautiful months of the year. It is also one of the busiest.

PLANT

- Evergreens and flowering shrubs may be planted or moved if you didn't do this last month.

- Plant new roses anytime between February 15th and April 15th. When buying rose bushes choose ones that have 3 – 5 healthy canes; if they are not already "cut back", cut them to 12" – 15" when planting.

- Perennials, ferns, hostas, and wildflowers – continue to divide and replant perennials. Hardy perennials, such as coneflower (*Echinacea*), coralbells (*Heuchera*), foamflower (*Tiarella*), aster, chrysanthemum, and black-eyed Susan (*Rudbeckia*), need to be planted so that the crown is almost sitting on top of the soil.

- Summer- and fall-flowering bulbs – hybrid Asiatic, Oriental, and trumpet lilies (*Lilium*), rain lily (*Zephyranthes*), canna, calla (*Zantedeschia*), crinum lily, blackberry lily (*Belamcanda*), naked lady (*Lycoris*), spider lily (*Hymenocallis*), alstroemeria, crocosmia, gladiolus, allium, tuberose (*Polianthes*), iris, liatris, and oxalis are planted now. [Martagon, Turk's-cap, and Madonna lilies are planted in early fall; Asiatic hybrids can be planted in either spring or fall.]

- Hardy cyclamen – plant the large corm in a depression in the soil under a tree, and barely cover with dirt. The cyclamen will find its own depth, and should not be disturbed once planted. It likes dry shade, slightly alkaline soil; flowers from early fall to early winter.

- Gladioli – put out first planting early in month and continue at two week intervals through the end of May for succession of bloom. Before planting, soak corms for three hours in solution of Lysol®, 1½ tablespoons to 1 gallon of water, to prevent thrips.

- Plant clematis and other perennial vines now. They like their faces in the sun and their feet in the shade; add lime to the soil amendments.

- Plant cool-weather vegetables out in the garden now – beets, broccoli plants, Brussels sprouts, cabbage plants, carrot seeds, cauliflower plants, English peas, Irish potatoes, lettuce, onion sets, radish seeds, snap peas, and turnip greens.

- Outdoor containers – weather permitting. Pansies, snapdragons, ornamental kale, and other cool weather annuals may be planted in outdoor pots or in the ground.
- Start caladium tubers indoors; do not put outside until the soil is warm and nighttime temperatures are above 50°.
- Do not put out warm-weather annuals yet, as the last frost date is April 15th.
- Lawns may be sodded. Treat lawns with a pre-emergent weed killer to control crabgrass.

FERTILIZE

- Most of the garden.
- Trees – if not done in January or February.
- Tulips and daffodils – apply small amounts of super-phosphate, bone meal, or 0–20–20 early in month to increase size of flowers for next year.
- Gardenias – scatter garden sulfur around, a handful to each plant.
- Hydrangeas – if you want to turn pink flowers blue, sprinkle aluminum sulfate around plants. To turn blue flowers pink, use lime.
- Peonies – scatter wood ashes or super-phosphate around plants.
- Clematis – apply 1 cupful lime per plant.
- Boxwood – fertilize and lime, if you didn't do so in February. (See recipes in the Shrubs – Boxwood article)
- Camellias – top-dress with prepared azalea-camellia fertilizer. Do not over-fertilize.
- Roses – start fertilizing roses now on a routine basis.
- Fertilize and prune spring-flowering shrubs when they finish blooming.
- Fertilize summer-flowering shrubs now for a good bloom, if not done in February.

PRUNE

- Crape myrtles and altheas may be pruned or moved in February or March.
- Prune floribunda roses severely now to about 12" – 15" tall; prune grandifloras to about 24". Consult *Shrubs – Roses*. Cut out any borers and seal cuts with white glue. If desired, you can use these clippings to start new bushes which will be rooted and ready to plant in the garden by November. (See *Garden Care – Propagation* for details)
- Evergreens – if pruning was not completed in February, finish as early in this month as possible.

115

- Ivy – cut back hard, whether on wall or used as a ground cover. It will be bare at first but will soon come out. It will kill trees if allowed to climb. Ivy likes lime, but tolerates all soils.
- Liriope and monkey grass – cut back to 2" – 4" with a weed eater or lawn mower so fresh new foliage can grow.

SPRAY

- Peony, lily, and clematis as they emerge. If they had blight last season, spray with a fungicide. Repeat twice at ten-day intervals.
- Lilac, ivy, vinca minor, and other plants that suffer from leaf spot with a fungicide.
- Camellia – for scale with a dormant oil spray.
- Azalea – for blight with a fungicide.
- Rose – after pruning, give final dormant spray, such as Volck® oil. After new leaves appear, give regular treatment throughout the growing season for insects and diseases. (See *Shrubs – Roses* for more details)
- Holly and boxwood – if you see small insects flying around, they are either the boxwood leafminers or the holly leafminers. Spray with an insecticide every ten days.
- Azalea and pyracantha – check leaves for lacebugs. Spray with insecticide.
- Hosta – Spread kitty litter, Fuller's earth, or slug bait around hostas to help prevent slugs. A dish of beer attracts slugs.

MULCH

- Replenish mulch on beds 2" deep as needed. Remove leaf covering from the garden gradually. Too-heavy covering will smother plants just coming up; too-sudden removal may expose them to frost.
- Start a compost pile with the leaves you rake from the beds. Shred them with a mower for faster decomposition. Throughout the season, add grass clippings and non-woody pruning trimmings. Try not to introduce weed seeds or diseased material. (See *Garden Care – Soil Basics – Making Compost* for details)

COLD FRAME

- Slips of many perennials may be rooted – carnations, pinks, shasta daises, etc.
- Root cuttings of azalea, camellia, holly, rose, and other shrubs. Place under glass jar in the garden. (See *Garden Care – Propagation*)

MISCELLANEOUS

- Begin hand-weeding the beds.

116

- Rake up bird seed hulls from under bird feeders as they will kill anything under them. While it costs a bit more, "No-Mess" birdseed has no sunflower hulls.

- Sweet peas must be supported by a trellis or twine.

- Pick dead flowers from tulips and daffodils because seed production weakens next year's bulbs. To assure next year's bloom, do not cut bulb foliage before it turns yellow and dies.

- Hang a hummingbird feeder as hummers begin arriving in the Mid-South the second to third week in March.

- Divide or repot any overgrown houseplant. After repotting, cut back weak, leggy portions to encourage new growth. Then increase fertilizer. Apply an application every two weeks.

- Have your sprinkler system turned on for the season toward the end of the month. The back-flow-preventer valve needs to be checked and certified, according to city sanitation code, and your sprinkler company can file that for you.

- If a baby bird falls out of the nest, put it in the bushes, or where cats can't easily get to it, and wait and see. Usually the mother is nearby and will attend to him. If he appears badly injured, contact a wildlife rescue agency.

MARCH BLOOM

Spring Bulbs & Perennials – epimedium, bletilla orchid, Virginia bluebells (*Mertensia*), glory-of-the-snow (*Chionodoxa*), helleborus, celandine poppy (*Stylophorum*), ajuga, daffodil, merrybells (*Uvularia*), primula, tulip, pachysandra, Jacob's-ladder (*Polemonium*), wild sweet William (*Phlox*), brunnera, columbine (*Aquilegia*), bleeding-heart (*Dicentra*), lungwort (*Pulmonaria*), trillium, early iris, violet

Vines – Carolina jessamine (*Gelsemium*), some clematis, akebia

Shrubs – azalea (*Rhododendron*) ['Festive', 'Salmon Beauty', 'Christmas Cheer', 'Coral Bell', 'Snow'], camellia, florida anise (*Illicium*), red buckeye (*Aesculus*), quince (*Cydonia*), fragrant honeysuckle (*Lonicera*), pieris, forsythia, kerria, pearlbush (*Exochorda*), loropetalum, *Mahonia bealei*, photinia, sweet box (*Sarcococca*), Thunberg spirea, boxwood (*Buxus*), witch-hazel (*Hamamelis*), *Viburnum x burkwoodii, Viburnum x juddii, Viburnum carlesii*

Trees – fruit trees: crabapple (*Malus*), pear (*Pyrus*), apricot, cherry, peach, plum, 'Higan' cherry, and flowering almond (all are *Prunus*), saucer magnolia, star magnolia, dogwood (*Cornus*), serviceberry (*Amelanchier*), and redbud (*Cercis*)

117

APRIL

April is the busiest month and one of the most beautiful with gardens ablaze with color. Do not forget that the last frost date is April 15th. You can work in your garden if the ground is not too wet.

Go to a garden center and look for some new varieties of plants. Treat yourself to something unusual.

PLANT

- Roses – plant anytime between February 15th and April 15th. It is very important to mulch and water newly-planted roses. (See *Shrubs – Roses*)

- Buy azaleas now while they are blooming so you can select compatible colors which do not clash.

- Transplant seedlings of perennials and annuals from cold frame into garden. If transplanted early, they get a good start before it gets hot.

- Gladiolus – make additional planting, as mentioned above, for extended bloom season.

- Vegetables – plant warm-weather vegetables in the ground now: bush snap beans, pole snap beans, sweet corn, radishes, tomato plants, lettuce. (See *Vegetables*)

- Put tender bedding plants, like impatiens and geraniums, out after April 15th.

- Caladium, canna, ginger lily (*Hedychium*), herbs, tomatoes, and peppers should be planted at the end of the month when the ground is warm.

- Start tender elephant's-ear bulbs in pots indoors (there are also hardy varieties which may be left in the ground in Zone 7). Plant them outside around Mother's Day.

- Zinnia – wait until late April or early May when the ground is warm for planting zinnia seeds. They are best grown from seed where you want them in the garden, as they are not easily transplanted from a cold frame. Alternatively, buy six-packs or flats of nursery-grown zinnia plants.

- Soak moon flower vine seeds in water. When the hard outer shell becomes soft, nick seed with a knife to aid in germination. Plant in the ground.

- This is the latest you can plant evergreen grasses like fescue.

CONTAINER PLANTS FOR OUTDOORS

- For shady terraces, plant pots of angel wing begonia (a variety with silver-spotted leaves), caladium, impatiens, fibrous begonia, geranium, ferns, coleus, and torenia. Caladiums are available in red, pink, or white with green veins – the

118

latter shows up particularly well at night. Since caladiums are very tender, they should not be put out until the soil is warm.

- For sunny terraces, plant pots of periwinkle (*Vinca*), fan flower (*Scaveola*), million bells (*Calibrachoa*), marigolds (*Tagetes*), petunias, black-eyed Susan vine (*Thunbergia*), and dusty-miller (*Senecio*).

- Geraniums (*Pelargonium*) need partial shade. In the heat of the Mid-South, many "full sun" flowers need partial shade.

FERTILIZE

- Roses – fertilize on a regular basis.

- Spring-blooming camellias and azaleas – after they bloom, with azalea-camellia fertilizer.

- Epsom Salt may be applied sparingly to the garden, especially berried shrubs and roses, for healthier plants. This supplies magnesium, an essential nutrient.

- Perennials – sprinkle a slow-release fertilizer around plants now if you didn't do so in February or March.

- Spring bulbs – after blooming, if you didn't do this in March.

- Lawns – see the *Lawns* chapter for details.

SPRAY

- Whiteflies can start attacking shrubs, perennials, and annuals now. Use insecticidal soap to control the adults followed by neem oil to control the immature larval form.

- Spray azalea and pyracantha for lacebug immediately after blooming if you notice an infestation.

- Spray roses for black spot and aphids on a regular schedule.

- Spray holly and boxwood for leafminer every 10 days. If you used dormant oil spray in the winter, this treatment will probably not be necessary. Avoid over-spraying toxic chemicals; good garden maintenance will eliminate the need for many sprays.

- Spray perennials, peonies, clematis, euonymus, and vinca minor with a fungicide if powdery mildew is a problem.

- Use a systemic on hollyhocks to treat lacebugs and rust if plant is infected.

- Spot control lawn weeds with an herbicide.

MULCH

- The whole garden (except iris and boxwood) should have about 2" of pine bark chips, pine needles, shredded leaves, or shredded hardwood mulch on the beds. Do not pile too deeply around stems and trunks.

119

- Do not mulch irises as doing so causes them to rot.
- Do not over-mulch boxwood.

PRUNE

- Azaleas – prune during and immediately after blooming. 'Kurumes' hold onto unsightly faded flowers which should be picked off.
- Flowering shrubs – prune as soon as they have finished blooming, or while in bloom for arrangements.
- Peonies and roses – disbud for specimen blooms.

PROPAGATE

- Shrubs (especially azalea, winter jasmine (*Jasminum*), climbing rose, and magnolia) and many vines may be propagated by "layering". (See *Garden Care – Propagation* for details)
- Continue to propagate cuttings of houseplants.
- Stock of many bedding plants may be increased by cuttings, especially dwarf ageratum, torenia, and verbena.

APRIL BLOOM

Perennials – ajuga, amsonia, wild ginger (*Asarum*), astilbe, bleeding-heart (*Dicentra*), bletilla orchid, brunnera, calanthe orchid, candytuft (*Iberis*), celandine or wood poppy (*Stylophorum*), columbine (*Aquilegia*), daffodil, daylily (*Hemerocallis*), epimedium, forget-me-not (*Myosotis*), grass pinks (*Calopogon*), crested iris, iris spp., jack-in-the-pulpit (*Arisaema*), lady's mantle (*Alchemilla*), lily-of-the-valley (*Convallaria*), lungwort (*Pulmonaria*), mayapple (*Podophyllum*), meadow rue (*Thalictrum*), merrybells (*Uvularia*), helleborus, peony (*Paeonia*), pansy, primrose (*Primula*), ranunculus, saruma, scilla, shooting star (*Dodecatheon*), Solomon's-seal (*Polygonatum*), sweet William (*Phlox divaricata*), foamflower (*Tiarella*), trillium, tulip, vinca, violet

Vines – akebia, clematis, crossvine (*Bignonia*), honeysuckle (*Lonicera*), Lady Banks rose, wisteria

Shrubs – azalea (*Rhododendron*) ['Delaware Valley', 'Glacier', 'Fashion', 'Pink Ruffles', 'Hino', natives], barberry (*Berberis*), beautybush (*Kolkwitzia*), red buckeye (*Aesculus*), anise (*Illicium*), leucothoe, pieris, pearlbush (*Exochorda*), Carolina silver-bell (*Halesia*), deutzia, fothergilla, chokeberry (*Aronia*), lilac (*Syringa*), kerria, gardenia, sweetshrub or Carolina allspice (*Calycanthus*), oakleaf hydrangea, some spirea, tree peony, weigela, viburnum [*V. carlesii, utile, nudum, juddii, burkwoodii, plicatum tomentosum, cassinoides, & opulus*]

Trees – dogwood (*Cornus*), red buckeye (*Aesculus*), Japanese snowbell (*Styrax*), umbrella magnolia, common quince (*Cydonia*), royal paulownia

MAY

May is the month of the poppy, iris, peony, and rose. The first half of May is mild and pleasant; by the end of the month, the weather is hot and humid and remains so until October. Get your planting done early in the month.

PLANT

- Annuals and perennials – plant early in the month if you didn't do so in April. Keep well watered.
- Chrysanthemum – transplant rooted cuttings into garden.
- Vegetables – bush and pole snapbeans, bush and pole lima beans, cantaloupes, sweet corn, cucumbers, eggplants, okra, parsley, peppers, squash, tomatoes, watermelons.
- Caladium and elephant's-ear – plant outside if you didn't do so in late April.
- Gladiolus - make additional planting, as mentioned above, for extended bloom season.
- Plant hyacinth bean vine (*Lablab*) seeds, which, incidentally, was Thomas Jefferson's favorite vine.
- Bermuda grass seed – best time to sow.

FERTILIZE

- Azaleas and spring-blooming camellias after they flower with azalea-camellia food, if it hasn't been done.
- Roses – fertilize on a regular basis.
- Lawns – if not done in April.
- Spring-flowering shrubs – prune and fertilize after flowering.
- As soon as blueberries finish blooming, give them an azalea-camellia fertilizer. If you fertilized in February before bloom, this should be a second light application.
- Perennials and annuals – give a light dose of Milorganite® and/or fish emulsion and Super-Thrive® which contains vitamins, plant hormones, and trace nutrients.

121

SPRAY

- Arborvitae and junipers – watch for bagworm. If infested, spray with an insecticide. Picking off "bags" is often sufficient.

- Azaleas – if you have an infestation, spray for lacebug, if not done in April.

- Mimosa – spray at end of the month for worms.

- Canna – spray with systemic insecticide for leaf roller, which grossly disfigures foliage by preventing the leaves from unfurling and crusting them with brown scabs. A small worm secretes glue which "rolls" the leaf closed; if you unroll the leaf you will see him. Cut off and dispose of affected leaves; spray. Alternatively, plant ginger lilies (*Hedychium*) which give a similar tropical effect and are not bothered by pests. Cannas bloom earlier and longer than ginger lilies, however.

- Roses – continue to spray according to schedule.

- Watch out for aphids, thrips, and slugs. Sprinkle slug bait pellets around hostas and any other plants that have the tell-tale slime trail and holes in the leaves. Be careful if you have pets that might eat the pellets.

- Examine boxwood and holly for leafminer. The leaves will have pin holes and tunnels caused by larvae.

- Gardenias – watch out for sooty mold on gardenia leaves which indicates whiteflies. After spraying with an insecticidal soap, spray with neem oil.

- Hosta – spray with a mixture of ½ cup of ammonia to 4 cups of water to stop snails. Spray early morning, in the cool of the day. This also has some fertilizing effect, as ammonia is oxidized to nitrate.

PRUNE

- Climbing roses – prune as soon as they have finished blooming. Cut some of the oldest wood back to the ground or to a strong new shoot. New canes will soon come out which will produce next year's flowers. Climbers need no other pruning except removal of dead or diseased wood. New plants may be started from the clippings. Train canes horizontally for best flowering and thickest foliage.

- Bulbs and bearded iris – cut seed pods as soon as they form because they sap the plant's strength.

- Clean up boxwood by removing all the dead leaves from the interior branches. Shake out dead foliage and rake up debris. Major pruning is done in winter.

- Start evergreen and deciduous shrub cuttings now to increase the number of plants. (See *Garden Care – Propagation*)

- Annuals – pinch the tops out of fast-growing annuals to make them bushy.

MULCH

- Mulch around larkspur and poppies before they flower if you plan to let them self-sow. That way, seeds fall on newly-mulched beds for bloom next May. Alternatively, you can wait and mulch after the plants bloom, and you have harvested the dried brown seedpods in June. Plan to sow the collected seeds in August or September for next spring bloom. Don't allow seeds to be covered with mulch; they will not germinate.

MISCELLANEOUS

- Repel deer by placing bars of Irish Spring® soap near the plants.
- Stake tall plants, like lilies, early, before heavy blossoms or the weather beats them down.
- Put tomato cages around peony plants to help support the branches with heavy blooms.

MAY BLOOM

Perennials – astilbe, arum, bugloss, baptisia, bleeding-heart (*Dicentra*), bletilla orchid, butterfly weed (*Asclepias*), calanthe orchid, coneflower (*Echinacea*), camassia, celandine or wood poppy (*Stylophorum*), columbine (*Aquilegia*), coreopsis, cornflower (*Centaurea*), delphinium, elephant's-ear (*Taro* or *Colocasia* or *Alocasia*), 'Becky' Shasta daisy (*Leucanthemum*), gaura, foxglove (*Digitalis*), hosta, Indian pink (*Spigelia*), bearded iris, Jupiter's beard (*Centranthus*), Asiatic lily, Madonna lily, meadow rue (*Thalictrum*), peony, penstemon, pinks (*Dianthus*), phlox, poppy (*Papaver*), 'Mrs. Moon' pulmonaria, rose, *Salvia*, saruma, sweet William (*Phlox*), foamflower (*Tiarella*), verbascum, veronica

Vines – clematis, wisteria, and honeysuckle (*Lonicera*) bloom for several weeks. Trumpet vine (*Campsis*) flowers all summer

Annual vines – cardinal vine (*Ipomoea*), hyacinth bean (*Lablab*), black-eyed Susan vine (*Thunbergia*), and gourds (*Cucurbita*) flower all summer

Shrubs – azalea (*Rhododendron*) ['Scintillation', *R. macrantha, gumpo, calendulaceum*], abelia, anise (*Illicium*), bottlebrush buckeye (*Aesculus*), beauty berry (*Callicarpa*), gardenia, deutzia, Chinese indigo (*Indigofera kirilowii*), Japanese snowball (*Viburnum*), oakleaf hydrangea, smooth hydrangea, mock orange (*Philadelphus*), pomegranate (*Punica*), rhododendron,

123

rose, spirea, tree peony, arrowwood viburnum, linden viburnum, Virginia sweetspire (*Itea*), weigela

Trees – catalpa , golden-chain tree (*Laburnum*), Kousa dogwood (*Cornus*), hardy orange (*Poncirus*), magnolia grandiflora, sweet bay magnolia, tulip poplar (*Liriodendron*)

JUNE

By June, the temperature is in the 80°s and 90°s, and rain is scarce. The garden should already have about 2" of pine bark or pine needle mulch on all the beds. Weeding, watering, and deadheading are the main chores.

PLANT

- Daylily – may be seen in bloom and planted at this time. They may be planted or transplanted almost any time of year; very durable plants.
- Iris – good time to divide and replant bearded type. Cut foliage back to about 6" after moving.
- Naked lady and spider lily bulbs (*Lycoris*) can be planted now and through the fall, if you didn't do this in March. Add a little bulb fertilizer.

FERTILIZE

- Bermuda and zoysia grass with a well-balanced fertilizer such as 10–10–10 and water thoroughly.
- June-flowering azaleas – fertilize and prune right after they bloom.
- Azaleas and camellias should be watched the rest of the summer for yellowing leaves ("chlorosis") which indicates magnesium or iron deficiency. Epsom salts or Ironite® will green up a plant. Be sure your soil is acidic so iron will be available to the plant; Mir-acid® or garden sulfur is good for this. Do not confuse this yellowing of leaves with the whitish, speckled condition caused by lacebug.

SPRAY

- Spray roses every 7 to 10 days.
- Spray whiteflies on gardenias and hydrangeas with insecticidal soap. As soon as the first spray dries, spray with neem oil to kill the larvae; or, spray with Sevin®.
- Check azalea and pyracantha leaves that are spotty and mottled for lacebug or whitefly. Spray with an insecticide.

124

- Canna – spray again for leaf roller if there is an infestation.
- Dust flowers and ornamental shrubs with Sevin® to control insects late in the afternoon so that you do not hurt pollinating bees.
- Hostas – control slugs and snails by pouring stale beer in shallow containers and place under plants. Sprinkling diatomaceous earth around hostas will help control slugs. Alternatively, a dilute ammonia and water solution is effective against slugs.
- Sprinkle Sevin® to control grubs in soil. Moles eat grubs and create unsightly tunnels in the lawn and beds, so eliminating their food source helps keep them out of your yard.

WATER

- Continue to water all plants, including your lawn, during dry spells. It doesn't hurt most plants to completely wet the foliage to help plants deal with the heat.
- Try to keep water off the foliage of mildew-prone plants like phlox, roses, zinnias, and euonymus.

PRUNE

- Chrysanthemum tips should be pinched out when plants are 6" – 8" high. For more compact plants, pinch once or twice more later in season until July 15th before the buds form.
- Annuals and perennials – pinch and deadhead leggy plants to encourage bushiness and re-blooming. Spindly plants often benefit from light application of 20–20–20 fertilizer. Stake tall annuals as necessary.
- Clematis – cut back autumn-blooming clematis for late-September bloom. (See *Vines – Clematis* for more)
- Southern highbush blueberries ripen in late May and early June. You may need to drape netting over the bush to prevent birds eating all the berries. Prune the bushes after picking to remove twiggy canes.
- Shearing boxwood is best done in late May or early June. If you are growing boxwood as a hedge or topiary, you need to start shearing now after new spring growth has hardened off. These clippings may be rooted for plant increase. Thin out and clean up boxwood in January with the "thin, shake, and rake" strategy. (See *Shrubs – Boxwoods*)

MISCELLANEOUS

- Collect seeds from the dried pods of wildflowers that bloomed in March or April, such as wild columbine (*Aquilegia*), wild blue phlox, wood poppy (*Stylophorum*), etc., and broadcast fresh seed where you want more plants.

- Cut off and harvest poppy pods when they are brown but before they crack and spill seed. Pull out the spent plant as it will just get shabbier. The decorative pods can be used in dried arrangements. The tiny seeds can be sown in September where they are to flower next May. The seeds can be used in salad dressing or muffins.

- Keep weeds under control in flower beds by using mulch and hand-weeding. It's easier to weed after a rain, or use a sprinkler the day before.

- Cut flowers in the early morning and place in a bucket of very warm water for conditioning. Place in a cool place. They can be arranged later in the day.

JUNE BLOOM

Perennials – alstroemeria, astilbe, balloon flower (*Platycodon*), bee balm (*Monarda*), blackberry lily (*Belamcanda*), butterfly weed (*Asclepias*), coreopsis, cornflower (*Centaurea*), coneflower (*Echinacea*), daylily (*Hemerocallis*), elephant's-ear (*Taro* or *Colocasia* or *Alocasia*), feverfew (*Tanacetum*), coralbells (*Heuchera*), hosta, Indian pink (*Spigelia*), gaura, gladiolus, hollyhock (*Alcea*), Japanese iris, Turk's-cap lily, Madonna lily, lizard's tail (*Saururus*), meadow rue (*Thalictrum*), phlox, 'Mrs. Moon' pulmonaria, black-eyed Susan (*Rudbeckia*), scabiosa, 'Becky' Shasta daisy (*Leucanthemum*), verbena, salvia, germander (*Teucrium*), veronica, voodoo lily (*Sauromatum*), water lily (*Nymphaea*)

Shrubs – abelia, bottlebrush buckeye (*Aesculus*), summersweet or sweet pepperbush (*Clethra*), butterfly bush (*Buddleia*), gardenia, hydrangea, rose, St.-John's-wort (*Hypericum*), yucca

Trees – golden-rain tree (*Koelreuteria*), chaste tree (*Vitex*), mimosa (*Albizia*), sourwood (*Oxydendrum*), sweet bay magnolia

JULY

It continues to be hot and humid with little rain. Water regularly, continue to weed, and watch for black spot and powdery mildew. Annuals are at their peak in mid-summer.

PLANT

- Seedlings – transplant second crop of flower seedlings into beds if you started them in March or April.

- Ground covers – start root cuttings to make more plants. This works well for pachysandra, sedum, and ajuga.

- House plants – start leaf, stem, or root cuttings for houseplants. Ivy, wandering Jew, philodendron, and begonia can be propagated this way.

- Vegetables – fall cabbage, parsley seeds, collards.

FERTILIZE

- Camellias – do not fertilize after July 1st.

- Dahlias – for extra special blooms.

- Perennials – if you used a time-released fertilizer in February or March, it is time for another light application. You may want to use a bloom booster, cottonseed meal, cow manure, soil soup, or fish emulsion for this feeding. Refer to *Garden Care – Fertilizers* for more details.

- Lawns – fertilizers applied in early spring are used up by now, so fertilize lightly if you didn't do so in June.

SPRAY

- Roses – continue to spray.

- Azalea, camellia, boxwood – spray for lacebug, whitefly, and spider mite if infested.

- Evergreens – spray for scale with a seasonal dormant oil, or horticultural oil, designed to be used in hot weather.

- Mimosa – watch for fresh hatching of worms in mimosa trees and spray with insecticide.

- Arborvitae and juniper – check for bagworm, pick off, and dispose; spray if infestation is bad, or call a professional.

- Boxwood – continue to watch for leafminer and treat with insecticide.

- Vegetables – if insects are a problem, spray with a "safe-for-vegetables" insecticide, like Sevin® or pyrethrin. Follow directions carefully.

- Grubs – continue to control with Sevin® or beneficial nematodes if grubs are a problem.

PRUNE

- Roses – prune lightly about July 1st to encourage new growth for fall bloom. Deadhead roses and cut back the cane to the bud above a five leaflet to encourage new shoots. Clippings may be used to start new plants.

- Ferns – cut broken, withered fronds to ground at the end of July. Fresh fronds will appear for fall garden.

- Continue to deadhead annuals and perennials.

- Continue to pinch and fertilize chrysanthemums for bushy growth until July 15th; then stop and allow flower buds to form.

- Hybrid clematis will set more flowers if you remove the seed clusters. Some gardeners, however, prefer to keep the decorative seed pods.

MISCELLANEOUS

- Biennial seeds – Canterbury bells (*Campanula*), foxglove (*Digitalis*), and sweet William (*Phlox*), should be allowed to go to seed in the garden, as the parent plant dies after flowering. The new seedling plants will produce flowers the following year.

- Cut flowers in the early morning while they are still at their best quality and soak in very warm water. Re-cut the stems before arranging. Refer to *Preparing Flowers for Arrangements – Fresh Flowers* for details on treating specific flowers.

- Raise blades on lawn mowers. Grass should not be closely cut in hot, dry weather.

- Rooted boxwood and deciduous shrub cuttings that were started in May should be potted now and allowed to grow for a season before planting in the ground. Some rooted cuttings may be ready to plant in the ground by November. Viburnum is best planted in the ground when young as it can be difficult to transplant when large.

JULY BLOOM

Perennials – blackberry lily (*Belamcanda*), butterfly weed (*Asclepias*), canna, calla (*Zantedeschia*), cardinal flower (*Lobelia*), spiderflower (*Cleome*), coneflower (*Echinacea*), cosmos, dahlia, daylily (*Hemerocallis*), elephant's-ear (*Taro* or *Colocasia* or *Alocasia*), hosta, gaura, gladiolus, coralbells (*Heuchera*), hibiscus, hybrid lily (*Lilium*), Madonna lily, liatris, liriope, lycoris, lythrum, montbretia, phlox, rudbeckia, salvia, scabiosa, Shasta daisy (*Leucanthemum*), tuberose (*Polianthes*), verbena, veronica

Berries – arum has showy, red seed-stalks

Shrubs – abelia, althea, buddleia, clethra, hydrangea

Trees – crape myrtle (*Lagerstroemia*), chaste tree (*Vitex*), sourwood (*Oxydendrum*)

AUGUST

Work in the garden pretty much follows the pattern of July, with weeding, watering, and deadheading. Nurseries and garden shops usually put their perennials on sale during this month. Do not prune woody shrubs now.

PLANT

- Seeds of calendula, columbine (*Aquilegia*), English and Shasta 'Becky' daisy (*Leucanthemum*), forget-me-not (*Myosotis*), sweet William (*Phlox*), violet (*Viola*) – broadcast seeds for next spring bloom. Start pansy seeds in seed trays inside as pansies do not like the heat. Sow seed of poppy (*Papaver*) and larkspur (*Consolida*) now through October, if you saved the seedpods rather than allowing them to self-sow.

- Shasta daisy – root cuttings.

- Vegetables – fall cabbage, kale, turnip greens.

- Plant store-bought chrysanthemums for fall color, if you did not hold chrysanthemums over from last year (and have been pinching and fertilizing them).

- Rooted shrub cuttings should be moved from the cold frame into pots if you did not do so in July. When they are large enough, plant in the ground.

FERTILIZE

- Roses – the first week in August should be the last time you fertilize for this year.

- Fertilize container plants with an all-purpose fertilizer.

- Do not fertilize spring-flowering shrubs and broad-leaved evergreens.

SPRAY

- Azalea, camellia, boxwood – for spider mite, whitefly, and lacebug if there is an infestation.

- Perennial phlox and zinnia – with a fungicide at first sign of powdery mildew. Alternatively, use an all-purpose spray which includes control for red spider. Interestingly, powdery mildew is worse in hot, dry weather while most other fungus diseases are worse in wet conditions.

129

- Dahlia – red spider and chewing insects.
- Cannas – spray for leaf roller if there is an infestation.
- Whiteflies can infest almost any shrubs or flowers in the garden, and are controlled with insecticidal soap and neem oil.

PRUNE

- Torenia, browallia, impatiens, begonia, and verbena – shear for fresh crop of bloom.
- Native fern – cut shaggy and broken fronds at ground level.
- Phlox – do not let phlox drop seed; deadhead as soon as possible. When a phlox reseeds, the flowers on the new plants don't have the same color.
- If your crape myrtle has developed seed pods at the tips of the branches, use a pole pruner to cut these clusters and your tree may re-bloom. Some gardeners prefer to leave the seed heads for the birds to eat.

WATER

- Continue to water the entire garden and lawn. Water early in the morning so foliage will dry in the sun and minimize water-requiring fungus diseases like Botrytis rot, root rot, and downy mildew.
- Water container plants daily in this intense heat.

LAWN

- Mow fescue lawns at 3½" and common Bermuda at 2½" – 3".

MISCELLANEOUS

- Starting this month, place your potted amaryllis bulb in a cool, dark place and let it dry out completely. The amaryllis must have a 2 – 3 month dormant period so that it will bloom at Christmas.
- Continue weeding and deadheading.

AUGUST BLOOM

Annuals – angel's-trumpet (*Brugmansia* and *Datura*), spiderflower (*Cleome*)

Perennials – butterfly weed (*Asclepias*), canna, calla (*Zantedeschia*), cardinal flower (*Lobelia*), coneflower (*Echinacea*), crinum, dahlia, elephant's-ear (*Taro* and *Colocasia* and *Alocasia*), gladiolus, ginger lily (*Hedychium*), hardy begonia, sneezeweed (*Helenium*), coralbells (*Heuchera*), hosta, Japanese anemone, liatris, lily, lobelia, phlox, black-eyed Susan (*Rudbeckia*), salvia,

(*Aegopodium* and *Euphorbia*), pink rain lily (*Zephyranthes*), veronica, verbena

Vines – clematis, trumpet vine (*Campsis*)

Shrubs – althea, butterfly bush (*Buddleia*), hydrangeas

Berries – mahonia has blue berries now, and nandina has red

Trees – crape myrtle (*Lagerstroemia*), chaste tree (*Vitex*)

SEPTEMBER

Continue to weed and water during the late summer heat. Powdery mildew is worse in hot, dry weather and can affect almost any plant in the garden. Do not prune any shrubs now; the new growth would be cold-damaged. This is the time to harvest most herbs. Cut and dry upside down in the attic or garage. September is LAWN month. Seed, reseed, fertilize, and water. Ginger lilies (*Hedychium*), cannas, elephant's-ear (*Taro* and *Colocasia* and *Alocasia*), fatsia, and callas (*Zantedeschia*) are blooming now and give a lush tropical feeling to the garden.

PLANT

- Daylily.
- Martagon, Madonna, and Turk's-cap lilies in early fall.
- Phlox and Shasta daisy – root cuttings.
- Vegetables – plant cell-packs of cabbage, broccoli, Brussels sprouts, lettuce, all spinach, and turnip greens. Plant onion sets and garlic cloves now for next summer. Sow seeds of mustard, turnip, and radishes.
- Winter grass – sow rye, blue grass, and fescue grass seed early in the month for winter lawn. Cut and soak lawns before reseeding and soak each week until grass is 3" high. In bare places, seed comes up much better if dirt is loosened before planting, which helps prevent seeds washing away. New seed may also be covered lightly with sand or straw. Remove straw when grass germinates; sand will blend into the lawn.
- Plant ornamental cabbage and pansies for winter color.
- Wildflowers – sow wildflower seeds for next year.

FERTILIZE

- Too late to fertilize evergreens.
- Flowers – use a foliar fertilizer spray for a quick boost for your flowers. With cooler evenings, some perennials will re-bloom if they were deadheaded.

131

- Lawns – spot-apply 40 – 50 lbs. of pelletized dolomitic lime per 1,000 square feet of evergreen lawn (approximately 31' x 31' area).

WATER

- Camellias need extra water to set buds. Spray foliage as well as the ground when camellias are about to bloom.
- This is a dry month so water the entire garden well and regularly.

SPRAY

- Rose – continue to spray for black spot with a fungicide.
- Spray for powdery mildew, or use dusting sulfur.
- Check hollies and pyracantha for insects and spray with insecticide.
- Spider mite and whiteflies are often bad in September. Check underneath the leaves for insects, and treat with an insecticide followed by a spray of neem oil.

PRUNE

- Harvest herbs for winter use – if you don't plan to pot up your herbs next month, cut the stems of basil, rosemary, and dill seed heads and wash. Hang upside down to air dry in a cool place for use during the winter months. Do not dry in the oven or you will lose essential oils.
- Cut back summer-flowering perennials to encourage root growth. Continue to deadhead and groom plants, removing tired and dead ones to keep your border tidy.
- Dahlias and large-flowered chrysanthemums can be disbudded for fewer but larger flowers. Keep faded blooms cut off of all plants to prolong bloom.
- Collect seeds from hollyhock and cleome. Save and plant in March.
- Take cuttings of coleus, geranium, begonia, impatiens, and tender salvia. Root them in water or in damp Pro-mix.
- Prune out old blackberry and raspberry canes.
- Do not prune azaleas or camellias.

MULCH

- Add to your compost pile – alternating grass cuttings and shredded dead leaves. Do not use dead weeds or diseased foliage in your compost pile.

MISCELLANEOUS

- Place catalog orders for spring-blooming bulbs such as daffodil, tulip, scilla, jack-in-the-pulpit, hyacinth, narcissus, crocus, and so on, to be delivered in the fall for November planting time.

- Stop watering Christmas cactus plants and place in dark area until the first of November to get them ready for Christmas bloom.
- Do not leave tomatoes on the vine to ripen. Pick them when they show good color so the worms and squirrels won't get them.
- Put out a hummingbird feeder in early September to welcome them back to the garden. They are attracted to trumpet vine and other blooming flowers.
- Check all house plants that have been outside for insects and spray with insecticide. Repot if necessary and then bring inside.

SEPTEMBER BLOOM

Perennials – perennial aster, canna, calla (*Zantedeschia*), chrysanthemum (*Dendranthema* or *Leucanthemum*), coneflower (*Echinacea*), elephant's-ear (*Taro* and *Colocasia* and *Alocasia*), gladiolus, ginger lily (*Hedychium*), sneezeweed (*Helenium*), Japanese anemone, hardy begonia, lobelia, liriope, garden phlox, leopard plant (*Ligularia*), toad lily (*Tricyrtis*), spider lily (*Hymenocallis*), black-eyed Susan (*Rudbeckia*), white rain lily (*Zephyranthes*), salvia, veronica, verbena

Vines – coral vine (*Antigonon*), trumpet vine (*Campsis*), morning-glory (*Ipomoea*), autumn clematis

Shrubs – althea, butterfly bush (*Buddleia*), rose

Trees – crape myrtle (*Lagerstroemia*).

Berries – viburnum, holly (*Ilex*), nandina. Nut trees like pecan and walnut are bearing green nuts.

OCTOBER

October is a rewarding month in the garden. The light frosts seem to give perennials and annuals a second wind. Toad lilies, leopard plants, chrysanthemums, asters, ginger lilies, and roses grace the garden now. Fall chores of dividing and re-planting perennials, general clean-up, and deadheading can be started this month and finished in November. Do not prune any shrubs now; it would stimulate new growth which will be winter damaged.

133

PLANT

- Perennials – plant Shasta daises (*Leucanthemum*), Siberian iris, phlox, and many other perennials.

- Divide and re-plant spring-blooming perennials – bearded iris, hosta, daisy, perennial foxglove (*Digitalis*), black-eyed Susan (*Rudbeckia*), celandine poppy (*Stylophorum*), merrybells (*Uvularia*), coneflower (*Echinacea*), phlox, and ferns. Perennials which DO NOT respond well to division include bleeding-heart (*Dicentra*), false indigo (*Baptisia*), helleborus, lily, balloon flower (*Platycodon*), trillium, hardy cyclamen, and Virginia bluebells (*Mertensia*); once planted, leave them alone.

- Divide, move, and plant peonies – make sure you have a large root-ball when moving peonies as they resent disturbance. Sweeten the soil with lime and plant where they will get morning sun. Plant the roots with five pink buds called eyes, almost on top of the ground. Peonies need to have a long cold spell to bloom and that is why they are surface-planted.

- Biennials – transplant healthy seedlings of English daisy, forget-me-not (*Myosotis*), foxglove (*Digitalis*), and pansy into their permanent locations.

- Bulbs – after soil has cooled, plant *Chionodoxa*, allium, crocus, daffodil, scilla, and other small bulbs of spring. Caution: do not plant tulips before November 15th, preferably December 1st. Some lilies are planted in spring, some in fall. In either case, plant as soon as you receive them as they are not truly dormant.

- Martagon, Madonna, and Turk's-cap lilies in early fall in a prepared bed.

- Annuals – broadcast seeds of cornflower (*Centaurea*), larkspur (*Consolida*), poppy (*Papaver*), and Queen-Anne's-lace (*Daucus*) where they are to bloom, mixing seeds with sand to ensure even distribution.

- Hardy begonia – to increase your stand, remove the bulbils from the branch tips, and scatter them where you want new plants.

- Herbs – pot up basil, chives, cilantro, parsley, sage, and sweet marjoram for the sunny window. Cut back and fertilize. Mint and rosemary are reliably hardy left in the ground.

- Evergreen propagation – dip cuttings in a hormone powder, such as Rootone®. Pot up in Pro-mix and place the pot in the compost pile, or out in the garden covered with leaves to keep it warm. Water well. Cuttings should be rooted by spring.

- Plant pansies, snapdragons, and ornamental cabbage now for winter color if you didn't do so last month.

- Plant crimson clover and/or Australian winter peas in the area where you grow vegetables; these are nitrogen-fixing plants that will help build the soil for next year's vegetables.

134

FERTILIZE

- Lawns – if not done in September.
- Fertilize your tropical house plants.

SPRAY

- Azalea and pyracantha – check leaves for spider mite and lacebug. Use an insecticide.
- Hosta – put out last application of slug bait to kill the eggs.

WATER

- Winter grass – keep moist to aid germination of seed spread last month.
- Azaleas – water moderately; do not let dry out.
- Camellias – water foliage frequently as in September; do not let soil dry out.
- Whole garden – plants survive freezing weather much better if their roots are hydrated. Water thoroughly during dry fall months.
- Sprinkler system – toward the end of the month, have the system shut down and winterized.

MISCELLANEOUS

- Saving annuals – make 4" cuttings of begonia, coleus, and geranium plants if you want to hold them over until next spring. Put in water until roots form and then pot up and keep inside.
- Store tender bulbs – dig up gladiolus, tuberose, dahlia, certain elephant's-ear, and caladium now and store them in a dry place until spring. Leave about five inches of the stems with each tuber. Many gardeners prefer to plant new bulbs each spring as they are relatively inexpensive.
- Houseplants – check for insects before you bring your house plants inside. Use a systemic insecticide to control mealy bugs and scale.
- Angel's-trumpet, citrus trees, tender palms, split-leaf philodendrons – bring pots of tender ornamentals inside before frost, and over-winter in sunny window.
- Christmas cactus – continue to dry out your cactus in a dark room.
- Use shredded, fallen leaves for compost – do not use whole leaves as mulch around perennials as they mat down when wet and cause crown rot, root rot, and harbor insect larvae. Some of the whole leaves may remain where they fall under trees and large shrubs in more naturalized areas, and will eventually become leaf mold.
- Lawns – if grass seed has germinated, remove straw covering. Do not cut your Bermuda grass and zoysia now; the taller grass will protect the grass roots.
- Greenhouse – it is time to light the pilot on your gas heater if you have one.

135

OCTOBER BLOOM

Perennials – perennial aster, canna, chrysanthemum, black cohosh (*Cimicifuga*), colchicum, dahlia, ginger lily (*Hedychium*), Japanese anemone, leopard plant (*Ligularia*), lobelia, salvia, toad lily (*Tricyrtis*), veronica

Shrubs – camellia, rose, encore azalea

COLORFUL FALL FOLIAGE

Shrubs – smokebush (*Cotinus*), burning bush (*Euonymus*), fothergilla, loropetalum, witch-hazel (*Hamamelis*), bottlebrush buckeye (*Aesculus*), amsonia, Virginia sweetspire (*Itea*), oakleaf hydrangea, barberry (*Berberis*), cotoneaster, nandina, azalea, possumhaw viburnum (*V. nudum*)

Trees – ginkgo, sweet gum (*Liquidambar*), black gum (*Nyssa*), all maples (*Acer*), dogwood (*Cornus*), oak (*Quercus*), American hornbeam (*Carpinus*), hop hornbeam (*Ostrya*)

BERRIES

Shrubs – common privet (*Ligustrum*), viburnum (many), juniper, nandina, beauty berry (*Callicarpa*), holly (*Ilex*), pyracantha. Porcelain berry vine (*Ampelopsis*) has blue berries now. Clematis has interesting feathery seed heads. Arum has red berry stalks

Trees – magnolia grandiflora cones, crape myrtle (*Lagerstroemia*), dogwood (*Cornus*). Pecans, walnuts, and hickories are ripe for harvest if the squirrels have not eaten every one.

NOVEMBER

November is another big clean-up and fall-planting month; finish any projects you didn't complete in October. Clean up garden before it gets too cold. Pull up all spent annuals, cut dead blooms off most perennials, rake some leaves out of beds if there is a heavy covering. Mark the spot where dormant or late-sprouting perennials and bulbs are located, so you don't disturb them next spring. Divide and transplant spring-blooming perennials now. Add new, or transplant existing, trees and shrubs now.

The highlight of the garden is camellia. Watch the growth habit of different varieties. Some grow tall and spreading, some medium and compact, some quite dwarf. Buy plants in bloom in the nurseries.

Toad lilies, with their orchid-like flowers, and hardy begonias will still be blooming in shady areas until there is a killing frost.

PLANT

- Plant perennials, shrubs, evergreens, and small trees now – viburnum, spirea, kerria, forsythia, deutzia, quince, and all trees prefer fall planting. Azaleas – plant early enough for them to get established before severe cold, or wait for early spring. Best time is before blooming. Always water a shrub 24 hours before it is planted; keep well watered until established.

- Divide and re-plant perennials – use a garden fork and sharp shooter to divide clumps of hosta, southern shield fern, wood poppy, and phlox.

- Start planting spring-flowering bulbs. Daffodils – as soon as possible. Tulips – do not plant before November 15th. Lilies – bulbs from catalogs arrive at this time, and are also available at nurseries; plant immediately.

- Dig out all unhealthy-looking evergreens or flowering shrubs and prepare ground for replacements.

- Rose cuttings – Thanksgiving week is a favored time for moving rooted cuttings taken in March – July into the garden. Select well-drained location. Cover cuttings with glass jars or bank sides of row with wheat straw which lets in light, air, and water but protects from cold. Caution: do not transplant established roses before December 1st. Early spring planting is preferred.

- Dill seeds – sow outside for spring growth, or you can wait and buy young plants in spring.

FERTILIZE

- Top-dress entire garden with a no-nitrogen fertilizer, such as 0–20–20, to winterize. Alternatively use a combination of bone meal and wood ashes and a little dolomitic lime on all the beds. Water in thoroughly. Mulch beds now as well with pine bark chips or pine needles.

- DO NOT fertilize shrubs, roses, or perennials at this time with nitrogen-containing fertilizers, as nitrogen encourages new growth which will be immediately damaged by cold weather.

SPRAY

- Dormant oil – spray evergreens, deciduous shrubs, and ornamental trees with dormant oil on a mild, windless day to control future scale. Especially beneficial for boxwood, camellias, hollies, and azaleas.

137

PRUNE

- Roses – look for stem borer, cut out, and paint stem with white glue. Do not severely prune your roses now or you risk winter damage.

- Dogwood – cut out borers.

- Annuals and perennials – spent annuals should be removed. Some perennials should be cut back, some left alone; consult the *Flowers* chapter.

- Hardy cannas, elephant's-ear, hedychium, calla, acanthus, Solomon's-seal, and similar rhizomatous plants should keep their dead or shabby foliage until spring to protect underground bulb and root system from freezing or rotting.

- Hollow-stemmed or square-stemmed perennials – Many of the salvias, like Mexican bush sage (*Salvia leucanthum*), should not be cut back in fall. They are reliably perennial if you leave them alone and cut back when new growth emerges in the spring.

- Generally, if it is blooming at first frost, leave the foliage on for the winter. If it bloomed much earlier and died back naturally, feel free to cut the old flower stalk back. This would include hosta, foxglove, etc.

- Leave some coneflower (*Echinacea*) and black-eyed Susan (*Rudbeckia*) seed heads for the birds to enjoy.

HOUSE PLANTS

- Christmas cactus – move plants into bright light. Water and fertilize.

- Poinsettia – move plants into bright light. Water and fertilize.

- Paperwhite narcissus bulbs can be forced indoors now for holiday bloom. (See *Flowers – Bulbs – Forcing spring bulbs for indoor bloom* for details)

- Amaryllis may be started for Christmas bloom now, and placed in dark room.

- Jerusalem cherry is poisonous if eaten so keep out of reach of children and pets.

- Keep house plants misted as central heating can be very drying.

MULCH

- Whole garden – spread 2" layer of pine bark chips, shredded leaves, pine needles, or aged compost over all the beds, keeping mulch away from stems. Also treat with 0–20–20 fertilizer. Do not smother plants or allow a lot of fallen leaves to remain in branches or crowns of shrubs.

- Roses – remove old mulch around roses and replace it with fresh mulch to inhibit spread of disease. Spray with a fungicide to help prevent black spot next season.

- Do not mulch iris or boxwood.

- Leaves – do not dispose of leaves. Save them for the garden. They may be utilized in two ways: 1) half-rotted hardwood leaves make perfect mulch for azaleas and camellias or, 2) added to the compost pile. Chop leaves with lawn mower for speedier decomposition. Alternate green and dry materials with two shovels full of soil and ½ cup of fertilizer such as 13–13–13 or 5–10–15. Sprinkle but do not soak with water. Turn and mix with garden fork to aid in decomposition. Use aged compost for the fall mulching.

COLD FRAME

- Cuttings of perennials and herbs may be put in at this time.

FREEZE PROTECTION

- Heaving – sometimes plants heave out of the ground during a long cold spell. Gently push the plant back in the ground and re-cover with soil and mulch.
- Gardenias and boxwood that are prone to winter bronzing can be covered with burlap.
- Pansies – place newspaper on top of newly planted pansies to protect them from hard freezes.
- Roses – protect by mounding organic mulch, straw, compost, or chopped leaves about 12" high around the rows to protect the graft union.

MISCELLANEOUS

- Dig and store tender bulbs – caladium, canna, gladiolus, Peruvian daffodil, and tuberose if you didn't do this in October. These should be hung indoors in mesh bags to protect from frost. Some varieties of these bulbs are hardy in the ground in Zone 7 and may be left alone.
- Vegetable bed – November is too late to plant crimson clover as a cover crop to add nitrogen to your vegetable garden. Australian winter peas can be planted now and are excellent soil builders and winter covers.
- Poison ivy removal – wearing gloves, cut the plant down to the ground and dispose of it in a plastic bag. Dig up and dispose of the root. Toxic oils are at a minimum now.
- Lawns – put out grub-control now to control moles.

NOVEMBER BLOOM

Perennials – chrysanthemum, hardy cyclamen, toad lily (*Tricyrtis*), leopard plant (*Ligularia*), ginger lily (*Hedychium*)

Shrubs – camellia, eleagnus, witch-hazel (*Hamamelis*)

Berries – viburnum, nandina, holly (*Ilex*)

139

DECEMBER

December is a good month for taking inventory, for reviewing the year's successes and failures, and for deciding what to do about the latter. If a plant has failed, the cause usually comes to light with digging. Often, it is too-deep planting, lack of or too much water, root rot, the wrong sun exposure, or over-accumulation of mulch and fallen leaves. We all learn by bitter experience.

The gardener can rest because it is too late to plant anything except some bulbs and trees, too early to get serious about pruning, and it is probably raining. You've already mulched, fertilized with 0–20–20, and cleaned up the garden. This is a time for bird watching, for enjoying camellias, hardy cyclamen, and berried plants, and preparing for the holidays.

PLANT

- Tulips
- Trees
- Spring-flowering bulbs

FERTILIZE

- Lawns – apply pelletized dolomitic or agricultural lime. Do not use quick lime.
- Use wood ashes from your fireplace, a good source of potash (or potassium), as fertilizer for roses and clematis. Ashes may be added to the beds anytime in winter.

MISCELLANEOUS

- Holiday decorations – clippings of arborvitae (*Thuja*), Leyland cypress (*X Cupressocyparis*), Japanese cedar (*Cryptomeria*), nandina, mahonia, cleyera, aucuba, holly, magnolia, and boxwood can be used to decorate your house for the holidays. They dry out quickly so it helps to keep them in water.
- Check paperwhite narcissus bulbs that are being forced for Christmas bloom. Bring them out of their cool dark place when they have 6" of green growth. If they have grown tall, stake with a small bamboo to prevent falling over. Misting helps paperwhites last through the holidays.
- Keep your bird feeder filled.
- Cut camellia blossoms (all varieties) before a hard freeze and bring them inside for arrangements.
- Drain gasoline from all garden engines, especially your leaf blower.

DECEMBER BLOOM

Shrubs – camellia, sweet olive (*Osmanthus*)

Bulbs – hardy cyclamen, winter aconite

Berries – aucuba, all hollies, nandina, juniper, viburnum

141

Photo by David Nester

Fresh flowers from the cutting garden are arranged twice weekly by members of the Memphis Garden Club – Foyer Urn – The Dixon Gallery and Gardens

Photo by Whitney McNeill

The Art & Flower Show, presented biannually by the Memphis Garden Club, features floral interpretations of notable artwork.

Photo by Whitney McNeill

A handsome container planting anchors this cutting garden and invites the visitor through the vine-covered arbor. — The Dixon Gallery and Gardens

Art has always had a place in the garden. Dale Chihuly, internationally renowned glass artist, exhibited this fanciful glass sculpture in the entrance courtyard. – The Dixon Gallery and Gardens

A formal garden, with its dignified geometry and layers of green, is a beautiful space within the landscape. – The Dixon Gallery and Gardens

Graceful bronze swimmers atop this formal fountain provide a lovely focal point across the lawn for visitors inside the museum. – The Memphis Brooks Museum of Art

The Goddess Iris presides over her realm. – Memphis Botanic Garden

Photo by David Nester

A shady bench in the secret garden offers a perfect place to enjoy conversation or quiet solitude. – The Dixon Gallery and Gardens

Photo by David Nester

Asiatic and Oriental lilies return every year. Planted with lily-of-the-valley, deutzia, white hydrangea, and Japanese anemone, white flowers adorn this Celtic cross for many months. – Private residence in Memphis

Photo by David Nester

An expanse of lawn separates the formal areas near the house from the naturalistic pathways and flower borders. This manmade creekbed provides a beautiful means of assuring good drainage. – The Dixon Gallery and Gardens

Photo courtesy of Memphis Botanic Garden

The rose garden in full bloom is spectacular. – Memphis Botanic Garden

Photo by David Nester

A naturalistic fieldstone waterfall is shaded by a Japanese maple.
— Memphis Zoo

Photo courtesy of Memphis Botanic Garden

Water lilies and water hyacinth soften the geometric lines of the fountain.
— Memphis Botanic Garden

Monarda fronts a graceful crape myrtle in this sunny border. — Memphis Zoo

Coneflowers and daisies provide long-lasting color in this native garden.
— Memphis Zoo

Tropical foliage creates a bold and dramatic statement. The plants pictured are hardy in the ground in Zone 7.
– Memphis Zoo

Photo by David Nester

A bronze deer with mayapple at his feet is at home in this dappled woodland of pachysandra, ivy, and fern; a planting that is elegantly beautiful and low-maintenance.
– The Dixon Gallery and Gardens

Photo by David Nester

'Daniel Weeks' and 'Flaming Torch' ginger lilies (*Hedychium*) perfume the garden in late summer. – Private residence in Memphis

'Miyazaki' toad lily (*Tricyrtis*) blooms in October with an orchid-like flower in every leaf axil of this lovely arching shade perennial. – Private residence in Memphis

A shady woodland path is flanked with hosta and 'Annabelle' hydrangea.
– Memphis Botanic Garden

A native azalea blooms beside the teak footbridge at this peaceful water feature.
— The Dixon Gallery and Gardens

Photo courtesy of Newton Reed

Photo courtesy of Memphis Botanic Garden

The fiery red Japanese maple warms the autumn garden.
— Memphis Botanic Garden

The bones of the garden and its architectural elements are accentuated in the lovely snow. – Memphis Botanic Garden

Riverwoods State Natural Area
is a gift to the State of Tennessee from the Memphis Garden Club
as part of our conservation effort.

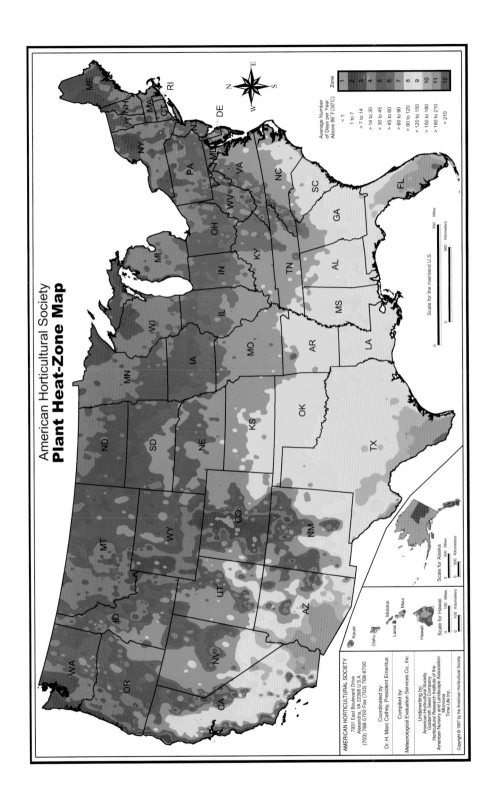

American Horticultural Society
Plant Heat-Zone Map

AMERICAN HORTICULTURAL SOCIETY
7931 East Boulevard Drive
Alexandria, VA 22308 U.S.A.
(703) 768-5700 Fax (703) 768-8700

Coordinated by:
Dr. H. Marc Cathey, President Emeritus

Compiled by:
Meteorological Evaluation Services Co., Inc.

Underwriting by:
American Horticultural Society
Goldsmith Seed Company
Horticultural Research Institute of the
American Nursery and Landscape Association
Monrovia
Time Life Inc.

Copyright © 1997 by the American Horticultural Society

Zone	Average Number of Days per Year Above 86°F (30°C)
1	< 1
2	1 to 7
3	> 7 to 14
4	> 14 to 30
5	> 30 to 45
6	> 45 to 60
7	> 60 to 90
8	> 90 to 120
9	> 120 to 150
10	> 150 to 180
11	> 180 to 210
12	> 210

Scale for the mainland U.S.
0   500 Miles
0   500 Kilometers

Scale for Alaska
0   500 Miles
0   500 Kilometers

Scale for Hawaii
0   100 Miles
0   100 Kilometers

Kauai   Oahu   Molokai   Lanai   Maui   Hawaii

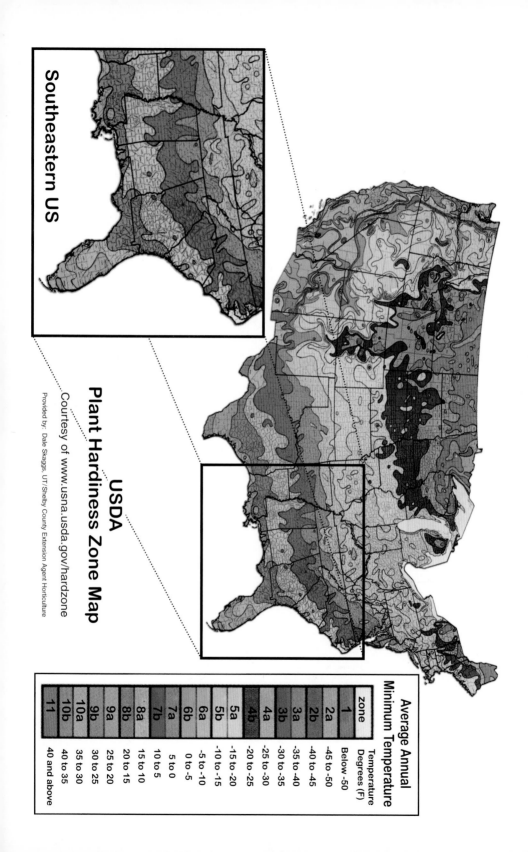

Southeastern US

USDA
Plant Hardiness Zone Map

Courtesy of www.usna.usda.gov/hardzone

Provided by: Dale Skaggs, UT/Shelby County Extension Agent Horticulture

Average Annual Minimum Temperature

zone	Temperature Degrees (F)
1	Below -50
2a	-45 to -50
2b	-40 to -45
3a	-35 to -40
3b	-30 to -35
4a	-25 to -30
4b	-20 to -25
5a	-15 to -20
5b	-10 to -15
6a	-5 to -10
6b	0 to -5
7a	5 to 0
7b	10 to 5
8a	15 to 10
8b	20 to 15
9a	25 to 20
9b	30 to 25
10a	35 to 30
10b	40 to 35
11	40 and above

LAWNS

SELECTING THE RIGHT GRASS

When selecting the right grass for your lawn there are several factors that must be considered. Is your lawn shady, in part sun, or in full sun? Is your lawn going to get high traffic from children, pets, or other recreations?

All the grasses below require a soil pH of around 6.5. All benefit from deep, infrequent watering which aids in root development and therefore drought-tolerance. In the extreme heat of summer, lawns need deep watering twice a week; in the cooler spring and fall, once a week is sufficient. Early morning is the preferred time to water.

POPULAR GRASSES FOR MID-SOUTH LAWNS

Bermuda Grasses are fast growing, drought tolerant, wear resistant, and well-adapted to the Mid-South. Bermudas prefer plenty of sun (6 hours or more) and well-drained soil, but will tolerate a variety of drainage situations. Common Bermuda requires frequent mowing and, although it makes a beautiful turf, it can become an invasive pest to adjacent landscaped beds if not kept in check. Hybrids types are generally finer textured than common Bermuda and less invasive. The hybrid varieties that perform well in the Mid-South area are 'T-10', 'Tifway II', 'Sahara', 'Shanghai', and 'Celebration'. Preferred mowing heights are ¾" to 1½" for common Bermuda, and ½" to 1" for most hybrids.

Zoysia Grasses form a very wear-resistant, thick, tightly-knit turf that almost feels like plush carpet underfoot. Zoysia is more shade tolerant and less invasive than the Bermudas. The more common 'Meyers Z-52' variety needs at least 4 hours of strong sun. There are newer varieties, such as 'Palisade', 'Zeon', 'Zorro', and 'Cavalier' that can survive in only 2 to 3 hours of sun. Zoysia needs well-drained soil, and if over-watered will begin to rot and die out. It should be mowed at 1½" to 2" in height.

143

As zoysia is slow to establish, laying sod is the best approach, and while expensive, sod creates an instant finished lawn. Zoysia can also be established from seed or by planting 4" plugs about 6" apart. Establishing a new zoysia lawn from seed can be somewhat tricky, so it is advisable that you work closely with the turf specialist at your local garden center for the variety best suited for your yard.

Fescues are best used in the Mid-South in shady areas where neither Bermuda nor zoysia will grow. Tall turf-type fescue *blends* are recommended for the best overall 12 month performance, as the mixture of seeds offers better combined shade tolerance, disease resistance, heat tolerance, etc. than a single variety. Turf-type tall fescues are easily established from seed, and September and October are the best months to sow them so the grasses will mature prior to the onset of hot weather the next year. Fescues can also be planted in the spring, but should be limited to spot-seeding or light over-seeding. A pH of 6.5 is preferred, although these fescues can tolerate a pH as low as 5.75.

Turf-type tall fescues should be mowed to 2" to 2½" during most of the year; in the extreme heat of summer leave at least 3" tall. This increased leaf surface area picks up more light rays filtering through the trees. This in turn makes the grass more drought-resistant and heat-tolerant. Water is critical to the survival of fescues and other shady lawn grasses during the summer. Fine-leaved fescues, such as creeping red fescue, make a prettier turf than the tall fescues but are not as heat-tolerant. Therefore they are not used as much in the Mid-South as they are in Kentucky and farther north.

ALTERNATIVE LAWNS

Clover (*Trifolium*) was included in grass seed mixes prior to 1950, and has many virtues. It feels good underfoot, is drought-tolerant, needs no fertilizing (as it is a "nitrogen-fixer" and gets nutrition from the air), improves and aerates the soil with its root system, requires less mowing as it is naturally low-growing, and does not turn yellow from dog urine. See *Garden Care – Dogs and Yellow Spots on Lawns*. This last trait alone makes it attractive to pet owners. Additionally, clover has rather pretty flowers and attracts bees. If you don't want honeybees around, keep the flowers mown.

The reduced expense for watering, fertilizing, and mowing makes clover a more economical ground cover than traditional lawn grasses. It is as easy to grow as a weed and is not fussy about sun or soil. Clover will not take as much foot-traffic as Bermuda and other rhizomatous grasses, but it will spread and fill in bare spots, unlike some other grasses which require re-seeding. While clover is an unconventional lawn, it has a lot going for it and works well in certain applications.

Other ground covers to consider using as alternative lawns, and which offer many of the advantages of clover, are wild violets, wild strawberries, and ground ivy or creeping-charley.

ESTABLISHING A NEW LAWN

Most grass types used for lawns in the Mid-South are available in seed or sod. Whichever method you choose, proper planning will be your key to success. There are several steps that should be followed in preparing the ground for either seed or sod.

Test the soil: Gather soil from several spots of the area to be planted. Take the samples from about 4" deep and mix them together to obtain average readings; a quart of soil is usually adequate. Next, take the sample to a soil testing lab, or obtain forms and boxes from the agricultural extension service. The sample can then be sent off for testing. Soil testing is very important since it will identify nutrient deficiencies.

Remove existing vegetation and debris: Spray the area with a non-selective herbicide containing glyphosate to kill all unwanted weeds and grasses. More than one application may be required to kill the undesirable vegetation. Lightly till the area and rake out the dead vegetation.

Prepare the grade: A new lawn should be graded so it slopes away from the house. If possible, change the grade to provide better drainage. In leveling, do not alter the existing grade around large trees as burying roots or removing existing soil could cause severe damage to the tree. Run a rotary tiller back and forth across the area until there are no large dirt clods. Now add soil conditioners such as finely ground pine bark, organic humus, composted manure, and sand to amend the clay soil. If the test indicated a need for lime and/or fertilizer, add those at this time. Till these in to a depth of 4" – 6" and level the soil by raking and lightly rolling. When you think the soil is level, use a heavy lawn roller to remove air pockets and firm up the planting area. You are now ready to plant.

Seeding: Sow the grass seed over the prepared bed. Use a hand-seeder or a fertilizer spreader, as long as you can calibrate it for seeds. Sow ½ of the needed seed over the bed, then go back and seed with the second half at right angles to the first seeding. This criss-crossing pattern virtually eliminates missed spots. Lightly rake, just barely covering the seed with loose soil, then roll the lawn again to firm the planting. A light layer of sand or straw can be spread on top of the seeded lawn to help prevent erosion and maintain even soil moisture which is essential for good germination.

145

POUNDS OF SEED NEEDED PER 1,000 SQ. FT.

Bermuda	2 – 4 lbs.
Zoysia	1 – 2 lbs.
Turf-type tall fescue	7 – 10 lbs.

Water: It is essential to keep the newly-seeded area evenly moist on a daily basis through the germination period until you have a good stand of grass all over. You may find it necessary to water lightly a couple of times a day to maintain this critical moisture level depending on weather conditions and time of year. Use a light mist, as you do not want to wash your seeds away.

Sod is the best way to go if it is within budget. The big advantage is that it gives an instant lawn. Prepare the area for sodding exactly as was described for seeding, except make the final grade about ¾" to 1" lower along the edge where the lawn will meet the paved surface. When laid, the sod should be at the same level as existing driveway or sidewalk. Water the area lightly prior to sodding. This encourages the roots of the sod to seek out moisture very quickly. Lay out the sod on the prepared ground so the joints butt together. Fill any gaps with sand. Use a lawn roller to help level the sod and press the roots into the soil. Water 2 or 3 times a week until the sod is well rooted, usually in about 2 weeks.

Spot sodding or plugging may be done as a cost-effective method of sodding. Prepare the ground as described above. Cut the sod mat into plugs 3" – 4" square, and plant these 1" – 2" deep and 6" – 12" apart. The closer they are the sooner the gaps will fill in. Bermuda spreads faster than zoysia. Fescues, being clumping grasses, are not suited for this method.

RENOVATING AN EXISTING LAWN

To renovate an old lawn first test the soil pH. Apply lime to increase alkalinity and sulfur (or iron sulfate) to increase acidity. If you have been following a good lawn care program, and the quality of the turf is just not as good as it should be, it's probably time to renovate the lawn. Excessive build up of thatch (over ½") in Bermuda and zoysia lawns is the most common reason for lawn decline.

De-thatching: Thatch is the excessive build up of undecomposed grass clippings that mat between the soil surface and the growing grass tips, and can smother your lawn. A little thatch is helpful in conserving moisture and stabilizing soil temperatures. Too much thatch can harbor insects and diseases, and prevent water and nutrients from penetrating into the root zone. For less severe thatch buildups, it is sometimes possible to speed the rate of grass clipping decomposition by using compost teas. This adds beneficial microorganisms which break down the thatch. In cases of severe thatch buildup, it is best to have a professional lawn service (or an energetic do-it-yourselfer) "de-thatch" the lawn with a verticut machine and remove all debris by raking or vacuuming.

Aerating: Have the lawn aerated after mechanical de-thatching or just before spraying with the compost tea. An aerator is a large drum covered with hollow projecting tines. When the aerator is rolled across the lawn, small plugs of soil are removed in a regular pattern, and the soil cores are left on the ground. The microorganisms in the soil plugs are then able to decompose the grass clippings which form thatch. Aerating allows water, food, and air to move into the root zone. Aerating should be done about once a year in the spring.

INSECTS AND DISEASES

If you follow a proper lawn maintenance program, insects and diseases are usually not a problem. However, if they do occur, it is best to consult the turf specialist at you garden center since controls of these are sometimes difficult. Follow all directions carefully paying particular attention to label precautions.

MONTHLY GUIDE FOR BERMUDA & ZOYSIA GRASSES

January – Mid-March	Apply herbicide for control of chickweed, wild onions, late-germinating Poa annua, and wild violets.
February – March	Apply pre-emergent herbicide to control crabgrass and certain other summer-germinating weeds and grasses.
Mid-March – May	Apply a broadleaf herbicide for control of clover, dandelion, and other broadleaf weeds.
Early April	Bermuda grass – Apply a complete lawn food containing controlled-release nitrogen.
Early May	Zoysia grass – Apply a complete lawn food containing controlled-release nitrogen.

147

Early May – Mid-Sept.	Apply herbicide for control of crabgrass, nutgrass, and certain other weeds and grasses.
Mid-May – August	When daytime temperatures are 80°F and above, apply herbicide for control of crabgrass, dallisgrass, and many other noxious grasses. Repeat at 7 to 14 day intervals if necessary.
Early to Mid-June	Bermuda lawns – apply a complete lawn fertilizer that provides controlled-release nitrogen.
Early to Mid-July	Zoysia lawns – apply a complete lawn fertilizer that provides controlled-release nitrogen.
Late August – Sept.	Apply pre-emergent herbicide for control of poa annua and certain other winter-germinating weeds and grasses.
Mid-September	Apply a winterizing fertilizer (like 0–20–20) to Bermuda and zoysia lawns to encourage root growth and help prevent winter damage. Do not use a nitrogen fertilizer at this time of year.
October – January	Have a pH test run and apply lime if necessary.

MONTHLY GUIDE FOR SHADY LAWN GRASSES

September – October	This is the best time of the year to plant fescues and other cool-season grasses, whether establishing a new lawn or over-seeding an existing shady lawn. Feed new shady lawn grasses with starter fertilizer or organic soil activators. Feed existing shady lawn grasses with lawn fertilizer containing controlled-release nitrogen. Apply lime if needed.
November – December	Keep fallen leaves off the shady lawn as best you can. They will smother the grass if allowed to remain all winter.
March	If necessary, over-seed areas of the thin turf. Feed shady lawn grasses with lawn food containing

	controlled-release nitrogen or an organic lawn food.
March – May	Spray established shady lawn grasses with carfentrazone-based herbicides for control of broadleaf weeds.
Mid-April – Mid-May	Use a pre-emergent herbicide for control of summer-germinating weeds and grasses.
May	Apply a complete lawn fertilizer containing controlled-release nitrogen.
May – June	Apply lawn fungicide to prevent turf diseases. If necessary, spot spray established shady lawn grasses for crabgrass and other grassy weeds with a spray approved for fescue and other cool-season grasses.
June – August	Keep these grasses mowed high (3") all through the summer and apply compost tea or feed with liquid seaweed to improve the shade grass's heat-tolerance.

TREES

CHOOSING A TREE

In choosing a tree, limit your selection to trees that are hardy in the Mid-South and suited to your sun/shade conditions. Sitka spruce or aspen, for example, would be a poor choice. Consider how long the tree will live, how fast it will grow, and its ultimate size relative to the size of your property. Almost all species of trees have cultivated varieties, or "cultivars", that are usually superior to the wild species, or at least their size, growth habit, leaf pattern, etc., are uniform and predictable.

What is the purpose of the tree in your landscape? Do you want to shade the south side of your house with a large spreading deciduous (loses its leaves in winter) tree like an oak, tulip poplar, or sycamore? You will have shade in the summer and light in winter, but it will take some years to grow fifty feet tall.

If you need a fast-growing deciduous tree and if gorgeous lavender flower clusters and large catalpa-like leaves appeal to you, then consider the royal paulownia. If you already have a canopy of large trees and need a small accent specimen near the patio, then crape myrtle (*Lagerstroemia*), Kousa dogwood (*Cornus*), redbud (*Cercis*), Japanese maple (*Acer*), or styrax might be good choices.

Perhaps you want to screen an unpleasant view, and you have the space; then consider the evergreen queen of them all, *Magnolia grandiflora*, or the handsome but smaller Japanese cedar (*Cryptomeria*). If you select a conifer, give it plenty of room to grow as they look best in their full natural habit rather than stunted on one side because they have been competing for sunlight and space. A row of slim columnar evergreens such as 'Emerald' arborvitae (*Thuja*) are nice fronting a wall.

151

Does the tree under consideration produce flowers, fruit, or seedpods that will be objectionable? Some people find this to be true of sweet gum (*Liquidambar*) and mimosa (*Albizia*). Others find the leaf form and fall color of sweet gum so lovely, and the ferny tropical foliage and fuzzy pink flowers of mimosa so romantic, that they don't notice the spiny gumballs and flower litter on the ground.

Consider also if the tree is prone to dropping branches, like loblolly pine or river birch, which can be damaging to perennials below. Beware of brittle-limbed trees, like Bradford pears (*Pyrus*), as they are likely to split in a wind storm and can do an amazing amount of property damage. On the other hand, a Bradford pear is ideal in most other respects – it has lovely white flowers in spring, pristine foliage, great fall color, handsome bark, medium-fast growth rate, and good disease resistance. If your location is sheltered from wind, the pear might be an excellent choice.

CULTURE AND CARE

SITE CONSIDERATIONS

In hot climates, the shade cast by large trees is very helpful in lowering your utility bill and extending the life of your air conditioner and shingles. This is especially true for older houses which are poorly insulated. A large tree has a canopy 40' or more in diameter and can be 70' – 100' tall. Such a tree will shade your house if planted 20' – 50' away on the south side of your property, keeping in mind that the sun moves from east to west across the southern sky. To provide shade, the tree does not need to be right against the house.

Never use trees as foundation planting because branches will abrade your shingles and gutters, and "raised roots" may damage foundation footings. Fallen leaves must be swept out of roof valleys and gutters on a regular basis. Further, constant shade and dampness promotes paint failure and rotting of the wooden gable and siding boards; this is especially likely if the shingles above have been damaged by tree limbs.

Watch any construction grading done around trees. Fine trees have been killed by dirt being dumped on top of their roots, or by having too much of their roots cut away.

It is especially important to remember when designing driveways, fences, and gates, that at some point a tree man with a crane may need access to your yard. Always have a professional tree man assess your big trees every few years and remove high dead branches and thin a too-dense canopy. Properly maintained trees are far less likely to be damaged in a bad storm.

PLANTING, WATERING, AND FERTILIZING

Trees are sold in three forms: bare-rooted, balled-in-burlap, and container-grown. Select a medium-sized tree, not the largest one available. A large tree requires two years of attention before it regains its former vigor. In this length of time a smaller tree will have caught up with its growth.

Many roots are cut when a tree is removed from its natural growing spot, and it may suffer from the shock. Choose a tree with an adequate root ball. A well-formed root system is symmetrically branched with the main roots growing down and out to provide trunk support. Kinked or circling roots can cause weak trunk support and restrict the movement of water and nutrients. Ideally, buy container grown trees in pots coated with copper sulfate to stop circling.

Reject any tree with broken branches or injured bark, which is an open invitation to disease. If the trees are in leaf, avoid any with wilted leaves or with leaves smaller than the variety usually bears, indicating poor root systems.

The details of planting, watering, and fertilizing trees are discussed in the *Garden Care* chapter. Some people advocate pruning back about 1/3 of the foliage to balance the root system, which is sometimes damaged or compromised in transplanting. The other school of thought, however, is to leave all foliage when planting because photosynthesis feeds the root system and helps the plant establish more quickly.

PRUNING

It is a very good policy to have a tree man prune big trees every few years to remove high dead limbs and let more light into the beds below. The few hundred dollars spent on big tree maintenance will save you thousands in storm damage repair. As this is inherently dangerous work, hire bonded and insured workmen.

The "high shade" and "dappled shade" created by limbing-up and thinning the tall canopy trees is ideal for a great many shrubs and flowers, and you should notice an improvement in the overall demeanor of your shade garden. It will be able to breathe.

Do not prune during period when sap is rising. This will cause them to "bleed" too much. If a limb has been removed from a tree, trim the bark smoothly to form an oval wound as close to the trunk as possible. It is not necessary to apply tree paint to the cut surface.

PEST CONTROL

Well-tended trees are less susceptible to pests and diseases than neglected ones and, if attacked, recover faster.

Borers are attracted by the odor of a wounded tree. You might try placing mothballs or yellow laundry soap around the base of the tree to discourage borers; don't do this if you have dogs and cats in the yard.

Gouty oak gall in oak trees is caused by a gall-forming wasp. It is an interesting bit of biology: the wasp injects its eggs into the vein of an oak leaf, along with a special growth hormone which stimulates the oak to make a brown golf-ball-sized mass of spongy-woody tissue, or gall, at that stem tip. The developing larvae feed on this spongy tissue and do not continue to sap strength from the tree once the gall is formed. The larvae eventually emerge from the gall as a mature wasp. The tree is not really harmed unless the infestation is very severe. Insecticides are generally ineffective, and cutting off the galls is the best, albeit usually unfeasible, method of control.

If a pest problem should arise, call a professional arborist. Trees are too tall for you to prune or spray effectively with home equipment anyway.

ORNAMENTAL VALUE

The trees listed below have showy flowers and/or fruit and are good garden choices. Select a tree that won't get too big for your space. A tree grown in the open will get larger and have a more handsome branch structure and crown than one grown in a woods competing for sun and space.

FLOWERING TREES

Basswood *Tilia*	Magnolia *Magnolia*
Bottlebrush buckeye *Aesculus*	Oriental magnolia
Catalpa *Catalpa*	Royal paulownia *Paulownia*
Chaste tree *Vitex*	Red buckeye *Aesculus*
Crape myrtle *Lagerstroemia*	Redbud *Cercis*
Dogwood *Cornus*	Serviceberry *Amelanchier*
Fringetree *Chionanthus*	Silver-bell *Halesia*
Golden-rain Tree *Koelreuteria*	Snowbell *Styrax*
Hawthorn *Crataegus*	Tulip poplar *Liriodendron*
Horsechestnut *Aesculus*	Yellowwood *Cladrastis*

FLOWERING FRUIT TREES

Apple *Malus*	Peach *Prunus*
Apricot *Prunus*	Pear *Pyrus*
Cherry *Prunus*	Persimmon *Diospyros*
Crabapple *Malus*	Plum *Prunus*

Japanese Bitter Orange *Poncirus*	Pomegranate *Punica*
Pawpaw *Asimina*	

WHY LEAVES CHANGE COLOR IN THE FALL

Deciduous shrubs and trees turn gold, maroon, red, or orange in autumn, and many perennials yellow-up as they die back in fall. Without going into much detail, a plant's green color is due to the chlorophyll molecules in its leaves. Chlorophyll is really a dye molecule which changes color, from green to colorless, depending on the angle of the sun, the cool temperatures, and the duration of daylight. In autumn, when the sun is lower in the sky and sets earlier, the chlorophyll molecule is still present but it becomes colorless instead of green.

This "unmasks" the red, yellow, orange, and maroon dye molecules that were always there so they now become visible. The familiar "carotene", which is responsible for the color of carrots, is one of several orange molecules in autumn leaves. If the tree has been well watered in summer, the various dyes will be more intensely colored, and it will be a beautiful autumn.

Evergreens have a different strategy for remaining green, and many have a tough waxy layer which makes the leaf's chlorophyll less sensitive to the changing sunlight angle. Some evergreens have a substance like car antifreeze in their leaves.

TREES FOR FALL COLOR

Ash *Fraxinus*	Japanese maple *Acer*
Beech *Fagus*	Red buckeye *Aesculus*
Black gum or tupelo *Nyssa*	Red maple cultivars *Acer*
Chinese pistache *Pistacia*	Scarlet oak *Quercus*
Crape myrtle *Lagerstroemia*	Maple (all) *Acer*
Dogwood *Cornus*	Serviceberry *Amelanchier*
Ginkgo *Ginkgo*	Sumac *Rhus*
Hickory *Carya*	Sweet gum *Liquidambar*

155

EVERGREENS AND CONIFERS

First, about the terminology, "evergreen" and "conifer" is not necessarily the same thing. Conifer refers to plants that bear cones as their reproductive means. To confuse things, some conifers such as juniper and yew have cones that look more like berries. Further, not all conifers are evergreen; some such as larch and cypress lose their leaves in fall. And finally, Southern magnolias are evergreen and bear a cone-like fruit but are not conifers. Behold the wonderful diversity of nature.

Textures may be coarse or fine; densely branched or sparse and sculptural. Colors range from shades of green, yellow, blue, orange, and purple. Many are bi-color or change colors through the seasons. Although conifers are welcome additions to the landscape for their diversity in texture and color, they have been largely underused or poorly sited.

Conifers can be used as specimens to highlight a spot in the garden, as screens, in containers, in rock gardens, and in the mixed border. Their forms may be rounded, pendulous, narrow, upright or spreading. Many new dwarf conifers have come on the market and may be easily used in any garden. (Refer to *Garden Care–Pruning Needle-Leaved Evergreens and Conifers* for more details on growing)

The most popular conifers for the Mid-South are pine (*Pinus*), juniper (*Juniperus*), cedar (*Cedrus*), cypress (*Taxodium*), China fir (*Cunninghamia*), Japanese cedar (*Cryptomeria*), arborvitae (*Thuja*), Leyland cypress (*Cupressocyparis*), false cypress (*Chamaecyparis*), and Japanese plum yew (*Cephalotaxus*).

156

TABLE OF TREES

TABLE 13. TREES OF THE MID-SOUTH

Key:	Bf – Bird food	E – Evergreen
	B – Broad-leaf evergreen	F – Showy Flower
	C – Coniferous	* – Very desirable
	D – Deciduous	

SCIENTIFIC NAME/ COMMON NAME	KEY	HEIGHT	COMMENTS
Acer **Maple**	D		Many excellent garden trees in this species. All are good. Sun or part shade. Moist, well-drained soil.
Acer circinatum **Japanese Maple**	D,*	3' – 10'	Native to Pacific Northwest and similar to Japanese Maples but leaves not usually as deeply incised. Takes sun, shade, moist, or dry. 'Little Gem' is 3' with orange fall color. 'Monroe' has incised leaves and grows 10'. 'Pacific Fire' foliage starts lime green, turns yellow, then red.
Acer japonicum **Japanese Maple**	D,*	10' – 15'	'Aconitifolium' has deeply dissected leaves and is very beautiful. 'Green Cascade' is weeping form. 'O Taki' can take more sun. All have brilliant fall color.
Acer palmatum **Japanese Maple**	D,*	2' – 20'	Slow growing. Part shade. Brilliant coloring early spring and fall. Desirable. Many excellent new varieties with green, purple, or variegated foliage. Very sculptural quality. 'Aka shigitatsu sawa', 'Higasa yama', 'Oridono nishiki', and 'Butterfly' are variegated and 12' tall. 'Bloodgood', 'Shaina', 'Fireglow', and 'Emperor' have red foliage on 10' – 20' trees. 'Kamagata' is 3' dwarf. 'Arakawa', 'Beni maiko', 'Beni shi en', 'Osakazuki', 'Shigarami', 'Shishigashira' and

157

Scientific Name/ Common Name	Key	Height	Comments
			'Trompenburg' are all good.
Acer palmatum dissectum **Japanese Maple, Dissectum**	D,*	4' – 5'	Finely cut leaves divided into segments. Scarlet in fall. Extremely slow growing and very elegant. 'Crimson Queen', 'Garnet', 'Filigree', 'Inaba shidare', 'Orangeola', 'Seiryu', 'Sekimori', 'Spring Delight', 'Tamuke yama', 'Viridis' and 'Waterfall' are all good.
Acer rubrum **Red Maple**	D	50' – 70'	Scarlet, orange in fall. Good street or park tree. 'October Glory', 'Autumn Blaze', 'Autumn Flame', and 'Fairview Flame' do best in the South. 'Red Sunset' is new; fast grower, red to gold fall color, weak wood.
Acer saccharinum **Silver Maple**	D	60' – 100'	Softwood. Native to eastern U.S. Good roadside ornamental. Fast grower. Has shallow spreading root system so not good for small garden. Yellow, red autumn foliage.
Acer saccharum **Sugar Maple**	D,*	100'	Hardy all over Eastern U.S. Source of maple syrup. Does not tolerate pollution. Autumn foliage gold, orange, scarlet. Best varieties for the South are 'Commemoration', 'Green Mountain', and 'Legacy'; they all have thicker, waxier leaves that don't tatter and burn in our heat and drought.
Acer shirasawanum **'Golden Full Moon' Maple**	D,*	to 20'	'Aureum' and 'Autumn Moon' Yellow foliage turns crimson in fall. Small, slow-growing rounded tree. Good in containers
Aesculus parviflora **Bottlebrush Buckeye**	D,F, *	8' – 12'	12" – 18" long white flowers in June. Clean butter yellow fall foliage. Tolerates shade and wet areas. Excellent landscape value. Spreading habit.

158

SCIENTIFIC NAME/ COMMON NAME	KEY	HEIGHT	COMMENTS
Aesculus pavia **Red Buckeye**	D,F, *	10' – 20'	Native. Bright red spiky flower in early spring. Hummingbirds love it. Handsome palmate foliage. The buckeye nut is a good luck charm.
Albizia julibrissin **Mimosa**	D,F	20' – 35'	Tropical looking ferny foliage with fragrant pink threadlike flowers. Blooms May – August. Sun, average soil. Can be messy.
Amelanchier **Serviceberry, Sarvis**	D,F, Bf	20' – 30'	Many varieties. Early bloomer. White spring blossom. Yellow, orange, or red fall foliage. Fall berry loved by birds. Lovely, small, under-story woodland tree. Native.
Aralia spinosa and *Aralia elata* **Devil's-walking-stick, Japanese Angelica Tree**	D	10' – 20'	Thick-stemmed spiny shrub or small tree with lovely compound leaves giving a handsome effect. Tends to sucker. Best for natural areas, as very thorny. *Aralia elata* has some variegated cultivars.
Asimina triloba **Pawpaw**	D,Bf	20' – 30'	Native. Fast grower. Banana-like fruit. Yellow fall foliage.
Betula nigra **River Birch**	D,Bf	60' – 80'	Stream and river banks. Fast growing. Bark orange and scaly. Tolerates poor drainage. Do not plant near house or terrace as roots tend to surface. Yellow fall foliage. Messy. Improved varieties 'Heritage' and 'Dura Heat' have less leaf shed, good bark, stronger limbs.
Carpinus caroliniana **American Hornbeam, Blue Beech, Ironwood**	D	40'	Leaves pest-free and resemble elm. Yellow in fall. Slow grower. Grown from Maine to Texas. Tolerates poor drainage.
Carya **Hickory**	D	to 100'	Many species. Food for wildlife. Wood used for smoking meat and fish, and for tools. Yellow fall foliage. Not used much in landscaping because long tap root makes

159

Scientific Name/ Common Name	Key	Height	Comments
			transplanting difficult. Prefers moist, loam, but is adaptable. Native, climax forest tree, along with oaks.
Carya glabra **Pignut Hickory**	D	50' – 60'	Beautiful gold fall foliage. Difficult to transplant due to long taproot, but worth trying to grow. Nuts are not very tasty. Native.
Carya illinoinensis **Pecan**	D,Bf	to 100'	Dull yellow fall foliage. Many varieties; consult local nursery. Excellent nut loved by man and squirrel. Troubled by caterpillars and bag worms. Not hardy north of Zone 7.
Carya ovata **Shagbark Hickory**	D,Bf	60' – 80'	Interesting bark "plates" that appear to be loose at top and bottom. Dull yellow fall color. Sweet, edible nuts. Native.
Carya tomentosa **White Hickory**	D,Bf	50' – 60'	Deep golden yellow fall color. Edible nut. Adaptable but prefers moist, well-drained soil. Native.
Catalpa bignonioides **Catalpa**	D, F	40'	Forest-sized. Attracts worms. Showy white flower in early summer. Long slender seed pods. Very large, heart-shaped leaves. Wind firm.
Cedar, Red See **Juniper** (*Juniperus*)			Red cedar is a juniper rather than a true cedar (*Cedrus*), and we cannot explain why it is not called red juniper.
Cedrus deodara **Deodar Cedar, Himalayan Cedar**	C,E	40' – 70' can be 100+'	Dark blue green needles. Handsome, graceful, drooping branches. Large accent or background tree. Fast growing; can be short lived.
Cedrus atlantica **Atlas Cedar, Cedar**	C,E	40' – 60' can be 100'	Feathery, bluish green needles. Also pendulous form. Handsome specimen tree when given enough space. Extract of bark used in aromatherapy.

SCIENTIFIC NAME/ COMMON NAME	KEY	HEIGHT	COMMENTS
Cedrus libani **Cedar-of-Lebanon**	C,E*	40' – 60' can be 100+'	Closely resembles *C. deodara* but darker green and larger. Very handsome, long-lived tree. Sunny, open location. No serious pests.
Celtis laevigata **Hackberry**	D,Bf	100'	Wide-spreading, airy branches. Thrives in poor soil. Native. Disease and insect free. Yellow fall foliage. Not particularly ornamental or desirable.
Cephalotaxus fortunei **Chinese Plum Yew**	E	15' – 20'	Horizontal, slightly pendulous branches. Graceful. Hard to find.
Cephalotaxus harringtonia **Japanese Plum Yew**	E,*	5' – 10' shrub or 20' – 30' tree	Hardy; thrives in shade or part sun. Slow growing, but beautiful. *Var. drupacea*, 'Duke Gardens', 'Fastigiata', and 'Prostrata' are a few good cultivars. Excellent shrub or tree. Use instead of *Taxus* Yew.
Cercidiphyllum japonicum **Katsura**	D	to 50'	Round 4" leaves. Scarlet and yellow in fall. Rich, moist soil. Female, spreading; male, columnar. Also great weeping forms.
Cercis canadensis **Redbud**	D,F, *	25'	Native, showy purplish pink flowers. Blooms before dogwood. Volunteers from seed. Fast grower, short-lived. Lots of cultivars to choose from: 'Forest Pansy'– purple leaf turns green; 'Silver Cloud'– variegated type; 'Lavender Twist'– weeping redbud; 'Alba'– white flowers; 'Tennessee Pink'– pink.
Cercis texensis **Redbud**	D,F, *	20'	Redbud with leathery glossy leaves with undulating margins. 'Oklahoma'– red blooms, 'Texas White'– white blooms. 'Traveler' is shrub-sized with pink flowers.
Chamaecyparis **False Cypress,**	C,E, *		Many varieties, sizes, and colors. Check local nursery.

161

Scientific Name/ Common Name	Key	Height	Comments
White Cedar			
Chionanthus virginicus **Fringetree, Old-man's beard**	D,F, *	30'	Good ornamental. Fragrant, white feathery flower in spring.
Chionanthus retusus **Chinese Fringetree**	D,F, *	15' – 20'	Spreading, rounded, small tree with beautiful white flowers. Sun to part shade. Garden soil. Fine tree.
Cladrastis kentukea **American Yellowwood**	D,*	30' – 50'	White panicles, like wisteria. Fragrant. Deep-rooted. Drought-resistant. Blooms profusely every other year. Prune only in summer as it bleeds severely if pruned in winter or spring. Yellow fall color. Native.
Cornus **Dogwood**	D,F, bf,*		A beautiful, flowering small tree for any garden. Anthracnose disease is destroying dogwoods all over the country. Look for resistant varieties.
Cornus kousa and Cornus kousa x C. florida **Asian Dogwood, Kousa Dogwood**	D,F, *	10' – 30'	June bloom. Pointed white bracts. Larger scarlet fruit. Flowers appear with leaves. Variegated cultivars are available. Very resistant to borers, mildew, and anthracnose. Tolerates more sun. Best white is 'Milky Way', best pink 'Satomi', and best variegated 'Samaritan'.
Cornus plena **Double-Flowered Dogwood**	D, F	20'	Double-flowered form of *C. florida.*
Cornus 'Rutban' **'Rutban' Dogwood**	D,F, bf,*	20' by 25'	Rutgers University developed this cross between *C. florida x C. kousa*. Highly resistant to dogwood borer, and anthracnose (*Discula distructiva*). Varieties include 'Stellar Pink' and other 'Stellar' hybrids, 'Aurora', 'Celestial', and 'Constellation'. Drought and sun tolerant; don't plant in heavy shade.

SCIENTIFIC NAME/ COMMON NAME	KEY	HEIGHT	COMMENTS
Cornus florida **Flowering Dogwood**	D, F, Bf,*	to 30'	Many cultivars. White and pink bracts in March or April before leaves. Scarlet leaves in fall. 'Cherokee Brave' is best pink; 'Cherokee Princess' is best white. Both introduced by Univ. Tenn. to be resistant to Anthracnose which is destroying this favorite native tree. Other *Cornus* species are less susceptible to this disease.
Cornus mas **Corneliancherry Dogwood**	D,F, Bf,*	20' – 25'	Good small tree. Yellow bract flowers. Valuable in shady place. Can stand dry soil. Also variegated. Check local nursery.
Cornus nana **Dwarf Dogwood**	D, F	5' – 6'	Dwarf form of *C. florida.*
Cornus pendula **Weeping Dogwood**	D, F	20'	*Weeping form of C. florida.*
Cotinus coggygria **Smoketree, Smokebush**	D,*	to 15'	Coppery purple leaf, feathery plumes in May and June. Hardy.
Cotinus obovatus **American Smoketree**	D	to 30'	Brilliant orange scarlet fall foliage. One of the best for intense fall color
Crataegus laevigata **Hawthorn**	D,Bf	25'	Hawthorn of English literature. White flowers in May. Red fruit. Thorny. Subject to caterpillars.
Cryptomeria japonica **Cryptomeria, Japanese Cedar**	C,E, *	50' – 60' can be 100+'	Pyramidal growth. Background tree. Distinctive greenery. Angular foliage. Many good cultivars – 'Black Dragon', 'Yoshino', 'Globoso Nana' is dwarf form.
Cunninghamia lanceolata **China Fir**	C,E, *	30' – 75'	Handsome. Hardy in Zones 7 & 8. Spiny, blue-green, medium-fine textured foliage. 1½" cones. Moist, acid, well-drained soil, protected from wind. Timber tree in China.

163

SCIENTIFIC NAME/ COMMON NAME	KEY	HEIGHT	COMMENTS
Cupressocyparis leylandii **Leyland Cypress**	C,E	60' – 70'	Has become very popular in Mid-South. Sun, rich moist soil. Magnificent evergreen with fine, feathery foliage forming a pyramidal outline. Some cultivars have gold foliage. 'Castlewellan Gold', 'Gold Rider', 'Naylor's Blue'. Subject to bagworms and fungus disease. Great salt tolerance. Used as Christmas trees.
Cydonia sinensis **Chinese Quince**	D,Bf	20'	Insignificant pink bloom. Spring. Grown for edible fruit, good for jelly and preserves. (See *Chaenomeles* in *Shrubs* for flowering quince)
Diospyros kaki **Japanese Persimmon**	D,Bf	40'	Large, orange, edible fruit. Very attractive tree. Hardy Zones 7, 8, 9.
Diospyros virginiana **Persimmon**	D,Bf	to 40'	Fall fruit edible, good for birds and wildlife. Very hard wood, used for golf clubs. Yellow to red fall foliage.
Fagus grandifolia **American Beech**	D,Bf *	50' – 90'	Light gray bark. Young trees retain leaves all winter. Leaf similar to elm. Climax tree.
Ficus carica **Common Fig**	D,Bf	to 30'	Many varieties. Grown for fruit. Can be tender. Consult local nursery.
Firmiana simplex **Chinese Parasol Tree, Phoenix Tree**	D	50'	Palmate leaf 12" across. Resembling sycamore. Grown in South for shade. Lemon yellow flower in Zones 8 & 9.
Fraxinus **Ash**	D,F, Bf	30' – 90'	Many varieties. Hardy. Rapid growth. Yellow leaves in fall. Emerald Ash Borer may become a problem.
Ginkgo biloba **Ginkgo, Maidenhair Tree**	D,*	120'	Hardy. Prehistoric. Very handsome ornamental. Yellow in fall. Good on city streets or parks. Wind firm. Only one species. Female has foul-smelling fruit. Many good male cultivars like 'Princeton Sentry'.

164

SCIENTIFIC NAME/ COMMON NAME	KEY	HEIGHT	COMMENTS
Gleditsia triacanthos **Honey Locust**	D	35' – 70'	Thornless varieties. Yellow in fall. Tolerates pollution. Fast grower. Reseeds and spreads.
Gordonia lasianthus **Loblolly Bay**	B,E, *	60'	Not hardy above Zone 7. White flowers, glossy dark green leaves.
Halesia tetraptera **Carolina Silver-bell, Silver-bell Tree, Lily-of-the-valley Tree, SnowdropTree**	D,F, *	35'	Branches in spring become lined with white bell-shaped flowers. Low-branched, graceful small tree. Azaleas grow well below them. Well-drained acid soil. Yellow fall color. Native. 'Rosea', 'Variegata', 'Arnold Pink'.
Holly – *Ilex* See *Holly* article in *Shrubs* chapter			
Ilex decidua **'Warren's Red' Deciduous Holly**	D,Bf	10' – 15'	Foliage resembles common privet. Wonderful red berries all winter. Very disease resistant.
Ilex opaca **American Holly**	B,Bf	40' – 50'	Not for foundation planting. Subject to leafminer. Fertilize heavily for masses of berries.
Juglans nigra **Black Walnut**	D,Bf	50' – 150'	Valuable for nuts. Do not plant ornamentals or vegetables underneath. Roots produce a substance toxic to some plants. Hellebores will grow under walnut trees.
Juniperus **Juniper**	E,Bf, *	1' to 50'	Many species and varieties. Foliage mostly gray green. Many forms from columnar to ground cover. Subject to rust, fungi, galls, bagworms. Remove rust galls. Juniper berries flavor gin.
Juniperus virginiana **Common Red Cedar**	C,E	to 50'	Many cultivars; site in full sun with good drainage. Wood is used to line closets as it is moth-repellent.
Koelreuteria paniculata **Panicled Golden-rain Tree, Varnish Tree.**	D,F, *	30'	Large clusters of tiny yellow flowers in July. Golden rain is the falling of yellow florets. Very ornamental. Large brown seed pods in fall. Choice

165

SCIENTIFIC NAME/ COMMON NAME	KEY	HEIGHT	COMMENTS
Pride of India			small specimen tree.
Lagerstroemia indica **Crape Myrtle**	D,F, Bf,*	15' – 25'	Useful, small ornamental with beautiful bark. Blooms mid-June through September; white, pink, lavender, or magenta. Be careful of vibrant colors clashing with surrounding perennials. Do not treat as shrub. Dwarf varieties available. Blooms 100 days. (See *Garden Care– Pruning* for specifics on shaping)
Lagerstroemia indica **'Choctaw' Crape Myrtle**	F*	15' – 20'	Beautiful flowering specimen with 8' – 10' spread. Pink flowers. Yellow-red in fall. Very hardy.
Lagerstroemia indica **'Sarah's Favorite' Crape Myrtle**	F*	20' – 25'	Spreading 15' – 20' with white flowers in summer and beautiful peeling bark. Red fall color. Very hardy and choice.
Lagerstroemia indica x fauriei **Crape Myrtle**	D,F, *	6' – 35'	These hybrids created by the National Arboretum have superior disease resistance, better fall foliage; and beautiful, exfoliating barks. Blooms 80 – 100 days. Check local nurseries.
Liquidambar styraciflua **Sweet Gum**	D,Bf	60' – 75'	Quick growth. Crimson, purple, and scarlet fall foliage. Winged bark. Trashy fruit balls. Maple-like leaf. Pest free. Good lumber for furniture and plywood. Likes river bottoms or moist garden soil. 'Rotundiloba' is a seedless sweet gum with glossy, rounded leaves and no gumballs.
Liriodendron tulipifera **Tulip Poplar, Tulip Tree**	D	to 100'	Green and apricot flower in late spring. Fine forest tree. Not easily transplanted. Subject to root rot, aphids, and mildew. Tennessee state tree.
Maclura pomifera **Osage Orange**	D	50' – 60'	Large, fast-growing, pest-free. Large round green fruit not edible. Invasive

SCIENTIFIC NAME/ COMMON NAME	KEY	HEIGHT	COMMENTS
			roots.
Magnolia	D,E, *	10' –100'	Many excellent species for the South.
Magnolia acuminata **Cucumbertree, Cucumber Magnolia**	D,F, *	50' – 80'	Early, very large foliage; greenish flower. Seed pod resembles cucumber. Pyramidal shape in youth; large spreading when mature. Many cultivars.
Magnolia acuminata var. subcordata **Yellow Cucumber Magnolia**	D,F	20' – 30'	Smaller overall than one above; yellow flower in April; glossy dark green leaves. Several cultivars.
Magnolia denudata (formerly M. heptapeta) **Yulan Magnolia**	D,F	25' – 40'	Large, coffee-cup-sized white flowers before leaf-out. Early bloomer. Bloom often caught in late freeze.
Magnolia grandiflora **Southern Magnolia**	E,F,*	to 100'	Large leathery leaf. Huge white fragrant flower, 8" – 12" diameter. Roots surface. Red fruit. Many cultivars. Most popular is 'Little Gem', with smaller leaves and smaller flowers; blooms from summer until winter; great for espalier. Other varieties 'Bracken's Brown Beauty', 'Claudia Wannamaker', and 'D.D.Blanchard'.
Magnolia liliiflora **'Nigra'** *(formerly M. quinquepeta* **'Nigra'***)* **Lily Magnolia**	D,F	to 12'	Red purple flowers appear before foliage. Subject to mildew. Used in hybridizing.
Magnolia macrophylla **Bigleaf Magnolia**	D,F	20' – 40'	Leaves 2½' long. Very large fragrant, rumpled white flower. Very dramatic, but difficult to incorporate into small landscape due to coarseness.
Magnolia stellata **Star Magnolia**	D,F, *	to 15'	Sweet-smelling, narrow-petaled flowers, 3" diameter. Often shrub form. Blooms early; white flowers appear before foliage. Often freeze-

167

Scientific Name/ Common Name	Key	Height	Comments
			damage to flowers. 'Stardust' is 8' – 10' tall and blooms early spring.
Magnolia stellata 'Rosea' *x M. liliiflora* 'Nigra'. **Star Magnolia 'Little Girl' Hybrids'**	D,F,*	10' – 15'	Star Magnolia hybrid developed to be later-blooming and avoid frost damage. Some summer blooms. 'Jane' and 'Ann' are the most popular.
Magnolia virginiana **Sweet Bay Magnolia**	D or E, F,*	to 60', often smaller	Grayish leaves. Small fragrant white flowers. Red fruit. 'Tensaw', 'Appalachi' and 'Greenbay' are all good.
Magnolia x soulangiana **Saucer Magnolia, Tulip Magnolia**	D,F,*	15' – 20'	Prolific bloomer. Fragrant white flower, streaked with orchid. Some subspecies dark reddish purple. Flowers appear before foliage. Creates dense canopy. Branches wildly if pruned incorrectly.
Malus **Apple**	D, F	to 30'	Many varieties. Check local nursery.
Malus prunifolia **Crabapple**	D,F, Bf,*	10' – 25'	Sun, many varieties. Showy spring flower, easy to grow. 'Calloway' outstanding for red fruit and disease resistance. Best for South. Do not cut off lower branches until well established.
Melia azedarach **Chinaberry**	D,Bf	30' – 40'	Fast grower, weak-wooded, short-lived. Good for quick shade. Lacy foliage, purple flowers, yellow fruit. Considered "weed" tree by some.
Metasequoia glyptostroboides **Dawn Redwood**	D,*	50' – 100'	Extremely handsome. Resembles cypress. Fast-growing.
Morus alba	D,Bf	50'	Edible fruit that stains; birds love it.

168

SCIENTIFIC NAME/ COMMON NAME	KEY	HEIGHT	COMMENTS
Common Mulberry			There are more desirable trees than the mulberry, but it has charm. Roots surface; attracts worms. Several varieties.
Myrica cerifera **Wax Myrtle**	E,Bf, *	15' – 25'	Ornamental evergreen tree, not fussy about soil. Sun to part shade. Female tree produces blue berries loved by birds, but you need a male for pollination. Host plant to red-banded hairstreak butterfly. Remove suckers to avoid thicket. Sculptural bonsai-like natural shape, or can be sheared into topiary.
Nyssa sylvatica **Black Gum, Sour Gum, Black Tupelo**	D,Bf *	60' – 90'	Handsome tree. Slow growing. Scarlet in fall. Well-drained site. Nice form. Transplanting is best from containers.
Osmanthus americanus **Devilwood**	B,F, *	20' – 30'	Leaves 7" long. Fragrant, greenish flowers in early spring. Hard wood. Can be kept as a shrub with pruning.
Osmanthus fragrans **Sweet Olive**	B,F, *	20' – 30'	Dark green shiny foliage. Fragrant, white flowers. Blooms fall and winter. Can be kept as a shrub. Needs protected location.
Ostrya virginiana **Hop Hornbeam**	D	20' – 50'	Very hard wood. Hardy, pest-free. Slow grower. Yellow in fall. Native.
Parrotia persica **Persian Ironwood, Persian Parrotia**	D,F, *	20' – 40'	Excellent lawn or street tree. Red tassel-like flowers cover bare branches in late winter. Outstanding fall color of yellow, orange, and scarlet. Attractive bark in winter. Full sun. Wide-spreading, rounded form.
Paulownia tomentosa **Royal Paulownia, Royal Empress Tree**	D,F, *, Bf	to 40'	Very fast-growing tree with showy, violet flower panicles in spring. Big catalpa-like leaves which create dense shade. Large clusters of nut-like fruits

169

SCIENTIFIC NAME/ COMMON NAME	KEY	HEIGHT	COMMENTS
			which can self-sow. 'Americana' is non-invasive. Hardy in Zones 6 – 9. Wood is highly valued by the Japanese.
Pinus **Pine**	C,E	1' –100'	100 species. Needle-like leaves in cluster. Hard, woody cones. Tolerates poor soil, prefers well-drained, sandy loam. Plant nursery grown trees rather than digging from woods. Fast-growing.
Pinus densiflora **Japanese Red Pine**	C,E	to 100'	Fast grower. Widespread. Hardy. Blue-green needles.
Pinus mugo **Mugo Pine, Swiss Mountain Pine**	C,E	1' – 3'	Shrubby, dense. Good for bonsai. Slow grower.
Pinus parviflora **Japanese White Pine**	C,E	50'	Dense, bluish needles form tufts at tips of branches.
Pinus resinosa **Red Pine**	C,E	to 80'	Upright and dome-like. Hardy. Dark green, glossy needles.
Pinus strobus **Eastern White Pine**	C,E, *	to 100'	Graceful. Picturesque in age. Symmetrical, pyramidal. Soft bluish-green needles. Needs water in dry weather. May be short-lived in the South due to heat stress. Very desirable timber tree.
Pinus strobes pendula **White Pine 'Pendula'**	C,E	2' – 3'	Umbrella-shaped.
Pinus strobus fastigiata **White Pine 'Fastigiata'**	C,E	20' – 70'	Narrow, upright growth. Beautiful cultivar. About 3 times taller than wide when mature.
Pinus strobus nana **White Pine 'Nana'**	C,E	1' – 2'	Bush form. Compact, mounded.
Pinus strobus prostrata **White Pine 'Prostrata'**	C,E	3' – 8'	Low, trailing branches.
Pinus sylvestris	C,E,	to 70'	Spreading, drooping branches. 2½"

170

SCIENTIFIC NAME/ COMMON NAME	KEY	HEIGHT	COMMENTS
Scotch Pine	*		cones. Stiff, bluish-green needles. Very hardy.
Pinus taeda **Loblolly Pine**	C,E	90'	Fast grower. Tolerates poor soil. Sheds lower limbs with age.
Pinus virginiana **Virginia Scrub Pine, Jersey Pine, Spruce Pine, Poverty Pine**	C,E	15' – 40'	Does well in poor, dry, clay or sand where little else will grow. Pioneer species. Basis of the Christmas tree industry.
Pistacia chinensis **Chinese Pistache**	D,Bf *	30' – 35'	Typical nut-tree foliage; turns brilliant orange or red in fall. Flower not showy. Tolerant of poor soil and urban conditions. Awkward in youth, handsome in maturity.
Platanus occidentalis **Sycamore, Buttonwood, Plane Tree**	D	70'	Large, fast-growing; will outgrow small spaces. Dull yellow fall foliage; attractive peeling bark. Wood good for butcher blocks. Leaves not good for compost.
Poncirus trifoliate **Trifoliate Orange, Japanese Bitter Orange**	D,F	to 20'	Hardy to New Jersey. Fragrant white flowers. Small, orange, very acidic fruit. Big thorns. Variety 'Flying Dragon'.
Populus deltoides **Eastern Poplar, Eastern Cottonwood**	D	75' –100'	Many varieties; check nursery. Fast grower, short-lived, soft wood. Roots can damage drains and walks. Found in low places and along river banks. Native. Flowers in March or April.
Prunus **Cherry and related fruits**	D,F, *	15' – 30'	Beautiful, fast-growing ornamental for any garden. Many cultivars.
Prunus mume **Japanese Apricot**	D,F, *	to 20'	Excellent winter-flowering species. Check local nursery. Many varieties. 'Bonita', 'Peggy Clarke', 'Matsubara Red'.
Prunus cerasifera **Cherry Plum,**	D,F	15' – 30'	Most popular varieties are 'Krauter Vesuvius', 'Newport', and

171

SCIENTIFIC NAME/ COMMON NAME	KEY	HEIGHT	COMMENTS
Myrobalan Plum			'Thundercloud'.
Prunus persica **Peach**	D,F	to 15'	Many varieties; see local nursery. White to pink flowers in spring. Also dwarf varieties. Prone to diseases and insects.
Prunus serotina **Black Cherry**	D,F, Bf	50' – 75'	Birds love berries. Fast grower. White flower in spring.
Prunus serrulata **Japanese Cherry**	D,F, *	to 30'	Unsurpassable. Blooms with daffodils. Upright or weeping. Tufts of pink flowers. 'Okawe' is most borer-resistant and blooms very early; very hardy.
Prunus subhirtella **'Higan' Cherry**	D,F, *	20' – 40'	'Higan cherry' is mostly grown as var. *pendula,* weeping cherry, and *autumnalis,* which flowers in spring and again in fall.
Prunus triloba var. multiplex **Double Flowering Plum, Flowering Almond**	D,F	to 20'	Many varieties. Early bloom. Pale pink flower. Susceptible to insects and disease. There are better *Prunus* trees. Green or purple leaves.
Prunus yedoensis **'Yoshino' Cherry**	D,F, *	20' – 40'	Very popular, large, flowering cherry. Early March bloom. Pink or white flowers. 'Shidare Yoshino' is a weeping variety. Can be short lived, splitting apart like a Bradford pear. Branches become horizontal with age; very picturesque.
Pterocarya stenoptera **Chinese Wingnut Tree**	D,*	to 30'	Ornamental, fast grower, pinnate leaf. Attractive, pale, green-winged nut chains in May. Moist soil. Tolerates hot summers.
Pterostyrax hispida **Fragrant Epaulette Tree**	D,*	20' – 30'	Hard to find, but has lovely white flower panicles in May-June. Sun to part shade in moist, well-drained acid soil. Japanese. Hardy.

SCIENTIFIC NAME/ COMMON NAME	KEY	HEIGHT	COMMENTS
Pyrus calleryana **Pear**	D,F	to 15'	Flowering pears are weak-wooded and overused in today's landscape. However the 'Bradford', 'Aristocrat', 'Chanticleer' (or 'Cleveland Select') are fast, easy to grow and beautiful in all seasons with few insect or disease problems, and therefore not a bad choice. Prune out crossed limbs to help prevent breaking in wind.
Quercus Species **Red Oaks**			Many varieties. Life span of 90 – 120 years. Dominant hardwood. No finer tree than an oak. Leaves are pointed and lobed. Some varieties subject to gouty oak gall (caused by wasps). Shallow-rooted and can fall in heavy winds. Keep pruned to help prevent this. Acorns feed wildlife.
Quercus coccinea **Scarlet Oak**	D,Bf	60' – 80'	Scarlet in fall. Likes dry location. Erect and symmetrical. Holds leaves in winter.
Quercus falcata **Southern Red Oak**	D,Bf	70' – 80'	Common in the South. Brown in fall; leaves hold late. Native, but seldom used by nurseries. *Q. falcata* var. *pagodifolia* is more handsome. Lobed pointed leaves.
Quercus nigra **Water Oak**	D,Bf *	60' – 70'	Holds leaves in winter. Fast grower. Not known for fall color. Vulnerable to wind-throw.
Quercus nuttallii **Nuttall Oak**	D,Bf *	60' –100'	Broadly pyramidal. Orange to red fall color. Takes wet soil. Great southern native oak.
Quercus palustris **Pin Oak**	D,Bf *	60' – 70'	Pyramidal head. Long pendulous branches. Red in fall. Fast grower. Subject to leaf gall. Holds brown leaves in winter. Use on dry sites.
Quercus phellos **Willow Oak**	D,Bf *	40' – 60'	Narrow leaves. Pendulous branches. Fast grower. Pale yellow fall foliage.

173

Scientific Name/ Common Name	Key	Height	Comments
			Any soil. Subject to leaf gall.
Quercus rubra **Red Oak**	D,Bf *	60' – 75'	Red fall foliage. Rapid grower. Subject to leaf gall.
Quercus velutina **Black Oak**	D,Bf	80' +	Fast grower. Dull orange in fall.
Quercus Species **White Oaks**	D	to 100'	Very desirable tree. Life span is 400 – 600 years. Many desirable species. Characterized by rounded-lobed leaves. Valuable lumber tree.
Quercus alba **White Oak**	D,Bf *	to 100'	Handsome. One of the most noble of hardwood trees. Should be planted in large open spaces. Russet fall foliage. Holds leaves in winter. Wind firm. Lives 400 – 600 years.
Quercus imbricaria **Shingle Oak**	D,Bf	to 60'	Round topped in age. Russet in fall. Holds leaves in winter.
Quercus lyrata **Overcup Oak**	D,Bf *	40' – 60'	Tolerates the worst soils, poorly drained or dry. Wind firm. Very uniform habit. Great oak for our area.
Quercus macrocarpa **Bur Oak,** **Mossycup Oak**	D,Bf	50' – 80'	Has a very large acorn. Insect and disease-resistant. Dull, yellow fall foliage. Drops leaves in winter. Wind firm.
Quercus michauxii **Basket Oak**	D,Bf	80' –100'	Also called Swamp Chestnut Oak. Likes moister soil. Red fall foliage and wind firm. Lives 400 – 600 years.
Quercus prinus **Chestnut Oak**	D,Bf	70'	Likes dryness. Shapely leaf. Dull orange in fall.
Quercus robur fastigiata **English Oak**	D,Bf	50' – 80'	Very upright, columnar, subject to mildew. Cultivar 'Regal Prince' is mildew resistant.
Quercus stellata **Post Oak**	D,Bf *	50' – 60'	Retains brown leaves all winter. Use on dry sites. Stately and long-lived. Hardy from Zone 3 southward.

174

SCIENTIFIC NAME/ COMMON NAME	KEY	HEIGHT	COMMENTS
Rhus **Sumac**	D,Bf	30'	Beautiful red foliage in fall. Red, fuzzy fruit clusters. Architectural presence. Many varieties; there are improved shrub varieties also. Some poisonous, rank. Great winter food source for wildlife.
Robinia pseudoacacia **False Acacia, Black or Yellow Locust**	D, F	40' – 80'	Spiny branches. Fragrant white flowers. Suckers. Avoid poisonous thorns. Nice purple flowered form called 'Purple Robe'.
Salix discolor **Pussy Willow**	D,*	10' – 20'	Good for flower arrangements. Easily propagated in water. Catkins appear before leaves. 'Nigra' is new variety.
Sassafras albidum **Sassafras**	D,*	30' – 60'	Fragrant, greenish blossom. All parts aromatic. Tea from roots is a medicinal tonic. Showy orange and red fall foliage. Needs good drainage. Native.
Styrax americana **American Styrax**	D,*	25' – 30'	Native. Lovely, white bell flowers in spring. Good substitute for dogwoods.
Styrax japonicus **Styrax, Japanese Snowbell**	D,*	30'	Sprays of bell-like, fragrant, white flowers in late spring. Good for arrangements. Slender, horizontal branches. Native. Needs protection. Slow grower. Underused ornamental.
Styrax obassia **Fragrant Styrax**	D,*	25' – 30'	Fragrant, white flower clusters like lily-of-the-valley. Sun to part shade. Understory tree. Specimen tree with rounded leaves and controlled growth habit.
Syringa vulgaris **'Descanso Hybrid' Lilac, French Lilac Hybrids**	D,F	8' – 15'	Heat-tolerant, low-chill cultivars: 'Angel White', 'Blue Boy', 'California Rose', 'Lavender Lady', 'Blue Skies'. Zone 7 – 9.
Taxodium ascendens **Pond Cypress**	C,D	70' – 80'	Medium-sized tree with a pyramidal crown, clear bole, and often buttressed base, generally smaller than bald cypress.

175

SCIENTIFIC NAME/ COMMON NAME	KEY	HEIGHT	COMMENTS
Taxodium distichum **Bald Cypress**	C,D*	70' – 80'	Handsome. Forest-sized. Good in large garden. Forms knees only under water. Longest-lived tree in Eastern U.S. Variety 'Autumn Gold' best for fall color.
Thuja occidentalis **Eastern Arborvitae, White Cedar**	C,*	2½' – 20'	Loamy, well-drained soil. Sunny. Lovely columnar habit. Gets bare in center. Best compact variety is 'Emerald', 'Nigra'; best large is 'Green Giant'.
Thuja orientalis or Platycladus orientalis **Oriental Arborvitae**	C,*	18' – 25'	Best for South. Dense, compact column when young, becoming more open with age. Best yellow-foliaged cultivar is 'Aurea Nana'. Has "dead zone" in center so don't over-prune.
Thujopsis dolobrata **False Arborvitae**	C	3' – 50'	Lacy green foliage on flattened mounds should not be sheared. 'Nana' is 3' dwarf. Many cultivars are available, including large trees.
Tilia americana **American Basswood, American Linden**	D,Bf *	70' – 90'	Fragrant, white flowers in summer; yellow, fall foliage; heart-shaped leaf. Fast grower; broad, shade tree. Bee forage tree.
Tsuga canadensis **Canadian Hemlock**	C,E	25' – 50'	Feathery conifer. Cool, damp location. Many species. Consult local nurseries. 'Pendula' is weeping variety. Not as stately as in northern climates.
Ulmus alata **Winged Elm**	D	10' – 20'	Winged bark. Twigs are corky. Dry soil. More of a shrub than a tree.
Ulmus parvifolia **Allée Elm**	D	70'	Graceful, 60' spread. Yellow to pink fall color. New to area; fast-growing, disease resistant. 'Elmer II'
Vitex agnus-castus **Chaste Tree,**	D,F, *	to 25'	Biblical tree. Purple-blue spiky flower in June-July. Pungent odor. Gray green palmate foliage. Beautiful.

176

Scientific Name/ Common Name	Key	Height	Comments
Vitex			White variety available.
Zelkova serrata **Zelkova**	D	50' – 80'	Very drought tolerant once established. Wine-red in fall; good bark; disease resistant. 50' Spread. Sun. 'Village Vase'.

177

SHRUBS

CHOOSING A SHRUB

Both trees and shrubs are woody plants and can be evergreen or deciduous. Trees generally have a single trunk, while shrubs have multiple trunks and can range in size from 6" – 20'. They are used as accent specimens, foundation plantings, hedges, background of the flower border, and cover for birds and wildlife.

Evergreen shrubs can be *needle-leaved and coniferous,* like red cedar, mugo pine, arborvitae, and Japanese plum yew, or *broad-leaved* like camellia, aucuba, boxwood, holly, and azalea, to name a few. Broad-leaved evergreens are the mainstay of the garden, and many are extremely hardy, undemanding, and pest-resistant.

Deciduous shrubs, on the other hand, offer seasonal interest; flowers and foliage in spring or summer, brilliant color in fall, and interesting bark or seedpods in winter. Birds and wildlife depend on the bounty of deciduous shrubs and trees.

Shrubs can be allowed to grow naturally and informally, or they can be sheared into formal shapes. Plants massed in a staggered pattern, forward and back, and low and high, create a soft natural background or border. The most interesting shrub borders are not planted in straight rows, but are designed with curves and bays that are lovely when under-planted with low-growing annuals, perennials, and bulbs.

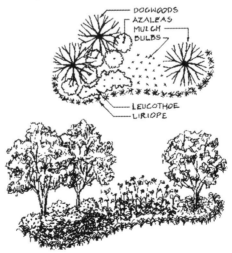

Flowering shrubs and trees can be grouped to create a natural scene.

179

Hundreds of varieties of shrubs grow in the Mid-South but the best choices for the home landscape will be the dozens available at local nurseries or garden centers. Stroll around and see what appeals to you in the way of foliage color and texture. With careful selection, it is possible to have something in bloom every month of the year.

Planting instructions for shrubs are discussed in the *Garden Care* chapter. In the Special Articles on azalea, boxwood, camellia, gardenia, holly, hydrangea, rose, and viburnum, which follow at the end of this chapter, any specific culture requirements will be described.

When purchasing, select young plants because older plants suffer shock when moved. Be sure to plant shrubs far enough apart to allow for future growth even though they are small now. For the few years it will take the bushes to mature, you can cover bare earth with annuals and perennials. Water deeply once a week until established and during dry spells.

HEDGES

Many shrubs may be grown as hedges, but not all should be pruned into formal shapes. For example, a line of forsythia or loropetalum against a fence creates a lovely hedgerow, but they both look better left in their natural, arching habit. Many "non-flowering" broad-leaved evergreens make superb hedges but look better left in their natural shapes or lightly shaped; aucuba, cleyera, and foster holly (*Ilex*) are a few.

Some flowering shrubs to consider for hedges are azaleas, camellias, hydrangeas, Virginia sweetspire (*Itea*), and viburnum. Prune after blooming with heading and thinning cuts to control size, rather than shearing into formal shapes. See *Garden Care–Pruning.* Cutting blossoms to bring indoors is a good way to accomplish this pruning. Be aware that some flowering shrubs are deciduous, and decide whether or not bare branches in winter will be a problem in your landscape.

To create formal or clipped hedges, use evergreens with small leaves which will respond to clipping, and thicken into smooth, unbroken shapes. Examples would include boxwood (*Buxus*), privet (*Ligustrum*), 'Compacta' holly (*Ilex*), box-leaf euonymus, and English yew (*Taxus*). Japanese plum yew *(Cephalotaxus),* which is better adapted to our heat than *Taxus*, has a different growth habit and is not as well suited to formal shearing.

When creating a hedgerow, spacing varies according to the particular plant. Small, quick growing shrubs, like small privets, should be planted 9" apart, the average evergreens 18" apart, and tall shrubs 24" apart.

SHRUBS BY SIZE AND SUN/ SHADE REQUIREMENTS

The following is a helpful list of good garden shrubs sorted according to size and sun/ shade requirements. Most shrubs can be pruned to any size desired, but if the plants selected are in the proper size range for their use in the landscape, you're spared a lot of work.

1' – 4' shrubs would be suitable for lining a walkway, for containers, in flower borders, or planting under a window.

4' – 6' shrubs might be used as specimens, the back of a flower border, foundation planting, or hedging along the driveway.

6' – 12' shrubs could be used along the back fence to block an unpleasant view and create privacy, or as foundation planting against a large blank wall.

The list is arranged by *Scientific Name* (Common Name). The height range, in many cases, refers to a particular species of shrub, and other species of the same genus may be considerably larger or smaller.

TABLE 14. SHRUBS BY SIZE AND SUN/ SHADE REQUIREMENTS

1' – 4' SHRUBS BY SUN/ SHADE REQUIREMENT

Key: ■ = full shade,   □ = partial shade,   ½ = half shade,   ☼ = full sun

1'–4' SHRUBS	■	□	½	☼	1'–4' SHRUBS	■	□	½	☼
Abelia **Abelia**			½	☼	*Hydrangea macrophylla* **Bigleaf Hydrangea**		□	½	
Aucuba 'Nana' **Aucuba**	■	□			*Hydrangea serrata* **Mountain Hydrangea**		□	½	
Abeliophyllum distichum **White Forsythia**			½	☼	*Hypericum* **St.-John's-wort**			½	☼
Aronia melanocarpa **Black Chokeberry**		□	½	☼					
Berberis **'Crimson**			½	☼	*Ilex crenata* **'Helleri'**		□	½	☼

181

1'–4' SHRUBS	■	□	½	☼	1'–4' SHRUBS	■	□	½	☼
Pygmy' Barberry					Japanese Holly				
Berberis julianae Barberry				☼	*Ilex crenata macrophylla* Japanese Holly				☼
Berberis verruculosa Warty Barberry				☼	*Ilex crenata* 'Soft Touch' Japanese Holly				☼
Buxus microphylla Boxwood – dwarf varieties		□	½		*Ilex crenata* 'Rotundifolia', 'Green Luster' Round Leaf Holly			½	☼
Buxus sempervirens Common Boxwood		□	½		*Ilex glabra* 'Nordic' Inkberry			½	
Camellia Ackerman Hybrids Camellia		□	½		*Ilex glabra* 'Shamrock' Inkberry		□	½	☼
Caryopteris Blue Spirea				☼	*Ilex vomitoria* 'Nana' Dwarf Yaupon				☼
Cephalotaxus harringtonia 'Prostrata' Japanese Plum Yew	■	□	½		*Itea* 'Henry's Garnet' Sweetspire				☼
Chamaecyparis False Cypress – dwarf varieties				☼	*Jasminum nudiflorum* January Jasmine		□	½	☼
Clethra 'Hummingbird' Summersweet	■	□	½	☼	*Juniperus* 'Blue Rug', 'Bar Harbor', 'Procumbens', 'Nana' Juniper			½	☼
Cotoneaster dammeri Bearberry			½	☼	*Leucothoe* Doghobble morning sun only	■	□	½	

1'–4' SHRUBS	■	□	½	☼	1'–4' SHRUBS	■	□	½	☼
Cotoneaster									
Cotoneaster salicifolia **Willowleaf Cotoneaster**			½	☼	*Loropetalum* **Loropetalum**	■	□	½	
Deutzia **'Nikko' Deutzia**			½	☼	*Nandina* **Heavenly Bamboo** dwarf varieties	■	□	½	☼
Deutzia gracilis **Deutzia**		□			*Philadelphus* **Mock Orange –** dwarf varieties				☼
Euonymus **Euonymus** several varieties		□	½	☼	*Pinus Mugo* **Mugo Pine –** dwarf varieties				☼
Euonymus fortunei **'Microphyllus' Wintercreeper**		□	½	☼	*Prunus* **'Otto Luyken', 'Zabel' Cherry Laurel**	■	□	½	☼
Euonymus japonica microphylla **Box-leaf Euonymus** several low-growers		□	½	☼	*Rhododendron* **Azalea**		□	½	
Fothergilla gardenii **Fothergilla**		□	½	½	*Sarcococca* **Sweet Box**	■	□	½	
Hydrangea arborescens **'Annabelle' Smooth Hydrangea**		□	½		*Spiraea* **'Anthony Waterer', 'Gold Flame', 'Gold Mound', 'Little Princess' Spirea**		□	½	☼

183

4' – 6' SHRUBS BY SUN/ SHADE REQUIREMENT

Key: ■ = full shade, □ = partial shade, ½ = half shade, ☼ = full sun

4'–6' SHRUBS	■	□	½	☼	4'–6' SHRUBS	■	□	½	☼
Abelia **Abelia**		□	½		*Ilex cornuta burfordi* **'Dwarf' Burford Holly**		□	½	
Acanthopanax sieboldianus **Variegated Five-Leaf Aralia**	■	□			*Ilex crenata* **Japanese Hollies-** several cultivars		□	½	☼
Aucuba **'Picturata',** **'Goldust' Aucuba**	■	□			*Ilex glabra* **Inkberry Holly –** several cultivars		□	½	
Aucuba japonica **Japanese Saw-Tooth Aucuba**	■	□			*Illicium* **Florida, Ocala, or Henry Anise**	■	□	½	
Berberis **'Rose Glow'** **Barberry** & others			½	☼	*Juniperus* **Juniper** – many			½	☼
Berberis julianae **Wintergreen Barberry**			½	☼	*Kerria* **Japanese Rose**	■	□	½	
Berberis verruculosa **Warty Barberry**			½	☼	*Leucothoe* **Doghobble** – morning sun only		□	½	
Buddleia **Butterfly Bush**			½	☼	*Ligustrum* **Privet** – many			½	☼
Lonicera fragrantissima **Winter Honeysuckle**			½	☼	*Loropetalum* **Loropetalum**		□	½	
Callicarpa **Beauty Berry**			½		*Mahonia bealei* **Oregon Grapeholly** – can get bigger	■	□	½	
Camellia japonica **Japanese Camellia** – can get bigger		□	½		*Nandina* **Heavenly Bamboo**		□	½	☼
Camellia sasanqua **Sasanqua**		□	½		*Pieris* **Dodd's Pieris,**		□	½	

4'–6' SHRUBS	■	□	½	☼	4'–6' SHRUBS	■	□	½	☼
Camellia – or bigger					**Andromeda**				
Camellia **Ackerman hybrid Camellias**		□	½		*Pinus mugo* **Mugo Pine**		□	½	
Cephalotaxus harringtonia **Japanese Plum Yew**	■	□	½		*Prunus schipkaensis* **Schip Laurel** – can get bigger		□	½	
Clethra alnifolia **Summersweet**	■	□	½		*Prunus laurocerasus* **Cherry Laurel** – can get bigger	■	□	½	☼
Cleyera **Cleyera**		□	½		*Rhododendron* **Azalea**		□	½	
Euonymus **Euonymus** – several varieties		□	½	☼	*Rosa* **Roses** – many			½	☼
Euonymus alata **'Compactus' Burning Bush**		□	½	☼	*Sarcococca confusa* **Sweet box**	■	□	½	
Forsythia **Forsythia**		□	½	☼	*Spiraea* **Spirea** – many		□	½	☼
Fothergilla major **Large Fothergilla**		□	½		*Vaccinium* **Blueberry**			½	☼
Hydrangea **'Mariesii Variegata' Hydrangea**	■	□			*Viburnum* cultivars **'Eskimo', 'Cayuga' 'Summer Snowflake', etc. Viburnum**		□	½	☼
Hydrangea arborescens **Smooth Hydrangea**		□	½		*Viburnum davidii* **David Viburnum**		□	½	☼
Hydrangea macrophylla **Bigleaf Hydrangea**		□	½		*Viburnum nudum* **'Count Pulaski' Viburnum**		□	½	☼
Hydrangea quercifolia		□	½		*Viburnum utile* **'Conoy' Viburnum**		□	½	☼

4'–6' SHRUBS	■	□	½	☼	4'–6' SHRUBS	■	□	½	☼
Oakleaf Hydrangea									
Ilex **Holly** – many				☼	*Weigela florida* **Weigela**		□	½	☼

6' – 12' SHRUBS BY SUN/ SHADE REQUIREMENT

Key: ■ = full shade,   □ = partial shade,   ½ = half shade,   ☼ = full sun

6'–12' SHRUBS	■	□	½	☼	6'–12' SHRUBS	■	□	½	☼
Acer palmatum – **Japanese Maple** some varieties; a tree		□	½		*Ilex* **Holly** – many			½	☼
Aesculus pavia **Red Buckeye**		□	½	☼	*Ilex vomitoria* **Yaupon Holly**			½	☼
Aesculus parviflora **Bottlebrush Buckeye**		□	½	☼	*Illicium parviflorum* **Anise**	■	□	½	
Berberis julianae **Wintergreen Barberry**			½	☼	*Juniperus* **Juniper** – several			½	☼
Buddleia **Butterfly Bush**			½	☼	*Juniperus virginiana* **Red Cedar**			½	☼
Calycanthus **Sweetshrub**	■	□	½		*Ligustrum* Weeping and **Common Privet** – many			½	☼
Camellia japonica **Japanese Camellia**		□	½		*Mahonia bealei* **Oregon Grapeholly**	■	□	½	
Camellia sasanqua **Sasanqua Camellia**		□	½		*Osmanthus fortunei* **Fortune's Osmanthus**		□	½	

186

6'–12' SHRUBS	■	□	½	☼	6'–12' SHRUBS	■	□	½	☼
Chaenomeles **Flowering Quince**			½		*Photinia fraseri* **Photinia**			½	☼
Chamaecyparis **False Cypress** – certain varieties			½		*Photinia glabra* **Photinia**			½	☼
Clethra acuminata **Cinnamon Summersweet**	■	□	½		*Prunus schipkaensis* **Schip Laurel**			½	☼
Clethra alnifolia **Summersweet**	■	□	½		*Rhododendron* **Azalea**		□	½	
Cleyera **Cleyera**		□	½		*Spiraea* **Vanhoutte and Bridalwreath Spirea**		□	½	☼
Elaeagnus **Eleagnus**		□	½	☼	*Thuja occidentalis* **American Arborvitae 'Emerald', others**			½	☼
Euonymus alatus **'Compactus' Burning Bush**			½	☼	*Vaccinium* **Blueberry**			½	☼
Hamamelis **Witch-hazel**		□	½		*Viburnum odoratissimum* **'Awabuki' Viburnum**, many others		□	½	☼
Hibiscus syriacus **Althea**		□	½	☼	*Viburnum plicatum var. tomentosum* **Doublefile Viburnum**	■	□	½	
Hydrangea paniculata grandiflora **Pee Gee Hydrangea**		□	½		*Viburnum pragense* **Prague Viburnum**	■	□	½	
Hydrangea quercifolia **Oakleaf**		□	½		*Viburnum rhytidophyllum* **Leatherleaf**	■	□	½	

6'–12' SHRUBS	■	□	½	☼	6'–12' SHRUBS	■	□	½	☼
Hydrangea					**Viburnum**				
Ilex **Holly** – many varieties			½	☼	*Vitex* **Chaste Tree**		□	½	
Ilex glabra **Inkberry Holly**			½		*Weigela florida* **Weigela**		□	½	☼

FLOWERING SHRUBS

The Mid-South is rich in flowering shrubs of great beauty and diversity. The exact time of bloom for the different varieties depends to a large extent on the weather, and therefore will vary slightly from year to year.

CULTURE

Flowering shrubs may be planted anytime from the first frost in the fall through the middle of April. They need at least 6 – 8 hours of sun a day and at least an inch of water a week to develop their best blooms. Fertilize in the spring with all-purpose fertilizer, and again in November with 0–20–20. Keep 1" – 2" of mulch on shrubs at all times. Prune *spring-flowering shrubs,* which bloom on old wood, immediately after flowering by thinning and heading. Prune *summer-flowering shrubs* while dormant from January to early March before spring growth starts, as they bloom on new wood. See the section on *Pruning* in *Garden Care.*

Most spring-flowering shrubs, especially flowering quince and forsythia, can be cut as soon as buds show a little color, brought into the house, and put in warm water to force blooms.

Table 15 gives both evergreen and deciduous flowering shrubs by month of bloom. The scientific name, if different from the common name, is given to facilitate finding the plant in *Table 18: Shrubs of the Mid-South.*

188

TABLE 15. FLOWERING SHRUBS BY MONTH OF BLOOM
Note: If common and scientific names are the same, it is given once.

JANUARY	
Camellia	Winter Jasmine (*Jasminum*)
Persian Ironwood (*Parrotia*)	Wintersweet (*Chimonanthus praecox*)
Winter Honeysuckle (*Lonicera fragrantissima*)	

FEBRUARY	
Almond (*Prunus glandulosa*)	Sweet Box (*Sarcococca*) fragrant, but inconspicuous
Camellia	Spiraea, Thunberg
Forsythia	Saucer Magnolia (*Magnolia soulangiana*) also a tree
Mahonia	Star Magnolia (*Magnolia stellata*)
Pussy Willow (*Salix discolor*)	Witch-hazel (*Hamamelis virginiana, H. vernalis, H. mollis*)

MARCH	
Camellia	Photinia
Bridalwreath (*Spiraea prunifolia*)	Quince, Flowering (*Chaenomeles speciosa*)
Fothergilla	Spicebush (*Lindera benzoin*)
Kerria	Spirea (*Spiraea*)
Loropetalum	*Viburnum carlesii*
Mahonia	Witch-hazel (*Hamamelis mollis*)
Pearlbush (*Exochorda racemosa*)	

APRIL	
Anise (*Illicium*)	Kerria
Azalea (*Rhododendron*)	Lilac (*Syringa*)
Azalea, Native	Loropetalum
Barberry (*Berberis*)	Quince, Common (*Cydonia oblongata*)
Buckeye, Red (*Aesculus pavia*)	Spirea (*Spiraea cantoniensis*)
Chokeberry (*Aronia*)	Vanhoutte Spirea (*Spiraea vanhouttei*)
Deutzia gracilis	Japanese Snowbell (*Styrax japonicus*)

Fothergilla 'Mt. Airy'	Sweetshrub *(Calycanthus fertilis & C. florida)*
Hydrangea, Oakleaf *(Hydrangea quercifolia)*	Viburnum, Doublefile *(V. plicatum tomentosum)*

MAY	
Agarista	Kirilow Indigo *(Indigofera kirilowii)*
Anise *(Illicium floridanum)*	Mock Orange *(Philadelphus)*
Azalea *(Rhododendron)*	Pomegranate *(Punica granatum)*
Blueberry *(Vaccinium)*	Rose – many
Deutzia	Spirea
Gardenia	Viburnum, Linden *(Viburnum dilatatum)*
Hardy Orange *(Poncirus trifoliata)*	Viburnum, Arrowwood *(V. dentatum)*
Honeysuckle *(Lonicera)*	Virginia Sweetspire *(Itea virginica)*
Hydrangea, Oakleaf *(Hydrangea quercifolia)*	Weigela
Japanese Snowball *(Viburnum plicatum)*	Kirilow Indigo *(Indigofera kirilowii)*

JUNE	
Althea *(Althaea)*	Hydrangea, Mophead *(H. macrophylla & H. serrata)*
Abelia	Hydrangea, Oakleaf *(H. quercifolia)*
Azalea, Gumpo; some native azaleas	Kirilow Indigo *(Indigofera kirilowii)*
Buckeye, Bottlebrush *(Aesculus parviflora)*	Rose – many
Swamp Leatherwood *(Cyrilla)*	Spirea, 'Anthony Waterer'
Beautybush *(Kolkwitzia)*	St.-John's-wort *(Hypericum)*
Butterfly Bush *(Buddleia)*	Virginia Sweetspire *(Itea)*
Elderberry *(Sambucus canadensis)*	Yucca
Gardenia	

JULY	
Althea	Gardenia
Beauty berry *(Callicarpa)*	Hydrangeas, 'Tardiva' and 'Pee Gee'
Bottlebrush Buckeye *(Aesculus*	Lavender Cotton *(Santolina)*

190

parviflora)	
Butterfly Bush (*Buddleia*)	St.-John's-wort (*Hypericum*)
Crape Myrtle (*Lagerstroemia*)	Summersweet (*Clethra*)
Swamp Leatherwood (*Cyrilla*)	Hydrangea, Mophead (*H. macrophylla & H. serrata*)
Hydrangea, Lacecap (*H. Macrophylla & H. serrata)*	Hydrangea, Oakleaf (*H. quercifolia*)
AUGUST	
Althea	*Hydrangea paniculata*
Bluebeard (*Caryopteris*)	St.-John's-wort (*Hypericum*)
Butterfly Bush (*Buddleia*)	Summersweet (*Clethra alnifolia*)
Crape Myrtle (*Lagerstroemia*)	
SEPTEMBER	
Althaea	Crape Myrtle (*Lagerstroemia*)
Bluebeard (*Caryopteris*)	Rose – re-bloomers
Butterfly Bush (*Buddleia*)	
OCTOBER	
Butterfly Bush *(Buddleia)*	Fatsia
Camellia	Tea Plant (*Camellia sinensis*)
Eleagnus *(Elaeagnus)*	Witch-hazel, Common *(Hamamelis virginiana)*
NOVEMBER	
Camellia	Wintersweet (*Chimonanthus*)
Sweet Olive *(Osmanthus)*	
DECEMBER	
Camellia	Wintersweet (*Chimonanthus*)
Sweet Olive *(Osmanthus)*	

SHRUBS FOR FALL COLOR & BERRIES

Many deciduous shrubs offer splendid fall color as well as nuts or berries. Refer to the *Trees* chapter for *Why Leaves Change Color in the Fall.*

TABLE 16. SHRUBS FOR FALL COLOR

Amsonia (see *Flowers–Perennials*)	Azalea
Barberry (*Berberis*)	Buckeye (*Aesculus*)
Burning Bush (*Euonymus alata*)	Cotoneaster
Fothergilla	Nandina
Oakleaf Hydrangea	Smokebush (*Cotinus coggygria*)
Sumac (*Rhus*)	Virginia Sweetspire (*Itea virginica*)
Viburnum	Witch-hazel (*Hamamelis*)

TABLE 17. SHRUBS AND TREES FOR BIRD FOOD

Ash (*Fraxinus*)	Apple (*Malus*)
Barberry (*Berberis*)	Beauty Berry (*Callicarpa*)
Beech (*Fagus*)	Birch (*Betula*)
Black Cherry (*Prunus*)	Black Chokeberry (*Aronia*)
Black Gum (*Nyssa*)	Blackberry (*Rubus*)
Blueberry (*Vaccinium*)	Chinaberry (*Melia*)
Coralberry (*Symphoricarpos*)	Cotoneaster
Chokecherry (*Prunus*)	Cranberry, American Highbush (*Viburnum trilobum*)
Crabapple (*Prunus malus*)	Devil's-walking-stick (*Aralia*)
Dogwood (*Cornus*)	Elderberry (*Sambucus*)
Euonymus	Fig (*Ficus*)
Hackberry (*Celtis*)	Hawthorn (*Crataegus*)
Hickory (*Carya*)	Holly (*Ilex* – many)
Hydrangea, Mophead and Lacecap	Inkberry (*Ilex* glabra)
Juniper (*Juniperus*)	Privet (*Ligustrum*)
Linden (*Tilia*)	Mahonia
Mulberry (*Morus*)	Nandina
Oak (*Quercus*)	Oakleaf Hydrangea (*Hydrangea*

	quercifolia)
Paulownia	Pawpaw (*Asimina*)
Pear (*Pyrus*)	Pecan (*Carya*)
Photinia	Plum (*Prunus*)
Sapphireberry (*Symplocos*)	Serviceberry (*Amelanchier*)
Snowberry, Common (*Symphoricarpos*)	Sumac (*Rhus*)
Sweet Gum (*Liquidambar*)	Viburnum (many)
Walnut (*Juglans*)	

TABLE OF SHRUBS

TABLE 18. SHRUBS OF THE MID-SOUTH

KEY: E – Evergreen   SE – Semi-evergreen
D– Deciduous   V – Variegated

SCIENTIFIC NAME/ COMMON NAME	KEY	HEIGHT	FLOWER COLOR/ BLOOM TIME	SUN/ SHADE	COMMENTS
Abelia grandiflora **Abelia**	SE	to 10'	Pinkish-white/ early summer to frost	Sun to part shade	Pinkish- white flowers on arching branches, leaves green in summer, bronze in winter.
Abeliophyllum distichum **White Forsythia**	D	2' – 3'	White/ mid spring	Sun to light shade	Not a true forsythia, but it has similar flowers in white. Equally easy to grow.
Acanthopanax sieboldianus 'Variegatus' **Variegated Five-Leaf Aralia**	D,V	4' – 5' x 4' – 5'	Greenish white/ late spring	Light to full shade	Hard to find but beautiful, five-lobed leaves with cream variegation. Arching stems, rounded habit. Carefree plant to brighten shade. Small greenish white flowers. (aka

193

Scientific Name/ Common Name	Key	Height	Flower Color/ Bloom Time	Sun/ Shade	Comments
					Eleutherococcus sieboldianus 'Variegatus')
Aesculus parviflora **Bottlebrush Buckeye**	D	10' – 30'	White/ mid summer	Partial shade	White spike flower; beautiful foliage forms dense mound. Any good soil; difficult to transplant. Slow grower.
Aesculus pavia **Red Buckeye**	D	6' – 12'	Red/ spring	Partial shade	Native, handsome plant with large palmate leaves. Red flowers in April are loved by hummingbirds.
Agarista populifolia (formerly *Leucothoe populifolia*) **Agarista**	E	to 12'	Cream/ late spring	Part shade to shade	A lax, arching, multi-stemmed, evergreen shrub, Agarista likes moist rich soil and room to spread. Good companion for anise or rhododendron. Flower is fragrant cream-colored raceme.
Aralia elata 'Variegata' **Variegated Aralia** or **Japanese Angelica Tree**	D, V	8' – 15'	White/ summer	Sun or shade	Spreading shrub with pinnate leaflets forming huge 4' by 3' leaves. Hand-some cream variegation. Large umbels of small white flowers followed by black berries.
Aronia arbutifolia **Red Chokeberry**	D	6' – 10'	White/ spring	Sun or shade	Adaptable shrub. Red fruit, orange fall color.

194

SCIENTIFIC NAME/ COMMON NAME	KEY	HEIGHT	FLOWER COLOR/ BLOOM TIME	SUN/ SHADE	COMMENTS
Aronia melanocarpa **Black Chokeberry**	D	3' – 6' x 3' – 6'	Pinkish white/ spring	Sun or shade	Tolerates wide variety of growing conditions. Glossy black fruit. Orange to red fall color.
Aucuba japonica **Aucuba**	E, V	to 6'	Tiny brown flower/ late spring	Light to full shade	Inconspicuous whitish or maroon flower. Large, glossy, toothed evergreen leaves, solid or variegated. Reliable, easy, and pest-free in shade. Bright red berries in fall. Roots in glass of water. 'Picturata', 'Gold Dust', 'Rozannie' and 'Japanese Saw Toothed' are popular.
Azalea (*Rhododendron*) See Special Article after this table.					
Bambusa **Bamboo**	E	to 20'	Evergreen	Sun to shade	Many nice clump-formers which are not invasive. Lend a nice tropical look.
Berberis **Barberry**	E & D	4' – 8'	Reddish foliage, yellow flowers/ spring	Sun to light shade	Leaf color can be red, pink, yellow, bronze, green or variegated. Many varieties, some dwarf, check local nurseries. Tiny yellow flowers, thorns, fall color. Barrier hedge.
Berberis julianae **Wintergreen**	E	6' – 8'	Yellow/ spring	Sun to part	Good for barrier hedge. Leave in

195

Scientific Name/ Common Name	Key	Height	Flower Color/ Bloom Time	Sun/ Shade	Comments
Barberry				shade	natural habit for best look. Good fall color. 'Spring Glory'
Berberis thunbergii **Dwarf Yellow Japanese Barberry**	D	1½' x 3'	Yellow foliage, Pink to white/ spring	Sun to light shade	Small, rounded shrub with bright yellow foliage. Flowers pink in bud opening to white. Red berries. 'Bonanza Gold'
Berberis thunbergii var. *atropurpurea* **Japanese Barberry, Purple-leaf type**	E	1' – 2' x 2' – 3'	Purple foliage	Sun to light shade	Dense branches make it useful as hedge, barrier, or grouping. 'Crimson Pygmy' (also sold as 'Little Gem' and 'Nana') is most popular.
Berberis verruculosa **Warty Barberry**	E	3' – 6'	Golden yellow/ spring	Sun to light shade	Leaves are lustrous, dark green above, whitish beneath; turn purple or bronze in winter. Yellow flower followed by purplish fruit.
Buddleia alternifolia **Butterfly bush**	D	8' – 12'	Lavender/ mid-summer	Sun to light shade	Clustered spikes of fragrant lavender-purple flowers; wide-spreading, arching branches. Attracts butterflies. Good for cutting. Cut back to 1'-2' in spring. 'Argenta' has gray foliage and lavender flowers, blooming in spring.

196

Scientific Name/ Common Name	Key	Height	Flower Color/ Bloom Time	Sun/ Shade	Comments
Buddleia davidii **Butterfly bush**	D	8' – 12'	Purple, rose, cream/ summer-fall	Sun to light shade	Long-blooming. Similar to above, many varieties. 'Black Knight', 'Lochinch', 'Honeycomb' are all good.
Buxus **Boxwood** See Special Article after this table.					
Callicarpa americana, Callicarpa alba **Beauty berry** or **French Mulberry**	D	4'	Orchid berries/ late summer – fall	Sun to part shade	Insignificant flowers; large bright orchid or lavender whorls of berries; leaves golden in fall. Native.
Calycanthus fertilis **Sweetshrub** or **Pale Sweetshrub**	D	2' – 6'	Chocolate/ mid-spring	Sun to part shade	Slightly fragrant, chocolate-colored flowers. Often mistaken for *C. floridus*. Lacks brownish fuzz on leaf.
Calycanthus floridus **Common Sweetshrub** or **Carolina Allspice**	D	6' – 8' x 6' – 8'	Chocolate/ mid spring	Sun to part shade	Sweet-scented, chocolate-colored flowers; brownish fuzz on underside of fragrant leaves. Native. Rich damp soil, will tolerate partial shade. 'Athens' is an improved variety with white flowers, lustrous dark green foliage, turning yellow in fall.

197

Scientific Name/ Common Name	Key	Height	Flower Color/ Bloom Time	Sun/ Shade	Comments
Camellia See Special Article below.					
Caryopteris x clandonensis **Bluebeard** or **Blue Spirea** or **Blue-mist shrub**	D	2' – 3'	Violet blue/ fall	Sun to part shade	Violet-blue flowers, gray-green foliage. Mulch in winter.
Cephalotaxus harringtonia **Japanese Plum Yew**	E	5' – 10' shrub or 20' small tree		Light to full shade	This evergreen aristocrat has lustrous, dark green foliage in sun or shade. Much better performer in the South than *Taxus* species. Gorgeous shrub. Also available as low-growing prostrate variety.
Cercis canadensis **Eastern Redbud**	D	20' – 30'	Magenta/ early spring	Sun to medium shade	Native. Lovely heart-shaped leaves and early spring magenta flowers. Several good cultivars. Short-lived tree.
Cercis chinensis **Chinese Redbud** or **Judas Tree**	D	to 10'	Magenta, purple, white/ early spring	Sun to medium shade	Bright magenta flowers blooming on stem and trunk of this large shrub. 'Alba' has white flowers; 'Avondale' has deep purple.
Chaenomeles speciosa **Flowering Quince**	D	6' – 10'	Rose pink/ early spring	Sun to part shade	Broad-spreading shrub with dense mass of spiny branches. Red flowers before leaves. Yellow fruit. Barrier bush. *Chaenomeles*

SCIENTIFIC NAME/ COMMON NAME	KEY	HEIGHT	FLOWER COLOR/ BLOOM TIME	SUN/ SHADE	COMMENTS
					japonica is similar but smaller. *Cydonia* is edible quince.
Chimonanthus praecox **Wintersweet**	E	to 10'	Yellow & maroon/ winter	Sun to part shade	Straw-yellow flowers marked with maroon; spicy perfume; coarse and dense foliage; irregular branch form. Average garden soil; good for cutting.
Clethra alnifolia **Summersweet** or **Sweet Pepperbush** or **Clethra**	D	4' – 6'	White/ summer	Light to full shade	Fragrant, white bottlebrush flowers lasting 4–6 weeks. Shade; wet, peaty or acidic soil. 'Hummingbird' Clethra is a superb small shrub. Native. Underused.
Clethra alnifolia **'Rosea' Clethra**	D	4' – 6'	Pink/ summer	Light to full shade	Long-lasting pink flowers. 'Pink Spires' and 'Rosea' are both good.
Cleyera japonica (or *Ternstroemia gymnanthera*) **Cleyera** or **Ternstroemia**	E	3' – 7'	Fragrant, but tiny/ spring	Sun to partial shade	New foliage is reddish turning glossy green; leathery texture. Handsome in arrangements. Pest free, acid soil. Excellent shrub; good hedge.
Cortaderia selloana **Pampas Grass**	E	15'	Feathery/ spring	Sun	Large ornamental grass. 1' – 3' flower plumes. Good for drying. Many other varieties.
Corylus avellana	D	to 7'	not	Sun to	Twisted, corkscrew-

199

Scientific Name/ Common Name	Key	Height	Flower Color/ Bloom Time	Sun/ Shade	Comments
Harry Lauder's Walking Stick			noticeable	light shade	like branches, desirable for flower arrangements, slow growing. In the Filbert family, but produces no nuts. 'Contorta'.
Cotinus coggygria **Smokebush**	D	6' – 12' x 6' – 12'	Feathery mauve/ summer	Sun to part shade	Purple or green leaves. Best in border but used as specimen. Blossom has smoky airy effect in June. Unusual.
Cotoneaster apiculatus **Cranberry Cotoneaster**	D	1½' – 2'	Pink/ mid-spring	Sun	Pink flowers, crimson fruit in fall. Dense growth habit; needs no pruning. Suitable for low hedges.
Cotoneaster dammeri **Bearberry Cotoneaster**	E	1½'	White/ mid-spring	Sun	White flowers, red berries in fall, prostrate form. Low and spreading.
Cotoneaster divaricatus **Spreading Cotoneaster**	D	3' – 5'	Pink/ mid-spring	Sun	Pink flowers, crimson berries in fall. Small, round, highly-polished, dark green leaves. Desirable for specimen plant or hedge.
Cotoneaster horizontalis **Rockspray** or **Rock Cotoneaster**	SE, E	3'	Pink/ mid-spring	Sun	Pink flowers followed by red berries. Low, spreading habit. Many cultivars.
Crape Myrtle (*Lagerstroemia*) See *Trees*.					

200

Scientific Name/ Common Name	Key	Height	Flower Color/ Bloom Time	Sun/ Shade	Comments
Cryptomeria japonica **Cryptomeria** or **Japanese Cedar**	E	2' – 40'	N/A	Sun to part shade	Lovely arborvitae-like foliage. Many cultivars from dwarf shrubs to trees. 'Globosa Nana'.
Cydonia oblonga **Common Quince**	D	15' – 20'	White to red/ late winter	Sun to light shade	White to red flowers appear before leaves. Blossoms easily forced in winter. Many varieties, spreading or erect. Sun, any soil. Fruit makes good jelly or cooked with applesauce.
Cyrilla racemiflora **Cyrilla** or **Titi** or **Swamp Leatherwood**	E, SE	10' – 15' x 10' – 15'	White/ summer	Sun to medium shade	Large shrub or small tree of great beauty. Long, thin leaves with long, thin panicles of white flowers. Handsome, sculptural form.
Danae racemosa **Alexandrian Laurel** or **Poet's Laurel**	E	3' – 4'	Not showy/ early spring	Partial shade to shade	Inconspicuous white flower; red berries in fall; glossy, spiny leaves. Not a true laurel.
Daphne x burkwoodii **'Carol Mackie' Daphne**	E	3' – 4' x 3' – 4'	Pinkish white/ late spring	High to part shade	Can be temperamental. Very fragrant flowers, cream edge on leaves. Loam, moist.
Daphne odora **Winter Daphne**	E	3' – 4' x 3' – 4'	Pinkish white/ winter	Part shade	Very fragrant flowers in mid-winter. Glossy, dark, evergreen foliage. 'Aureo-Marginata' has gold edge on leaf.

201

Scientific Name/ Common Name	Key	Height	Flower Color/ Bloom Time	Sun/ Shade	Comments
					'Leucantha' is non-variegated. Not too moist in summer. Alkaline loamy soil. Can die for no reason.
Deutzia gracilis **Deutzia**	D	2' – 4'	White/ mid-spring	Sun to part shade	Clusters of pure white flowers on slender, delicate, arching stems. Pest resistant.
Deutzia scabra **'Pride of Rochester'** **Deutzia**	D	6' – 8'	White/ mid-spring	Sun to part shade	Good cultivar. Double, white flowers brushed with pink.
Elaeagnus pungens **Thorny Eleagnus**	E	10' – 15' x 10' – 15'	Fragrant, small, white/ fall	Sun or shade	Tiny flower, silvery-green underside of leaf. Many varieties; requires frequent shaping. Good screening material. Species is fast grower. 'Fruitlandii'.
Elaeagnus pungens **'Variegata'** or **'Aurea'** **Eleagnus**	E, V	10' – 15'	Fragrant, small white/ late summer	Sun or shade	Leaves light green, margined yellowish white and yellow, respectively. Any soil. Pest free. Easily transplanted. Slower growth than species.
Elaeagnus x ebbingei **'Gilt Edge'** **Eleagnus**	E, V	8' – 10'	White, small/ late summer	Sun to light shade	Dense, upright, evergreen shrub with large, oval, bright green leaves silver beneath and edged in yellow. Fragrant, thorn-less.
Euonymus alata **Winged**	D	to 8'	White, small/	Sun to part	Insignificant flower, gorgeous scarlet

SCIENTIFIC NAME/ COMMON NAME	KEY	HEIGHT	FLOWER COLOR/ BLOOM TIME	SUN/ SHADE	COMMENTS
Euonymus or **Burning Bush**			spring	shade	leaves in fall, winged bark. 'Compacta' and 'Rudy Haag' are good varieties.
Euonymus americana **Hearts-abursting-with-love** or **Straw-berry Bush**	D	4'	Hot pink/ mid-spring	Sun to part shade	Hot pink flowers; fruit with orange seed, dark red fall foliage.
Euonymus atropurpurea **Wahoo**	D	to 25'	Small/ spring	Sun to part shade	Insignificant flower, yellow, fall foliage, scarlet fruit.
Euonymus fortunei **Wintercreeper Euonymus**	E	1' – 6' or larger	White, small/ spring	Sun to part shade	Evergreen; trailing, or climbing; 2" leaves. Orange-yellow berries in fall. Good, quick cover for fence. Var. 'Coloratus' has lovely purple foliage in winter. 'Vegetus' is tall, bushy, and big-leaved. 'Kewensis is tiny-leaved ground cover. 'Emerald Gaiety' can be ground cover, vine, or bush.
Euonymus japonica aureo-variegata **Japanese Euonymus**	E, V	8' – 10'	Cream, tiny/ spring	Sun to part shade	Insignificant flower, variegated yellow leaves. 'Ovatus Aureus', 'Gold Spot'.
Euonymus japonica aureo-variegata var. **'Silver King' Euonymus**	E, V	8' – 10'	Cream, tiny/ spring	Sun to part shade	Insignificant flower, variegated white leaves.

203

Scientific Name/ Common Name	Key	Height	Flower Color/ Bloom Time	Sun/ Shade	Comments
Euonymus japonica microphylla **Box-leaf Euonymus**	E	½' – 2'	Cream, tiny/ spring	Sun to part shade	Insignificant flower; dwarf, compact, evergreen foliage. Similar to boxwood. Also variegated form.
Exochorda racemosa **Pearlbush**	D	6'	White/ early spring	Sun to part shade	Waxy, white clusters of flowers. Strong, rank grower. Does very well here.
Fargesia rufa **Rufa Clumping Bamboo**	E	8'		Light to medium shade	Non-invasive, clump former from China. Elegant upright fountain habit.
Fargesia nitida **Hardy Clump Bamboo**	E	8' – 12'		Light to medium shade	Non-invasive clump former of great beauty. Any well drained soil. Hardy.
Fatshedera lizei **Fat-headed Lizzie**	E, V	3' – 5'	Green-white/ fall	Light to deep shade	A cross between *Fatsia japonica x Hedera helix*, it forms a semi-climbing evergreen shrub or vine in the shade. Fat-headed Lizzie produces 10" panicles of green-white flowers in autumn.
Fatsia japonica **Fatsia**	E	4' – 8'	Green white/ fall	Light to medium shade	Unusual, ball-like, white flowers; Dramatic, glossy, tropical-looking foliage shaped like large maple leaf. Not hardy north of Zone 7.
Forsythia **Forsythia**	D	1' – 8'	Yellow/ late winter	Sun to light shade	Yellow flowers; 'Lynwood Gold' is very fluorescent.

SCIENTIFIC NAME/ COMMON NAME	KEY	HEIGHT	FLOWER COLOR/ BLOOM TIME	SUN/ SHADE	COMMENTS
					Many varieties. Do not prune into ball. Can be forced in winter. Remove old canes to ground after blooming. See White Forsythia – *Abeliophyllum*.
Forsythia intermedia **Border Forsythia**	D	6'	Yellow/ late winter	Sun to light shade	Yellow, bell-like flower; handsome, fall foliage.
Forsythia intermedia spectabilis **Showy Border Forsythia**	D	6' – 10'	Yellow/ late winter	Sun to light shade	Showiest yellow flowers; handsome, fall foliage. Strong grower.
Forsythia suspense **Weeping Forsythia**	D	6' – 10'	Yellow/ spring	Sun to light shade	Blooms later than others.
Fothergilla gardenii **Dwarf Fothergilla**	D	4' – 5' x 4' – 5'	White/ early spring	Sun to medium shade	Small, rounded shrub with white bottlebrush flowers, good summer foliage, and great fall color of red, yellow, & orange. Native. 'Mt. Airy' & 'Blue Mist' are good choices. Excellent shrub.
Fothergilla major **Large Fothergilla**	D	6' – 10'	White/ mid- spring	Sun to medium shade	Handsome native shrub with white bottlebrush flowers, blue-green foliage, and excellent yellow to red fall coloration. Underused, pest free.

205

SCIENTIFIC NAME/ COMMON NAME	KEY	HEIGHT	FLOWER COLOR/ BLOOM TIME	SUN/ SHADE	COMMENTS
					Requires well-drained acid soil.
Fuchsia magellanica **Hardy Fuchsia**	D	6' – 10' x 6' – 10'	Purple & rose/ early summer	Partial to medium shade	Hardy to zone 6, Plant this fuchsia in good loam and keep evenly moist. Red and purple flowers are loved by hummingbirds. Mail order sources. Prefers cooler climate.
Gardenia jasminoides or G. augusta **Gardenia** or **Cape Jasmine** See Special Article below.	E	to 6'	White/ spring & summer	Sun to light shade	Large, white, waxy, very fragrant, flowers. Some bloom into fall. Needs protection in severe winter. Plant in sheltered spot. All gardenias subject to whitefly. New cold hardy cultivars.
Gardenia jasminoides **'Radicans'** **Creeping Gardenia**	E	1' – 2'	White/ late spring	Sun to light shade	Dwarf, prostrate. Acid soil, humus. Use chelated iron if leaves turn yellow. Requires sun for setting of buds.
Gardenia x hybrid **'Frostproof'** and others	E	3' – 4' x 3' – 4'	White/ late spring	Sun to light shade	Fragrant, small, single white flowers on cold hardy (zone 6) evergreen shrub with slender 2" leaves.
Hamamelis x intermedia **Hybrid Witch-hazel**	D	6' – 20' x 8' – 10'	Yellow to red/ late winter	Sun to part shade	Improved hybrids of an excellent shrub. Fragrant bloom in late winter. Handsome foliage turns gold in fall. Moist well

206

Scientific Name/ Common Name	Key	Height	Flower Color/ Bloom Time	Sun/ Shade	Comments
					drained soil. 'Arnold's Promise', 'Orange Beauty', 'Primavera'.
Hamamelis mollis **Chinese Witch-hazel**	D	10' – 15' x 10' – 15'	Yellow/ late winter	Sun to part shade	Fragrant flowers in late winter, good summer foliage, brilliant yellow in fall. Moist woodland, but very adaptable.
Hamamelis vernalis **Vernal Witch-hazel**	D	6' – 10' x 6' – 10'	Yellow, orange or red/ late winter	Sun to part shade	Fragrant flowers in late winter; yellow fall color. Suckering habit. Native.
Hamamelis virginiana **Common Witch-hazel**	D	6' – 15'	Yellow/ fall	Sun to part shade	Very fragrant pale yellow flowers; yellow fall foliage. Native.
Hibiscus syriacus **Althea or Rose-of-Sharon**	D	6' – 12'	White, rose, lavender/ late summer	Sun to light shade	White, lavender, or rose flower. Old-fashioned and reliable. Check local nursery and catalogs.
Hydrangea **Hydrangea** See Special Article below.					One of the very finest shrubs. Excellent new cultivars bloom on old and new wood for guaranteed blooms.
Hypericum calycinum **St.-John's-wort** or **Aaronsbeard**	E	1' – 1½'	Yellow/ early summer to fall	Sun to part shade	Blooms like single, yellow rose on low spreading plant. Good ground cover. Poor, sandy soil.
Hypericum frondosum **Hypericum** or **Golden St.-**	E	3'	Yellow/ mid-summer	Sun to light shade	Yellow, wild rose-like, 2" bloom; dull green leaf. 'Sunburst'

SCIENTIFIC NAME/ COMMON NAME	KEY	HEIGHT	FLOWER COLOR/ BLOOM TIME	SUN/ SHADE	COMMENTS
John's-wort					is good variety.
Ilex – **Holly** See Special Article below.					
Illicium floridanum **Florida Anise**	E	6' – 10' x 6'	Maroon/ spring	Light to full shade	Interesting, 1" – 2" spidery, maroon flowers. Medium green, beautiful foliage. Moist, rich soil. Deer resistant. Several cultivars. The culinary anise is *Illicium verum* – star anise; others are inedible.
Illicium henryii **Henry Anise**	E	6' – 8' x 6'	Red/ spring	Light to full shade	Densely pyramidal, broadleaf evergreen with handsome foliage. Showier red flowers than other Anises.
Illicium parviflorum **Ocala Anise**	E	8' – 12' x 8'	White/ late spring	Light to full shade	Beautiful olive-green foliage on this pyramidal shrub. White, spidery flowers. Less aromatic than others. Excellent in shade.
Illicium anisatum **Japanese Anise Tree**	E	6' – 19'		Partial shade	Rarely produces flowers. Desirable for light olive- green, elliptical leaves; aromatic, pest free. Lasts well in water for arrangements; roots easily in glass container.

Scientific Name/ Common Name	Key	Height	Flower Color/ Bloom Time	Sun/ Shade	Comments
Indigofera kirilowii **Kirilow Indigo**	D	2' – 3' x 3' – 4'	Pink & white/ mid-summer	Light shade	Low, dense, suckering shrub with lovely foliage and panicles of pink and white flowers which resemble wisteria
Itea virginica **Sweetspire** or **Virginia Willow**	E, SE	4' – 6'	White/mid-summer	Sun or shade	Fragrant, white flowers; fall color. Likes moist soil. Semi-evergreen. Native. 'Henry's Garnet' or the dwarf 'Little Henry'.
Jasminum floridum **Florida Jasmine Showy Jasmine**	E, SE	4' – 5'	Yellow/ mid-spring	Sun to light shade	Do not confuse with the evergreen vine Carolina Jessamine, (*Gelsemium sempervirens*). Yellow flowers, tri-lobed leaf. Good clipped to a low hedge overhanging a wall. Site in sheltered location
Jasminum nudiflorum **Winter Jasmine**	D	3' – 4'	Yellow/ late winter	Sun to light shade	Yellow blossoms before leaves appear. Young branches green in winter. Low spreading form. Can be forced indoors.
Juniperus chinensis pfitzerana **Pfitzer Juniper**	E	5' x 10'		Sun	Steel blue foliage; massive, shaggy form. Spreading habit. Poor soil.
Juniperus horizontalis **Creeping Juniper** or	E	1' – 2'		Sun	Small blue fruit that birds love. Woody, treelike trunk, gray green foliage.

SCIENTIFIC NAME/ COMMON NAME	KEY	HEIGHT	FLOWER COLOR/ BLOOM TIME	SUN/ SHADE	COMMENTS
Trailing Juniper					Coniferous evergreen that forms a low ground cover. Good in rock garden; sculptural, hardy.
Kerria japonica **Kerria** or **Japanese Rose**	D	4'	Yellow gold/ spring	Sun to part shade	Single or double yellow flower; neat, slender growth; sparse dark green foliage.
Kerria japonica pleniflora **Kerria**	D	5' – 7'	Orange gold/ spring	Sun to part shade	Double, orange pom-pom flowers. Growth too insubstantial and color too strong for foundation or border planting. Naturalizes well.
Kolkwitzia amabilis **Beautybush**	D	6' – 10'	Pink and yellow/ early summer	Sun to light shade	Upright, arching, vase-shaped shrub. Pretty, pink bell-shaped flowers on well-established plants. Otherwise, a coarse and seldom used shrub. Leaves dull red in fall.
Lagerstroemia **Crape Myrtle** See *Trees*		15' – 25'	Pink, red, roses, mauve, scarlet, white	Sun to light shade	Crape myrtles may be grown as multi-stemmed shrubs by pruning. Typically they are small trees. See *Garden Care–Pruning* for specifics.
Laurel See *Prunus;* also **Alexandrian Laurel** (*Danae*)					

Scientific Name/ Common Name	Key	Height	Flower Color/ Bloom Time	Sun/ Shade	Comments
Leucothoe axillaris **Leucothoe**	E	5'	White/ spring	Part to full shade	Bronze leaf in spring. Not very hardy.
Leucothoe fontanesiana **Drooping Leucothoe**	E	6'	White/ spring	Part to full shade	Lily-of-the-valley-like flower. Hardy. Sandy loam. Mail order sources.
Leucothoe populifolia or *Agarista populifolia* **Agarista**	E	to 12'	Cream/ late spring	Part shade to shade	Evergreen, multi-stemmed shrub with arching habit. Agarista likes moist rich soil and room to spread. Flower is fragrant cream-colored raceme.
Leucothoe recurva **Sweetbells**	D	10'	White/ mid to late spring	Part to full shade	Similar to above but more spreading habit. Can stand drier conditions
Leucothoe racemosa **Sweetbells**	D	10'	White/ late spring	Part to full shade	Same as above. Upright. Scarlet in fall. Very desirable.
Ligustrum japonicum var. *coriaceum* **Ligustrum** or **Glossy Privet**	E, V	to 4'	White/ early summer	Sun or shade	Small, curly, waxy leaf. Not hardy above Zone 7. Several other good Japanese privets; some variegated.
Ligustrum lucidum **Black Wax Privet**	E	to 25'	White/ early summer	Sun or shade	White, very fragrant flowers in racemes; dark green, shiny leaves; dark blue berries that birds like. Fast grower but wood is weak. May be used as a small tree. Useful for tall screen.

SCIENTIFIC NAME/ COMMON NAME	KEY	HEIGHT	FLOWER COLOR/ BLOOM TIME	SUN/ SHADE	COMMENTS
Ligustrum sinense var. **'Pendulum'** **Chinese Privet**	E, V	12' or more	White/ early summer	Sun or shade	Weeping privet, good for hedge. Variegated forms available.
Ligustrum vulgare **Common Privet**	D	15'	Cream, tiny/ early summer	Sun or shade	Rank, suckering, must be pruned or sheared. Tough, persistent plant.
Lindera benzoin **Spicebush**	D	4' – 7'	Yellow flower/ early spring red berry/ fall	Light to partial shade	Small shrub with fragrant foliage that turns gold in the fall. Early blooming with small, yellow flowers on bare stems. Host plant for butterflies; berries loved by birds. Moist woodland.
Lonicera fragrantissima **Fragrant Honeysuckle** or **Winter Honeysuckle**	SE	6' – 8'	White/ late winter	Sun to part shade	Spicy, fragrant, creamy white flowers. Fast-growing screen or hedge material. Many varieties. Branches easy to force in midwinter. Any soil; pest-free.
Loropetalum chinense **Loropetalum** or **Chinese Fringe-flower**	E	to 10'	White/ spring	Partial shade	Spidery, white flowers that resemble Witch-hazel. Small dark leaves of medium texture. Pest free. Foliage and bloom good for filler in arrangements.
Loropetalum chinense **'Rubrum'** **Loropetalum**	E	to 10'	Hot pink/ spring	Partial shade	Many new selections with purple foliage and striking pink flowers. 'Pizazz',

SCIENTIFIC NAME/ COMMON NAME	KEY	HEIGHT	FLOWER COLOR/ BLOOM TIME	SUN/ SHADE	COMMENTS
					'Plum Delight', and 'Burgundy' are a few. Fountain-form. Pest free.
Magnolia stellata **Star Magnolia** See *Trees*	D	10' – 15'	White/ late winter to early spring	Sun to part shade	Very early white starry flower, also pale pink; shrub, or tree. Dense foliage; branches oddly where pruned. Often frostbitten.
Mahonia spp. **Mahonia**	E	5' – 10'	Yellow/ spring	Partial to medium shade	Clusters of bright yellow flowers followed by blue-green, grapelike fruit, stiff, holly-shaped, spiny, leaves. Great architectural presence. When pruned, new foliage comes from top only.
Mahonia aquifolium **Oregon Grape**	E	5' – 6'	Yellow/ spring	Partial to medium shade	Large, coarse, spiny leaves. Irregular form. Showy yellow blooms in March followed by conspicuous blue-black fruit. Cut back older stems in early spring.
Mahonia bealei **Leather-Leaf Mahonia, Grape Holly**	E	7' – 10'	Yellow/ spring	Partial to medium shade	Large, coarse, leathery, blue- green foliage; yellow flowers in early spring followed by bluish berries. Moist soil. Keep cut to 4' – 6' to prevent legginess.
Mahonia fortunei	E	4'	Yellow/	Partial	Similar leaves, less

213

SCIENTIFIC NAME/ COMMON NAME	KEY	HEIGHT	FLOWER COLOR/ BLOOM TIME	SUN/ SHADE	COMMENTS
Chinese Mahonia			spring	to medium shade	spiny. Plant in protected area; not hardy above Zone 8.
Mahonia nervosa **Long-leaf Oregon Grape**	E	3'	Yellow/ spring	Partial to medium shade	Much smaller than above. Leaves turn bronze spring and fall. Blooms March
Nandina domestica **Nandina or Heavenly Bamboo**	E	5' – 6'	White/ late spring	Sun to medium shade	Small, white raceme flower; beautiful airy foliage; clusters of red berries in fall and winter; bronze in spring. Should be pruned by thinning, not lopping. Desirable. Trouble-free and reliable.
Nandina domestica nana purpurea **Dwarf Nandina**	E	1' – 1½'	White/ late spring	Sun to medium shade	Dwarf, thick foliage that is vivid bronze-purple.
Osmanthus americanus **Osmanthus or Devilwood**	E	20'	Greenish-white/ spring	Light to medium shade	Smooth, oval leaves; fragrant, greenish-white flowers; light gray bark. Open, loose growth. Fast grower; trouble-free. Cold-hardiest Osmanthus.
Osmanthus fortunei **Fortune's Osmanthus**	E	to 20' but can be kept at any height	White/ fall	Light to medium shade	Large, rounded shrub of great beauty. Small, white, fragrant flowers; profuse bloomer in early winter. Lighter green foliage, spiny and smooth leaves. A hardy hybrid;

Scientific Name/ Common Name	Key	Height	Flower Color/ Bloom Time	Sun/ Shade	Comments
					preferred to *O. fragrans.*
Osmanthus fragrans **Sweet Olive** or **Osmanthus**	E	10'	White/ winter	Light to medium shade	Tiny, white, very fragrant flowers. Upright growth habit. Not hardy below 10 degrees. Very desirable in winter gardens as it blooms freely throughout winter.
Osmanthus heterophyllus **Holly-Leaved Osmanthus**	E	15' – 20' some are only 2' x 2'	White/ fall	Light to medium shade	White or yellowish, fragrant flowers. Small, dark leaves resembling holly but leaves are opposite instead of alternate. Available with yellow variegation. Responds well to clipping. Peaty soil.
Parrotia persica **Persian Ironwood**	D	5' – 20'	Red/ late winter	Sun to light shade	Small, shrubby tree with red fall color, spidery red flowers on bare branches in late winter, handsome foliage. Not fussy about soil. Related to Witch-hazel.
Philadelphus **Mock Orange**	D	12'	White/ mid-spring	Sun to part shade	White and yellow, fragrant flowers on long graceful branches. Many varieties; check local nurseries or catalogs.
Photinia fraseri **Photinia**	E	15'	White/ spring	Sun to shade	White umbel flowers; red berries; new foliage is red. Will

215

Scientific Name/ Common Name	Key	Height	Flower Color/ Bloom Time	Sun/ Shade	Comments
					stand shade.
Photinia glabra **Photinia**	E	6' – 10'	White/ spring	Sun to part shade	Smooth leaf; can be kept in vivid red foliage by clipping every two weeks. Can be winter-killed.
Phyllostachys nigra **Black Bamboo**	E	8' – 18' x 3' – 7'		Light to medium shade	Clump-forming, non-invasive bamboo with striking black stems and green foliage. 18' by 7' in 7 years. Loam, easy to grow. Will spread slowly.
Pieris floribunda **Mountain Pieris**	E	to 6'	White/ spring	Light to medium shade	White Lily-of-the-valley-like flower; dull evergreen leaves. Other *Pieris* are better for this area.
Pieris formosa **Himalayan Pieris**	E	to 20'	Pink/ spring	Light to medium shade	Flowers tinged with pink; somewhat more tender than *Pieris* above. Not great in the South.
Pieris japonica **Japanese Pieris** or **Andromeda**	E	to 10'; usually 3' – 5'	White/ spring	Light to medium shade	Drooping panicles of white flowers. Larger and faster grower than *P. floribunda.* Dodd's hybrid 'Bridal Veil' is improved cultivar; best for the South.
Pieris japonica variegata **Variegated Pieris**	E, V	1½' – 3'	White/ spring	Light to medium shade	Dwarf form with white-edged leaves. Suitable for bonsai.

216

Scientific Name/ Common Name	Key	Height	Flower Color/ Bloom Time	Sun/ Shade	Comments
Pleioblastus auricomas **Dwarf Variegated Bamboo**	E, V	3'	Gold and green	Light to medium shade	Beautiful, upright, low-growing, non-invasive bamboo; easy in any soil. Variegated forms. Border or specimen.
Poncirus trifoliate **Hardy Orange**	D	15'	White/ late spring	Sun to light shade	White flowers, sour orange fruit, thorny. Very good to espalier on south or west wall.
Privet See *Ligustrum*					
Prunus Also see *Trees*					Many beautiful deciduous fruit trees and evergreen shrubs/ trees are in this genus.
Prunus glandulosa **Flowering Almond**	D	4'	Pink/ early spring	Sun to light shade	Pink "pom-pom" blooms, very hardy.
Prunus laurocerasus **Cherry Laurel** or **English Laurel**	E	12'	White/ spring	Sun to shade	Short clusters of inconspicuous, fragrant, white flowers, glossy leaf. Can be used as a hedge. Subject to borers. Many improved varieties.
Prunus laurocerasus 'Otto Luyken' **'Otto Luyken' Laurel**	E	3' – 4' x 6'	White/ spring	Light to full shade	Fine, compact habit, 4" dark green leaves. Formal appearance. Free-flowering, will take heavy shade. Most popular variety in our area.

217

Scientific Name/ Common Name	Key	Height	Flower Color/ Bloom Time	Sun/ Shade	Comments
Prunus laurocerasus 'Schipkaensis' **'Schip' Laurel**	E	4' – 5' x 6' – 7'	White/ spring	Light to full shade	Dark green leaves 4" long and 1" wide on a very hardy, refined species. Desirable.
Prunus laurocerasus zabeliana **'Zabelle' Laurel**	E	9'	White/ spring	Light to full shade	Inconspicuous flower, blue-black berries, horizontal branches. Not good for foundation planting.
Prunus virginiana **Chokecherry**	D	20' – 30' shrub or tree	White/ spring	Sun to part shade	Rugged shrub. Reddish fruit turns black when ripe. Eaten by birds though seeds are poisonous. Prefers Northern climate.
Pseudocydonia sinensis **Chinese Quince**	D	10' – 20'	Pink/ spring	Sun to part shade	Dense, oval shrub or small tree grown primarily for beautiful, flaking bark. Fireblight can be a problem.
Punica granatum **Pomegranate**	D	to 10'	Crimson/ mid-spring	Sun to part shade	Flame-colored, double flowers; delicious red fruit; handsome foliage. Not hardy in severe winters. Try in pot.
Pyracantha coccinea **Pyracantha** or **Scarlet Firethorn**	E	6' – 15'	White/ spring	Sun to medium shade	Many varieties. White flowers followed by red or orange berries; poisonous thorn; suitable for espalier. Acid soil. Subject to red spider and scale. *P. lalandei* has orange berries. 'Apache' and 'Mojave' have berries

218

SCIENTIFIC NAME/ COMMON NAME	KEY	HEIGHT	FLOWER COLOR/ BLOOM TIME	SUN/ SHADE	COMMENTS
					birds don't like; other cultivars are loved by birds.
Rhaphiolepis umbellate **Rhaphiolepis** or **Indian Hawthorn**	E	4' – 6' x 4' – 6' or larger	Pink or white/ mid-spring	Sun to part shade	Clusters of fragrant flowers; small, shiny leaf; dark blue berry in fall. Will not tolerate very cold winters. Interesting branch structure. Pest-prone. Improved cultivars.
Rhododendron **Rhododendron** See Special Article on Azaleas below.	E	to 15'	Various/ late spring	Light to medium shade	Many species and cultivars. Huge flowers in white, pink, red, yellow; large, handsome leaf. Rhodies best in Smokies; dislike extreme summer heat & fluctuating winter temperature. In Mid-South choose coolest spot in light shade; plant high. Avoid winter sun, especially afternoon. Rich, moist, acid soil. 'Capistrano', 'Yaku Princess' and 'Trinidad' are more heat- and cold-tolerant than most.
Rhus spp. **Sumac**	D	2' – 20'	Yellow/ spring	Sun to part shade	Many varieties, all native. Tiny yellow or green flowers before leaves in early spring; hairy, red fruit in late summer; brilliant red

219

SCIENTIFIC NAME/ COMMON NAME	KEY	HEIGHT	FLOWER COLOR/ BLOOM TIME	SUN/ SHADE	COMMENTS
					in fall. Pest-free; good for naturalizing as it spreads by suckers. Good source of food for wildlife.
Rhus glabra **Smooth Sumac**	D	10' – 15' x 10' – 15'	Greenish yellow/ mid-summer	Sun to part shade	Large suckering shrub; great texture, great fall color, and red fruit. Used along highway medians, it tolerates dry, poor soil. Native. Bird food. New hybrids are more restrained. 'Morden's Selection'.
Rhus typhina **Staghorn Sumac**	D	20'	Greenish yellow/ summer	Sun to part shade	Large clusters of greenish-yellow flowers; hairy, crimson fruit; hollow stem. Splendid, red fall color. Suckering; use for naturalizing waste areas. Tolerates poor, dry soil. 'Laciniata' is cut-leaf variety. Native.
Rhus vernix **Poison Sumac**	D	20'	Yellow/ early summer	Sun to part shade	Poisonous. Severe skin irritant; avoid any contact with eyes or mouth. 7 to 13 leaflets; bright scarlet in fall; flattened, round, gray fruit. Grows in marshes.
Rosa **Rose** See Special Article below.					

SCIENTIFIC NAME/ COMMON NAME	KEY	HEIGHT	FLOWER COLOR/ BLOOM TIME	SUN/ SHADE	COMMENTS
Salix discolor **Pussy Willow**	D	10'	Gray catkin/ late winter	Sun to part shade	Gray catkins. Severe pruning after blooming produces longest stems and largest catkins. Fast growing, also a tree.
Sambucus canadensis **Elderberry**	D	12' – 15'	White/ early summer	Sun to shade	Large, white flower cluster, followed by black berries. Favorite of birds. Rank, suckers freely. Can become weed. Berries used for wine, jam, and pies.
Santolina chamaecyparis-sus **Lavender Cotton**	E	1' – 2' x 2' – 4'	Yellow/ mid-summer	Sun	Lovely, silver foliage; yellow button flowers; remove faded flowers and prune to rejuvenate. Prefers drier, sandy soil, but tolerates well-drained clay. Good for rock garden.
Sarcococca confusa **Sarcococca** or **Sweet Box**	E	4' x 5'	Tiny white/ late winter to early spring	Light to full shade	Tiny, fragrant, white flower; very attractive, glossy, narrow, dark green leaves; reddish black fruit. Needs shade from hot sun, prefers garden loam but will tolerate dry shade. An elegant and underused shrub.
Sarcococca hookeriana var. *humilis* **Hooker's**	E	1½' x 3'+	Tiny white/ late winter to early	Light to full shade	Stoloniferous, spreading ground cover of great beauty. Fragrant flowers in

221

Scientific Name/ Common Name	Key	Height	Flower Color/ Bloom Time	Sun/ Shade	Comments
Sarcococca			spring		winter.
Sarcococca ruscifolia var. *chinensis* **Chinese Sarcococca**	E	to 6'	Tiny, white/ late winter to early spring	Light to full shade	Similar to *S. confusa* but has red berries.
Spiraea bumalda (cross between *S. albiflora* and *S. japonica*) **Bumald Spirea**	D	3' x 5'	Pink to Rose/ early summer	Light to medium shade	Pink or rose flowers; dwarf. Prune old branches in late winter before new growth starts; cutting off flowers promotes new flush of growth. 'Anthony Waterer' & 'Gold flame': leaves emerge russet-purple and become yellow-green. Yellow foliage provides nice contrast with other shrubs.
Spiraea japonica **Japanese Spirea**	D	4' x 6'	Pink/ late spring	Light to medium shade	Dainty, low-growing mass with pink flowers in late May. 'Gold Mound' is good yellow-leaf variety that does not burn in sun. Orange fall color.
Spiraea prunifolia **Bridal Wreath Spirea**	D	6' x 9'	White/ spring	Sun to part shade	Coarse, straggly, old-fashioned shrub. Double, white flowers; erect form. Less desirable than other spireas.

222

SCIENTIFIC NAME/ COMMON NAME	KEY	HEIGHT	FLOWER COLOR/ BLOOM TIME	SUN/ SHADE	COMMENTS
Spiraea reevesiana or *Spiraea cantoniensis* **Double Reeves Spirea**	D	4'	White/ spring	Sun to part shade	Clusters of white flowers. Bushy grower, not hardy in North. 'Lanceata' is good.
Spiraea thunbergii **Thunberg Spirea**	D	3' – 5'	White/ early spring	Sun to part shade	Dainty, white flowers; feathery branches; twiggy; orange to scarlet in fall.
Spiraea vanhouttei **Vanhoutte Spirea**	D	6' x 10'	White/ spring	Sun to part shade	Clusters of single, white flowers in profusion on fountain-like arching branches; most popular spirea.
Spiraea x cinerea **'Grefsheim' Spirea**	D	4' x 5'	White/ spring	Sun to part shade	Handsome, dense shrub with arching stems. Blooms in April.
Symphoricarpos albus laevigatus **Snowberry** or **Waxberry**	D	3' – 6'	Pink/ early spring	Sun to light shade	Tiny, pink flowers in early spring followed by clusters of white, waxy berries that cling until late fall. Tolerates any soil. Informal suckering shrub. Native.
Symplocos paniculata **Sapphireberry** or **Asiatic Sweetleaf**	D	10' – 20'	White/ late spring	Sun to part shade	Large shrub or small tree. White flowers precede true-blue berries, loved by birds. Any soil. Plant more than one for better fruiting.
Syringa persica **Lilac** or **Persian Lilac**	D	5' – 6'	Lavender/ spring	Sun to part shade	Very fragrant. Hardiest of all lilacs. Cut off spent flowers.

223

SCIENTIFIC NAME/ COMMON NAME	KEY	HEIGHT	FLOWER COLOR/ BLOOM TIME	SUN/ SHADE	COMMENTS
Syringa vulgaris **Common Lilac** or **French Lilac**	D	10' – 15'	Lavender to white/ spring	Sun to part shade	Fragrant flowers; old-fashioned; many varieties. Happier in North. All *Syringas* need alkaline soil, cool nights, and wood ashes. Periodically remove old stems after flowering to stimulate new growth.
Syringa vulgaris hybrid var. **'Descanso' Hybrid Lilac**	D, F	8' – 15' x 6' – 12'	Various/ spring	Sun to part shade	Heat-tolerant, low-chill-requirement cultivars for the South: 'Angel White', 'Blue Boy', 'California Rose', 'Lavender Lady' and others. Zones 7 – 9.
Taxus baccata repandens **English Yew**	E	4' x 5'		Light to full shade	Feathery, rich-green foliage. Low, spreading mound; good for informal masses or clipped hedges or border. Acid soil, good drainage; dislikes extreme heat. Try *Cephalotaxus* – Japanese Plum Yew instead for informal.
Taxus cuspidata **Japanese Yew**	E	to 20'		Light to full shade	Red fleshy berries in fall; vigorous spreading growth. Good for hedges; hardy.
Taxus cuspidata nana **Dwarf Japanese**	E	to 6'		Light to full shade	Dwarf; slow grower.

224

Scientific Name/ Common Name	Key	Height	Flower Color/ Bloom Time	Sun/ Shade	Comments
Yew					
Taxus x media **Hybrid Yew**	E	30'		Light to full shade	Cross between English and Japanese. Needlelike foliage; red, fleshy, one-seeded berries in fall.
Ternstroemia gymnanthera **Cleyera** or **Japanese Ternstroemia**	E	4' – 15' x 5' – 6'	Tiny white/ spring	Sun to medium shade	Oval-rounded, densely branched, evergreen. New foliage is bronze. Very handsome. Tiny fragrant flowers in May. See also under *Cleyera japonica*.
Thuja occidentalis **American Arborvitae** or **Eastern Arborvitae**	E	1' – 50'	Cones look like berries	Light shade	Many cultivars ranging from dwarf to giant. Lovely form and texture. Be careful pruning.
Thujopsis dolobrata **False Arborvitae**	E	3' – 50'	Cones look like berries	Light shade	Lacy green foliage on flattened mounds should not be sheared. 'Nana' is 3' dwarf. Many cultivars available, including large trees.
Vaccinium ashei **Rabbiteye Blueberry**	D, E	8' – 10'	Pale pink/ spring	Sun	Evergreen. Best species for the South, with lower chill requirements. Flower clusters before leaves, good berries, fall color. Plant more than one for pollination. Berries loved by wildlife and people.

SCIENTIFIC NAME/ COMMON NAME	KEY	HEIGHT	FLOWER COLOR/ BLOOM TIME	SUN/ SHADE	COMMENTS
Vaccinium corymbosum **Highbush Blueberry**	D, E	6' – 10' x 8' – 12'	Pale pink/ spring	Sun	Similar to above. Many cultivars. 'Sunshine Blue Dwarf' is good choice for small gardens growing 3' x 4' with good fruit and fall color.
Viburnum **Viburnum** See Special Article below.	E,D	4' – 25'	Pink, white/ spring	Sun to medium shade	Many species, all are good. Very easy, pest-free. Beautiful shrub. Big variety in leaf forms, flowers, berries, and growth habits in this genus.
Weigela florida **Weigela**	D	8' – 10'	Pink/ late spring	Sun to light shade	Rose-pink clusters of tubular flowers on arching "old-wood" branches. Many varieties.
Yaupon *Ilex vomitoria* see Special Article on Holly below.					
Yucca alnifolia **Yucca** or **Spanish Bayonet**	E	4' x 3'	White/ mid summer	Sun to light shade	Large spikes of creamy white, bell-shaped flowers, rising above sharp-pointed foliage. Makes interesting contrast in garden. Any well-drained soil; not bothered by heat, drought or pests. (See also under *Trees*)
Yucca glauca **Small Soapweed**	E	3' x 3'	White/ mid to late	Sun to light	Smaller and less sprouting than

SCIENTIFIC NAME/ COMMON NAME	KEY	HEIGHT	FLOWER COLOR/ BLOOM TIME	SUN/ SHADE	COMMENTS
			summer	shade	*Y. gloriosa*, below; leaves a brighter color.
Yucca gloriosa **Spanish Dagger**	E	6' – 8'	White/ mid to late summer	Sun to light shade	Stiff, pointed leaves atop fleshy stem. Large panicle of creamy white flowers.

SPECIAL ARTICLES ON SELECT SHRUBS

AZALEA

(RHODODENDRON)

These members of the *Rhododendron* genus are literally covered in spring with a profusion of flowers, ranging from pastel to vivid, in shades of white, yellow, orange, pink, coral, magenta, crimson, lavender, and purple. The flowers are single, double, or hose-in-hose (one flower inside another) forms and may be solid, striped or flecked. The new hybrids are more tolerant of sun and re-bloom in the fall. By planting a selection of varieties, one may have azaleas in bloom for three months in the spring and two months in the fall.

Many of the vivid colors clash when planted together, and too much of one strong color may be overpowering, so choose carefully. Intersperse bright colors with whites, grays, or other evergreens, or blend with soft pastels. Azaleas may be planted while in bloom to help in arranging pleasing color combinations. Fortunately, it is simple to correct mistakes because azaleas are easy to transplant.

Ranging in size from 12" dwarfs to 8' giants, both evergreen and deciduous azaleas afford numerous landscaping possibilities. They are used as specimens, edging for walkways, hedges, containers, and foundation plantings (consider your brick or siding color when choosing). The dark foliage of broadleaf evergreens and conifers makes a good background for azaleas. Many have nice fall color (reds, yellows, and pinks). The native deciduous azaleas, which may grow as tall as small trees, are valued for their light, airy, fragrant flowers and for the interesting structure of their bare branches.

Azaleas are most attractive in naturalized plantings in open wooded areas or under deciduous trees, with low-growing varieties placed in front of taller ones. As their own form is beautiful, they should be left to grow naturally and should never be sheared or mounded. Dwarf varieties, such as *Satsukis*, may be allowed to grow together to form a dense, high ground cover under a large, deciduous tree.

Certain varieties of azaleas make excellent Bonsai, while others are good greenhouse plants. A potted azalea received at Christmas should not be planted outside until mid-April. Check the variety before planting outside, for some florists' azaleas are greenhouse plants only.

CULTURE

Azaleas may be planted successfully in fall, winter, and spring, whenever the soil is workable. Fall planting is best, for this gives more time for the plant to become established. Spring planting, while azaleas are in bloom, makes it easier to arrange colors, but the new growth is apt to wilt so give extra water.

- Azaleas like filtered light and not full sun. They will not bloom abundantly under large shade trees unless the tree's branches are thinned to allow light through.
- Azaleas cannot grow in a heavy clay soil. Give them slightly acidic (pH of 4.8 – 6.0) sandy loam or woodland soil.
- Beware of too-deep planting.
- Over-accumulation of mulch and fallen leaves can smother plants.

Refer to *Garden Care – Planting Shrubs.* Beware of root-bound azaleas in containers and score the rootball with a knife before planting. Plant them "high" and mound loam and mulch around the raised rootball. Since azalea roots are right at the surface of the soil, heavy ground covers, such as ivy, will smother them and compete for moisture and plant food. Use specially prepared azalea–camellia food, and pine bark or shredded oak leaves as mulch. See *Garden Care* for more details on *Fertilizing, Watering, Pests, Propagation,* and *Pruning.*

ACIDITY AND CHLOROSIS

Azalea leaves should be rich green; if they begin to turn yellow with dark green veins, a condition known as "chlorosis", the plant needs iron. Use liquid chelated iron spray or Ironite® according to package directions. Iron is chemically available to plants in a slightly acidic soil of pH 4.8 – 6.0. For lowering the soil pH, use garden sulfur which increases soil acidity.

If the soil becomes too acidic, it locks up all the plant food. Therefore, do not add sulfur or iron until definitely needed. Have the soil tested.

The first stage of magnesium deficiency is similar to iron chlorosis. The leaves turn yellow. Later, reddish-purple blotches appear on the leaves which then turn brown on the tips and edges. Spread Epsom salts (magnesium sulfate) generously around the plant, or apply as a foliar spray (2 tablespoons per gallon of water).

PESTS AND DISEASES

Leaf Gall (Fungus) – Malformed, enlarged, thick, fleshy leaves; pale green changing to velvety grayish-white – a problem in wet seasons. Check for this in early April if we have a wet March. Pick off the galls and destroy. Spray plant and ground at first sign of trouble with a fungicide.

Petal Blight (Fungus) – Flower petals spotted, turning soggy and brown. Large-flowered and mid-to-late-season plants are most affected. Spray flowers and soil with a fungicide according to directions. The following spring, spray soil with a fungicide just before buds show color and spray again when flowers are open.

Dormant oil spray in February is good protection against pests.

Lacebug – Leaves grayish green with dark spots on underside. Spray with an insecticidal soap.

229

Red Spider Mite – Leaves appear stippled and off-color, turning brown. To check for red spider mite, hold a white paper under a branch and shake. Minute red spiders will drop onto paper. Spray with a miticide or an oil-based spray at 7-day intervals on underside of leaves.

Scale – White, cottony scales appear in forks of twigs and main stems. Spray with an insecticide. Indoor plants: remove with cotton swab and rubbing alcohol.

Whitefly – Adults fly from the leaves like dandruff when disturbed. Leaves become mottled yellow and have black sooty mold which grows on the sticky honeydew secreted by the insect. Spray with an insecticidal soap, and if that doesn't work use an insecticide.

PROPAGATION

Azaleas may be propagated from seeds, cuttings, layering, division, and grafting. Leave the seeds and grafting to the experts, but cuttings and layering are easy. See *Propagation* in the *Garden Care* chapter.

PRUNING

Azaleas require very little pruning as their natural shape is very appealing. Azaleas may be sheared into a formal clipped hedge, as is popular in Japan, but this is not usually done in the South. To control size, blooms may be cut for arrangements while the shrub is in flower or prune after it finishes blooming.

New growth tends to be on the outside of the plant, and sun and light need to reach the interior of the shrub for a full lush look. Therefore, prune as described in detail below for *Boxwood – thinning* if you want a graceful natural habit.

VARIETIES OF AZALEA

Given the number of varieties of azaleas, it is impractical to list them except by groups. Some are deciduous, the majority evergreen. Some are low and spreading, some are tall and spreading, and some are dominantly upright.

TABLE 19. VARIETIES OF AZALEA (*RHODODENDRON*)

Key: (E) – Early spring bloom from late-March to late-April,

(M) – Mid-spring bloom from mid-April to mid-May,

(L) – Late spring bloom from mid-May to mid-June.

EVERGREEN AZALEAS

BACK ACRES—Double or single flowers of substance and texture; mid–season to late–blooming. Multiple color forms such as solids with white, or nearly white, centers and colored margins. Heat and cold tolerant; evergreen foliage; very desirable.

White: 'White Jade' (M, L) flat-faced white, green in center

White Centers with Colored Margins: 'Margaret Douglas' (M,L) white to pink centers with salmon margins, 'Marion Lee' (M,L) white center with pink margin

Pink: 'Debonaire' (M) light pink, 'Saint James' (M) white throat with salmon margin, 'Tharon Perkins' (E) pale salmon

Red: 'Pat Kraft' (L) dark red, 'Target' (M) scarlet, 'Ben Morrison' (M) red

GLENN DALE HYBRIDS—Over 400 varieties cover the entire blooming season from April to June. Large flowers, wide range of colors, stripes, flecks, and variegated margins and throats. Attractive, glossy, dark green foliage; hardy; height varies from low and compact to tall.

White: 'Bold Face' (M), 'Delight' (E), 'Everest' (L), 'Geisha' (E), 'Glacier' (M), 'Helen Close' (M), 'Moonbeam' (L), 'Treasure' (M), 'Wavelet' (L)

Salmon, Pink, and Red: 'Allure' (E) pink, 'Aphrodite' (M) rose-pink, 'Aztec' (L) rose-red, 'Copperman' (L) orange-red, 'Crinoline' (L) rose-pink with ruffled margin, 'Fashion' (M) orange-red, 'Glamour' (M) rose-red, 'Grace Freeman' (M) violet-pink, 'Greeting' (M) salmon, 'Wildfire' (E) scarlet

Purple and Violet: 'Chanticleer' (L) purple, 'Dauntless' (L) purple, 'Muscadine' (M) rose-purple, 'Sarabande' (L) purple, 'Zulu' (M) purple, 'Martha Hitchcock' (M) purple

Very Dwarf: 'Eros' (L) orange-red, 'Pearl Bradford' (L) rose-pink, 'Sagittarius' (L) salmon-pink, 'Sterling' (L) rose-pink

INDICA (SOUTHERN INDIAN HYBRID) – Large flowers, wide range of colors; tall and fast-growing, open growth pattern; finished blossoms fall to ground; bloom early to mid-season; tender plants, apt to be damaged by cold. Very desirable.

231

White: 'Alba maculata' (M) white speckled with chartreuse, 'G.G.Gerbing' (M) white, 'Indica alba' (M) white and fragrant, 'Mardi Gras' (M) white with pink stripes

Lavender: 'George Lindley Tabor' (M) pale lavender flushed with purplish-pink, 'Gulf Pride' (M) light lavender

Purple: 'Formosa' (M) violet-red – does not bloom well for us

Pink: 'Pride of Mobile' (M) light to deep pink – does not bloom well for us

KURUME – Masses of bloom; dense, dark green spring foliage; large range of colors. *Kurumes* are hardier than *Indicas*. They are excellent for greenhouse, containers, and Bonsai. Blooms April – May. Varying in height, some slow growing, most reach 4' – 6', generally upright

White: 'Apple Blossom' (M) white variegated with pink, 'H.H.Hume' (M) hose-in-hose

Shades of salmon-pink or red: 'Christmas Cheer' (M) brilliant red, 'Coral Bells' (M) shell pink hose-in-hose, 'Glory' (M) pink, 'Hexe' (M) crimson-red hose-in-hose, 'Hino-Crimson' (M) crimson, 'Hinode-Giri' (M) vivid red, 'Pink Pearl' (M) salmon-rose hose-in-hose, 'Salmon Beauty' (M) salmon-pink hose-in-hose, 'Sherwood Red' (M) orange-red

SATSUKI HYBRIDS – Most *Satsukis* have large, single flowers; many different colors and forms. Shiny, dark green leaves. Tolerates more sun, but needs protection from hot afternoon sun. Very late blooming: May – June. Most grow low and spreading, thus excellent for foreground planting as well as Bonsai. For low edging, use very dwarf Gumpo.

'Gumpo' (L) white, light pink, or salmon-rose

'Gunrei' (L) variegated white with pink

'Macrantha' (L) pink or salmon-red, medium height

'Waka-bisu' (L) salmon-pink, hose-in-hose, medium height

ROBBIN HILL HYBRIDS – Large-flowered group similar to *Satsuki* but bloom in April and are more winter hardy. They are compact plants and most have some fall blooms. Most popular varieties are:

'Conversation Piece' (M) single 1" pink flowers with dots, blotches, and sectors of white, pink, and red all at the same time.

'Gillie' (M) single rose-salmon

'Gwenda' (M) pale pink ruffled 3" flowers, semi-dwarf

'Hilda Niblett' (M) perfect mound growth habit; pink and white flowers

'Watchett' (M) rich pink with ruffled margins

232

ENCORE AZALEAS – New hybrids that bloom in the spring and re-bloom in the fall. Memphis is on the northern end of their growing zones but with a little care the first year, they do very well.

'Autumn Royalty' – single purple blooms

'Autumn Rouge' – semi-double, pink to red

'Autumn Bravo' – semi-double, red

'Autumn Coral' – single coral

'Autumn Embers' – semi-double, orange-red

'Autumn Monarch' – semi-double coral

'Autumn Amethyst' – single purple

'Autumn Twist' – white with pink stripes

'Autumn Cheer' – single rose pink

GIRARD HYBRIDS – Excellent, large-flowered shrubs with bright colors for colder climates, but they do very well in the Mid-South. Most popular varieties are:

'Girard Crimson' (M, L) large crimson flowers, good winter color on compact plant

'Girard Fuchsia' (M) reddish purple florets are wavy and ruffled, foliage dark green and glossy

'Girard Hot Shot' (M) deep orange red

DECIDUOUS NATIVE AZALEAS

In general they require more sun. Flowers are trumpet shaped in terminal clusters with long showy stamens, many are fragrant. Mature plants can reach 8' or more. Hard to find; consult catalogs.

'Cumberland' – Rhododendron bakerii – scarlet-red flowers, July–August

'Flame' – R. calendulaceum – flowers orange-red, red, or clear yellow. May–June. (The Flame Azalea of the Great Smoky Mountains)

'Florida' – R. austrinum – fragrant golden flowers in late March or early April

'Oconee' – R. flammeum – flowers orange, red, strong pink, yellow, and salmon. Blooms early- to mid-April

'Piedmont' – R. canescens – fragrant flowers, white to deep pink. Late March

'Pinxterbloom' – R. *nudiflorum* – Honeysuckle fragrance; flowers are white, light pink, deep violet in April

'Plumleaf' – *R. prunifolium* – flowers red, orange-red, to orange. Very late blooming: July–August. Requires shade

'Swamp' – *R. viscosum* – spicy, fragrant white flowers. Hybrids may be pink, salmon, yellow. Blooms mid-May to early June

'Sweet' – *R. arborescens* – flowers white, fragrant. May–June

DECIDUOUS HYBRID AZALEAS

Large, spectacular flower clusters, many quite fragrant. Require more sun than evergreen azaleas; very desirable shrubs.

GHENT HYBRIDS – Large flower clusters of palest yellow through varying shades of salmon, pink, cream, ivory, red, orange, and flame. Single and double flowers bloom early- to mid-season; April–May. Plants tend to be leggy. They do not require as much acidity as other azaleas. 'Exbury', 'Slocock', 'Ilam', and 'Knaphill'

MOLLIS HYBRIDS – Less hardy than the Ghent azaleas, possibly more heat-resistant. Colors are yellow, orange, to orange-red, and growth is upright. They tolerate less acidic soil (lime lightly). Late mid-season bloom

MUCRONULATUM—Very early, lavender flowers which coincide with forsythia bloom. Tender; may be killed-back by a late spring freeze

234

BOXWOOD

BUXUS

Boxwood is truly an aristocrat among evergreen shrubs. They lend an air of elegant refinement wherever they are planted. The secrets to beautiful boxwood in this area are *perfect drainage* and *partial shade*. As for nomenclature, "boxwood" is both the singular and the plural; do not put an "s" on boxwood.

Boxwood are slow growing shrubs that initiate most of their new growth from buds at or near the ends or tips of the branches. Because of this growth habit, boxwood over time produces a great deal of growth on the outside of the shrub which tends to shade out the interior of the plant. To maintain good health, they should be pruned correctly to allow light and air inside the plant.

Boxwood does not like to be crowded. For maximum health it needs plenty of room with free circulation of air around it. It is best grown as a specimen, or as a well-spaced hedge.

CULTURE

Location is the key to success with boxwood. They thrive on the north side of the house, or in "high" shade or "dappled" shade in a well-drained location. This site offers protection from hot afternoon sun in summer and helps prevent foliage burn, or "bronzing", in winter. Bronzing, while not injurious to the plant, is not as pretty as the natural dark green color, and discolored branches may be cut off in early spring if desired.

Boxwood will flourish in any good garden loam and tolerates slightly acidic to slightly alkaline conditions (pH 6.5 – 7.2). In preparing the hole, incorporate plenty of humus, such as leaf mold or compost, also some sand and pine bark chips. If your soil is acidic, add dolomitic lime to the soil amendments.

Take care in planting not to set the ball too low. Let about 5" of the rootball be above grade, and mulch around it with 1" – 2" of pine bark chips or pine needles. In time, rain will wash dirt away from a "high rootball" and the bare roots will need to be re-covered with dirt or mulch. If your boxwood is planted level with surrounding grade, then keep the mulch at the dripline and not up to the main stem, as boxwood prefers very little mulch. Boxwood is easily transplanted in late fall or winter with a good ball of dirt around the roots.

Boxwood roots are near the surface so do not cultivate with a hoe. Hand-pull any weeds. Boxwood likes plenty of moisture in all seasons.

PRUNING

Boxwood can be pruned as needed during December through early spring. One of the objectives of pruning is to open the interior to light, air, and moisture; this

235

is done by *thinning*. Pruning should begin when the plant is young and continue every two years to maintain the vigor and shape of the plant.

To determine if boxwood are too thick, look beneath the exterior stems to check for dried, brown foliage and bare branches. This indicates little light is reaching the interior of the plant. One should be able to see inside the plant if standing a few feet away. When running your hand over the plant, the main stems should be flexible, not heavy and weighted down at the tips. Poke your head into the plant to see if light is entering the shrub. The light should be bright and evenly distributed. If it is dark, the plant needs thinning. Remember, boxwood's natural growth habit is cloud-like and billowy, although young plants tend to be tightly branched and round in form. As the plant matures it spreads into a more open, cloud-like form.

Thinning is a type of pruning that reduces the number of branches at the outer edge of the shrub, and is the technique most used with boxwood. Thinning produces flexible stems that are more resistant to breakage from ice or snow. (See *Garden Care – Pruning* for illustrations)

To thin boxwood, cut out 6" – 8" shoots from inside branches to create openings for sunlight. Thinning holes should be about 3" wide. No more than a third of the stem length should be removed from a branch. This encourages new leaves to grow the entire length of the branch. Use these same cuttings for Christmas decorations.

Many health problems of boxwood are the result of poor sanitation. The interior of the plant needs to be kept culturally clean of shed and diseased foliage and dead branches. This accumulated leaf litter becomes a breeding ground for insects and disease organisms if it is not removed from the center of the plant once a year.

The *"thin, shake, and rake"* approach gives the best results. First, thin to reduce the dense foliage and prune out any dead or diseased branches. Then, vigorously shake the branches to dislodge additional debris to the ground, and finally pick up fallen material with a rake or by hand and remove from the plant.

If this is not done, a build-up of debris will encourage aerial root growth on the branches which can be damaged during periods of stressful weather. When the crown is kept clean, the plant will get light and air circulation which reduces the chance of disease.

Heading Cuts and Renewal Pruning: *Heading cuts* are used to control shape and size, or to rejuvenate overgrown boxwood. As boxwood mature, they begin to take up more room and frequently outgrow their space. Reducing the overall size of the overgrown boxwood requires some drastic corrective pruning and results in an unsightly plant until the foliage fills in. Many old shrubs can be shaped by removing 6" – 8" of growth over the entire plant and thinning down into the interior stems to a point where new growth is visible. Prune above the new growth. In some cases, old shrubs should be cut back in stages over a two or three year period. In extreme cases, boxwood can be cut to the ground and allowed to generate new growth from the roots. It will take several years for them to regain any size.

236

Shearing: Boxwood are occasionally *sheared* to control the size or the shape of a box hedge or box topiary. While the effect can be spectacular, it is not the natural growth habit and results in dense foliage only on the tips of the plant and prevents any interior growth. Over time, this results in a green, leafy shell and can lead to the decline of the plant. If shearing is necessary, it should be accompanied by thinning to open the plant up to air, light, and moisture. Unlike other types of pruning, shearing is done after new growth has hardened off in late spring, early summer.

FERTILIZING

Boxwood likes neutral soil, a PH of 6.5 – 7.2; neither too acidic nor too alkaline. Before fertilizing, a soil test is a good idea. Apply a little dolomitic lime if the soil is too acidic. *Do not over-feed* boxwood; *feed once in late March or early April* before new leaves emerge. Choose one of the following for your annual fertilization:

The Dixon Gallery and Gardens' Recipe: 1 part 35–0–0 slow-release nitrogen fertilizer, 2 parts dolomitic lime, 4 parts dehydrated cow manure, and 4 parts Milorganite®. A shovelful of this mix is sprinkled around the drip line of each boxwood plant. Amounts will vary depending on the size of plant.

Recipe 2: Use Sta-Green® 12–6–6 according to package directions. If leaf edges are orange and/or gold-tipped, use Epsom salts to correct a magnesium deficiency; also use Epsom salts if leaf color is not a dark green.

Recipe 3: 1 tablespoon Super Thrive®, 2 tablespoons Halt® systemic, 4 tablespoons root stimulator, and 1 tablespoon Epsom salts in a gallon of water. Pour this mixture around your boxwoods once a week for 4 weeks and watch them green up nicely. Use this for a quick fix.

Well-rotted or dehydrated manure is excellent but do not allow it to build up too deeply over roots. Whichever fertilizer you choose, spread evenly over root area and a little beyond the edge of the branches (or dripline). Do not scratch in as shallow roots may be damaged.

PESTS

Leafminers are the major pest of boxwood in the Mid-South. Evidence of infestation consists of blistered spots on leaves followed by general decline of the shrub. Spray with a systemic pesticide containing Avermectin (such as Avid®) in late March or early April when eggs hatch. Spray again in June with a pesticide containing Imidacloprid (such as Marathon® or Merit®).

Southern red mites and boxwood mites are common boxwood pests, causing pale, speckled leaves. Treat by spraying in April and in mid-summer with a miticide or insecticidal soap, paying special attention to the undersides of leaves.

237

Boxwood root rot is caused by poor drainage. Planting the rootball "high" helps with this problem.

Over-wintering scale, leafminers and mites are treated in winter with a dormant oil spray such as Volck® Oil. Spray on a day when the temperature is not expected to fall to freezing.

PROPAGATION

Boxwood is easily rooted from cuttings. For this procedure a cold frame is not needed. Choose a spot in partial shade where the soil is loamy. The addition of 1 part sand to 2 parts soil makes a good rooting mixture. Clippings should be taken in late spring or early summer just as new spring growth has hardened off. Select cuttings 4" – 6" long. Pull clippings apart at the joints, leaving a "heel", or cut, just below a leaf bud. Trim off some of the bushy growth at the top, to reduce water loss due to respiration. Dip end in rooting hormone medium. Insert half the length of each cutting in the ground. From this time on, keep moist. With minimum care about 75% of the cuttings will root, sometimes more. They may be left in the cutting bed the first year. Cuttings may be transplanted bare-rooted to their permanent location when they are about 10" tall.

VARIETIES OF BOXWOOD

Tried-and-true varieties of box as well as newer cultivars are listed below. The sizes given will help in selecting the best species for your landscape use.

TABLE 20. VARIETIES OF BOXWOOD (*BUXUS*)

SCIENTIFIC NAME/ COMMON NAME	COMMENTS
Buxus harlandii **'Richard'**	Easily recognized by its longer leaf with notched tip. Recommended by Southern nurseries as the variety that best stands heat.
B. microphylla var. japonica **Japanese Boxwood**	Loose rounded shrub 3' – 6' high. Wide, rounded leaf; medium green. More resistant to heat, cold, and nematodes than other varieties.
B. microphylla var. japonica **'Morris Midget'**	Very slow-growing dwarf; excellent for edging. Dense green foliage. 'Morris Dwarf' is similar but denser.
B. microphylla var. japonica **'Wintergreen'**	Loose rounded shrub 3' – 6' high. Wide, rounded leaf; medium green. More resistant to heat, cold and nematodes than other varieties. Also known as **Korean**

SCIENTIFIC NAME/ COMMON NAME	COMMENTS
	Boxwood.
B. microphylla var. japonica **'Green Beauty'**	Compact, more tolerant of sun, clay soil and dog urine.
B. microphylla **Littleleaf Boxwood**	3' x 4', dense, round shrub, slow-growing.
B. microphylla **'Compacta'** (same as **'Kingsville'**)	Dwarf, compact, 8" – 10".
B. microphylla **'Curly Locks'**	Branches grow out at unusual, twisted angles; light green, curly leaves. Extremely slow growth, about 1/8" per year.
B. microphylla **'Green Beauty'**	Compact, more tolerant of sun and clay soil.
B. sempervirens **Common Boxwood** or **American Boxwood**	Many named cultivars.
B. sempervirens **'Arborescens'**	Upright, irregular form, dark green foliage, 6' x 3', large leaves.
B. sempervirens **'Argenteo-variegata'**	Leaves variegated with white.
B. sempervirens **'Aurea-pendula'**	Variable, creamy-yellow variegation. Large weeping shrub or small tree, 7' x 6'
B. sempervirens **'Aureo-variegata'**	Leaves variegated with yellow.
B. sempervirens **'Dee Runk'**	Narrowly upright habit, 6' x 2'. Perhaps the best columnar box.
B. sempervirens **'Elegantissima'**	Dark green leaves with white margins, 5' – 8' x 5' – 8' in 15 years.
B. sempervirens **'Fastigiata'**	Dark green, tall, and upright, conical with upright branches.
B. sempervirens **'Handsworthiensis'**	Large, oval, dark green leaf. Strong growing; wide form. Good hedge.
B. sempervirens **'Rotundifolia'**	Rich, bright green, rounded leaf; oval compact habit, 4' x 3' (10' x 8' in 20 yrs).
B. sempervirens	Does not grow well here. Use 'Justin

239

SCIENTIFIC NAME/ COMMON NAME	COMMENTS
'Suffruticosa' **English Boxwood**	Brouwers', 'Green Beauty', 'Green Velvet', or 'Morris Dwarf' instead.
B. sempervirens **'Varder Valley'**	Medium-sized shrub, 3' x 5'; blue-green leaf, broad habit with flattened top.
B. sinica var. insularis **'Justin Brouwers',** and **'Winter Gem'**	Small, medium-green leaf; hardy; somewhat open habit to 2' tall and twice as wide. Foliage turns yellowish brown in winter.
Buxus x hybrids **'Glencoe', 'Green Gem', 'Green Mountain', 'Green Mound',** and **'Green Velvet'**	A great group of compact, hardy boxwoods with good leaf color.

CAMELLIA

CAMELLIA

Camellias are beautiful, broad-leaved evergreen shrubs with dark, glossy foliage, native to woodlands. *Camellia sinensis* is the plant tea is made from, and has been cultivated in China for thousands of years.

Camellia flowers take many forms and come in variations of white, pink, and red. They are used in mixed borders, woodlands, foundation plantings, and as specimens. The *sasanqua* varieties may be espaliered against a wall. *Sasanquas* and the new Akerman hybrids have greater cold hardiness than the *japonicas*. Their combined blooming times extend from September through April.

CULTURE

Camellias, like azaleas, prefer filtered sunlight or partial shade, and a well-drained, acidic (pH 4.8 – 6.0), sandy loam. See *Garden Care – Amending the Soil.* Using azalea-camellia food, shredded oak leaves, and pine bark chips, all of which are acidic in reaction, will help keep the pH where you want it. If planted near masonry foundations or walls, test soil often for alkalinity and, if needed, adjust the soil pH. Bring the soil pH to between 5.5 and 6.0 with garden sulfur. (See *Garden Care – Altering the Soil pH)*

Because of the susceptibility of camellias to extreme cold, some gardeners prefer growing camellias in greenhouses. Many more varieties can be grown and the blooms enjoyed and exhibited far more successfully with this protection. However, early- and late-blooming varieties alike may be grown in the garden provided the site is well-chosen to offer protection from wind and morning sun in winter.

Do not plant against a western wall without shade or tree protection, as the radiated heat from the wall will be detrimental. A northern or eastern exposure is best, where there is protection from the hot midday sun. Avoid locations where there is heavy root competition. The ground should never be cultivated around camellias as their roots are shallow; mulch instead.

Planting too deep is the principal cause of failure with camellias. They should be planted in loose, loamy soil which will settle a couple of inches when watered. Pack amended soil firmly in the bottom of the hole before planting, and set the top of the ball 3" – 4" higher than surrounding ground level. Camellias must have good drainage. If necessary, dig the hole much deeper and put in coarse gravel or rocks to allow the excess water to drain away. Backfill, tamp lightly, and mulch with shredded oak leaves or pine bark chips.

Water well after planting and until camellia becomes established. Lack of sufficient moisture during August through November will cause bud drop. The

241

natural habitats of these plants are areas of heavy rainfall, so it is important to water each time to a depth of several inches.

Container-grown plants may be set out at any time during the growing season. Those balled in burlap should be planted during the winter season, October through March. Camellias may be planted when in bloom so you are sure of the flower color. Keep roots and leaves moist before planting.

Helpful Hint: To keep a camellia bloom, put 1 teaspoon water in the bottom of a brandy snifter or a glass bowl. Place bloom in snifter and cover the top with a glass plate or plastic wrap. It keeps longer.

PRUNING

Camellias respond to pruning and shaping. They can be pruned when cutting blooms or, when needed, immediately after the blooming period, which could be anytime from late fall until early spring depending on the variety. Remove dead, weak, spindly growth whenever found. On plants with heavy bud crops, disbudding results in larger and better flowers.

FERTILIZING

Fertilize twice a year – once in March and again in early June. Use specially prepared azalea-camellia fertilizer which may be purchased at garden stores. Do not over-fertilize camellias.

When leaves get yellowish instead of rich, dark green, the trouble is usually not enough acidity, which in turn makes iron and magnesium unavailable to the plant. This generally occurs in late summer. Treat with Ironite® or Epsom salts, and adjust soil pH with garden sulfur.

PESTS AND DISEASES

Camellias are subject to the following pests and diseases:

Scale, Aphids, Chewing Insects – use an insecticidal soap.

Leaf Gall – Pick off and dispose of deformed or thickened leaves. Damp weather increases this trouble, and dry weather stops it.

Spider Mites – Cause surface of leaves to lose color in a speckled pattern. Use a miticide and spray top and underside of foliage.

Flower Blight – Caused by *Sclerotinia camelliae*, a fungus disease that forms in the base of blossoms and affects only them. Blossoms turn brown, the petals have a veined appearance, and the rotted tissue becomes soggy. The infected flowers should be removed; dispose of all fallen blossoms and leaves. You may need a fungicide; ask your nurseryman for a recommendation. Apply to soil surface in fall, winter, or early spring before blooms appear.

242

VARIETIES OF CAMELLIA

The two best-known types are the *japonicas* and the *sasanquas*, but there are several other species and new hybrids that are worthy additions to the garden. *The Official Nomenclature Book of the American Camellia Society* lists over 30,000 varieties with descriptions and information on each. Consult local nurseries or catalogs for available varieties. By using several species you can have blossoms from September through winter until April. All prefer some shade from hot afternoon sun.

TABLE 21. VARIETIES OF CAMELLIA (*CAMELLIA*)

SCIENTIFIC NAME/ COMMON NAME	HEIGHT	FLOWER COLOR/ BLOOM TIME	COMMENTS
Camellia japonica **Japanese Camellia**	10' – 15' x 6' – 10'	White, red, pink, bicolor/ Sept. – April depending on cultivar	*Japonicas* produce beautiful flowers in many colors. Consider the bloom period and include in your collection early [fall], mid-season [winter] – not recommended outdoors – and late [spring] bloomers. This handsome evergreen has a large 5" x 2.5", dark, leathery ovate leaf. Slow-growing. Many good named varieties. Not as cold-hardy as some others, and can be killed in severe winters.
Camellia sasanqua **Sasanqua Camellia**	2' – 15' x 2' – 10'	White, red, pink, bicolor/ Sept. – Dec.	Its graceful form, profusion of bloom, dark green foliage, and ability to thrive in part sun or shade make it an excellent plant. Leaves and flowers are smaller than *japonica*. Blooms in fall –the flowers come early and are usually finished before the worst of winter. Slow-growing. Many good named varieties. Can be killed back in severe winters.
Camellia reticulata **Reticulated Camellia**	12'+	White to pink/ Dec. – April	Natural growth is more open than *japonicas*. They prefer more sunlight and can stand heat. Well adapted for containers, as they are

243

Scientific name/ Common Name	Height	Flower Color/ Bloom Time	Comments
			not very cold-hardy. Not grown as often as the other varieties.
Camellia hybrids **Ackerman Hybrids**	6' – 8' x 5' – 7'	White, red, pink, bicolor/ Nov. – April	Dr. William Ackerman and Dr. Clifford Parks developed these very useful hybrids by crossing *Camellia oleifera* with *C. hiemalis* or *C. sasanqua* to give superior heat and cold tolerance, albeit they have a slightly less graceful habit than either the *japonica* or *sasanqua*. The spring bloomers have names like 'April Blush', 'April Dawn', 'April Snow', 'Spring Promise' and 'April Kiss'. The winter series have names like 'Winter's Beauty', 'Winter's Snowman, 'Polar Ice', 'Snow Flurry', 'Winter's Hope', and 'Winter's Charm'.
Camellia oleifera **Tea-oil Camellia**	12' – 20'	White to pink/ Oct. – Dec.	A large shrub to 20' with glossy, dark green leaves and fragrant, 2" wide flowers in fall. The most cold-hardy *Camellia* (Zone 6), and one of the parents of many good, new, cold-hardy hybrids.
Camellia sinensis **Tea Plant**	4' x 4'	White, cream, pink/ Sept. – Nov.	Fragrant flowers and shiny green leaves on a compact shrub. Exhibits good cold-hardiness. This is the plant tea is made from and has been cultivated in China for centuries.

244

GARDENIA

GARDENIA

The gardenia (or Cape jasmine) is an evergreen shrub which has extremely fragrant flowers and glossy foliage, and can grow to 9', but is usually around 3' x 3'. The white, cream, or yellow flowers can be single or double. Bloom time ranges from spring to summer depending on variety, and some re-bloom in the fall. The "ever-bloomers" flower intermittently from spring to fall. Plant it near the house so the fragrant flowers may be enjoyed.

CULTURE

Gardenias like moist, acidic soil with lots of humus, much like azaleas and camellias. Add plenty of organic matter, such as compost or ground pine bark. Mulch plants instead of cultivating. Fall or spring is the best time for planting. If gardenias are happy in their location, they are carefree, prolific bloomers; if not, they malinger horribly. Gardenias need protection during severe winters, however, as extreme cold will split the bark causing the plant to die. A sheltered location in high shade with minimum competition from tree roots is best. Gardenias need some sun for setting of buds.

Feed gardenias in mid-March, using an acidic plant food, fish emulsion, or blood meal. Feed the shrubs again in late June to encourage extra flowers on ever-bloomers and faster growth. Do not fertilize gardenias in the fall. Doing so will stimulate tender growth, which may be winter-killed. Gardenias are prone to yellowing foliage; this can usually be corrected by acidifying the soil with Ironite® or Epsom Salt.

Prune shrubs after they have finished flowering to remove straggly branches and faded flowers; pruning at other times may remove latent flower buds. Keep gardenias well-watered throughout the growing season. Well-established gardenias can become very drought-tolerant however. Drip-irrigation will keep water off the foliage and blossoms, and prevent leaf spots. Gardenias resent root disturbance, so try to avoid transplanting. Recover roots with dirt and mulch promptly if winter-heaved.

PESTS AND DISEASES

Several insects and diseases are likely to show up on your gardenia.

Sooty mold may coat gardenia leaves in summer, it is usually due to an infestation of *whiteflies*. These sucking insects look like bits of cotton. While eating your leaves they excrete honeydew and this, in turn, supports the growth of the black fungus called sooty mold. Spray with insecticidal soap solution.

245

Small gray aphids, which cling to leaf undersides, are similar in habit.

Root rot caused by several different fungi can also be a problem, especially in poorly drained soils.

VARIETIES OF GARDENIA

There are approximately 250 species of gardenia worldwide, and most are native to tropical and sub-tropical regions of Asia. Consequently, they like heat and humidity and are well suited to greenhouse or indoor container culture.

The species most suitable for temperate regions is *Gardenia jasminoides* (or *Gardenia augusta*). Common gardenias are reliably ground-hardy in Zones 8 – 10; newer cold-hardy varieties are viable to Zones 7 and 6. Some of the new hybrids and more cold-hardy varieties are given in the following table.

TABLE 22. VARIETIES OF GARDENIA (*GARDENIA*)

SCIENTIFIC NAME/ COMMON NAME	COMMENTS
Gardenia jasminoides (or *Gardenia augusta*) **Common Gardenia** or **Cape Jasmine** or **Cape Jessamine**	The cultivars below belong to this species.
'August Beauty'	Grows 4' – 6' high and blooms heavily from mid-spring to fall. Small leaf and flower.
'Chuck Hayes'	Extra hardy type; Zones 6 – 10. Grows to 4' with glossy evergreen foliage and large, double flowers in summer.
'Daisy'	A more cold-hardy variety.
'Dirr's Hardy Select'	Cold-hardy.
'First Love'	Larger than 'August Beauty' with large flowers in spring.
'Fortuniana'	Large leaf, 4" double, carnation-like flower. Also known as *Gardenia fortunei*.
'Frostproof'	Has narrow, 2" long, evergreen leaves; small white flowers; and is cold-hardy.
'Golden Magic'	Reaches 3' tall and 2' wide, and has golden yellow flowers.
'Griffith's Select'	Grows 3' x 4'; has a small single blossom; cold-hardy.

SCIENTIFIC NAME/ COMMON NAME	COMMENTS
'Kleim's Hardy'	Is hardy to 10°F and grows to 3' tall with single flowers in summer.
'Mystery'	Is the best-known selection. It has 4" – 5" double white flowers, and can reach 6' – 8'. Not as cold-hardy as some.
'Radicans'	Grows to only 12" tall and spreads 2' – 3', with small, dark green leaves, and 1" wide, double flowers in summer. It is not very cold-hardy.

247

HOLLY

ILEX

Hollies belong to the genus *Ilex*, which includes over 400 species worldwide. There is great diversity among hollies with respect to leaf size and texture, berry color, growth habit, and so on; and good new cultivars are appearing every year. Whether used as a focal point, an anchor for the perennial border, privacy screening, wildlife refuge, floral arrangement material, or winter color, the genus *Ilex* offers a wide range of reliable and low-maintenance choices.

CULTURE

Almost all hollies are dioecious (male and female flowers are on separate plants) and pollination of the female is necessary for production of fruit. The fruit is technically a drupe, but is referred to as a "berry". Male plants in the vicinity pollinate the females (courtesy of bees). The ideal pollinator is a male of the same species as the female, but cross-pollination generally occurs among hollies with overlapping bloom periods. Many dwarf cultivars are propagated from male plants that do not produce fruit.

Hollies prefer slightly acidic soil and good drainage (although certain deciduous hollies, noted below, tolerate wet feet) and are planted in either spring or fall. The root ball should be planted level with or slightly higher than surrounding grade; creating a collar of soil and mulch around the root ball will facilitate watering during the first growing season. Hollies generally tolerate some shade, but most will perform best in sun. They are undemanding stalwarts of the garden.

PRUNING

Minimal pruning is necessary if an appropriate holly is selected for the site; the lists below and other sources provide guidance on the ultimate size and growth habit of specific varieties. If pruning is necessary or desired for purposes of shaping or restoration, it is best done in the winter or early spring while the plant is dormant. Hedges can be sheared more than once during the growing season to maintain a tidy appearance, but avoid pruning in the early fall which might subject tender new growth to freeze damage.

All too often, a gardener encounters a naturally tall holly planted at the foundation of a house. If removal is not an option, such a holly can be severely pruned to 6" – 12" above the ground in the late winter with acceptable re-growth obscuring the cuts by the end of the growing season. Alternatively, "tree-up" the overgrown holly by cutting off lower branches and shaping the top to keep it off the roof shingles.

FERTILIZATION

Fertilize hollies in the spring with a slow-release complete fertilizer having 4:1:2 or 3:1:2 ratios of nitrogen, potassium, and phosphorus, such as 18–6–12. If hollies look anemic, check the pH of the soil and the planting depth, but they are exceptionally durable and uncomplaining.

PESTS AND DISEASES

Pests and diseases are generally not serious problems for hollies given reasonable care. In the Mid-South, the most common problems are *scale, leafminers, mites, and root rot.*

Susceptibility is generally associated with poor soil drainage or aeration, improper planting, or inadequate fertilization. Horticultural oil and soap sprays will help control scale, mites and other pests. During the hot and dry summer period, use a miticide when mite damage is first noticed.

VARIETIES OF HOLLY (*ILEX*)

The Chinese hollies (*Ilex cornuta*) have a glossy, very spiny, dark green, leathery leaf and large red berries. Their upright growth habit and response to pruning make them excellent hedges. The spiny leaves keep out children and dogs. They generally grow too large for foundation planting.

The Japanese hollies (*Ilex crenata*) all have very small, smooth leaves, and black berries. They grow compactly, even when unpruned, and are often used as a boxwood substitute. This family produces many dwarf forms.

The following three tables list hollies according to their landscape use and mature size. Avoid having to prune for size-control by choosing a holly in the correct size range for your site.

TABLE 23. HOLLIES FOR SPECIMENS AND SCREENING HEDGES (EVERGREEN)

SCIENTIFIC NAME/ COMMON NAME	SPECIMEN & SCREEN	COMMENTS
Ilex **Red Holly™ series:** **'Festive',** **'Little Red',** **'Oak Leaf',** **'Cardinal',** **'Robin',** etc.	10' – 15' x 5' – 8'	Patented series of small, pyramidal, ornamental trees; lustrous green leaves; red fruit; reddish new growth; stature appropriate for small properties, large containers or mixed borders.

Scientific Name/ Common Name	Specimen & Screen	Comments
Ilex aquifolium **English Holly**	20' x 10'	Red fruit; glossy, very dark green, spiny, curled leaves. Most beautiful of all hollies. Give afternoon shade; and acid soil. Less hardy than others.
Ilex cassine **Dahoon Holly**	18' – 25' x 10' – 15'	Small, red or yellow fruit on stalks; narrow, light green, gray-backed leaves. Loose growth; prune to keep dense. Tolerates wet feet.
Ilex cornuta 'Burfordii' **Chinese 'Burford' Holly**	20' x 20'	Bright red fruit in abundance; smooth pale gray bark. Effective in limbed-up tree form.
Ilex cornuta **'Needlepoint' Chinese Holly**	15' x 10'	Red fruit; narrow leaves; conical habit. Also known as 'Willowleaf' and 'Anicet Delcambre'. Excellent for massing or screen.
Ilex latifolia **Lusterleaf Holly**	20' x 10'	Red fruit in clusters; spineless, magnolia-like, deep green leaves. Slow grower; bold, dense accent. Subject to scale.
Ilex opaca **'Old Heavyberry' American Holly**	30' x 20'	Abundant red fruit; dull dark green leaf; native to U.S. Loses most of its leaves in March.
Ilex vomitoria **Yaupon**	20' x 6'	Persistent, red fruit; small oval leaf; can be sheared into hedges if desired; or left to become a small graceful tree. 'Katherine' has yellow fruit.
Ilex vomitoria **'Pendula' Weeping Yaupon**	9' – 15'	Weeping tree form.
Ilex vomitoria fastigiata **Columnar Yaupon**	12'	Columnar tree form.
Ilex x **'Emily Bruner'**	20' x 15'	Abundant red fruit; lustrous, dark green leaves; pyramidal habit.
Ilex x **'Mary Nell'**	20' x 15'	Red fruit; glossy, green leaves; pyramidal habit.
Ilex x **'Nellie R. Stevens'**	20' x 15'	Red fruit; very shade tolerant; vigorous grower; dark green leaves.

250

SCIENTIFIC NAME/ COMMON NAME	SPECIMEN & SCREEN	COMMENTS
Ilex x aquipernyi **Aquipernyi Holly**	6' – 20' x 6' – 20'	Red fruit; lacy foliage. Hardier because cross between English *I. aquifolium* and American *I. pernyi*.
Ilex x attenuata 'Fosteri' **Foster's Hybrid Holly**	25' x 10'	Deep-red fruit; slender, graceful, pyramidal habit; responds well to shearing and/or limbing-up; small, dark green, softly-spiny leaves.
Ilex x attenuata **'Humes' Holly'**	30' x 10'	Any of Dr. Humes' hybrids are very desirable. Loose conical tree, spineless leaves of light green, fluorescent red berries.
Ilex x attenuata 'Savannah' **'Savannah' Holly**	30' x 20'	Abundant red fruit; outstanding light green leaves; less spiny. Benefits from fertilizer and Ironite application in the fall; broad pyramidal form.
Ilex x attenuata 'East Palatka' **'East Palatka' Holly**	30' – 40'	Smooth, light green leaf, scattered red berries. Vigorous grower. Tree. Similar to Foster and Savannah hollies.
Ilex crenata 'Rotundifolia' **Bigleaf Japanese Holly**	8' – 12'	Rapid grower, excellent for hedge. Upright, rounded habit.
Ilex glabra **Inkberry**	4' – 8' x 6' – 10'	Smooth, glossy leaves. Black berries. Good for naturalizing or clipping; suckering shrub. Cold-hardy. Likes moist, acidic soil; tolerates shade, best in sun. 'Nigra', 'Nordic', and 'Compacta' are good.
Ilex x koehneana **Koehne Holly**	20' x 15'	Bright red fruit; dense broad pyramid; heat and drought tolerant. 'Wirt L. Winn' and 'San Jose' are good cultivars.
Ilex pernyi **Pernyi Holly**	9' – 12' x 4' – 6'	Small-toothed leaf, large red berries. Medium, pyramidal size. Used in hybridizing. Spare, open growth.

251

TABLE 24. HOLLIES FOR FOUNDATION PLANTING AND LOW HEDGES (EVERGREEN)

SCIENTIFIC NAME/ COMMON NAME	LOW & MEDIUM HEDGES	COMMENTS
Ilex cassine myrtifolia **Myrtle Dahoon**	3' – 4'	Very small, narrow, dark green leaves, black berries.
Ilex cornuta 'Burfordii Nana' **Dwarf 'Burford' Holly**	6' x 6'	Dark red fruit; lustrous dark green leaves with single spine on most; dwarf, but too large under low windows; can be pruned almost to ground and sheared annually to maintain if height is a problem and removal not feasible.
Ilex cornuta 'Carissa' **'Carissa' Chinese Holly**	3' – 4' x 4' – 5'	Dense dwarf with single-spined leaves having translucent or off-white rim; waxy, dark green; heat and drought tolerant (as are other two Chinese hollies above).
Ilex cornuta cornuta **Dwarf Chinese Holly**	2' x 2'	Hybrid, no berries.
Ilex cornuta 'Rotunda' **'Rotunda' Chinese Holly**	4' x 8'	Viciously spiny leaves can make an effective barrier; medium green; very hardy; rarely fruits.
Ilex crenata 'Compacta' **'Compacta' Japanese Holly**	6' x 6'	Dense, globose habit; small, dark green, spineless, oval leaves; no fruit.
Ilex crenata 'Convexa' **'Convexa' Japanese Holly**	2' – 7' x 3' – 9'+	Dense with small, shiny convex leaves; black fruit; can be sheared for hedging; can be used as a boxwood substitute; part shade; susceptible to spider mites.
Ilex crenata 'Helleri' **'Heller's Japanese Holly**	2' – 4' x 2' – 5'	Mounding, compact habit useful for hedging or as a border for paths; stiff stems; medium green oval leaves, not glossy; fruit rare; can be sheared to maintain formal hedge. Japanese in feeling.
Ilex crenata hetzii	3' – 5'	Dark shiny green leaf, leaf larger

SCIENTIFIC NAME/ COMMON NAME	LOW & MEDIUM HEDGES	COMMENTS
Hetz's Japanese Holly		than *I.* 'Convexa'. Vigorous grower, semi-spreader, can be espaliered.
Ilex crenata microphylla **Microphylla Japanese Holly**	2' x 3'	Foliage lighter green than *I.* 'Convexa'*;* makes good, low hedge. Small, smooth leaves.
Ilex crenata nummularia **Nummularia Japanese Holly**	1' – 1½'	Small leaves, cloud form.
Ilex crenata 'Repandens' **'Repandens' Japanese Holly**	2' – 3' x 4' – 6'	Compact and spreading; narrow, lustrous; dark green leaves; no fruit.
Ilex crenata 'Steeds' **'Steeds' Japanese Holly**	6'+ x 4'	Pyramidal habit; minimal pruning required to achieve topiaried boxwood appearance; dark green lustrous leaves; no fruit.
Ilex vomitoria **'Schillings' or 'Stokes Dwarf' Dwarf Yaupon**	3' – 4' x 3' – 4'	Compact, mounded cushion; wine-colored new growth; small, light green leaves; no fruit; 'Nana' very similar but smaller and without wine-colored new growth; can be sheared to maintain formal hedge.

Note: Numerous other *Ilex crenata* cultivars are widely available; typically distinguished by habit and size but generally appropriate for foundation plantings and low hedges.

TABLE 25. HOLLIES FOR ACCENTS AND WINTER COLOR (DECIDUOUS)

SCIENTIFIC NAME/ COMMON NAME	SIZE	COMMENTS
Ilex decidua **Possumhaw Holly**	18' x 15'	Abundant and persistent red fruit; shiny green foliage prior to leaf drop; tolerates wet soil. 'Warren's Red' & 'Council Fire' have orange fruit and 'Finch's Golden' has yellow fruit; pollinators include 'Red

SCIENTIFIC NAME/ COMMON NAME	SIZE	COMMENTS
		Escort', but plentiful male *I. opaca* in the area generally suffice.
Ilex serrata **Japanese Winterberry**	6' x 10' or larger	Abundant red fruit ripening early and persisting during winter; cut branches effective in arrangements; 'Leucocarpa' has white fruit; male *I. serrata* needed for pollination; best in moist soil.
Ilex serrata 'Xanthocarpa' **'Xanthocarpa' Finetooth Holly or Japanese Winterberry**	6' – 12'	Deciduous holly from Japan and China; bears yellow berries. Moist soil.
I. serrata x *I. verticillata* hybrids **'Bonfire' and 'Sparkleberry' Winterberry hybrids**	10' x 12'	Abundant brilliant red fruit that persists; upright habit; pollinated by 'Apollo'; tolerates wet soil.
Ilex verticillata **'Aurantiaca' Winterberry Holly**	5' x 6'	Abundant, large orange fruit; 'Red Sprite' and 'Bright Horizon' have large red fruit; pollinators include 'Jackson' and *I. serrata* males.
Ilex verticillata **'Winter Red' Winterberry Holly**	8' x 8'	Bright red fruits persist; cut twigs last well in arrangements; 'Sunset' has red-orange fruit; 'Simpson's Early Male' blooms mid- to late-season and can pollinate "Southern" *I. verticillata* plants such as these.

HYDRANGEA

HYDRANGEA

Hydrangeas are the premier deciduous shrubs of the Southern garden. They are pest-free and easy to grow. The large, long-lasting flowers have great visual impact at quite a distance, and are breathtaking when massed. Your season of bloom can extend from spring through fall if you grow oakleaf, bigleaf (both mophead and lacecap varieties), and panicle hydrangeas.

In the past, a late spring frost could kill all flower buds that were beginning to swell on last year's wood, and there would be no flowers that year. Today's improved hybrids bloom on old *and* new wood, so you will always have blossoms.

CULTURE

Hydrangeas prefer high, light shade; some protection from wind and hot afternoon sun; and rich, acidic, sandy loam. A few varieties, including 'Tardiva' or 'Pink Diamond' (*H. paniculata*) can take full sun.

As the name implies, hydrangeas like a lot of water. The foliage on many hydrangeas will wilt in the hot, direct sun, regardless of how well-watered the plant is, and it perks back up when the sun passes. Hydrangeas will also look wilted when they do need water, so be aware that they are not as drought-tolerant as say, hollies.

Flower color is highly variable and if you do not care whether your flowers are blue, pink, or lavender, simply follow normal garden practices. The following information on changing soil pH is directed to the reader who wants a particular color.

FLOWER COLOR

The flower color of mopheads and lacecaps is determined by the concentration of free aluminum ions in the soil. Flowers are blue if aluminum ions are available to the plant and pink if aluminum ions are either not present or not chemically available. The chemical availability of aluminum ions is in turn dependent on the soil pH (alkalinity or acidity). The flowers of a given hydrangea variety might tend to be pink or tend to be blue, but their actual color will be the result of soil conditions. Hybridizers are working hard on developing hydrangeas that will have the advertised flower color regardless of soil pH.

To grow a **blue** hydrangea, ensure that aluminum is present by adding aluminum sulfate to the soil around the hydrangeas. Authorities recommend that a solution of ½ oz. (1 Tbsp.) aluminum sulfate per gallon of water be applied to plants (which are at least 2 – 3 years old) throughout the growing season. *Important*: water plants thoroughly in advance of application and put solution on cautiously, as too much can burn the roots.

255

In order for the aluminum to be chemically available to the plant, the pH of the soil should be acidic (5.0 – 5.7). Aluminum sulfate itself can be used to lower the pH of the soil; or use garden sulfur. Another method for lowering the pH is to add organic matter to the soil, such as pine bark chips or pine needles or shredded oak leaves. (See *What Effect Do the Various Soil Amendments Have on pH?* in the *Garden Care* chapter) If your soil is acidic and contains aluminum (which is very likely the case) the color of the hydrangea flower will automatically tend toward shades of blue and/or purple.

The choice of fertilizer will also affect the flower color. An (N–P–K) fertilizer low in phosphorus (P) and high in potassium (K) is helpful in producing a good blue color (25–5–30 is good). Super-phosphates and bone meal should be avoided when trying to produce blue. Planting hydrangeas near a concrete foundation or sidewalk will often affect the color since the pH of the soil may be raised considerably by lime leaching out of these structures, making it difficult to obtain blue.

For hydrangea blooms to be **pink,** the plants must *not* take up aluminum from the soil. If the soil naturally contains aluminum, one must try to keep it away from the hydrangea's system. Following are a few tricks that might work:

Add dolomitic lime several times a year. This will help to raise the pH. Shoot for a pH of about 6.0 to 6.3 (if it goes above 6.4, hydrangeas may experience an iron deficiency). Since hydrangeas take up aluminum best at lower pH levels, raising the pH will help to keep the bluing effect of aluminum out of the hydrangea's system.

Use a fertilizer with high levels of phosphorus, such as bloom boosters, in the range of 10–30–20 or 18–22–8. Phosphorus helps to prevent aluminum uptake in hydrangeas.

In areas with acidic soils containing aluminum which naturally produce blue hydrangeas, consider growing pink hydrangeas in large pots. If hydrangeas are grown in pots, it would be best to use soil-less mixtures, since these potting mixes would probably not have aluminum in them.

If you live in a hot climate, it is unlikely you will ever see a "true red" hydrangea. No matter how convincing those pictures in the catalogs are or how much lime is added to the soil, one can only achieve a very deep pink, but not a true red, at least here in the South. The new 'Lady in Red' hybrid has red leaf veins and either pink or blue lacecap flowers that age to burgundy.

One can rarely change the intensity of a color (how vivid or pale the color). The intensity develops for a number of reasons: the heredity of a particular hydrangea variety, weather conditions (hot or cold, humid or dry), health of the plant, and possibly other natural factors. Fertilizing hydrangeas once or twice a year may result in a little more saturated color simply because the health of the plant may be improved.

The **white** hydrangeas are white, and can NOT be changed to pink or blue by the grower. A few *H. macrophylla* such as 'Sister Theresa' and 'Teller White', and *H. serrata* 'Fuji Waterfall' have white flowers regardless of soil pH. Other white-flowered hydrangea species include *H. quercifolia, H. paniculata,* and *H. arborescens.* The flowers on oakleafs and paniculatas are often tinged with chartreuse, cream, or rose and change colors through the season.

PRUNING

Hydrangeas range in height from 2' – 12', and have a lovely natural habit. If you do not cut flowers for bouquets or drying, but leave them on the bush, the winter effect is quite beautiful and provides food for birds.

If your hydrangea has outgrown the space, a good way to accomplish size-pruning, as with azaleas, is to cut blooming branches for flower arrangements. Because hydrangeas grow freely from the base of the plant, old branches of any species may be cut to the ground. For pruning and management practices, the genus may be divided into four groups based on habits of growth and flowering.

Group 1: Those that flower terminally on current season's (new) growth: This includes *Hydrangea arborescens* 'Annabelle'; *H. paniculata* 'Tardiva' and *H. paniculata* 'Grandiflora' Pee Gee. Some newer *H. macrophylla* cultivars bloom on both old and new wood and may be size-pruned in late winter if necessary, without sacrificing all flowers.

The *paniculatas* should be pruned back in late winter or early spring if desired for size control. 'Annabelle', however, needs to be cut to 6" – 12" high in late winter so lush new growth will produce maximum flowers.

Group 2: Those which are low to medium height and produce new growth freely from the base of the plant: This includes *H. macrophylla* (the mopheads and lacecaps) and *H. serrata. Hydrangea macrophylla* flowers on strong buds that have wintered over (old wood). These plants bloom on old wood and should be pruned in mid-summer after they have flowered.

However, if the plant is overgrown and needs to be thinned, it is best to remove about a third of the old branches to the ground in mid-winter. Leave the old flower heads on the plant for protection. In late winter or early spring, when the new growth buds are swollen, cut back to strong new buds, removing weaker and older stems. Late spring frosts frequently damage flower buds on old-wood bloomers, and there are no flowers that year. Look for the new cultivars that bloom over a long period on both old and new wood. Re-bloomers are pruned after flowering.

Group 3: Those which form large shrubs, retaining a more permanent framework: This includes our native *Hydrangea quercifolia*, the oakleaf hydrangea. This species needs little pruning, other than removing old woody, diseased, spindly and damaged branches. This can be done whenever needed, although late winter or early spring is a good time to shape this plant.

Group 4: Those which climb by aerial rootlets: *Hydrangea petiolaris* and *Schizophragma* vines have a three-dimensional branching habit; over time, the branches reach out and away from the support and can be cut back closer to the main stem. This slow-grower will not require much shaping. However, normal pruning consists of cutting back unwanted extension growths as they are produced during the summer.

HYDRANGEAS AS CUT FLOWERS

Hydrangea flowers are beautiful in arrangements, either fresh or dried. For fresh arrangements, cut flowers in early morning when a majority of the florets have opened. Unless properly conditioned, hydrangeas tend to wilt in flower arrangements. Cut and split stems and immerse in boiling or hot water (or vinegar) for 30 seconds. Then immerse stems in deep, cold water adjusted to pH of 4.0 by adding 2 tbsp. of vinegar and 2 tbsp. sugar to quart of water to "harden" the flower.

Another method involves crushing the stems, burning the tips with fire, and then "hardening" overnight neck-high in tepid water.

A third method of conditioning requires the stem be cut and split, and the whole flower head and stem be submerged in cold water overnight.

For dried flower heads, cut flowers when the petals have a papery-feeling. Immerse stems with papery flower heads into an upright vase that contains about 2 inches of hot water. Allow stems to draw up the water; do not add more water once the vase is dry. Alternatively, dry by "hanging" as described in *Preparing Cut Materials for Flower Arrangements.*

VARIETIES OF HYDRANGEA

Bigleaf or French Hydrangeas (*Hydrangea macrophylla*) are broadly classified as either *mophead* (more formally known as *hortensia*) or *lacecap* and there are literally hundreds of named cultivars; they are late-spring to early-summer bloomers.

The *mophead* has large beautiful round clusters of sterile flowers borne at the branch tips. Older mophead varieties like 'Nikko Blue' and 'Ayesha' are very fine. Newer hybrids bloom on both old and new wood. The re-blooming mophead varieties like 'Penny Mac', 'Endless Summer', 'Lady in Red', and 'All Summer Beauty' are excellent choices.

The *lacecap* flower is smaller and flatter with a non-showy fertile center surrounded by the showier sterile flowers giving a pinwheel effect. Among the notable Bigleaf hybrids are the so-called 'Teller Series' which refers to twenty-six fine lacecaps developed in Switzerland. 'Blue Billow', 'Blue Wave', and 'Lilacina' are also good lacecaps.

Mountain Hydrangeas (*H. serrata*) are smaller woodland species from Japan. Several fine lacecap-flowered cultivars, such as 'Bluebird' and 'Preziosa', are available. 'Fuji Waterfall' is an exceptionally beautiful 4' x 5' shrub with white double-lacecap flowers and pristine foliage. They flower in early-summer.

Panicle Hydrangeas (*H. paniculata*) are large coarse shrubs, but cultivars like 'Tardiva', 'Pee Gee' (*H. paniculata grandiflora*), and 'Praecox' are much improved over the species in form, habit, and flower. They bloom later in the summer than other species.

Oakleaf Hydrangeas (*H. quercifolia*) are among the finest of all garden shrubs and can become quite large, say 10' x 10', or they can be as small as 3' x 4'. 'Alice', 'Snow Queen', 'Snowflake' and the dwarf 'Pee Wee' are all excellent choices. Oakleafs are early bloomers starting in May, and hold their flower bracts all season. The blooms change color through the season from white to greenish-rose to tan. Birds love to pick at dried flower heads.

Smooth Hydrangea (*H. arborescens*) is available in several cultivars, but the best is probably 'Annabelle'. This shrub is recommended by everyone who grows it. Cut it back to 6" – 12" in the spring, as it blooms on new wood. In summer, smallish, mophead flowers emerge chartreuse and turn white; has medium textured leaves; native.

Climbing Hydrangea Vines (*H. anomala petiolaris* and *Schizophragma hydrangeoides*) are slow growing woody vines for partial shade. They have cream colored lacecap flowers in early summer.

The list below gives some good choices in each of the hydrangea categories.

TABLE 26. VARIETIES OF HYDRANGEA (*HYDRANGEA*)

NAME	FLOWER TYPE	COLOR	SIZE	BLOOM TIME
Hydrangea anomala petiolaris **Climbing Hydrangea Vine**	Lacecap	white	Vine	spring
Schizophragma hydrangeoides **Japanese Hydrangea Vine**	Lacecap	white	Vine	early summer
Schizophragma integrifolium **Chinese Hydrangea Vine**	Lacecap	pale pink	Vine	early summer
Hydrangea arborescens **'Annabelle' Smooth Hydrangea**	Mophead	white	4' – 5'	summer
H. aspera sargentiana **Sargent Hydrangea**	Lacecap	white/ lavender	6' – 8'	summer
H. involucrata 'Tama Azasai', 'Hortensia'	Lacecap	light purple/pink	3' – 4'	summer
H. macrophylla **Bigleaf or French Hydrangea**	Mophead or lacecap	the following are all of		

Name	Flower Type	Color	Size	Bloom Time
		this species		
'All Summer Beauty'	Mophead	light pink/blue	4' – 5'	repeat bloomer
'Alpengluhen'	Mophead	rich red	4' – 5'	summer
'Amethyst'	Mophead	creamy pale purple	4' – 5'	summer
'Ayesha'	Mophead	pink cupped	4' – 5'	summer
'Beaute Vendomoise'	Lacecap	white/blue	5' – 7'	late summer
'Blushing Bride'	Mophead	white	5' – 7'	repeat bloomer
'Bouquet Rose'	Mophead	pink	2' – 3'	summer
'Endless Summer'	Mophead	blue	5' – 7'	repeat bloomer
'David Ramsey'	Mophead	blue/pink	4' – 5'	repeat bloomer
'Decatur Blue'	Mophead	blue/pink	4' – 5'	repeat bloomer
'Generale Vicomtesse de Vibraye'	Mophead	brilliant blue	5' – 7'	repeat bloomer
'Lady in Red'	Lacecap	white/burgundy	3' – 6'	repeat bloomer
'Lanarth White'	Lacecap	white/blue-white	4' – 6'	summer
'Mme Emile Moulliere'	Mophead	white/blue eye	5' – 7'	repeat bloomer
'Mme Faustin Travouillon'	Mophead	blue	5' – 7'	summer
'Nigra'	Mophead	blue/dark stems	4' – 6'	summer
'Nikko Blue'	Mophead	blue	4' – 6'	summer
'Otaksa'	Mophead	blue	3'	summer
'Paris'	Mophead	deep pink/purple	4' – 6'	summer
'Penny Mac'	Mophead	pink/blue	3' – 6'	repeat bloomer

NAME	FLOWER TYPE	COLOR	SIZE	BLOOM TIME
'Pia'	Mophead	pink	2' – 3'	summer
'Teller White'	Lacecap	white	4' – 6'	summer
'Tokyo Delight'	Lacecap	white/red	5' – 7'	summer
H. paniculata **Panicle Hydrangea**	Panicle	white to rose		
'Pink Diamond'	Panicle	white to rose	8' – 10'	late summer
'Pee Gee'	Panicle	white	8' – 10'	late summer
'Pee Wee'	Panicle	white, smaller	6' – 10'	late summer
'Tardiva'	Panicle	white	8' – 15'	late summer
H. quercifolia **Oakleaf Hydrangea**	Panicle	white		
'Alice'	Panicle	white	8' – 10'	spring
'Pee Wee'	Panicle	white	3' – 4'	spring
'Snow Queen'	Panicle	white	6' – 10'	spring
'Snowflake'	Panicle	white	7' – 8'	spring
H. serrata **Mountain** or **Serrata Hydrangea**	Lacecap	blue		
'Fuji Waterfall'	Double Lacecap	white	3' – 5'	summer
'Bluebird'	Lacecap	blue	3' – 5'	spring
'Grayswood'	Lacecap	white to mauve	5' – 6'	summer
'Preziosa'	Mophead	white to mauve	4' – 5'	summer
'Wilsons 7820'	Lacecap	pink to blue	3' – 4'	spring

261

ROSE

ROSA

The rose is the queen of flowers, long accepted as the symbol of love. Roses come in all colors; many are fragrant, some are evergreen, some deciduous. Rose bloom peaks during May and June and again in August to early fall. However, most modern roses bloom throughout the summer.

CULTURE

Most growers agree that there are five MUSTS for cultivating these beautiful flowers:

1. Roses must have good drainage; a raised bed is best.

2. Roses require at least 6 hours of sun. Full sun is best.

3. Roses must be fertilized and watered.

4. Roses require disease and insect control.

5. Roses require pruning and mulching.

PLANNING THE ROSE BED

Pick a well-drained location away from trees and other shrubs so that the roses will not have to compete for nutrients. A location with strong morning sun is preferable so the sunlight can dry any moisture on the bush, which helps prevent diseases. Ideally, the gardener should prepare the bed in the fall and let it rest until spring. A good general soil mixture for the rose garden is 1/3 native Mid-South soil (clay soil), 1/3 blended organic matter (which could include ground pine bark, compost, or well-rotted manure), and 1/3 coarse sand.

Buy roses from reputable local nurseries or mail-order companies recommended by the American Rose Society. Purchase grade #1 roses whenever possible, since these generally out-perform the #1 ½ and lesser graded roses. The rose bush should have at least 3 strong canes that are 12" to 15" long and no smaller than a pencil in diameter.

Many new hybrids have been developed for black spot resistance, improved fragrance, reblooming, thornlessness, and increased color range. Antique floribunda and polyantha roses, many of which have thrived at abandoned homesteads and cemeteries for years with no human intervention, are being re-introduced into the genetic mix for their hardiness and fragrance.

PLANTING

Roses may be moved in November or December, after they are completely dormant. Good times to plant new roses are late February – April before it gets too hot.

Roses require firm planting, good air circulation, and plenty of room for their roots to spread, so make sure each bush has ample room when fully grown (plant them at least three feet apart). In preparing roses for planting, remove all dead canes and any canes smaller than a pencil in diameter, leaving the three or four strongest canes that are spread out around the bud union (the bud union is the bulbous knot that the canes are growing from and is located just above the roots).

Do not use regular rose food when planting new roses. Use root stimulators, fish emulsion and seaweed blends or compost teas at planting time, and repeat a couple of times about one week apart. After the rose becomes established (usually a month after planting) and has good, new growth, you can begin the monthly cycle of feeding the roses.

Bareroot Roses: Dig the planting hole approximately 2' wide and 2' deep, and add 2" – 4" of gravel to the bottom. Make a mound of soil in the center of the hole and set the rose on top of the mound with the roots spread as evenly as possible around it. The mound should be high enough so that when the rose is set on top of the mound, the bud union is slightly higher than the soil surface (about one inch). With the rose in place, fill the hole with the soil mixture, lightly packing and firming the soil around the roots as you go.

When the hole is filled, water thoroughly with a root stimulator and water solution to remove any air pockets and settle the soil. This action will probably cause the soil level in the hole to drop, so keep adding soil and watering until the level in the hole is equal to or slightly higher than the surrounding soil. (Hint: Soak bareroot roses overnight in the root stimulator solution prior to planting).

Potted Roses: Dig a hole approximately 2' wide and 2' deep. Add approximately 2" – 4" of gravel to the bottom of the hole, and then add enough soil so that when the pot is placed in the hole, the bud union is about one inch above ground level. Cut the bottom of the pot and, holding it in place, lower the pot into the hole, and then remove the pot's bottom. Next, cut the pot on each side from bottom to top, and carefully remove the rest of the pot. Add enough soil to fill the hole, and tamp and firm the soil around the rose. Water the rose thoroughly with root stimulator solution and add more soil if the watering settles the soil below grade.

Raised beds effectively solve the drainage problem in soils with high clay content. A number of materials can be used for the retaining walls; raised beds should be a minimum of 12" deep. (See *Garden Care – Planting and Maintaining* for details)

After completion, fill the raised bed with the rose soil mix mentioned above, leaving room at the top for the added mulch layer. Many nurseries have similar soil mixes available, and all that is left for you to do is to add the final

263

touches such as lime, manure, alfalfa meal, rock phosphate, and green sand for potassium.

MAINTAINING ROSES

Roses need regular and frequent **watering** to continue producing beautiful blooms. Despite their water requirements, they must have good drainage because roses cannot stand "wet feet". It is best to water roses rather infrequently with deep, thorough soakings. Frequent, light watering keeps the feeder roots close to the surface so that they do not grow deep. This causes drought-intolerance, and really stresses roses during very hot weather.

Water roses twice a week if it does not rain; some find it necessary to water every couple of days during extremely hot weather. Water in the morning, if possible; avoid wetting the foliage in the afternoon or evening, which can lead to black spot or fungus problems. Soaker hoses buried beneath the mulch are an excellent means of watering roses. Overhead sprinklers may be used as long as the foliage can thoroughly dry before nightfall.

Disbudding develops one full-size flower on the stem of roses that bloom in clusters. Remove all but the dominant, central flower bud from each cluster to produce a large flower. On hybrid teas, remove any bud below the terminal bud for specimen blooms. Remove the largest and smallest bud from a floribunda cluster for specimen clusters.

Deadheading is the act of removing faded flowers to stimulate growth and create new blossoms. The general rule is to cut the old bloom off about ¼" above a five-leaflet. However, since first-year roses need to be treated more gently, cut just above the first set of three leaves when working with these bushes.

Popular rose **mulches** in the Mid-South are shredded pine bark mulch, pine straw, homemade compost, and stable manures. When mulching a rose bed, cover completely with mulch 1" to 2" deep, but adjust the depth of the mulch at the base of the rose so the bud union is approximately an inch above the mulch. Bareroot roses and roses just sprouting need extra protection, so lightly cover the bud union with mulch when planting, and uncover the bud union when leaves are plentiful.

Winter Protection: In September or October apply one half cup of 0–20–20 fertilizer around each bush. This will help thicken cell walls and make roses more winter-hardy.

In mid-November or after a couple of good hard freezes, prune bush roses back to about three feet. This is called "wind pruning" because it keeps the winter winds from rocking the roses in the soil and damaging the roots.

Next make a mound of mulch or fallen leaves 12" to 15" high up on the canes. This will protect the bud union from freezing and will help prevent dieback of the canes if exposed to extremely cold temperatures. Keep the mounded mulch in place throughout most of the winter and remove it when the roses are pruned back in the spring.

FERTILIZING

One of the most important aspects of successfully growing roses is having the soil pH fairly neutral, around 6.5 – 6.7. (See *Garden Care – Altering your Soil pH* for more)

In February, top dress the rose bed with a good organic fertilizer. Roses love manure (horse, cow, chicken, etc.), mushroom compost, and manure blended with alfalfa meal and humate, just to name a few.

In March, when the roses have 2" – 3" of new growth begin feeding them with prepared rose foods, which contain the proper nutrients for growing beautiful flowers. Fertilome Rose Food® and Espoma Rose Tone® are both very good for the Mid-South area. Feed roses monthly with the dry rose foods until mid-August; then stop so the shrubs harden off before winter. Water the granular fertilizer in immediately so it does not burn.

Roses can be given auxiliary feedings with liquid or water-soluble plant foods such as Monty's Joy Juice®, Miracle-Gro for Roses®, or a bloom booster. This can also be done monthly, two weeks after applying the dry food, but is optional. Since liquid plant foods do not last as long, they can be used until mid-September, then discontinue fertilizing and allow roses to harden off.

Other Feeding Tips:

- Osmocote® is a slow-release plant food that only needs to be applied once a season if monthly feedings are not possible.

- Apply a handful of magnesium sulfate (Epsom Salt) around each bush in March to encourage new basal breaks.

- Apply about a cup of alfalfa meal or pellets around each bush in the spring. Alfalfa contains a natural growth stimulant that will encourage greener growth and stronger stems.

PESTS AND DISEASES

Insect and disease control is another important aspect of growing roses successfully in the Mid-South. Most roses grown in this area will require regular treatments of insecticides and fungicides.

In January or February, on a day when it is not expected to freeze during the night, spray the rose canes and the rose bed with lime–sulfur or a combination of lime–sulfur and horticultural oil for control of over-wintering diseases and insects.

Around mid-March, when there are about 2" – 3" inches of new growth, begin spraying the roses on a weekly basis with rose sprays containing both insecticides and fungicides. Since insects and diseases can sometimes become resistant to a spray, it is a good idea to change products after 2 or 3 applications. In early summer, if the insects and diseases are under control, move to spraying every 2 – 3 weeks but remain observant, and if a problem arises, address it before the situation gets out of control. Spray early morning and not during the heat of the day

265

to avoid burning, and be sure the roses have been well-watered the day before spraying to avoid a possible chemical burn on the foliage.

An alternative to spraying is to apply a product containing the fungicide, insecticide, and fertilizer about every six weeks. These products are poured directly onto the soil around the rose and are absorbed into the plant through the root system. This type of "systemic" protection eliminates spraying and protects the plant from pests even during periods of rain.

Although most roses require regular spraying to control insects and diseases, there are new roses being introduced each year with better disease resistance, such as the 'Knockout' and 'Carefree' series. In selecting cultivars for long stems and perfect flowers, the hybrid tea roses had, over time, become odorless. Hybridizers have rediscovered the antique, fragrant, evergreen bush roses which have inherent disease-resistance. The introduction of this genetic material into modern roses has resulted in wonderful new cultivars that are relatively trouble-free and very fragrant. Check with your local nurseryman or catalogs for more information.

TABLE 27. COMMON ROSE PROBLEMS AND CONTROLS

Aphids	Acephate®, Neem Oil, Imidacloprid (Merit®), Permethrin®, Safer Soap®
Spider mites	Horticultural Oil, Neem Oil, Imidacloprid (Merit®), Permethrin®, Acephate® , Safer Soap®
Thrips	Acephate®, Imidacloprid (Merit®), Permethrin®, Spinosad
Beetles	Carbaryl (Sevin®), Permethrin®, Acephate®, Imidacloprid (Merit®)
Budworms	Imidacloprid (Merit®), Spinosad, Acephate
Rose cane borers	Carpenters' glue or nail polish
Black spot	Banner® (for prevention), Triforine, Daconil®, Liquid copper, Mancozeb®, Thiophanate Methyl, (Halt®, Cleary's 3336®), Remedy®, Neem Oil
Powdery mildew	Bayleton®, Banner®, Triforine, Liquid copper, Daconil®, Neem Oil
Mosaic virus	Prune out infected areas; sterilize pruners with disinfectant between each cut.

(The above products are generally available to the home gardener)

PRUNING

Roses must be pruned throughout the year. In early winter after a couple of freezes, cut back all long growth to keep the wind from rocking the plants loose. In mid-to-late February, cut back all dead wood, crossed canes, and weedy growth. Suckers (fast-growing shoots growing from below the graft) should be removed completely by breaking them off below the soil where they are connected to the trunk. The average pruning height for **floribundas** and **hybrid teas** is 15"–18", but taller growing varieties and **grandifloras** can be left at 24". Cut at a 45-degree angle ¼" above an outward-facing bud. Keep the center of the bush open by removing blind shoots, crossed canes and branches with sick, yellow leaves. Cut off lower leaves about 8" from the ground to let in air and make the bush easier to water. Paint cut ends with carpenter's glue, nail polish, or a similar sealer to prevent the invasion of stem borers.

Climbers and **ramblers** are pruned differently, since many of them bloom on previous season's growth. For a climber that only blooms once a year, prune immediately after blooming. In February, for climbers that bloom on old and new growth, first remove dead and diseased canes; then remove the oldest canes, leaving 5 to 8 of the strongest canes. These remaining canes should be tied to a trellis, wall or other support.

Miniature roses are not as demanding in their pruning requirements. Cut out all dead and dying tissue, cut back about halfway or more and attempt to prune slightly above outward facing buds, although this is not as critical as with hybrid teas. For additional information on pruning, please refer to the chart below on Roses.

VARIETIES OF ROSE

It is impractical to recommend named cultivars as there are so many. Rather the various types of roses are described in general terms.

TABLE 28. VARIETIES OF ROSE (*ROSA*)

NAME	HEIGHT	BLOOM	COMMENTS/ PRUNING
Climbing	10' – 50'	Depends on variety, many bloom all summer.	Train canes horizontally for more profuse blooms. Climbing roses do not climb naturally and must be tied to supports. Unsupported climbers are hybrid teas, Floribundas and Grandifloras. **Prune:** Remove all dead or weak wood. In summer as soon as flowers fade, shorten laterals (flowering stems originating from main canes) to 3½" to 6". Be sure

267

Name	Height	Bloom	Comments/ Pruning
			to cut to a twig containing 5 or 6 leaves. Varieties which bloom only once should have some of the older, dark canes cut back to the base. Do not let seedpods form on climbers.
Floribunda	2' – 4' average	Blooms are somewhat smaller than hybrid tea, single, semi-double, or double. Usually borne in clusters.	Hardy, prolific bloomer all summer. Use as an informal hedge or in flower border. Compact bush. Most are low-growing. **Prune:** Remove twiggy interior growth. Keep 6 to 8 canes and try to leave the bush open with enough room for flower clusters to develop.
Grandiflora	8' – 10'	Blooms prolifically from spring to frost. Produces quantities of flowers like a floribunda. Flowers usually clustered, but sometimes single. They often have the shape and larger size of the hybrid tea.	Tall, vigorous bush which is extremely hardy. Use as tall hedge or back-ground plant. **Prune:** Allow grandifloras to grow to their full size. After pruning in February, their cane height is about 3' to 4' and may support as many as 8 structural canes.
Hybrid Tea	2½' – 7' but most are 3' – 5'	Flowers are double, often fragrant on long, straight stems. Long-lasting blossoms, good for cutting. Most beautiful of all roses.	Should be in a bed for roses alone. **Prune:** Keep 3 to 6 strong, good canes. Canes should be well-spaced to allow good air circulation. Remove old non-producing canes at the bud union.
Miniature	4" – 13"	Some have solitary flowers. Others bear clusters. Most are not fragrant.	Natural dwarfs; good for edging in beds, and rock gardens, and as houseplants. Hardy. Need 6 hours of sun, but some shade is desirable.

NAME	HEIGHT	BLOOM	COMMENTS/ PRUNING
		Many bloom all summer.	Plant a little below nursery level (they have not been grafted) to promote root development. **Prune:** Maintenance varies with the variety. Most miniatures should be pruned to within 2" of the ground in February.
Old-fashioned	3' – 10', depending on variety	Very fragrant. Often blooms in early summer, generally only once.	Hardy, little maintenance, not as beautiful as newer varieties. Hard to find. See catalogs. **Prune:** Similar to hybrid tea.
Polyantha	3' – 4'	Clusters of small blooms. Blooms in spring and intermittently during summer. Very few are fragrant.	Very hardy, small leaves on compact plant. Can resist some drought conditions. **Prune:** Cut polyanthas back by one-third yearly.
Shrub	6' – 8'	Many are single. Most are fragrant. Not as much color variety as others. Older varieties bloom once in late spring. New varieties bloom all summer.	Tough, tolerates poor soil. Use for hedges. Disease-resistant. **Prune:** When young, prune only to shape. When mature, cut twiggy growth and very old, dark canes. Shorten other canes by one-third in February.
Tree Roses	to 5'	Depends on variety.	Man-made, grafted plants. Hybrid tea and grandiflora are most popular types. They are good for formal gardens and are very elegant. Trunk must be wrapped or painted with water-base paint to protect from hot summer sun. In winter, partially uproot the plant, lay it on its side and cover with soil, held in place by evergreen branches. They must be planted with a support stake. Place stake on hottest side (south or west).

269

NAME	HEIGHT	BLOOM	COMMENTS/ PRUNING
			Prune: Remove any growth from the trunk which is below the upper bud union.

VIBURNUM

VIBURNUM

Every garden should have at least one viburnum. These well-behaved members of the honeysuckle family can be either shrubs or trees, depending on how they are pruned. There are 120 – 150 species of *Viburnum* ranging in size from 2' – 30'; some are evergreen or semi-evergreen; some deciduous with outstanding fall foliage; some have fragrant flowers and showy berries; some are native, some exotic. Leaf size and texture varies greatly among the species. It can be rounded, lance-shaped, or toothed; glossy, velvety, or rough. Landscape uses include foundation planting, hedges, screens, specimens, and accents in the mixed border.

Mature specimens in full flower can be breathtaking. Flowering starts in early March and as late as June for some varieties. Viburnums have either white or pinkish flowers; some are exquisitely fragrant. The flowers themselves come in three distinct forms:

1) Flat clusters of florets,

2) Flat umbels outlined with larger flowers, resembling lacecap hydrangeas,

3) Dome-shaped, snowball-like clusters.

Prune after flowering to control size, if desired. Almost all viburnums produce attractive clusters of drupe-type fruits which are relished by birds and wildlife. However, most are not self-pollinating and will require another variety to cross-pollinate with in order to produce fruit. Fruit color can be yellow, orange, pink, red, blue, or black.

CULTURE

These are easy-to-grow shrubs, thriving in full sun to partial shade. They prefer a moderately fertile soil with a pH of 5.5 – 6.8, but are very adaptable.

When purchasing plants, choose a young specimen, since they can be difficult to transplant when they get older. Early spring is the best time for transplanting, giving them a full season to get adjusted.

Viburnum has no unusual culture requirements; water, fertilize, mulch, and prune as described in *Garden Care*.

PROPAGATION

Most commercially available viburnums are crosses and cannot be started from seed. You can propagate from softwood cuttings during the summer or simply layer branches in the fall. By spring there should be a new plant you can cut off and move.

271

PESTS

Viburnum are bothered by very few pests, which accounts for their ever-increasing popularity. Recently the Viburnum Leaf Beetle (*Pyrrhalta viburni* – Paykull) has been introduced into North America from Canada and is making its way south; it is capable of great damage and is being closely watched.

VARIETIES OF VIBURNUM

As there are so many excellent viburnums to choose from, your local nurseryman can help find the right one(s) for your landscape. The U.S. National Arboretum's Dr. Donald Egolf introduced 18 excellent cultivars, among them the *Viburnum utile* 'Conoy', *V. carlesii X V. x carlcephalum* 'Cayuga', and *V. plicatum* var. *tomentosum* 'Shasta'.

Awabuki viburnum is a large, handsome evergreen with dark, glossy foliage. Doublefile viburnum is one of the most elegant flowering shrubs with its horizontal layered habit and snow white flowers. Tea viburnum is a rather coarse shrub with outstanding red fruits.

Native species offer beautiful flowers (not fragrant), great fall color, and fruit for birds and wildlife. They are tough, hardy, undemanding, and pest-free. The tree-forms, like black-haw and maple-leafed viburnum, may require some pruning to achieve the desired shape, but are becoming popular replacements for dogwoods which are currently dying from anthracnose all over the Southeast.

Good choices for creating standards are *Viburnum plicatum var. tomentosum* 'Newport' (10' H x 12' W), *Viburnum carlesii* 'Compactum' (3' – 4' H & W), and *Viburnum* x *bodnantense* 'Dawn' (10' H x 6' W).

The list below is sorted according to deciduous forms (most are fragrant), evergreen varieties, and tree-forms.

TABLE 29. VARIETIES OF VIBURNUM (*VIBURNUM*)
Key: E = evergreen, Semi-E = semi-evergreen, D = deciduous

DECIDUOUS VIBURNUMS – MOST ARE FRAGRANT			
Viburnum x burkwoodii **Burkwood Viburnum**	Semi-E	8' x 8'	Round clusters of pink or white star-shaped flowers; extremely fragrant; red to black berries; dark red fall foliage that remains late. Not particular to soil or position; soil should not be too dry. Many varieties: 'Mohawk' is 8' – 10'; 'Anne Russell' is compact. Blooms in March.
V. carlesii **Koreanspice** or **Mayflower Viburnum**	D	5' x 5'	Most fragrant, pink buds open to white snowball clusters of flowers; dark green foliage can be either velvety or rough like sandpaper. Red fall foliage. 'Compactum' and 'Cayuga' are both good. Blooms in April.
V. x juddii **Judd Viburnum**	D	6' – 8' x 4' – 6'	More open in habit. Wonderful fragrance. Nice velvety texture, pale olive foliage. Very reliable. Blooms late March.
V. dentatum **Arrowwood Viburnum**	D	10' x 10'	This native grows wild in woodlands and bogs, full sun to part shade. Fast growing, suckering (new shoots were used for arrows by Indians). Creamy flowers in spring; great fall colors. Foliage is larval food for azure butterfly, fruit eaten by many birds. 'Morton' has round upright habit; purple fall foliage. 'Blue Muffin' has intense blue fruits; compact (3' – 5' tall) and makes great hedge or foundation plant. 'Synnestvedt' and 'Emerald Luster' are lustrous dark green.
V. dilatatum **Linden Viburnum**	D	5' x 8'	One of the showiest for both flowers and red fruit clusters. 'Catskill' only gets about 5' x 5'. Unpleasant smelling flower.

273

DECIDUOUS VIBURNUMS – MOST ARE FRAGRANT			
V. lantanoides (formerly *V. alnifolium*) **Hobble Bush**	D	8' x 12'	Native to eastern US. A bit rampant as branches take root wherever they touch soil. Moist shade. Flat white umbels in May followed by red fruit which ages to blue-black. Fuzzy leaves, red gold in fall.
V. lentago **Nannyberry**	D	12' x 10'	Prefers moist shade but will tolerate sun and dry soil. Coarse and suckering. Creamy lacecap-type flowers in mid-May. Fruits pass from green to yellow to pink to deep blue, and are loved by birds. Native.
V. macrocephalum **Chinese Snowball Viburnum**	D to Semi-E	6' – 10' x 6' – 10'	Dense, rounded shrub with 3" – 8" white, snowball flowers in May. Good for large gardens, spectacular in bloom. Will re-bloom in September. No fruit. Semi-evergreen.
V. nudum **Swamp-haw or Possumhaw Viburnum**	D	12' x 6'	Native Long Island to Florida. Full sun to part shade. White flowers in late May. Fruit changes from green to white, to pink, to blue. Reddish-purple in fall. 'Winterthur' has brighter red fall color, and is self-sterile so needs to be planted with another *V. nudum*.
V. opulus **European Cranberry Bush Viburnum**	D	8' – 12' x 10' – 15'	Not the showiest, but some good cultivars. 'Xanthocarpum' is an exceptional white lacecap-type with persistent yellow fruit. 'Nanum' is a slow-growing dwarf variety (2' x 3'). 'Roseum' has snowball flowers resembling hydrangeas that start out pale green and turn white. Fruits are plentiful and much loved by birds & wildlife.

DECIDUOUS VIBURNUMS – MOST ARE FRAGRANT			
V. plicatum **Japanese Snowball Viburnum**	D	6' – 10' x 6' – 10'	Cultivars below are better than the species. Flowers 2 weeks later than *V. p. v. t.,* below. 'Kern's Pink' (aka 'Roseace') has soft pink snowballs, purple edging on leaves, grows 6' – 10'H. 'Chyverton' is low & spreading (4'x15'); floriferous.
V. plicatum var. *tomentosum* **Doublefile Viburnum**	D	10' x 12'	Flowers in flat double rows; great orange-red fall color and red-black fruits. Some are fragrant. Very elegant, horizontal, layered habit; good against brick. 'Mariesii' has white lacecap flowers in May; red fruits; 6'x8'. 'Shasta' is excellent also: white flowers in May; red fruit; 6'x10'.
V. setigerum **Tea Viburnum**	D	8' – 12' x 6' – 8'	Tall, upright, multi-stemmed shrub with open, leggy habit. Produces stalked clusters of small, non-descript white flowers in spring. Outstanding orange to red fruits that ripen in Nov.

EVERGREEN VIBURNUMS			
V. awabuki **Awabuki Viburnum**	E	15' x 10'	Very beautiful shrub. Large, dark, lustrous leaves. White spring flowers, clusters of red fruit. Needs some shelter and good drainage to protect from winter damage. Derived from *V. japonicum,* confused with *V. odoratissimum.*
V. davidii **David Viburnum**	E	3' – 5' x 3' – 5'	Native to China. Most attractive. Dark green leaves; dark blue fruit. Tiny, tubular white flowers are borne on stem tips. Requires both a male and female to bear fruit.
V. x pragense **Prague Viburnum**	E	10' x 10'	Rounded, well-branched; a cross between leatherleaf and service

EVERGREEN VIBURNUMS			
			viburnums. Glossy, dark green leaves are narrow and deeply veined. Small, tubular white flowers form domed umbels.
V. rhytidophyllum **Leatherleaf Viburnum**	E	15' x 12'	Native to China. Semi-evergreen and can look shabby in winter. Large, flat cluster of yellowish-white flowers followed by red to black berries; deeply-veined leaves. Not hardy in North unless protected. 'Willowood' flowers in fall. 'Allegheny' is good variety; blooms in May.
Viburnum tinus **Laurustinus Viburnum**	E	6' – 12' x 3' – 6'	Slow-growing, erect to vase-shaped shrub with pink-white flowers in spring followed by blue berries in late summer. Useful as hedge or specimen. Not fussy about soil. Sun to light shade. Not as cold-hardy as some viburnum. 'Compactum', 'Clyne Castle', 'Variegata'.
V. utile **Service Viburnum**	E	4' – 6' x 4' – 6'	Parent of Burkwood and Prague, the Service Viburnum is heat-tolerant with narrow, evergreen leaves. 'Conoy', 'Chesapeake' and 'Eskimo' are good cultivars. Blooms early to mid-spring.

NATIVE TREE-FORM VIBURNUMS			
V. acerifolium **Maple-leafed Viburnum**	D	3' – 6' x 4'	Eastern woodland native. Fine border plant, open canopy casts dappled shade. Creamy umbels in May; black fruits loved by birds. Fall foliage is pink.

NATIVE TREE-FORM VIBURNUMS			
V. prunifolium **Black-haw Viburnum**	D	12' x 8'	Fine in sun or shade; tolerates dry soil. Good substitute for dogwood or crabapple. Pebbled bark, red leaf stems, and yellow stamens in white flowers are distinctive. Dark blue fruit makes jelly if birds don't eat them first. Red to purple fall foliage.
V. trilobum or *V. opulus* var. *americanum* **American Cranberry Bush**	D	8' – 15' x 12'	Large, sterile white flowers surround small fertile ones in center; bright red berries (not actual cranberries, but edible and may be used for jelly); burgundy red fall foliage. Makes good screen or hedge. Prefers cooler climate. Blooms in April.

VINES

Vines offer a variety of foliage texture and flower color, and many are evergreen. Vines can be pruned and trained for such uses as privacy screening, shading a pergola or arbor, and covering unsightly fences. Small-leaved vines can be trained onto wire supports in containers to create topiaries. Small annual vines are often used to drape gracefully from hanging baskets. Vines can also be useful in narrow areas where there is no space for shrubs. Clematis vines can be allowed to entwine through roses, fothergilla, sweetshrub, or viburnum to give twice the flowering effect.

Pay attention to the alleged size of the vine you are considering planting in your space. If unpruned, many vines will just keep on growing, and some develop a very substantial woody framework. A so-called 40' vine can swallow your house if left on its own for several years. By contrast, a 10' annual vine will never overwhelm you.

Give vines a suitable support on which to climb and consider the heft and vigor of the vine you want to plant. Use a 4" x 4" trellis or iron framework for heavy non-clinging vines, like Armand clematis or wisteria. Light-duty trellises and wire frames are fine for smaller, lightweight vines like 'Betty Corning' clematis or morning-glory vine. Or, simply use wall (or masonry) nails with flexible ties attached for securing small runners. Raffia, breathable plastic tape, or twine is good for tying vines. Remember: climbers need support, and clingers adhere to any surface.

PERENNIAL VINES

When planting, dig a large hole, adding humus, sand, pine bark chips, and a little slow-release fertilizer. Refer to *Garden Care* for general instructions. Water thoroughly and do not let vines dry out. A spring feeding before flowering is adequate.

279

If planting next to the house, keep in mind that the soil around a building may have a lot of concrete debris which will kill acid-loving plants. Remove construction debris and add good soil.

Pruning is important. Vines which flower on new growth must be pruned very early in spring, and all vines may be pruned immediately after blooming. Do not permit unrestrained growth to conceal interesting architectural features or damage your structure. Rampant vines can weave themselves under house siding, cornice or fascia boards, and pry them loose, creating leaks. If you have ever seen the stronghold of an old, neglected wisteria, akebia, or trumpet vine, you have some idea of the muscle-power of vines.

TABLE 30. PERENNIAL VINES FOR THE MID-SOUTH

SCIENTIFIC NAME/ COMMON NAME	COMMENTS
Actinidia kolomikta **Kiwi Vine**	Deciduous climber to 20'. White spring flowers are insignificant but fragrant. Foliage is attractive, heart-shaped, and variegated green with pink and white. Fruit borne on female plant in fall.
Akebia quinata **Five-leaf Akebia**	Semi-evergreen climber. Delicate curly foliage, mahogany flowers – fragrant. Invasive. Blooms early spring.
Ampelopsis brevipedunculata **Porcelain Berry Vine**	Variegated leaf with turquoise blue and green berries in the fall. Deciduous; climbs with tendrils; sun.
Antigonon leptopus **Coral Vine**	Climber. White or bright pink flowers. Hardy Zones 8 – 10; if grown in Zone 7, the evergreen leaves will die back. Mulch well over winter and it should re-sprout from root; or treat as annual and replant yearly. Sun, moist. Blooms all summer to fall
Bignonia capreolata **Cross Vine**	Evergreen in the South. Yellow trumpet flower; sun. Prune hard after flowering. Can get very large if allowed. Blooms early summer.
Campsis radicans **Trumpet Vine** or **Trumpet Creeper**	Creeper up to 30' but can get bigger. Orange and scarlet tubular flowers. Can be trained into standard. Sun. Rank growth pattern. Native vine. Attracts hummingbirds. Blooms all summer.
Celastrus scandens	Climber. Yellow or orange berry in fall,

SCIENTIFIC NAME/ COMMON NAME	COMMENTS
Bittersweet	inconspicuous flower. Deciduous. Blooms in spring
Clematis **Clematis** See Special Article below.	Many varieties; deciduous, woody climber. Handsome red, pink, white or purple flowers. Plant in sun with roots in shade or heavy mulch. Bloom time is variable, spring through fall.
Cocculus carolinus **Carolina Moonseed**	Deciduous, woody climber. Red fruit in clusters, attractive foliage. Keep moist. Blooms in summer.
Euonymus radicans **Euonymus**	Trailer or climber. Many varieties. Evergreen; look for scale-resistant varieties. Blooms in spring.
Ficus pumila **Fig Vine** or **Creeping Fig**	Thin, green, heart-shaped leaves. Clinging stems, desirable for foliage. May die back in winter but recovers. Does well in hanging baskets, topiary, or covering walls.
Gelsemium sempervirens **Carolina Jasmine** or **Carolina Jessamine**	Woody, evergreen; graceful climber. Very fragrant yellow flower; native. Sun. Blooms in mid-spring.
Glechoma hederacea 'Variegata' **Variegated Creeping-charley** or **Ground Ivy**	Good for hanging baskets. Hardy perennial.
Hedera helix and spp. **English Ivy** See Special Article below.	Many varieties, hardy evergreen creeper and climber. Blooms in spring.
Hydrangea anomala petiolaris **Climbing Hydrangea Vine**	Woody, deciduous clinger, shade- and moisture-loving. Slow-growing. Fragrant, white flower clusters in summer.
Jasminum floridum **Florida Jasmine**	Evergreen climber; arching stems clad in glossy trifoliate leaves. Yellow flowers. Sun or shade. Blooms in spring.
Jasminum humile **Jasmine**	Many varieties. 'Revolutum' is an evergreen climber. Yellow flower. Sun or shade. Blooms in spring.
Lonicera japonica **Japanese Honeysuckle**	Fragrant yellow flowers. Invasive. Blooms in June. There are many good new *Lonicera* cultivars which are better-behaved than the

281

SCIENTIFIC NAME/ COMMON NAME	COMMENTS
	species.
Lonicera sempervirens **Trumpet Honeysuckle**	Orange, yellow, or scarlet trumpet flowers; fragrant. Sun. Often used on mail boxes. Non-invasive native vine, keep pruned. Deciduous or evergreen depending on climate. Blooms in summer.
Lygodium japonica **Japanese Climbing Fern**	Dainty, lacy-leafed fern. Light to partial shade. Grows to 10'+. Can be invasive in deep South.
Lygodium palmatum **Climbing Fern**	Hand-shaped leaves on a delicate, ferny 8' – 15' evergreen vine. Shade.
Macfadyena uniquis-cati **Cat's Claw**	Evergreen clinger. 4" yellow trumpet flowers; Sun, dry soil. Very tender, prefers greenhouse. Blooms in spring.
Parthenocissus quinquefolia **Virginia Creeper** or **Woodbine**	Clinger. 5-leaved, often confused with poison ivy (3-leaved). Scarlet in fall. Insignificant bloom.
Parthenocissus tricuspidata **Boston Ivy** See Special Article below.	Fast-growing; sturdy.
Passiflora incarnata **Passion Flower** or **Maypop**	Climber. Marvelous lavender flower; edible fruit. Sun. Invasive native vine. Blooms in early summer.
Polygonum aubertii **Silver Lace Vine** or **Chinese Fleece Vine**	Twining native vine, 20'. Greenish-white, fragrant flowers in long, drooping panicles. Sun. Zone 5 – 10. Pest-free. Blooms in summer.
Rosa banksiae **Banksia Rose** or **Lady Banks Rose**	The only thornless climbing rose. Evergreen. Not hardy above Zone 7. Clusters of yellow, lavender, or white tiny roses. Blooms June – August.
Rosa laevigata **Cherokee Rose**	Evergreen climber, 15'. Fragrant, white single flowers, 2" – 3" across. Not hardy in North. Blooms in summer.
Schizophragma hydrangeoides **Japanese Hydrangea Vine**	Woody, deciduous, shade-loving. Faster growing than *Hydrangea anomala petiolaris*. White lacecap flowers in summer.
Smilax glauca	Climber. Spreads rapidly. Sharp prickles,

SCIENTIFIC NAME/ COMMON NAME	COMMENTS
Smilax	insignificant bloom. Undesirable. Sun. Blooms in summer.
Smilax lanceolata **Jackson Vine**	Evergreen, hardy climber; can be invasive. Good for out-of-water decoration. Blooms in spring.
Vitis rotundifolia **Muscadine Grape** or **Scuppernong** or **Southern Fox Grape**	Heavy green screen in summer. Many varieties; see catalogs. Grapes can be used for jelly or wine. Can be invasive. Native vine. Blooms in spring,
Wisteria floribunda **Japanese Wisteria**	Hardier than Chinese. Flowers white, lavender, pink; woody framework. Fast grower. Fertilize in fall. Blooms in spring. Magical effect in flower.
Wisteria sinensis **Chinese Wisteria**	Vigorous climber. Shorter racemes than *W. floribunda.* Bluish violet, fragrant flowers. Prune roots about 3' from main trunk for heaviest flowering. Can be trained into standard. Sun. All wisteria, if allowed to run rampant on gates, fences, and gutters, will pull them apart.

283

SPECIAL ARTICLES ON SELECT PERENNIAL VINES

CLEMATIS

CLEMATIS

The *Clematis* genus is unusually pest free, reliably perennial, and bears magnificent blooms in many colors, shapes, and sizes. Like boxwood, "clematis" is both the singular and the plural. Clematis prefer their heads in the sun and their feet in the shade. Give them 5 to 6 hours of sun, and either plant ground covers, perennials, or small shrubs in front of their trellis.

Dig a hole large enough to accommodate a mature rootball (about one cubic foot) and amend the soil to make **neutral-to-alkaline sandy loam** (pH 6.7 – 7.2) by adding dehydrated manure, sand, compost, a handful of bone meal, and some dolomitic lime. (See *Garden Care–Soil Basics* and *Garden Care–Altering the pH of Soil* for more detail) Set the crown a couple of inches below soil level since **clematis is planted deep**; latent buds will develop if the brittle woody stem gets damaged or broken. Clematis likes rich, well-drained soil. Apply 1 cupful of lime plus small amount of commercial fertilizer to each plant in spring. Keep well-watered in hot, dry weather. In winter, protect stems with covering of leaves, straw, or other loose material.

Provide support for climbing and carefully help fragile new growth to attach. The brittle woody stems of clematis should be protected at ground level with a half-circle of chicken wire or decorative wire cage to prevent their being damaged when weeding. Some clematis species, like *Clematis integrifolia,* are small, light-weight sprawlers rather than climbers; they are usually grown in the perennial border and allowed to drape over other flowers.

TABLE 31. VARIETIES OF CLEMATIS (*CLEMATIS*)

CLEMATIS HYBRIDS
Florida Group – Most hybrids have semi-double to double large flowers, bloom in late spring on last year's wood, and are pruned after flowering is completed. **'Bell of Woking'** – mauve, double; re-bloomer **'Duchess of Edinburgh'** – double, white with green shading; re-bloomer **'Kathleen Dunford'** – semi-double, rosy purple
Jackman Group – Popular, large-flowered variety, *C. jackmanii*, blooms on new

growth in July or August with some varieties flowering until frost. Stems can be cut back hard before buds swell; or the stems may be cut back to 4" – 6" from origin, thus allowing a larger framework to develop.

'Comtesse de Bouchard'– rose to rich pink; prolific bloomer; grows in partial shade

'Crimson Star'– large, bright red flowers

'Hagley Hybrids'– pink flowered; grows in partial shade

'Jackmanii'– popular, hardy grower, purple blossoms, 5" across

'Jackmanii alba'– white blooms, 5" across with bluish tinge

'Jackmanii rubra'– red variety of above

'Jackmanii superba'– dark violet-purple and larger

Lanuginosa Group – This group of hybrids derived from *C. lanuginosa* will flower as early as June if a portion of the previous year's growth is left. If cut back to within 2' – 4' of the ground each spring, new shoots will grow quickly and more abundant bloom can be expected later in the summer. Some within this group produce double flowers on old wood and single flowers on new wood.

'Henryii'– choice, pure white, 5", wax-like blooms, good for cutting; strong grower

'Elsa Spath'– profuse, intense blue flower

'Nelly Moser'– small red stripe on lavender petals; free-flowering; very popular

'Ramona'– large, lavender-blue flowers with dark anthers; June bloom on old wood

Patens Group – This group is derived from a wild Japanese species, *C. patens,* used in creating hybrids because of its long bloom period from May to July. Typically flowers on old wood; may have smaller re-bloom in late summer. Prune dead and broken growth in spring. After flowering, a portion of old shoots should be cut back severely to encourage them to branch, thus producing flowering wood for the next spring.

'Lasurstern'– deep lavender-blue

'Marie Boisselot'– large white blooms; vigorous and free-flowering

'The President'– popular, rich purple flowers

285

Viticella Group – This summer-flowering group of hybrids derived from *C. viticella* can be pruned back hard in the spring. If greater height is desired it is possible to retain the woody lower framework and reduce the previous season's growth to within 6" of their origins on the more permanent woody framework.

'Madame Julia Correvon'– red-flowered; cut to ground in spring

'Ville de Lyon'– flowers hot pink, 4" across; vine 6' – 10' tall

C. x **'Betty Corning'**– prolific, dainty, blue pixie hat blooms continuously from mid-spring to late-summer; 7'.

C. x **'Durandii'** – old cultivar; four dark-blue recurved sepals with yellow center; sprawling, rather than climbing; very long bloom period.

OTHER CLEMATIS SPECIES

Clematis armandii – **Armand clematis** is evergreen, 10' – 15', with clusters of fragrant, small, white 4 – 7 sepaled flowers in March – May on previous season's growth. 'Apple Blossom', 'Farquhariana' (pink form), and 'Snowdrift' are cultivars.

Clematis cirrhosa – **winter clematis** has glossy evergreen foliage and cream flowers in late winter. Needs little pruning; 10' long.

Clematis heracleifolia – non-climbing vine, 1' – 3', pale blue flowers. 'Mrs. Robert Brydon'– small, pale blue flowers in late summer.

Clematis integrifolia – small, non-climbing vine, 1' – 3', with blue pixie hat flowers in summer. Allow it to sprawl over perennials in the flower border. A favorite in sunny English gardens. Cut back to 6" in early spring.

Clematis montana – **anemone clematis** is a vigorous, almost rampant, vine to 30' with white or pink, 2" diameter, 4-sepaled flowers in May – June. Fine used to cover walls or arbors. 'Alexander' and 'Grandiflora' have white flowers; 'Elizabeth' and 'Superba' have pink flowers.

Clematis orientalis – **Oriental clematis** is more restrained (10' – 20') and has yellow flowers, 2" in diameter, in August – September. Often bears fruits while flowers are still opening. Similar to *C. tangutica,* but more delicate.

Clematis tangutica – **golden clematis** has tiny, golden bells in June – July; fall seed pods are good for arrangements. The most interesting yellow clematis available; 'Bill MacKenzie' is vigorous with larger yellow flowers. From China.

Clematis terniflora or *C. paniculata* – **sweet autumn clematis** is old-fashioned with fragrant, white, feathery flowers in August – October; very hardy and rampant grower to 20'. Needs strong support structure.

Clematis texensis –**Texas** or **scarlet clematis** has 1" nodding red chalice flowers. 'Duchess of Albany' has pink blooms from May – July. 'Countess of Onslow', 'Gravetye Beauty', and 'Major' are other cultivars. Almost shrub-like growth to 6' – 10'.

Clematis virginiana – **virgin's bower** is a handsome vine 15' – 20' with festoons of white 4-sepaled flowers from July – September. Climber; let ramble over slopes and rocky places.

Clematis viticella – **Italian clematis** has purple 1" – 2" diameter, 4-sepaled flowers in July – August. Grows to 10' with dainty, nodding, bell-like blooms. 'Abundance', 'Kermesina', 'Plena', and 'Rubra' are good cultivars.

PRUNING CLEMATIS

Flowering will diminish and bottom growth will be bare and leggy unless clematis is pruned every year or so. How to prune depends on the variety you grow. There are 3 categories of clematis for pruning purposes:

1. Spring Bloomers
2. Summer or Fall Bloomers
3. Repeat Bloomers

If you don't know which pruning category your clematis falls into or even what type of clematis it is, watch the plant for a season and check when and how often it blooms. Basically it comes down to whether the plant blooms on new or old wood, and then how large a plant you want your clematis to be. Here's a quick list of when clematis varieties bloom and what pruning category to put them.

SPRING BLOOM	SUMMER/ FALL BLOOM	REPEAT BLOOM
C. alpina	C. crispa	C. florida
C. armandii	C. x durandii	
C. cirrhosa	C. heracleifolia	
C. macropetala	C. integrifolia	
C. montana	C. x jackmanii	
C. patens	C. lanuginosa	
	C. orientalis	
	C. tangutica	
	C. terniflora or C. paniculata	
	C. texensis	
	C. viticella	

1. SPRING BLOOMERS

- Spring blooming clematis flower on last year's growth. Prune them back as soon as they finish blooming in the spring and they will have the whole season to put on new growth and set buds for next year.

- You can prune vigorous growers almost back to the ground if that suits your purpose, but it's not necessary.

- Slower growers should be treated more cautiously, pruning just enough to shape the plant or to keep it in bounds.

- If there is very old wood on the plant, avoid cutting into it, since it is less likely to re-sprout. That's another good reason to prune your vines regularly.

2. SUMMER AND FALL BLOOMERS

- Summer and fall bloomers flower on the current seasons' growth. You don't have to prune summer and fall bloomers at all, but they will continue to grow, probably becoming a tangled mess, and flowering will eventually diminish.

- Pruning seems beneficial and should be done either while dormant or when just waking out of dormancy.

- Clematis in this category can be hacked back to about 12", if necessary. Something like sweet autumn clematis (C. terniflora), that will reach out and swallow the rest of your garden, will benefit from this drastic pruning.

- However, if you have a summer or fall bloomer that you would like to remain long, perhaps to cover an arbor or grow through a tree, prune just to a healthy leaf bud.

- If you've been a bit negligent about pruning a summer or fall bloomer and would like to do some remedial pruning, you may sacrifice some of this year's blooms, but it should be worth it in the long run.

3. REPEAT BLOOMERS

- This group is a little tricky. Some clematis bloom profusely in spring and again sporadically later in the season. Others will offer a few blossoms in spring and a better show on new growth, later in the season. Either way, pruning in either season is going to cost a few blooms.

- The easiest approach is to watch the plant and determine which season offers the best display and then do your pruning accordingly.

- If spring is the big show, prune after the spring flowers have faded. You will lose some late season bloom, but gain next spring.

- Conversely, if late season is the show stopper, do your pruning while plant is dormant or in early spring.

- Whichever approach you choose, don't prune this class of clematis as severely as categories 1 & 2. Treat this pruning more like deadheading or a means to thin out the plant.

IVY

HEDERA AND *PARTHENOCISSUS*

Ivy *(Hedera)* is a hardy, shade-tolerant, evergreen vine. All ivy has two stages of growth. During the juvenile stage, the plants have attractive leaves with 3 to 5 lobes and aerial roots that cling to any surface. Upon maturity, the stems become thick and woody while the leaves change to an oval shape and inconspicuous flowers are followed by small poisonous berries. As ivy is usually clipped and slow to mature, few plants are seen in the adult stage.

Hedera helix, or **English Ivy**, is the most common with over sixty named varieties, some variegated. All ivy can be propagated by cutting or layering. It grows best in shade where the afternoon sun will not burn it. Ivy prefers rich, moist loam, but it will grow in ordinary garden soils. Although it is rather slow to establish, it will tolerate much abuse. Water ivy during dry spells. Feed it once a year with 6–10–10. In the unlikely event that there is an insect problem spray with an oil-based insecticide.

Ivy has many uses in the landscape. It is an excellent ground cover for shady areas, such as under trees where grass cannot survive. Ivy can be planted on slopes to prevent erosion. Ivy transforms an unsightly fence into a soft green screen. Its long trailing stems are perfect for hanging baskets, garden urns, and window boxes. The small-leaved varieties make excellent house plants and are desirable for large topiaries.

Do not let ivy grow up tree trunks as it will eventually kill the tree. Do not plant ivy in flower beds because it will smother annuals and perennials. When planted beneath azaleas, camellias, or other ornamental shrubs, ivy must be constantly thinned or it will rob the plants of nutrients and moisture. Plant shallow-rooted ground covers like pachysandra instead.

Ivy is lovely grown on the wall of a brick house, but this is not recommended because over a period of time it ruins the mortar. It has to be constantly trimmed, not only for neatness, but to keep it from stopping up gutters and rotting wood trim.

Prune ivy in early spring by shearing in order to maintain a well-groomed garden. When grown on walls, the heavy woody stems should be cut back to promote lacy new growth. If ivy is used as a ground cover, clip the plants rather close to the ground for denser, more attractive foliage. To make plants spread into bare areas, cover the middle of a trailing stem with dirt and keep it moist (a layering technique). Alternatively, place the cut stem in water and transplant it after it has rooted.

290

  Parthenocissus tricuspidata (also known as **Japanese creeper**, **Boston ivy** or **Japanese ivy**) is a flowering plant in the grape family (*Vitacea*) native to eastern Asia. It is a deciduous, woody vine growing to 50', with trilobed leaves 5" – 8" across. The flowers are inconspicuous, greenish clusters, usually hidden by foliage; the fruit is a small, dark-blue grape.

  Boston ivy, like its close relative the Virginia creeper, attaches by small, branched tendrils tipped with sticky discs and is frequently used to cover the façade of masonry buildings. While the plant does not penetrate the building surface but merely attaches with adhesive pads, nevertheless damage can occur from attempting to rip the plant from the wall. However, if the plant is killed first, such as by severing the vine from the root, the adhesive pads will eventually deteriorate to the point where the plant can be easily removed.

ANNUAL VINES

If you are looking for plants that offer maximum rewards for minimal effort, look no further than annual vines. Morning-glories are perhaps the most common annual vine, and for good reason: they grow quickly, are easy to maintain, and flower abundantly.

Even gardeners with limited space can enjoy annual vines because they'll grow vertically, requiring just a square foot or two of actual garden space. Note that some vines are more vigorous than others, so match the vine to the space you have, the support you're providing, and the look you want. Use vigorous annual vines to hide unattractive landscape features, such as chain link fences, or to provide a summertime screen between you and your neighbors. Use less vigorous ones in hanging baskets and window boxes, or trained up and around a window frame.

Unless you wish to let the vines sprawl over a stone wall or bank, you'll need to provide some type of support. Fortunately, most annual vines can be trained to a simple string trellis; no fancy or expensive wooden or metal structures are needed as with heavier, woody perennial vines.

The simplest support consists of a few vertical strands of heavy twine secured at the top to the eave, allowed to dangle to the ground, and trimmed so they reach a few inches above the soil line. Vines planted below will quickly find the strings and start climbing. Or, secure a mesh trellis (the kind sold to support peas, for example) to the siding, making sure there's a few inches between the wall and mesh to give the vines room to twine. A simple tepee made from three or more sturdy branches or bamboo poles is another simple solution.

TABLE 32. ANNUAL VINES FOR THE MID-SOUTH

SCIENTIFIC NAME/ COMMON NAME	COMMENTS
Ceanothus **California Lilac**	Espaliered shrub grown against a wall; regarded as coastal plant but known for its floral display.
Clerodendrum **Glory Bower**	Many species, all tender. Beautiful flower clusters in pink, scarlet, cream, bi-color. 12' long; sun to part shade.
Clerodendrum thomsoniae **Bleeding-heart Vine**	Tropical twining vine.
Cucurbita **Gourds**	Runners or climbers. Inedible fruits in many colors and shapes; when dried, serve many useful and decorative purposes. Sun, long growing season. Mulch. Blooms in spring.

SCIENTIFIC NAME/ COMMON NAME	COMMENTS
Dolichos lab-lab **Hyacinth Bean Vine**	Pea-like, pink flowers all summer. Edible pods used as food crop in Asia. Fast growing; full sun.
Ipomoea alba **Moonvine** or **Moonflower**	Climber up to 20'. Blooms at night. 6", fragrant, white flowers have clove-like scent. Sun. Soak seed overnight before planting. Vigorous. Native vine. Blooms in summer.
Ipomoea batatas **Sweet Potato Vine**	Grown from the edible sweet potato. Most attractive cultivars are 'Blackie' with black foliage, 'Marguerite' has chartreuse foliage, and 'Tricolor' has variegated pink, green, and white foliage. Sun. Non-flowering. Good groundcover or hanging basket material.
Ipomoea multifida **Cardinal Vine**	Climber to 20'. Small red and white morning-glory-like flower; lovely leathery leaf. Sun, light soil, native vine. Blooms in summer.
Ipomoea quamoclit **Cypress Vine**	Vigorous climber to 20'. Feathery leaves, red and white flowers. Sun, light soil. Red attracts hummingbirds; native. Blooms in summer.
Ipomoea violacea **Morning-glory Vine**	Many varieties. Vigorous climber. Red, white, blue; 'Heavenly Blue' is gorgeous color. Sun. Blooms in summer.
Mandevilla x amabilis **Mandevilla Vine**	Tropical, twining, evergreen vine; sun to part shade. Pink or white flowers. Can be houseplant with sufficient sunlight.
Phaseolus coccineus **Scarlet Runner Bean**	Vine to 12' with scarlet pea-like flowers. Full sun to part shade. Loved by hummingbirds. In the green bean family, it has edible pods and seeds. Blooms in summer.
Solanum dulcamara **Night Shade**	Climber. Poisonous, red berry, shiny oval leaves, violet flowers. Deciduous. Blooms in summer.
Solanum jasminoides **Potato Vine**	Twining vine; tropical; sun to part shade.
Thunbergia alata **Black-eyed Susan Vine**	Popular for its manageable size and abundant flowers. Bears dark-throated orange, yellow, or white blossoms. Fertile soil in a lightly shaded location. Can reach up to 8 feet in length.

293

SCIENTIFIC NAME/ COMMON NAME	COMMENTS
	Perfect for hanging baskets and window boxes. Blooms in summer.
Trachelospermum jasminoides **Confederate Jasmine**	Tropical, evergreen, twining vine. White flowers.
Tropaeolum majus **Nasturtium**	Less vigorous climber; 8' – 12'. Yellow, orange. Good vine for cool greenhouse. Blooms in early summer; winter in greenhouse.

FLOWERS – PERENNIALS

PLANNING THE FLOWER BORDER

Perennials for the flower border range in size from 3" to 7', and are available in every color of the rainbow. Some bloom for months and others for only a few days. Some are evergreen, some die back in the heat of the summer to re-emerge in early spring (known as *spring ephemerals*), and some die back for the season at first freeze. The most interesting borders use a combination of long-blooming, easily-managed perennials, bulbs, and annuals.

The *Considerations for Landscaping* chapter has tables listing flowers, shrubs, and trees to use in sun and shade beds, and offers plant recommendations for various types of gardens. Below are suggestions for planning your flower border:

- Provide a strong *background* such as a shrubbery border, a wall or fence, or the side of the house. Hybrid tea roses are usually grown in a bed in the open, rather than backed by a wall, and will be discussed in *Shrubs – Roses*.

- *Plan the area on paper first.* Consult the following tables for height, color, bloom time, and sun requirements. Maybe the look of an English cottage garden appeals, or you might prefer the understated beauty of a silver and green variegated woodland garden. Perhaps you like masses of one flower. You may want to use a certain color palette, or you may want tall plants to hide an ugly fence. Playing with your design on paper will be very helpful.

- Plants should be *used in groups* of three or more, repeated at rhythmic intervals throughout the border. **Plant flowers together which have similar soil, water, and sun requirements.** If you are more of a plant collector, try to arrange your "ones" of various plants in a way to create a pleasing contrast, or a repetition of color or form. If a plant gets rather large, like a baptisia, use only one in an area, and repeat through the border if desired.

- *Make the border wide enough* (suggested width, 5' – 6') to accommodate several depths of planting. In general, place shorter flowers in front and taller flowers at the back. Use tall, airy, see-through plants like gaura, tall verbena (*Verbena bonariensis*), and meadow rue (*Thalictrum*) in front and middle of the bed to give depth. Allow spaces to walk in the border to stake, trim, etc. without trampling the flowers. Stepping stones are very practical and understated.

- *Laying out beds and borders*: For straight lines follow a string stretched between stakes. For irregular lines and curves, outline the bed with a hose, and then dig along its edges.

- In *prominent beds*, choose perennials with *attractive disease-resistant foliage* which looks good in or out of bloom. Examples would include 'Powis Castle' artemisia, baptisia, heuchera, hosta, helleborus, tiarella, heucherella, Japanese anemone, hardy begonia, ferns, pachysandra, liriope, vinca minor, and lamb's-ears (*Stachys*). Use coarser plants, which may be uninspiring when not in bloom, for the cutting bed or a more distant area.

- Emphasize the *easy, reliable, pest-free perennials* such as helleborus, epimedium, hosta, celandine poppy (*Stylophorum*), arum, hardy begonia, toad lily (*Tricyrtis*), and fern for *shade*. Use amsonia, black-eyed Susan (*Rudbeckia*), coneflower (*Echinacea*), 'Becky' daisy (*Chrysanthemum* or *Dendranthema*), daylily (*Hemerocallis*), iris, lily, salvia, and verbena for *sun*.

- A few plants with short bloom time but spectacular flowers, such as Oriental poppy (*Papaver*), foxglove (*Digitalis*), and peony (*Paeonia*) should certainly be included. The perennials whose foliage disappears completely after flowering like the spring ephemerals [mayapple (*Podophyllum*), bloodroot (*Sanguinaria*), toothwort (*Dentaria*), Virginia bluebells (*Mertensia*), wake robin trillium (*Trillium*), bleeding-heart (*Dicentra*), etc.] and bulbs like daffodil and hyacinth can be over-planted with other ground covers or annuals. Perennial hardy begonia comes up late and is a good choice for this, as are shade annuals. Daylilies are a good cover for fading daffodil foliage.

- *Avoid rampant growers.* Oftentimes the species is overly prolific, but hybrid cultivars are better behaved. Obedient plant (*Physostegia*) and showy evening primrose (*Oenothera*) can be invasive, but that might not be a problem in a distant bed.

- Use *perennial ground covers* as a low massed carpet or for filling in around taller perennials. Good ones include ivy (see Special Article in *Vines*), asarum ginger, pachysandra, epimedium, vinca minor, pratia, spotted nettle (*Lamium*), yellow archangel (*Lamiastrum*), ajuga, creeping jenny (*Lysimachia*), mondo grass (*Ophiopogon*), liriope, and stonecrop sedums.

- An edging or massing of *annuals* is effective for long season of bloom and to cover fading spring bulbs. They are especially useful in a new garden where the main perennials are still small. Annuals like impatiens, lantana, pentas, Mexican heather, and many of the begonias offer good foliage and flowers all summer. The neutral silver of dusty-miller and 'Powis Castle' artemisia are good for tying various colors together in the border. Buy annuals in 6-packs or flats at your nursery. Zinnias are best grown from seed sprinkled in a sunny bed of ordinary soil in mid-April.

- In a *very narrow, shady border,* as between a driveway and building, one type of plant massed might be more attractive. Easy-care, low-growing options would be evergreen autumn fern (*Dryopteris*), mondo grass (*Ophiopogon*), liriope, cast iron plant (*Aspidistra*), or helleborus. If you want something taller, try a Japanese climbing hydrangea (*Schizophragma*). In a *narrow sunny border*, you could espalier a pyracantha, or plant a disease-resistant climbing rose with a clematis vine intertwined on the same trellis.

- *Keep the border neat* with the taller plants firmly supported and staked as needed. Cut off faded blooms to promote new ones. (See *Deadheading* in *Garden Care*) Pinch back leggy stems to promote bushier growth. Mark all dormant plants and bulbs with a stake or label to avoid injuring or digging them up when working the bed.

- *Rule of Thumb for dividing perennials*: If it blooms in the spring, divide in the fall. If it blooms in the fall, divide in the spring. .

CULTURE OF PERENNIAL FLOWERS

WATER – Soak ground thoroughly (do not sprinkle) early in the day so plants are dry by nightfall. Keep beds mulched.

FERTILIZE – Excessive nitrogen causes luxuriant foliage and few blooms. When preparing the bed dig in 3 – 4 oz. of 0–20–20 per 100 square feet. For established beds give each mature clump a handful of 5–10–5 once in early February or March and again 4 to 6 weeks later. In general, use an organic top dressing (compost, Milorganite®, dehydrated manure, cottonseed meal, fish emulsion, bone meal) for long-range care, and chemical fertilizers for quick pickups.

DIVISION – Some perennials need dividing every three or four years to maintain their vigor, such as iris, aster, chrysanthemum, and daisy. Peony, crinum lily, baptisia, epimedium, helleborus, balloon flower (*Platycodon*), hardy cyclamen, Virginia bluebells (*Mertensia*), and bleeding-heart (*Dicentra*) seldom if ever need dividing. (See *Garden Care – Vegetative Propagation* for more ways to increase plant stock)

PEST AND DISEASE – A garden that is not overcrowded, that is clean of debris and infected plants, and is properly fed and watered is relatively trouble free. If problems arise, use products that control specific insects and diseases. (See *Garden Care – Pests and Disease)* Avoid powerful broad-spectrum insecticides that destroy beneficial as well as harmful insects.

TABLE OF PERENNIALS

Special Articles on Chrysanthemum, ground covers, herbs, hosta, and ornamental grasses follow at the end of this table.

TABLE 33. PERENNIAL FLOWERS, GROUND COVERS, HERBS, AND ORNAMENTAL GRASSES FOR THE MID-SOUTH

KEY: P = Perennial – A plant that lasts for more than two years in the garden, but does not have a woody trunk.

e = Evergreen – A plant whose foliage remains green year round.

H = Herb – A plant used for seasoning food, teas, medicines, and potpourris.

gc = Ground Cover – A plant which grows low and tends to fill in and spread when planted in masses.

V = Variegated – A plant with white, yellow, chartreuse, pink, red, purple, maroon, silver, gray, or blue foliage, or foliage patterned in these colors.

Z = Zone refers to the Cold-Hardiness Zone Map and the Heat Zone Map. See color pages for Zone Maps.

SCIENTIFIC NAME/ COMMON NAME	KEY	HEIGHT	FLOWER COLOR/ BLOOM TIME	SUN NEEDS	COMMENTS
Acanthus mollis x latifolius **'Summer Beauty' Bear's Breeches, Acanthus**	P, e	1' – 3'	Purplish/ spring	Partial shade	Grown primarily for beautiful foliage. May not flower in Mid-South. Species *A. mollis* is not heat tolerant, so look for hybrids in catalogs. Rich moist soil; good drainage. Old foliage withers away as new leaves form in September and remain green all winter. Acanthus leaf motif used on Corinthian columns and other art forms.
Achillea millefolium	P	1' – 3'	White, hot pink, red,	Sun	Pungent, feathery leaf; any soil. Long

298

SCIENTIFIC NAME/ COMMON NAME	KEY	HEIGHT	FLOWER COLOR/ BLOOM TIME	SUN NEEDS	COMMENTS
Yarrow			yellow/ summer		lasting bloom. Easily dried for arrangements. Native.
Achillea x **'Coronation Gold' Yarrow**	P	3'	Golden yellow/ early summer	Sun	Same as above.
Achillea x **'Gold Plate' Yarrow**	P	3' – 4'	Gold/ early summer	Sun	Same as above.
Achillea x **'Moonshine' Yarrow**	P	2'	Lemon yellow/ late spring	Sun	Finely dissected, feathery foliage; dry, lean soil.
Acorus calamus **Calamus Root, Sweet Flag or Sweetflag**	P	5' – 6'	Green - seldom flowers/ early summer	Sun to part shade	Sacred to American Indians and Chinese for medicinal and hallucinogenic properties. Similar to iris, but grows in bogs.
Acorus gramineus **Dwarf Sweetflag, Golden Sweetflag**	P, e, gc, V	8" – 10"	Lime and cream variegated foliage/ spring	Light to medium shade	Grass-like foliage. May be used in water gardens. Moist rich soil. Spreading evergreen clump. Lovely. 'Ogon' or 'Variegatus'
Acorus gramineus **Japanese Miniature Sweetflag**	P, e, gc, V	2" – 4"	Gold foliage/ evergreen	Part sun to shade	Moist well drained soil. Good ground cover. 'Minimus Aurea'
Aegopodium podagraria **Bishop's Weed, Goutweed**	P, e, gc, V	1'	White/ summer	Sun to part shade	White parsley-like flower, variegated foliage. Good for edging, spreads rapidly.

299

Scientific Name/ Common Name	Key	Height	Flower Color/ Bloom Time	Sun Needs	Comments
Ajuga genevensis **Ajuga, Bugleweed**	P, e, gc	1" – 3"	Blue/ spring	Part sun to medium shade	Hardy creeper. 6" spike of brilliant blue flowers. Beautiful with celandine poppy in April.
Ajuga reptans **Ajuga, Bugleweed**	P, e, gc	1" – 3"	White, pinkish/ spring	Part sun to medium shade	Many varieties; bronzed to dark purple leaf; white to rose flower. All subject to fungus.
Ajuga **'Chocolate Chip' Ajuga**	P, e, gc	2"	Blue/ spring	Part sun to shade	New cultivar that is true dwarf at 2" tall and showier flower. Evergreen bronze foliage.
Alchemilla mollis **Lady's Mantle**	P	12" – 18"	Lime green/ early spring – April	Sun to part shade	Velvety foliage, medium clump, well-drained moist soil; short-lived but reseeds; woodland beauty.
Amsonia hubrectii **Arkansas Amsonia, Narrow Leaf Amsonia**	P	2' – 3'	Pale blue/ Mid-spring, April - May	Full sun to part shade	Fine textured; clump forming; small blue flowers; yellow fall foliage is outstanding, grows into large mass; moist, humusy soil; native.
Amsonia tabernaemontana **Bluestar, Willow Amsonia, Dogbane**	P	2' – 3'	Sky blue/ late spring	Sun	Damp garden soil. Reliable. Grows into a large clump over time. Native.
Anemone See under *Bulbs* also.					
Anemone	P	2' – 3'	Red-violet	Sun	Nice foliage when not

300

Scientific Name/ Common Name	Key	Height	Flower Color/ Bloom Time	Sun Needs	Comments
hupehensis **'September Charm' Anemone**			tint/ fall, Sept-Oct		in flower. Good late season bloom. Does not flop like taller ones below
Anemone hybrids **Japanese Anemone**	P	3' – 4'	White, rose pink/ late summer – fall	Part shade	Deep moist soil; flowers held high above attractive foliage; clumps increase; 'Robustissima' is a vigorous pink; 'Honorine Jobert' is a beautiful white.
Anemone sylvestris **Snowdrop Anemone**	P	10" – 18"	White/ spring	Part shade	Light, rich, well-drained soil. Pretty single flowers followed by woolly fruit.
Aquilegia caerulea **Columbine**	P	1' – 3'	Blue/ spring	Partial shade	Sandy loam. All columbines are prone to leafminers which disfigures the foliage but does not kill the plant. Z (3–8/ 8–1)
Aquilegia chrysantha **Golden Columbine**	P	2' – 4'	Yellow/ spring	Sun to part shade	Spectacular in flower; long-spurred; ordinary well-drained soil. Z (3–8/ 8–1)
Aquilegia hybrids: **Columbine hybrids: 'McKana', 'Musik', 'Song Bird', 'Windswept'**	A/ P	1½' – 3'	Various/ spring	Sun to part shade	Lovely spurred flowers; subject to leafminer; relatively short lived and hybrids do not come true from reseeding; ordinary well-drained soil. Z (3–8/ 8–1).
Aquilegia	P	1' – 3'	Yellow &	Partial	Moist woodland

Scientific Name/ Common Name	Key	Height	Flower Color/ Bloom Time	Sun Needs	Comments
canadensis **Wild Columbine, Canadian Columbine**			red/ spring	shade	habitat; reseeds; delicate looking yellow and red flowers, erect clumps. Native. Z (3–8/ 8–1).
Artemisia dracunculus sativa **French Tarragon**	P, h	2' x 3'	small, greenish/ late summer	Sun	Culinary herb. French tarragon is more flavorful than the common Russian tarragon, and both are hard to grow in the Southern humidity and heat. See *Tagetes lucida* – Spanish or Mexican tarragon as a tasty alternative.
Artemisia hybrids **Artemisia, Wormwood**	P	3' – 4'	Silvery gray foliage; tiny white flowers/ mid–late summer	Sun to part shade	'Powis Castle' is best one for the South. Beautiful silver foliage combines well with other colors; lean, ordinary, dry, well-drained soil. Valued for feathery, aromatic foliage.
Artemisia lactifolia **White Mugwort**	P	4' – 6'	Creamy white/ summer	Sun	Moist, rich soil. Upright habit, back of border 'Guizho'.
Artemisia vulgaris **Artemisia, Wormwood**	P	6" – 10" x 1' – 3'	Yellow-green variegated foliage	Sun to part shade	'Oriental Limelight' is a lovely variegated form for containers or ground. Lean, ordinary, dry, well-drained soil. Feathery foliage.
Asarum canadense **Wild Ginger**	P, gc	4"	Maroon/ spring	Partial shade	Flower at ground level; moist, leaf mold. Good ground

SCIENTIFIC NAME/ COMMON NAME	KEY	HEIGHT	FLOWER COLOR/ BLOOM TIME	SUN NEEDS	COMMENTS
					cover; some evergreen, some deciduous varieties. Native. Many other *Asarum* are good garden plants, but some are slow to spread.
Asclepias tuberosa **Butterfly Weed**	P	1½' – 3'	Orange, yellow/ summer	Sun	Thrives in garden soil. Good cut flower. Attracts butterflies and hummingbirds. Native.
Aspidistra elatior **Cast Iron Plant**	P, e	2' – 3'	White/ summer	Shade	Tropical-looking, broad, dark green elliptical leaves. Will grow in deep shade. Likes moisture but tolerates dry shade. Plant in masses for best effect. Slow growing but reliable in pots or ground.
Aster hybrids **Aster**	P	6" – 5'	Lavender, blue, pink, rose, and white/ late summer-fall	Sun to light shade	Average soil, not too rich. Sow seeds or set out plants of named varieties in early spring. Divide most varieties every other spring. Tall varieties need staking. Can be weedy-looking. *A. frikartii* 'Wonder of Staffa'; *A. novi-belgii* 'Woods Dwarfs'.
Astilbe **Astilbe**	P	2' – 3'	White, pink, red, lavender/	Partial shade	Ferny delicate foliage and tall fluffy spire flowers in spring.

303

SCIENTIFIC NAME/ COMMON NAME	KEY	HEIGHT	FLOWER COLOR/ BLOOM TIME	SUN NEEDS	COMMENTS
			May–June		Rich moist soil with humus. Divide in fall every two or three years for increase and to retain vigor. Many named cultivars. Z (4–8/ 8–1)
Baptisia alba **White False Indigo**	P	3'	White/ early summer	Sun	Average soil, pea-like bloom. Less hardy than *B. australis*.
Baptisia australis **False Indigo**	P	3' – 4'	Blue to violet/ mid-spring to early summer	Sun to part shade	Can be substituted for delphinium and lupine in hot climates. Pinch faded flowers to extend bloom time. 12" spike of pea-like flower. Blue-gray foliage is attractive all season. Native.
Baptisia. tinctoria **Yellow Wild Indigo**	P	2' – 3'	Yellow/ mid-spring to early summer	Sun to part shade	Lupine-like bloom. Native.
Begonia grandis **Begonia, Hardy**	P, gc	1' – 2'	Pink/ late summer – fall	Partial to full shade	Showy, angel-wing leaf, red on underside; large pink panicle flowers. Self sows by bulbils in moist dappled shade. Hardy. Dies back in winter and late to emerge in spring. Fabulous woodland plant.
Boltonia asteroides **Boltonia**	P	3' – 4'	White with yellow centers/	Sun	Average, well drained soil. Self-supporting in sun, may need staking in shade.

SCIENTIFIC NAME/ COMMON NAME	KEY	HEIGHT	FLOWER COLOR/ BLOOM TIME	SUN NEEDS	COMMENTS
			late summer		Daisy-like flowers. 'Snowbank'.
Calamagrostis x acutiflora **Feather Reed Grass**	P,	3' x 2'	Pink turning cream then tan/ early summer	Sun to part shade	Strong vertical accent grass with 5' slower spikes emerging pink, then cream then tan. Useful for dried arrangements. Hardy and carefree plant. Moist, well-drained ordinary soil. 'Karl Foerster' & 'Avalanche' are good cultivars.
Caltha palustris **Marsh Marigold**	P	1' – 2'	Yellow/ spring	Partial shade	Live in bogs or water gardens. Beautiful foliage, cheerful yellow spring flowers. Worth the trouble to grow.
Carex spp. **Sedge**	P, e, gc, V	4" – 20"	Yellow, variegated chartreuse / ever-green	Part to full shade	Ornamental grass-like plants from Japan and New Zealand provide color and texture in the shade garden. Mail order sources have many varieties.
Carex morrowii **Golden Sedge**	P, e, gc, V	12"	Variegated yellow/ evergreen	Light to full shade	Nice golden variegated clump-forming, grass-like plant for shady spots. 'Aurea Variegata'
Ceratostigma plumbaginoides **Leadwort**	P, gc	8" – 12"	Dark blue/ June–Sept	Sun to light shade	Rich, well-drained soil. Spreading ground cover; rock gardens. Good plant for sun. Late to emerge in spring.

305

Scientific Name/ Common Name	Key	Height	Flower Color/ Bloom Time	Sun Needs	Comments
					Gentian blue flowers. Bronzy red fall foliage.
Chelone lyonii **Pink Turtlehead**	P	2' – 3'	Dark rose/ late summer, August	Sun to shade	Clump-forming. Moisture-loving. Rich, woodland soil. Z (3–8/ 8–1).
Chelone obliqua **Turtlehead**	P	2' – 3'	Pink/ late summer	Partial shade	Clump-forming, moisture-loving. Rich woodland soil. Z (3–8/ 8–1).
Chrysanthemum, Dendranthema, or *Leucanthemum* See Special Article below.	P	2" – 36"	all colors but blue	Sun to light shade	One of the oldest cultivated plants. Many variations in flower form. 'Becky' is the best daisy for the South.
Chrysoganum virginianum **Green and Gold**	P, gc	6" – 8"	Yellow/ early spring	Partial to full shade	Tolerates sun if kept moist. Good shade ground cover with yellow daisy-like flowers. Native.
Coreopsis verticillata **Threadleaf Coreopsis**	P	10" – 26"	Yellow/ summer-fall	Sun to light shade	Light, airy foliage. 'Zagreb' best in our area. 'Moonbeam' also. Long bloom. Deadhead. Z (4–9/ 9–1).
Cortaderia selloana **Dwarf Pampas Grass**	P	3' x 3'	White/ late summer	Sun	'Pumilla' is a wonderful dwarf variety 3' tall with 5' plume of feathery white. Useful in small gardens. Very hardy.
Cypripedium **Lady's Slipper Orchid,**	P	6" – 15"	Pink/ spring	Partial shade	Acid woods; endangered species. Native but can be

SCIENTIFIC NAME/ COMMON NAME	KEY	HEIGHT	FLOWER COLOR/ BLOOM TIME	SUN NEEDS	COMMENTS
Moccasin Flower					difficult to grow. Requires certain soil fungus to thrive. Do not dig from wild unless it is threatened by a bulldozer.
Daucus carota **Queen-Anne's-lace, Wild Carrot**	P	to 6'	White/ summer	Sun	Good for cutting; dries well. Weedy. Native.
Dendranthema see *Chrysanthemum* or *Leucanthemum* **Chrysanthemum, Daisy** See Special Article below.					Several chrysanthe-mums have been reclassified and there is still discussion as to the correct genus for some species.
Dentaria laciniata **Toothwort**	P	4" – 6"	White/ spring	Part shade	Woodland ephemeral. Charming white flowers in early spring. Naturalizes easily in loamy garden.
Dianthus allwoodii hybrids **Pinks**	P	12" – 20"	Various pink, rose, white, red, salmon/ summer	Sun	Good in the South. Well-drained alkaline soil. Small carnation-like flower.
Dianthus gratianopolitanus **'Cheddar Pinks'** **Dianthus**	P,e	9" – 12"	Rose, pink, violet-red; ever-gray foliage/ early–late spring	Sun	Best *Dianthus* for the South. 'Bath's Pink' (10", May), 'Fire Witch' (6", May–Aug), 'Mountain Mist'. Ever-gray foliage. Average soil, somewhat alkaline. Rock garden or sunny

Scientific Name/ Common Name	Key	Height	Flower Color/ Bloom Time	Sun Needs	Comments
					border. Z (3–9/ 9–1).
Dicentra eximia **Fringed Bleeding-heart**	P	10" – 18"	Pink/ spring – summer	Partial shade	Leaf mold, moist, well-drained soil. Native. Similar to *D. spectabilis* but has fernier foliage and smaller flowers. Can be short-lived if not happy. Z (4–8/ 8–1).
Dicentra spectabilis **Old-fashioned Bleeding-heart**	P	2½' – 3'	Pink/ spring	Partial shade to shade	Beautiful foliage; pink and white hearts dangle from stem in mid-spring. Good garden soil. Long lived perennial which doesn't need dividing. May die back in mid-summer heat.
Digitalis mertonensis **Strawberry Foxglove**	P, e	15" – 30"	Pink, rose, yellow/ late spring	Light shade	True perennial foxglove. Smaller than hybrids. Rich moist soil. Z (3–8/ 8–1). See *Annuals* also.
Disporum sessile and *D. flavum* **Fairy Bells**	P	1' – 2'	White, yellow/ spring	Partial shade	Woodland plant similar to Solomon's-seal or *Uvularia*. Well-behaved shade plant. Reliable and underused.
Disporopsis pernyi **Evergreen Solomon's-seal**	P, e, gc	6"	White/ spring	Light to medium shade	Small evergreen woodland plant similar to Solomon's-seal with glossy foliage and small white flowers in early spring.
Echinacea pallida	P	to 3'	Pale	Sun	Long drooping rays;

SCIENTIFIC NAME/ COMMON NAME	KEY	HEIGHT	FLOWER COLOR/ BLOOM TIME	SUN NEEDS	COMMENTS
Coneflower			orchid/ summer		prominent dark center. Garden soil. Native.
Echinacea purpurea **Coneflower**	A/ P	2' – 4'	Purple, white/ mid-summer to mid-fall	Sun	Broad coarse oval leaves. Holds up well in heat; garden soil. Many varieties: 'White Swan', 'Bravado', 'Magnus', 'Bright Star', 'Robert Bloom'. Used in herbal medicine. Native. Z (3–9/ 9–1).
Echinops ritro **Globe Thistle**	P	5'	Steel blue/ summer	Sun	Globular flower heads; dark green, prickly leaves. Long-lived, heat and drought tolerant. 'Veitchii's Blue'. Z (3–9/ 9–1).
Epimedium hybrids **Epimedium, Bishop's Hat, Barrrenwort**	P, e, gc	10" – 15"	Yellow, pink, white/ spring	Part sun to shade	Excellent, trouble-free, evergreen plant for partial shade. Pixie-like yellow, white, red, or pink flowers; heart-shaped leaf. Some spreading, some clump-forming; slow grower. Cut off old foliage in late winter so early spring flowers can be seen and fresh new foliage can emerge. Wood-land or rock garden.
Equisetum **Horsetail Reed**	P, e	1' – 5'	Green/ summer	Part sun to shade	Ancient, evergreen, vertical reed which can be grown in

Scientific Name/ Common Name	Key	Height	Flower Color/ Bloom Time	Sun Needs	Comments
					garden or pond. Best to confine roots as it can be invasive. Has Oriental feeling.
Eryngium planum **Flat Sea Holly**	P	2' – 3'	Blue/ summer	Sun	*E. planum* stands up to heat and humidity better than other *Eryngium.* Good in dried arrangements. Ordinary to poor garden soil. Dry.
Eupatorium coelestinum **Hardy Ageratum, Hardy Mist Flower**	P	1½' – 3'	Blue/ late summer to late fall	Sun to part shade	Any soil. Native to eastern U.S. Rampant grower. Z (2–9/ 9–1).
Eupatorium maculata **Joe-Pye weed, Smokeweed**	P	5'	Purple/ fall	Sun to part shade	Any soil. Large and coarse; long-flowering. Some good new cultivars are smaller and better suited to the garden. 'Gateway' Z (2–9/ 9–1).
Farfugium japonicum or *Ligularia* **Leopard Plant**					See below under *Ligularia*
Gaillardia grandiflora **Blanket Flower**	P	1' – 3'	Yellow, orange, red/ June to frost	Sun to light shade	Hardy prairie-type perennial; likes ordinary soil, sun, well-drained. Drought resistant, native. Z (3–8/ 8–1).
Gaura lindheimeri **White Gaura**	P	3'	White, pink/ May – Sept.	Sun to part shade	Light, airy plant with butterfly-shaped flowers. Tolerates heat and humidity.

SCIENTIFIC NAME/ COMMON NAME	KEY	HEIGHT	FLOWER COLOR/ BLOOM TIME	SUN NEEDS	COMMENTS
					'Whirling Butterflies', 'Siskiyou Pink'. Z (5–9/ 9–1)
Geranium hybrids **Geranium**	P	1' – 2'	Blue, violet, rose/ spring – summer	Sun to part shade	'Johnson's Blue', 'Patricia', 'Gravetye', many new offerings. Can be short-lived. Z (4–9/ 9–1).
Geranium maculatum **Wild Geranium, Spotted Cranesbill**	P	to 2'	Pink/ spring	Sun to part shade	Basal rosette of deeply lobed leaves. Leaf mold. Native. Z (4–9/ 9–1).
Geranium sanguineum **Bloody Cranesbill**	P	9" – 15"	Magenta/ spring	Sun to part shade	Tolerant of heat and cold. Many cultivars. 'Striatum' is pink with crimson veins and long-blooming. 'New Hampshire Purple'. Z (4–9/ 9–1).
Geranium x cantabrigiense **Cambridge Geranium Hybrids**	P, e, gc	6" – 8"	White streaked with pink/ spring – summer	Sun to part shade	'Biokovo' is handsome ground cover (white, April–May). 'Karmina' (red-violet, May–June) Evergreen. Z (4–9/ 9–1).
Geum **Geum**	P	12" plant 18" flower stem	Bright orange, red, yellow/ mid-spring to mid-summer	Sun	Good garden soil. Several varieties: 'Lady Stratheden', 'Mrs. Bradshaw', *G. borisii.* Z (5-9/ 9-1).
Hakonechloa macra Aureola	P, V	1' x 2'	White & cream	Part shade	This woodland native of Japan prefers high

311

Scientific Name/ Common Name	Key	Height	Flower Color/ Bloom Time	Sun Needs	Comments
Golden Hakone Grass			stripes on spring green leaves		shade. Variegated grass-like foliage on a neat 1' clump that spreads slowly to brighten shade. Excellent.
Helenium autumnale **Sneezeweed**	P	3' – 5'	Yellow, orange, mahogany / late summer/ late summer	Sun to light shade	Does not cause sneezing. Cut back to control size in July. Similar to sunflower. Z (4–8/ 8–1).
Helianthus angustifolius **Sunflower**	P	1' – 10'	Yellow/ summer	Sun	Any soil; grow for bird food. Native.
Heliopsis helianthoides **Sunflower Heliopsis**	P	2' – 6'	Yellow, orange/ summer	Sun to light shade	'Summer Sun' is best for Southern heat. Not as weedy as species. Z (3–9/ 9–1).
Helleborus foetidus **Bearsfoot Helleborus**	P, e	1½' – 2'	Light green often rimmed in purple/ late winter – spring	Partial shade	Rich, moist well-drained soil. Should not be disturbed once established. Beautiful, unique foliage and long lasting flower bracts. 'Wesker Flisk'. Can be short lived, but reseeds freely when happy. Z (4–9/ 9–1).
Helleborus orientalis **Helleborus, Lenten Rose, Christmas Rose**	P, e	12" – 15"	White, lavender, green, rose, speckled, pink, cream,	Part sun to shade	Excellent, trouble-free plant that holds flower bracts for 6 months. Flower resembles a downward-facing dogwood blossom (hybridizers are

SCIENTIFIC NAME/ COMMON NAME	KEY	HEIGHT	FLOWER COLOR/ BLOOM TIME	SUN NEEDS	COMMENTS
			maroon/ late winter – spring		working to make hellebores hold their heads up). Peony-like, evergreen, leathery, palmate foliage. Moist, neutral-to-slightly-alkaline, humusy soil. Slow to establish, so do not disturb once planted. Sends up new foliage in late fall, and flowers in winter. Cut back weather-beaten leaves in late January. Long-lived; reseeds freely. 'Pine Knot Strain', 'Royal Heritage', 'Sunshine', and other new hybrids have larger range of flower color and are quicker to establish. Z (4–9/ 9–1).
Hemerocallis **Daylily** See Special Article in *Bulbs.*	P	1' – 3'	All colors but blue/ spring – fall, depending on cultivar	Sun to light shade	Many new hybrids; some bloom all summer. Easy in any soil. Z (3–10/ 10–1).
X Heucherella hybrids **Heucherella**	P, e	1' – 2'	White, pink, red/ spring	Part shade	*X Heucherella* is an inter-genus hybrid between *Heuchera* and *Tiarella.* All heucherella are sterile and are thus profuse and repeat bloomers. Starry flowers are a

313

Scientific Name/ Common Name	Key	Height	Flower Color/ Bloom Time	Sun Needs	Comments
					mix of the parents' flowers. The "X" is not pronounced, just written.
Heuchera americana **Coralbells, Alumroot**	P, e	18" – 24"	White, pink, green/ late spring – summer	Partial shade	Grown mainly for the gorgeous low evergreen foliage. Acid soil, partial shade. Native. Many new purple and silver variegated cultivars: 'Purple Palace', 'Veil', 'Silver Shadows', etc. Also new amber and pink foliage cultivars like 'Amber Waves'. Z (4–8/ 8–1).
Heuchera sanguinea **Coralbells**	P, e	12" – 18"	Dainty pink, red, coral, white, lime green/ late spring	Sun to part shade	Good garden soil. Neat edging plant. Grown for foliage, spike flower. Native. Many new cultivars. 'Chatterbox'. Short-lived. Z (4–8/ 8–1).
Hibiscus coccinia **Red Swampmallow**	P	7' – 12'	Red/ summer	Sun	Tall, long-blooming, tropical effect. Hardy. Z (5–10/ 10–1).
Hosta **Hosta** See Special Article below.	P	3" – 40"	Pale or deep blue, white, lavender/ late May – Oct. depending on cultivar	Partial shade	A mainstay of the shade garden for beautiful mounding foliage. Hundreds of named cultivars with variegated foliage: green & white, green & blue, green & yellow, blue & yellow, etc. Small, medium, and large

SCIENTIFIC NAME/ COMMON NAME	KEY	HEIGHT	FLOWER COLOR/ BLOOM TIME	SUN NEEDS	COMMENTS
					plants. Pleated foliage on some. Rich, moist, woodland. All subject to slugs.
Iris **Iris** See Special Article in *Bulbs*.	P	3" – 3'	Purple, blues, white, yellow, corals, pinks/ late spring	Sun to light shade	Many varieties of many species. Z (4–9/ 9–1).
Juniperus horizontalis **Trailing Juniper, Creeping Juniper**	P, e, gc	1' – 2'	Evergreen / spring	Sun	Small blue fruit that birds love. Woody, tree-like trunk, gray-green foliage, coniferous evergreen shrub. Good in rock garden, sculptural, hardy. See *Shrubs* and *Trees* for other juniper species.
Kalimeris pinnatifida **Mrs. Lawrence's Mystery Plant, Japanese Aster**	P	18"	White/ June – Oct	Sun or Shade	A favorite of late garden designer Gertrude Lawrence; slowly spreading, small daisy-like flower all summer. Works well in borders.
Kirengeshoma **Yellow Wax Bells**	P	2' – 3' x 3'	Yellow/ spring	Light shade	Lovely Japanese perennial with maple-shaped leaves. Bell-like flowers in spring. Does not flower well in too-deep shade.
Lamium galeobdolon or *Lamiastrum*	P, gc	9" – 15"	Yellow/ spring	Partial sun to shade	Spreads by stolons in shade. Silver variega-tion brightens dark

315

Scientific Name/ Common Name	Key	Height	Flower Color/ Bloom Time	Sun Needs	Comments
Yellow Archangel					areas of garden. Cut back if it becomes leggy. 'Herman's Pride', 'Variegatum'.
Lamium maculatum **Spotted Nettle**	P, gc	8" – 12"	Red to purple, white/ spring	Partial to deep shade	Spreads by stolons. 'Beacon Silver', White Nancy' add splash of silver to shady areas. Can look shabby in extreme heat.
Lavandula angustifolia **Lavender**	P, h	2' – 3'	Purple/ summer	Full sun	Light, limy, well-drained, sandy soil. Fragrant, used in sachet. 'Hidcote Blue', many new cultivars. Z (5–8/ 8–1).
Leucanthemum x superbum **'Becky' Shasta Daisy** (also called *Chrysanthemum* or *Dendranthema x superbum*)	P	18" – 30"	White/ June – Sept	Sun	Many varieties. 'Becky' is best for this area. Large clumps need dividing for rejuvenation. Heavy feeder. Deadhead for more blooms. Z (5–8/ 8–1).
Ligularia dentate or *Farfugium dentate* **Bigleaf Ligularia, Leopard Plant, Golden Groundsel**	P, V	2' – 3' x 3' – 4'	Gold, yellow/ Oct – Nov	Part to full shade	'Britt Marie Crawford' has black, glossy, rounded leaves and late-season yellow, daisy-like flowers. Keep very moist in the shade garden. Herbaceous. Recent name change to *Farfugium*.
Ligularia tussilaginea or	P, V	18"	Yellow/ November	Light to full	Rich green, glossy, round leaves with

SCIENTIFIC NAME/ COMMON NAME	KEY	HEIGHT	FLOWER COLOR/ BLOOM TIME	SUN NEEDS	COMMENTS
Farfugium japonicum **Leopard Plant**				shade	dappled yellow spots. Yellow daisy-like flower in mid-fall. Shade and moisture lover. Bold. 'Aureomaculata' has yellow spots.
Lilium **Lily** See Special Article in *Bulbs.*	P	1' – 7'	Many/ Spring – fall depending on cultivar	Light to partial shade	Many hardy species and hybrids. Beautiful flowers. Z (5–8/ 8–1).
Lippia citriodora **Lemon Verbena**	P, h	12"	White	Sun	Moist soil. Terminal white flowers, lemon-scented foliage. Shrub in South, pot plant in North; move to green-house in winter.
Liriope muscari **Liriope**	P, e, gc, V	10" – 18"	Purple or white/ late summer	Sun or shade	Green or variegated, broad grass-like foliage, lavender or white spike flower. Hardy and undemand-ing. Good for large areas or edging borders. Cut back in February before spring growth with lawnmower. Several varieties: 'Okina' has frosted blue foliage. 'Peedee Ingot' has gold foliage. Average soil.
Lobelia cardinalis **Cardinal flower**	P	2' – 4'	Red/ summer	Partial shade	Spike flowers, 6" – 12"; moist, woodland. Native. Hybrids have

317

Scientific Name/ Common Name	Key	Height	Flower Color/ Bloom Time	Sun Needs	Comments
					improved bloom. 'Fan Scarlet'. Z (3–9/ 9–1).
Lobelia siphilitica **Great Blue Lobelia**	P	2' – 3'	Blue, mauve, rose, white/ late summer	Partial shade	Spike flowers in moist, light shade. Native.
Lychnis chalcedonica **Maltese Cross**	P	2' – 3'	Scarlet/ summer	Sun	Old-fashioned. Cultivated since the Crusades. Well-drained but moist average soil.
Lysimachia nummularia **Creeping Jenny**	P, e, gc	2" – 4"	Gold/ green	Sun to shade	Fast-growing evergreen. Great in containers or around water features.
Lythrum virgatum **Purple Loosestrife**	P	2' – 3'	Pink magenta/ summer	Sun	New varieties like 'Morden's Pink', 'Morden's Gleam', 'and Dropmore Purple' are improved over species. Avoid old magenta color. Moist soil. Cut back after flowering.
Majorana hortensis **Sweet Marjoram**	P, h	2'	Herb	Sun	Keep pruned to 7" or 8" in hedge or ball, keep well mulched. Used for seasoning.
Mazus pumilio **Creeping Mazus**	P, gc	3"	Blue-violet tint/ April – May	Light to medium shade	Good groundcover between stepping stones. Will not tolerate much foot traffic. Underused.
Mazus reptans **Mazus**	P, e, gc	2" – 4"	Lavender, white/ early	Sun to part shade	Plant between stepping stones, but don't walk on it.

318

SCIENTIFIC NAME/ COMMON NAME	KEY	HEIGHT	FLOWER COLOR/ BLOOM TIME	SUN NEEDS	COMMENTS
			spring		Charming and underused ground cover. Heat and cold tolerant. Fast grower, easily controlled.
Melissa officinalis **Lemon Balm**	P, h	2'	Herb	Sun to part shade	Moist soil. Lemon scented, used for seasoning. Winters well.
Mentha **Lemon Mint, Apple Mint, Curly Mint, Orange Mint, Peppermint, Pineapple Mint, Chocolate Mint, Spearmint**	P, h	1' – 2'	White/ summer	Sun to part shade	Rich damp area, some shade as leaves lose color and flavor in full sun. Suggestion: plant in tubs to confine creeping roots. Pinch off blossoms for a bushier plant and to prevent reseeding.
Mertensia virginica **Virginia Bluebells**	P	to 2'	Blue/ spring	Partial shade	Buds and fading flowers are pink; leaf mold, lime. Spring ephemeral. Native.
Miscanthus sinensis **Maiden Grass**	P, V	3'	Yellow-orange tone/ October	Sun	Variegated grass, tan in winter. Clump forming ornamental grass. Good varieties include 'Morning Light', 'Minuett', 'Adagio', 'Andante', 'Cabaret', 'Little Kitten', 'Little Zebra', and so on.
Miscanthus sinensis purpurascens **Pink Eulalia Grass**	P, V	3' x 3'	Reddish/ late summer	Sun	Ornamental grass clump with reddish inflorescence in late summer. Effective all season.

319

Scientific Name/ Common Name	Key	Height	Flower Color/ Bloom Time	Sun Needs	Comments
Mitella diphylla **Bishop's-Cap, Miterwort**	P, gc	12"	White/ spring	Partial to medium shade	Similar foliage to *Tiarella* and *Heuchera*. Ground cover for moist woodland in partial shade. Loamy soil.
Monarda didyma **Bee Balm, Monarda, Oswego Tea, Bergamot**	P	2' – 3'	Red, rose, pink/ early summer	Sun or partial shade	Moist, well-drained, not-too-rich soil. Remove faded flowers to prolong blooming. Attracts hummingbirds and bees. Good cut flower. 'Jacob Cline', 'Gardenview Scarlet', 'Marshall's Delight'. Z (4–9/ 9–1).
Monarda fistulosa **Wild Bergamot**	P	to 2'	Lavender/ summer	Sun	Ordinary soil. Native. Z (4–9/ 9–1).
Muhlenbergia capillaris **Hairy Awn Muhly**	P	3' x 3'	Reddish purple/ late summer	Sun	Narrow, green, grass-like foliage on 3' clump. In August fluffy pink inflorescence appears.
Muhlenbergia lindheimeri **Lindheimer's Muhly**	P	3' x 3'	Tan/ late summer	Sun	Narrow, blue, grass-like foliage of this Texas native makes an attractive clump. 6' plumes of reed grass-like (*Calamagrostis*) inflorescence in August. Can take the heat.
Nepeta x faassenii **Faassen's Nepeta, Catnip**	P	1' – 2'	Blue, purple, white/ early to mid-	Sun to light shade	Well-drained ordinary soil. 'Six Hills Giant', 'Blue Wonder'. Some cats roll in it bliss-fully. Z (4–8/ 8–1).

SCIENTIFIC NAME/ COMMON NAME	KEY	HEIGHT	FLOWER COLOR/ BLOOM TIME	SUN NEEDS	COMMENTS
			summer		
Oenothera fruticosa **Primrose** or **Sundrops**	P	1' – 2'	Yellow/ summer	Sun	Hairy leaves; 2" wide yellow flowers. Ordinary soil on the dry side. Best cultivars are *O. fruticosa* ssp. *glauca* such as 'Cold Crick', 'Summer Solstice', & 'Erica Robin'. Native.
Oenothera speciosa **Showy Evening Primrose**	P	1' – 2' x 1' – 2'	Pink, white/ late spring	Sun	Stoloniferous and spreading. Can be an invasive nuisance in rich soil. Full sun and ordinary soil are best. 'Siskiyou', 'Woodside White' and 'Ballerina Hot Pink' are better than species. Native.
Ophiopogon japonicus **Mondo Grass** or **Monkey Grass**	P, e, gc, V	4" – 10"	White/ spring	Sun or shade	Dwarf variety similar to liriope. Cobalt blue berry in fall. Hardy. Forms sod-like mat. Useful for edging. Average soil; vigorous spreader in rich humusy soil. Many new varieties: 'Little Tabby', 'Torafu', 'Bluebird'.
Ophiopogon planiscapus Nigrescens **Black Mondo Grass**	P, e, gc	6" x 12"	Pink on black foliage/ summer	Part shade	Lovely, dramatic black grass-like foliage with pink flowers and black berries. Good for edging. 'Arabicus'.
Origanum vulgare	P, h	2½"	Herb	Full	Well-drained soil.

SCIENTIFIC NAME/ COMMON NAME	KEY	HEIGHT	FLOWER COLOR/ BLOOM TIME	SUN NEEDS	COMMENTS
Oregano				Sun	Used for seasoning. Pinch off spent blossoms for bushier plant and to prevent going to seed.
Pachysandra procumbens **Native Pachysandra**	P, e, gc	6" – 12"	Greenish, purplish/ spring	Part sun to deep shade	Mottled leaf larger than *P terminalis*. Good garden soil. Will spread to form nice ground cover. 'Allegheny'
Pachysandra terminalis **Pachysandra**	P. e, gc	6" – 12"	White/ spring	Part sun to deep shade	Attractive foliage. 'Silver Edge' is variegated variety. Hardy. Easily propagated from cuttings. One of the best ground covers for shade.
Paeonia **Peony** See under *Bulbs* and Special Article	P	1' – 2'	Many/ spring	Sun to part shade	Well-loved heirloom plant. Z (3–8/ 8–1).
Panicum virgatum **Blue Switch Grass**	P	30"	Yellow-orange tone/ October	Sun to light shade	'Heavy Metal'. Metallic blue grass-like leaves ½" – ¾" wide on compact upright plants. Foliage is amber in fall, beige in winter. Airy yellowish flowers in fall are useful in arrangements. Native.
Panicum virgatum **Purple Foliage Switchgrass**	P, V	2' – 3' x 2' – 3'	Reddish-purple foliage, crimson bloom/	Sun to part shade	'Shenandoah'. Grass-like foliage emerges reddish-purple in spring, has crimson flowers in summer,

SCIENTIFIC NAME/ COMMON NAME	KEY	HEIGHT	FLOWER COLOR/ BLOOM TIME	SUN NEEDS	COMMENTS
			summer		and maroon foliage in fall on this non-invasive clump-former. Decorative, tough.
Patrinia scabiosifolia **Scabious Patrinia, Japanese Patrinia**	P	3' – 6'	Yellow/ summer to fall	Sun to light shade	Does well in heat and humidity. Small flowers on tall airy branches. 'Nagoya' is 2' – 3' tall and blooms July – Sept.
Patrinia triloba **Patrinia**	P	3' – 4'	Yellow/ July	Sun to part shade	Dainty yellow flowers carried over glossy ivy-like foliage.
Pennisetum orientale **Fountain Grass**	P	3' x 2'	Dusty rose/ May – frost	Sun	Ornamental grass with showy pink plumes all season on this clump-former. Blue-green foliage stays fresh-looking all season.
Penstemon barbatus **Beard-tongue, Common**	P	1' – 1½'	Pink, red, white/ June – July	Sun	Acid soil with humus. Good drainage. Sensitive to winter wetness. Good cut flower. Native. Many species. Z (4–9/ 9–1).
Penstemon digitalis **Beard-tongue**	P	3'	White/ spring	Sun	'Husker Red' is best variety. White foxglove-like flower with maroon stems and maroon-tinged foliage. Z (4–9/ 9–1).
Penstemon smallii **Beard-tongue**	P	2½'	Lavender/ spring – summer	Sun	Many other hybrid varieties; check catalogs. Garden soil, slightly sandy. Native.

323

Scientific Name/ Common Name	Key	Height	Flower Color/ Bloom Time	Sun Needs	Comments
					Z (4–9/ 9–1).
Persicaria amplexicaule **Mountain Fleeceflower, Knotweed**	P	2' – 3'	Red-violet/ July – Oct	Sun to light shade	Blooms for 4–5 months with spikes of rose flowers. Reliable, not fussy about growing conditions. 'Taurus' and 'Firetail' are good.
Petasites japonicus **Fuki, Dinosaur Food**	P	2' – 3'	White/ spring	Partial to full shade	Moist woodland or water garden. Huge 2' round leaves. Tropical looking but very hardy. 'Giganteum'. See catalogs.
Phlox divaricata **Woodland Phlox**	P, gc	12"	Lavender, blue, white, rose/ early spring	Partial shade	Slowly spreading, stoloniferous, woodland plant. Buy mildew-resistant varieties. Native.
Phlox maculata **Spotted Phlox, Wild Sweet William**	P	2' – 3'	Mauve-pink, lavender/ spring	Partial shade	Garden soil. Native. Spider mites a problem for phlox. New hybrids: 'Miss Lingard', 'Rosalinde'.
Phlox paniculata **Garden Phlox**	P	1' – 4'	Magenta, white, blue, salmon, red, scarlet/ summer	Sun	Old-fashioned flower; buy mildew-resistant varieties. Many new cultivars: 'David' & 'Mt. Fuji' are white. Z (4–8/ 8–1).
Phlox stolonifera **Creeping Phlox**	P, gc	½' – 1'	Lavender, violet/ spring	Partial to full shade	Better for the South than *P. subulata*. Stoloniferous, woodland spreader. Very nice plant.
Physostegia	P	1' – 4'	Pink,	Sun or	Flower spikes 8" –

SCIENTIFIC NAME/ COMMON NAME	KEY	HEIGHT	FLOWER COLOR/ BLOOM TIME	SUN NEEDS	COMMENTS
virginiana **Obedient Plant, False Dragonhead**			White/ late summer – early fall	shade	10". Easily grown, can become invasive. New cultivars are better behaved.
Platycodon grandiflorus **Balloon Flower**	P	1' – 2½'	Blue, white/ June – Oct	Sun or part shade	Good drainage. Easily grown from seed sown in garden in early spring. Has tap-root so do not trans-plant. Z (4–9/ 9–1).
Podophyllum peltatum **Mayapple**	P	to 18"	White/ spring	Partial shade	Waxy flower borne on double leafed stem; spring; garden soil. Spring ephemeral; dies back in summer. Spreading. Native.
Polemonium reptans **Greek Valerian, Creeping Polemonium, Creeping Jacob's-ladder**	P, V	8" – 15"	Blue/ spring	Partial shade	Drooping flower in clusters; leaf mold. Missouri native woodland wildflower. Not the same Jacob's-ladder as *P. caeruleum* which does not do well here. Also available variegated.
Polygonatum biflorum **Solomon's-seal**	P	to 3'	Creamy white/ early spring	Partial shade	Flowers hang below leaf axil; likes humus and leaf mold. Native.
Polygonatum commutatum **Great Solomon's-seal**	P	3' – 7'	White-green/ spring	Partial shade	Takes up a lot of space; too big for most gardens. Good at edge of moist wood-land. Outstanding plant. Native.
Polygonatum odoratum	P	1½' – 2½'	Creamy white/	Partial shade	'Variegatum' is a premier shade plant.

325

SCIENTIFIC NAME/ COMMON NAME	KEY	HEIGHT	FLOWER COLOR/ BLOOM TIME	SUN NEEDS	COMMENTS
Variegated Solomon's-seal			April		Tolerates dry shade but prefers even moisture. Woodland conditions. April bloom.
Pontederia cordata **Pickerel Weed**	P	1' – 4'	Lavender/ spring – summer	Partial shade	Likes bogs or water gardens. Spreads without being invasive. Lovely, dark green, arrow-shaped leaves with purple spike flower.
Pratia angulata **Pratia, Blue Star Creeper**	P, gc, e	1"	White with blue veins/ spring	Part sun to light shade	Semi-evergreen ground cover from New Zealand with round green leaves on black zigzag stems. White lobelia-like flowers in spring to early summer. Tolerates wet sites.
Pratia pedunculata **Pratia, Blue Star Creeper**	P, gc. e	1"	Pale blue/ spring to summer	Part sun to part shade	Ground cover from New Zealand; will tolerate some foot traffic, plant between stepping stones. In the lobelia family.
Primula vulgaris **English Primrose**	P	6" – 9"	Yellow, white, greenish/ spring	Light to medium shade	Likes moist rich dirt. This is one of the more heat-tolerant *Primulas* among the 400 species. Charming in woodland or rock garden. Can be short-lived.
Pulmonaria saccharata **Bethlehem Sage,**	P	9" – 18"	Pink to blue/ early spring	Partial shade	Good plant for front of shady border. 'Mrs. Moon', 'Margery

Scientific Name/ Common Name	Key	Height	Flower Color/ Bloom Time	Sun Needs	Comments
Lungwort					Fish', 'Roy David-son'. Rich moist soil. Must be well drained; hates wet feet in winter. Z (4–8/ 8–1).
Rosa **Rose** See Special Article in *Shrubs–Roses.*					
Rosmarinus officinalis **Rosemary**	P, H	15"	Blue, white/ spring to summer	Sun	Garden soil, good drainage. Dark, needle-like leaves. Propagate from cuttings. 'Arp' rosemary is good garden plant.
Rubus calycinoides **Creeping Raspberry**	P, e, gc	12" – 16"	White/ spring	Sun to shade	Fast-spreading once established. Round bright green textured leaves that turn burgundy in fall.
Rudbeckia fulgida **Black-eyed Susan, Orange Coneflower**	P	1' – 2'	Golden yellow with black or brown center/ all summer	Sun	Garden soil. Many varieties: Good cut flower. Long bloom period; reliable perennial, rather coarse. Native.
Rudbeckia nitida **Coneflower**	P	7'	Yellow/ late summer – fall	Sun	'Herbstsonne' is an excellent large cone-flower. May need staking. Native.
Rudbeckia triloba **Three-Lobed Coneflower**	B/P	2' – 3'	Yellow/ summer	Sun	Yellow petals with raised central black disc. Underused native. Reliable biennial.
Rudbeckia x	P	2'	Yellow/	Sun	Good cultivar for the

327

SCIENTIFIC NAME/ COMMON NAME	KEY	HEIGHT	FLOWER COLOR/ BLOOM TIME	SUN NEEDS	COMMENTS
'Goldsturm' **Rudbeckia**			summer		garden. Average soil. Moist.
Salvia **Sage,** **Salvia**	P	1' – 4'	Blue, purple, red, white/ summer – fall	Sun	Over 700 species of sages and salvias. Annual salvias are in *Annuals*. The following are short-lived perennials; long-lived where happy. Leave dead foliage on through winter for protection. Z (4–9/ 9–1).
Salvia azurea **Azure Sage**	P	2' – 4'	Azure blue/ fall	Sun	Garden soil; good for cutting. Tolerant of heat and humidity. Native. Z (4–9/ 9–1).
Salvia greggii **Greg's Salvia,** **Texas Sage**	P, e	1½' – 3'	Various/ summer – fall	Sun to light shade	Texas native; heat, humidity, & drought tolerant. Long-blooming. Hummingbirds & butterflies love it. Great plant. Leave dead foliage through winter. 'Cherry Queen', 'Alba', 'Furman's Red', 'Desert Blaze'. Z (4–9/ 9–1).
Salvia guaranitica **Blue Anise Sage**	P	4' – 6'	Deep blue/ all summer	Sun	Average well-drained soil. Divide every 3 years to maintain vigor. *Salvia x* 'Indigo Spires' is 3' tall and blooms for months. 'Purple Majesty'. Z (4–9/ 9–1).

SCIENTIFIC NAME/ COMMON NAME	KEY	HEIGHT	FLOWER COLOR/ BLOOM TIME	SUN NEEDS	COMMENTS
Salvia haematodes or *Salvia pratensis* **Meadow Sage**	P	1' – 3'	Purplish-blue/ summer	Sun to light shade	Average soil, evenly moist. Several cultivars: 'Rosea', 'Alba'. Z (4–9/ 9–1).
Salvia leucantha **Autumn Sage**	P	3' – 4'	Blue-violet, white/ Oct – Nov	Sun	Late-flowering, with dozens of blue and white blooms from October – frost. Velvety, fragrant foliage is pest and disease resistant. 'Blue on Blue'. Leave dead foliage through winter. Z (4–9/ 9–1).
Salvia nemorosa **Salvia Woodland Sage**	P	1½' – 2'	Deep violet blue/ all summer	Sun	'May Night' is a garden-worthy salvia, compact and heat-tolerant, with blue flower spikes over a long season. Prefers ordinary, well-drained soil. 'East Friesland'. Z (4–9/ 9–1).
Salvia officinalis **Garden Sage, Common Sage**	P, H	2'	Herb/ summer	Sun	Aromatic leaves used dried for cooking. Propagates from cuttings. Cut back to half its height each spring. Z (4–9/ 9–1).
Salvia x superba **Hybrid Sage**	P	1' – 4'	Violet blue, purple/ summer	Sun	'Purple Rain', 'Plumosa', and many others. Z (4–9/ 9–1).
Sanguinaria canadensis **Bloodroot**	P	3" – 6"	White/ early spring	Partial shade	Small woodland ephemeral blooms before trees leaf-out, dies back in summer. Pretty foliage. Native.

329

SCIENTIFIC NAME/ COMMON NAME	KEY	HEIGHT	FLOWER COLOR/ BLOOM TIME	SUN NEEDS	COMMENTS
					Sap used as dye and paint.
Saponaria officinalis **Soapwort, Bouncing Bet**	P, h	1' – 2'	Pink/ spring – fall	Sun	Well-drained garden soil. Leaves give "cleansing" sap when bruised. Rock garden. Native.
Sarracenia purpurea **Pitcher Plant**	P	4" – 3'	Rosy, yellow, greenish/ summer	Sun to part shade	Carnivorous native bog plant. Special growing require-ments; only rainwater or distilled water; no fertilizer; consumes insects. Unusual and hardy. Z (6–8).
Saruma henryii **Saruma**	P	1' – 2'	Light yellow/ spring	Partial shade	From China, great in woodland. Heart-shaped, fuzzy leaf with pale yellow flowers in early spring. Pest-free and reliable. See catalogs.
Satureja montana **Winter Savory**	P, H	14"	Herb	Sun	Pinch tips for bushier plants. Propagate from cuttings or root division. Aromatic, good for seasoning. Cut and dry branches by hanging upside down.
Saxifraga stolonifera **Strawberry Geranium Strawberry Begonia**	P, gc	6" – 15"	White, pink or scarlet/ late spring	Partial to full shade	Silver-mottled, green-gray, geranium-like leaf. Propagates by runners. Good for rock gardens; dies back in winter.
Sedum	P, e,	1" – 10"	White/	Sun to	Many varieties; hardy

SCIENTIFIC NAME/ COMMON NAME	KEY	HEIGHT	FLOWER COLOR/ BLOOM TIME	SUN NEEDS	COMMENTS
Sedum, Stonecrop, Live-forever	gc		summer	part shade	in any soil, succulent leaf and stem; best in rock gardens.
Sedum kamtschaticum **Kamtschat Stonecrop**	P, e	4" – 9"	Yellow/ summer	Sun	Well-drained, ordinary soil. Rock garden. 'Weihenstephaner Gold'.
Sedum spectabilis x **'Matrona' Sedum**	P, e	2'	Ivory/ late summer to fall	Sun	Burgundy foliage, whitish flower. Good for design. Z (3–10/ 10–1).
Sedum spectabilis x **'Rosy Glow' Sedum**	P, e	2'	Pink, rose/ late summer to fall	Sun	Good selection. Z (3–10/ 10–1).
Sedum spectabilis x **'Autumn Joy' Sedum**	P, e	1' – 2'	Pink/ late summer to fall	Sun	Popular variety. Good, long-lasting bloomer. Z (3–10/ 10–1).
Sedum ternatum **Native Sedum**	P, gc	5"	White/ April – May	Light to medium shade	Low-growing, reliable sedum. Likes well drained soil in part shade.
Selaginella uncinata **Peacock Moss**	P, gc	6" – 12"	Green/ spring	Partial shade	A low, spreading habit, with metallic aquamarine arbor-vitae-like foliage overlaid on a green background. Coloring is most prominent on new spring foliage. See *Selaginella braunii* under *Ferns*. Charming ground cover for woodland.
Silene virginica	P	1' – 2'	Scarlet/	Sun	Loose clusters of star-

331

Scientific Name/ Common Name	Key	Height	Flower Color/ Bloom Time	Sun Needs	Comments
Fire Pinks			summer		shaped flowers; open woods and rocky slopes. Native.
Sisyrinchium angustifolium **Blue-eyed Grass**	P	to 12"	Violet blue/ spring	Sun	Garden soil; easily transplanted, multiplies. Native.
Smilacina racemosa **False Solomon's-seal**	P	to 3'	Creamy white/ spring	Partial shade	Foliage similar to Solomon's-seal. Tapering spike flower; leaf mold. Native.
Solidago cultivars **Goldenrod**	P	1½' – 3'	Yellow/ summer	Sun to part shade	Humusy or ordinary, well-drained soil. 'Cloth of Gold', 'Golden Thumb', 'Crown of Rays'. Z (5–9/ 9–1).
Spigelia marilandica **Indian Pink, Pinkroot**	P	1' – 2'	Red tube with yellow lining/ May – June	Partial shade	Rich soil. Propagation by root or seed; good for cutting. Native.
Spiranthes odorata **Ladies Tresses**	P	1' – 2'	White/ Sept.	Sun to part shade	In the *Orchid* family, this plant does not have showy blossom, but is a woodland native. Rich moist soil in part shade is best. 'Chadd's Ford'.
Stachys byzantina **Lamb's-ears**	P, gc	1' – 1½'	Purple/ late spring	Sun to part shade	The pale silver-green velvety foliage is more attractive than flowers; remove them as they form, or cut after blooming. 'Countess Helene von

SCIENTIFIC NAME/ COMMON NAME	KEY	HEIGHT	FLOWER COLOR/ BLOOM TIME	SUN NEEDS	COMMENTS
					Stein' and other improved cultivars. Moist, well-drained, average soil. Reliable.
Stokesia laevis **Stokes' Aster**	P	1' – 1½'	Blue, lavender, white/ summer	Sun to light shade	Well-drained soil. Good for cutting. Many new cultivars. 'Blue Danube'.
Stylophorum diphyllum **Celandine Poppy, Wood Poppy**	P	1' – 1½'	Bright yellow/ early spring	Partial shade	2" flower; silvery seedpods, lovely foliage. Rich moist soil. Wonderful plant. Native.
Tagetes lucida **Spanish Tarragon**	P, H	3' – 4'	Yellow/ fall	Sun	Substitute for French tarragon. Good garden plant.
Teucrium chamaedrys **Germander**	P, e, gc, H	1'	Red-violet tint/ June	Sun	Nice evergreen foliage on short woody perennial. Easily shaped and pruned. Mint-like flowers. Cats love it.
Thalictrum aquilegifolium **Columbine Meadow-Rue**	P	2' – 3'	Shades of purple, white, pink/ late spring	Partial shade	Rich moist soil. Heat tolerant. 'White Cloud', 'Purpureum'.
Thalictrum polygamum **Woodland Meadow Rue**	P	6' – 8'	White/ late spring	Partial shade	Rich moist soil. Panicles of white flowers on tall airy plant. Underused.
Thermopsis caroliniana **False Lupine**	P	2' – 4'	Yellow/ early spring	Sun – partial shade	Rich moist soil. Blooms early with yellow, lupine-like flowers for 3 – 4 weeks. Similar to *Baptisia* but smaller.

SCIENTIFIC NAME/ COMMON NAME	KEY	HEIGHT	FLOWER COLOR/ BLOOM TIME	SUN NEEDS	COMMENTS
					Cut back after bloom.
Thymus vulgaris **Thyme**	P, H, gc	8"	Herb – avoid flowering	Sun	Light, sandy, lime soil. Small leaved. Keep well-clipped to prevent woody growths. Can be potted and put in sunny window for winter. For drying, cut before or at flowering time; hang upside down. Propagate from seeds or cuttings.
Tiarella cordifolia **Foamflower**	P, gc	6" – 12"	White/ early spring	Partial shade	Tiny, white spike flowers, dies back in summer heat; leaf mold. Stoloniferous. Native. Z (4–9/ 9–1).
Tiarella wherryi **Wherry's Foamflower**	P	1' – 1½'	White, pinkish/ early spring	Partial shade	Similar to above but showier. Clump-former. Woodland conditions. Z (4–9/ 9–1).
Tovara virginiana (or *Polygonum virginiana* or *Persicaria virginiana*) **Painter's Palette**	P, gc	10" – 15"	Red/ late spring	Sun to part shade	Pretty oval green leaf with cream splotch overlaid with maroon chevron. Nicely spreading ground cover. To control spread, pick some but not all of the spiky heuchera-like flowers.
Tradescantia virginiana **Spiderwort**	P	to 2½'	Brilliant blue, white/ spring to early summer	Sun	Any soil; closes at night. Related to Wandering Jew; low and sprawling. Some long-blooming new cultivars. Native.

SCIENTIFIC NAME/ COMMON NAME	KEY	HEIGHT	FLOWER COLOR/ BLOOM TIME	SUN NEEDS	COMMENTS
					Z (5–9/ 9–1).
Tricyrtis formosana (or *T. stolonifera*) **Formosa Toad Lily**	P	1' – 3'	Pale purple/ late summer – early fall	Partial shade	Rich moist soil. Toad lilies are wonderful and underused in the shade garden. Arching branches with flowers in the leaf axils as well as tip. Orchid-like, long-lasting bloom. 'Amethyst-ina' among others.
Tricyrtis hirta **Common Toad Lily**	P	1' – 4'	Purple or crimson spots over white/ fall	Partial shade	Moist, rich soil. *T. hirta* is erect or slightly arching with terminal flowers resembling orchids in September and October. Toad lilies can look a little tatty by summer's end. 'White Towers', 'Lilac Towers'.
Tricyrtis hirta x T. formosana **'Miyazaki' Toad Lily,**	P	2'	Purple spots over white/ fall	Partial shade	'Miyazaki' has a lovely, graceful, arching habit. Orchid-like flower in every leaf axil in October. Super and underused. See catalogs. Rich moist soil. Also 'Miyazaki Gold'.
Tricyrtis macropoda **Toad Lily**	P	2' – 3'	Lavender/ fall	Partial shade	More upright in habit. Flower clusters borne terminally. 'Togen', White Flame', 'Seiryu'.
Trillium erectum **Stinking**	P	to 1'	Dark red/ early	Partial shade	Leaf mold. Name is misleading; a

335

Scientific Name/ Common Name	Key	Height	Flower Color/ Bloom Time	Sun Needs	Comments
Benjamin			spring		charming ephemeral woodland native. Dies back in summer heat.
Trillium catesbaei **Rose Trillium**	P	10" – 12"	Rose pink, white/ early spring	Partial shade	Leaves have wavy margin, flower is below leaf canopy. Charming, woodland native. Spring ephemeral.
Trillium grandiflorum **Great White Trillium**	P	to 12"	White changing to pale pink/ early spring	Partial shade	Leaf mold. Woodland ephemeral. May die back in heat of summer. Native.
Trillium luteum **Yellow Trillium**	P	8" – 12"	Yellow/ early spring	Partial shade	Mottled leaf; beautiful plant. Woodland ephemeral, leaf mold. Native.
Trillium sessile **Sessile Trillium, Toad Trillium, Wake Robin**	P	to 12"	Red, purple/ early spring	Partial shade	Mottled leaf; leaf mold. Spring ephemeral; dies back in summer. Many varieties. See catalogs. Native.
Uvularia grandiflora **Merrybells, Bellwort**	P	18"	Yellow/ early spring	Partial shade	Bell-like flower; resembles Solomon's-seal. Slowly increasing clump. Leaf mold. Excellent, trouble-free plant; underused. Buy from catalogs. Native.
Uvularia sessilifolia **Merrybells**	P	12"	Greenish yellow/ early spring	Partial shade	Same as above.
Verbascum	P	1' – 2'	Violet,	Sun to	Ordinary soil, well-

SCIENTIFIC NAME/ COMMON NAME	KEY	HEIGHT	FLOWER COLOR/ BLOOM TIME	SUN NEEDS	COMMENTS
hybrids **Verbascum, Mullein**			pink, cream, rose, salmon/ June – Sept.	light shade	drained. Spires of colorful flowers from wooly basal rosette. 'Summer Sorbet', 'Jackie in Pink', 'Caribbean Crush'.
Verbena bonariensis **South American Verbena, Tall Verbena**	P	3' – 4'	Rose-violet/ summer – frost	Sun to light shade	Best massed in cutting garden. Cutting increases branching. See-through, airy plant for mid-border. Ordinary garden soil.
Verbena canadensis **Clump Verbena**	P	8" – 18"	Dark purple/ early spring – summer	Sun	'Homestead Purple'. Excellent cultivar for the South. Long-flowering. Native.
Veronica noveboracensis **Ironweed**	P	3' – 7'	Red-violet/ late summer – fall	Sun	Tall, durable plant for back of the border. Flower head is 6" – 8" across consisting of 30 – 50 flowers. Cut back a month after emergence to control size, if desired.
Veronica peduncularis **'Georgia Blue' Veronica**	P, e, gc	12"	Blue/ March	Sun	'Georgia Blue'. Good low-growing evergreen. Burgundy foliage in winter. From Georgia in Russia. Well-drained garden soil.
Veronica spicata **Veronica, Speedwell**	P	1½' – 2'	Violet blue/ mid-summer to fall	Sun to part shade	Garden soil, good drainage a must. Underused. 'Sunny Border Blue' is an excellent plant. 'Silver Anne' is a

337

Scientific Name/ Common Name	Key	Height	Flower Color/ Bloom Time	Sun Needs	Comments
					beautiful, warm pink. Z (3–8/ 8–1).
Veronicastrum virginicum **Culver's Root**	P	3' – 5'	White, lavender/ June	Sun to light shade	Handsome plant if given sun. Native. 'Alba' and 'Lavendelturm' are improved over species
Vinca major **Vinca, Greater Periwinkle**	P, e, gc	1' tall – to 20' long	Lavender/ spring	Sun or shade	Dark green oval leaves on long runners. Vine-like but used as ground cover. Species can be rampant in rich soil. Look for hybrids.
Vinca minor **Periwinkle, Vinca**	P, e, gc	6"	Lavender, blue and white/ spring	Partial shade	Garden soil. Useful as ground cover. Variegated variety good for window boxes and hanging baskets. Can become invasive, but not as badly as *Vinca major*. Native.
Viola **Violet**	P, e, gc	6"	White, yellow, lavender, purple, purple and white/ spring	Partial shade	Many varieties. Native. Can become invasive weed, but is a charming, small, evergreen ground cover.
Yucca filamentosa **Yucca, Adam's-needle**	P, e	2' – 4'	White/ summer	Sun	6' spike of many bell-shaped flowers, sharp leaves; garden soil, many other varieties. See *Shrubs* for others.

SPECIAL ARTICLES ON SELECT PERENNIALS

CHRYSANTHEMUM

CHRYSANTHEMUM, DENDRANTHEMA, LEUCANTHEMUM

Chrysanthemums are one of the oldest cultivated plants, grown by the Chinese since 500 B.C. They have undergone extensive hybridizing through the years, especially in the last few decades, for traits such as flower form, disease resistance, earlier bloom time, and longer-lasting flowers.

Two main categories are: 1) *garden mums* which are reliably hardy in the border, and 2) *florist's mums* which are best grown in a protected environment. Varieties come in shades of white, yellow, pink, lavender, red, orange, and bronze; every color except blue. For named varieties check catalogs.

Over a decade ago, botanists reclassified the genus of many *Chrysanthemum* species as either *Dendranthema* or *Leucanthemum*. Some are now being changed back to the original name, however, so there is confusion in the literature. They are members of the Aster (*Asteracaea*) family. This all makes little difference to the gardener who will probably always call them daisy or chrysanthemum.

CULTURE

Chrysanthemums should be planted in sunny or high shade beds. If grown in too much shade, they will become leggy and lose lower leaves. They prefer sandy loam kept evenly moist, but will grow in ordinary garden soil if fertilized occasionally. Before planting prepare the soil by spading in a 3" layer of well-rotted or dehydrated manure, or compost to which super-phosphate has been added.

Feed lightly every 2 weeks with a good balanced all-purpose fertilizer. Do not fertilize after buds show color. Keep well watered.

PINCHING BACK AND DISBUDDING

If you want mums with long stems for flower arrangements, do not pinch back. Nor should you remove buds from the *pompom* or *cushion* varieties. On the largest-flowering types it is best to remove all buds except for the one on top in order to obtain specimen blooms rather than many smaller ones.

To double the crop of flowers and promote bushiness on most garden mums, pinch out the tip of each stem, including the top set of leaves, when plants are 6" – 8" tall. When they reach a foot tall, pinch them again. After July 15th, stop pinching and allow flower buds to develop.

339

Chrysanthemum can be tricky to over-winter successfully. Do not cut off dead foliage until spring and avoid planting where the ground stays wet all winter.

PROPAGATION

Chrysanthemums may be divided for increase, or propagated from cuttings rooted either in water or in a soil-less mixture, like Pro-mix. If cuttings are from last year's growth, choose shoots farthest from the center of the plant. Treat the cuttings with a rooting hormone before planting in Pro-Mix. For maximum garden display in the fall, start cuttings in April. (See *Garden Care – Propagation* for details)

DISEASES AND PESTS

Leaf spot – Use a fungicide.

Cucumber beetles in fall – Use an insecticide, such as Sevin.

VARIETIES OF CHRYSANTHEMUM

There are hundreds of named varieties of mums, and many are grown for flower show competitions. A few good perennial (**P**) garden mums are listed below.

TABLE 34. VARIETIES OF CHRYSANTHEMUM
(*CHRYSANTHEMUM, DENDRANTHEMA, LEUCANTHEMUM*)

SCIENTIFIC NAME/ COMMON NAME	KEY	HEIGHT	FLOWER COLOR/ BLOOM TIME	SUN NEEDS	COMMENTS
Chrysanthemum leucanthemum superbum or *Leucanthemum x superbum* **Shasta Daisy**	P	1' – 2'	White/ June – Oct	Sun	Many varieties. **'Becky'** is best for the South. Large clumps need dividing for rejuvenation. Heavy feeder. Deadhead for more blooms. Z (5–8/ 8–1).
Chrysanthemum x rubellum or *Dendranthema* **'Clara Curtis'** Daisy	P	1' – 2'	Deep pink/ late summer	Sun	Also *D.* **'Mary Stoker'**. Ordinary soil; free-flowering. Z (5–8/ 8–1).
Chrysanthemum or *Leucanthemum vulgare* **Ox-eye Daisy,**	P	to 2'	White with yellow center/ summer	Sun	Any soil. Good for cutting. Reseeds. Will naturalize. Sun. Z (5–8/ 8–1).

SCIENTIFIC NAME/ COMMON NAME	KEY	HEIGHT	FLOWER COLOR/ BLOOM TIME	SUN NEEDS	COMMENTS
Field Daisy					
Dendranthema arcticum **Arctic Daisy**	P	1' – 1½'	White, red, pink, gold, russet/ fall – frost	Sun	A very beautiful group of border mums, making a spreading mound of large, single daisy-like flowers. They bloom over a long period and are very hardy.
Dendranthema grandiflora or *Chrysanthemum x morifolium* **Chrysanthemum hybrids**	P	1' – 4'	Varies by hybrid type	Sun	Some of the better garden and florists' mums are in this category.
Anemone– flowered	P	2' – 3'	Pink, russet, lavender, gold, etc/ fall – frost	Sun	Have single or double blossoms with pincushion-like centers. Best in greenhouse.
Button	P	1' – 2'	Yellow, orange, russet, lavender, pink, rose, burgundy, white/ fall – frost	Sun	Flowers are less than 1" across and have petals that hug the center of the flower so tightly that they look as if they have been trimmed. They bloom in long-stemmed clusters. Compact plants. Hardy and late-flowering.
Cushion or Azalea	P	1'	Yellow, orange, russet, pink, rose, lavender, burgundy, white/ late	Sun	Offer the advantage of early and continuous bloom, but many of them have the unpleasant habit of retaining their faded flowers, which spoils

341

Scientific Name/ Common Name	Key	Height	Flower Color/ Bloom Time	Sun Needs	Comments
			summer		the effect.
Daisy	P	2' – 3'	Yellow, orange, russet, lavender, pink, rose, burgundy, white/ fall	Sun	Single-flowered chrysanthemums have daisy-petaled blossoms with slightly rounded central disks. Good garden mum.
Decorative	P	2' – 3'	Yellow, orange, russet, lavender, pink, rose, burgundy, white/ fall – frost	Sun	Vigorous plants produce large, showy, 5" – 6" fully-double flowers. Best in greenhouse.
Korean hybrid	P	1' – 2'	Yellow, orange, russet, lavender, pink, rose, burgundy, white/ fall – frost	Sun	This daisy-flowered variety is one of the best garden mums. Some clump-formers, some spreaders. Have semi-double blossoms as well as singles. Hardy, reliable. Z (5–8/ 8–1).
Pompom	P	1'	Yellow, orange, russet, pink, rose, burgundy, white/ fall	Sun	Has a blossom about 1½" – 2" across, borne in clusters on long stems throughout the fall. They may be yellow-centered, single type with loosely arranged petals or heavily petaled doubles.
Quilled	P	2' – 3'	Yellow, orange, russet,	Sun	Similar to spoon mums, except ends of petals are closed. Best

Scientific Name/ Common Name	Key	Height	Flower Color/ Bloom Time	Sun Needs	Comments
			pink, rose, burgundy, white/ fall		in greenhouse.
Spider or Fuji	P	2' – 4'	Yellow, orange, russet, lavender, pink, rose, burgundy, white/ fall	Sun	Fuji mums have wide-spreading, flat-headed flowers of great beauty. Best in greenhouse.
Spoon	P	2' – 3'	Yellow, orange, russet, pink, rose, burgundy, white/ fall – frost	Sun	The 3" – 5" flowers have spreading, flat-headed, tubular petals; the ends of the petals flare into the shape of a spoon and are often lighter in color than the rest of the petal. Best in greenhouse.

343

GROUND COVERS

Ground covers are low-growing plants used to blanket the ground, and are among the most practical and beautiful landscape materials. They can prevent erosion on banks and are useful in shady areas where grass will not grow. They also help to eliminate weeding and preserve moisture in flower beds. Ground covers are being used in more creative ways than ever before in container gardening and hanging baskets, zero-lot-line landscaping, and in raised beds and borders.

In the past only a few varieties such as **liriope, mondo grass** (*Ophiopogon*), **vinca minor, pachysandra, ivy** (*Hedera*), **ajuga**, and **creeping jenny** (*Lysimachia*) were available. Interesting new additions include **Japanese sweetflag** (*Acorus*), **spotted nettle** (*Lamium*), **yellow archangel** (*Lamiastrum*), **mazus** (*Mazus reptans*), **stonecrop sedums**, and **blue star creeper** (*Pratia*).

If you are planting a large bedding area, use the more common and available ground covers such as ajuga, ivy, vinca minor, and pachysandra. If you want a low maintenance, albeit unconventional, lawn you can abandon Bermuda and fescue and let your yard go to **clover, wild violets, creeping-charley,** or **wild strawberry**. While typically considered weeds, these ground covers require little fertilizer, infrequent mowing, are evergreen, and have seasonal flowers. **Crown vetch** has lovely foliage and pretty pea-like flowers but is a rampant groundcover best reserved for banks or natural areas.

Evergreen ground covers like **epimedium, wild ginger** (*Asarum*)**, lily-of-the-valley** (*Convallaria*)**,** and herbaceous native spring ephemerals are wonderful additions to the shade garden. Take into consideration when planting herbaceous perennials that they are considerably more maintenance than evergreen ground covers.

Annuals like **sweet potato vine** (*Ipomoea*) and **wandering Jew** (*Tradescantia*) are effective seasonal ground covers.

Moss is a good ground cover under trees, but dangerous on walkways. To remove slippery moss from brick walks use a solution of equal parts laundry bleach and water.

All ground covers may be fertilized in the spring and again about July 1st with Milorganite or cottonseed meal. Sprinkle fertilizer over them and quickly wash off their leaves with a gentle spray of water. Some ground covers are subject to fungus in periods of damp weather. If you discover a problem, consult your local nurseryman for specific recommendations.

HERBS

Botanists consider any plant that dies to the ground after the growing season to be an herb or herbaceous perennial. In ancient times any plant that was not a tree or a bush was called an herb. They can be perennial, biennial, or annual. Traditionally, herbs were used for medicinal and culinary purposes. Today they are also used in flower borders, scents, cosmetics, dyes, and insect repellants. Both "herb" and "erb" are acceptable pronunciations.

The herbs are listed in either the *Perennials* (P) or *Annuals* (A) tables in this chapter. Look for improved varieties of the following.

PERENNIAL AND ANNUAL HERBS

Basil (*Ocimum* – A)	**Rosemary** (*Rosmarinus* – P)
Chives (*Allium* – P, A)	**Sage** (*Salvia* – P, A)
Germander (*Teucrium* – P)	**Savory** (*Satureja* – P, A)
Lavender (*Lavandula* – P)	**Tarragon,** (*Artemisia, Tagetes* – P)
Mint (*Mentha* – P)	**Thyme** (*Thymus* – P)
Parsley (*Petroselinum* – A)	

Herbs may be mixed into the flower border or grown separately as a kitchen cutting garden. When laying out an herb bed, take into consideration accessibility for harvesting (which would be near the front) as well as aesthetic appearance of the foliage. Some herbs maintain fresh-looking foliage in extreme heat and humidity and others do not. Salvia, basil, mint, and parsley are good performers. Lavender and tarragon are more particular as to soil and drainage, and benefit from light shade. Shrubby herbs like germander and rosemary can be pruned to edge a formal parterre garden.

Soil should be porous, slightly sandy, not overly fertile, and have a neutral pH. *Drainage is a must for all herbs; plant in a raised bed if possible.* Most herbs require full sun, but several will tolerate part shade. Most herbs like a mid-summer application of 5–10–5 fertilizer. Pests are not often a problem; if red spider mites or whitefly attack, spray with warm soapy water.

You do not want herbs to flower if you intend to harvest them for kitchen use. Pinch off flower heads for a bushy, robust plant and to prevent going to seed. It is very important to harvest herbs early in the morning when the plants are richest in essential oils. They can be used fresh, frozen, or dried.

For dried herbs, wash and dry the branches, strip the leaves from the stems, place the leaves loosely on a shallow screened tray, and put in a shaded room. Stir them every morning so all will be exposed to air. In three or four days they should

345

be dry and ready to pack in airtight glass jars. If freezing, gather them as for dried, rinse dirt off, pat dry, and blanch leaves or freeze as is.

If you let your herb go to flower, the seeds are collected as soon as they are ripe and before they fall to the ground. They should be washed, dried, and packed away for future use. Herbs may be propagated by division, by seeds sown directly in the ground, or by softwood cutting.

HOSTA

HOSTA

Hostas are outstanding shade perennials grown primarily for foliage. For many years, they were in the *Funkia* genus in the *Liliaceae* (lily) family and were called plantain lily. Now they are classified in their own family, *Hostaceae*, and *Hosta* is the universally recognized genus and common name. They are well suited to our climate as they are native to Japan, Korea, and China.

Hostas range in size from 3" dwarfs to 40" giants with leaves over a foot wide. They produce white or purple trumpet-shaped flowers along stems held high above the foliage, from late May to October depending on the variety. Small hostas are useful for edging pathways or in the front of the shady border. Medium and large specimens are used in middle and back of the woodland border, around trees, and in containers.

CULTURE

Hostas may be planted any time the ground is workable. They prefer acidic (pH 5.5 – 6.5), well-drained, loamy soil, amended with compost, ground leaves, and ground pine bark, and they like plenty of water. Hostas planted under trees compete fairly well for moisture and nutrients. They also grow very well in raised beds.

The ideal site provides high or dappled shade, but full shade is acceptable too. Morning sun is tolerated, but afternoon sun is not. Thicker-leaved hostas can stand the heat better than thin-leaved ones. As a rule, blue-leaved and variegated hostas require more shade. Yellow and some green hostas can take more sun.

Hostas need a chill period and roots like to be cold in winter, so do not mulch until spring. Old, established hostas (over 4 – 5 years old) do not require much attention, but young plants benefit from a March application of a high-nitrogen, time-released fertilizer.

When the hosta shoots emerge in early spring, fertilize with Milorganite® and Osmocote®, and then mulch with ground pine bark. Never mulch the crown of the hosta, as that allows rot disease to develop. Sprinkle fertilizer granules around the root zone but not in the crown. An application of fish emulsion, liquid all-purpose food, or Milorganite® in early-summer helps keep the foliage looking its best. Faded flowers are usually removed which allows the hosta to spend its energy keeping the roots and leaves healthy. Never fertilizer late in the fall as new growth will be frost-damaged.

If voles are eating the roots and destroying your plants, you can pot hostas up and either submerge the pot in the ground, or set it under a tree. Hostas make excellent outdoor container plants and will over-winter successfully. Hostas in containers must be fertilized each year because frequent watering leaches minerals

347

out of the pots. Divide and repot, or transfer to a larger pot if it gets too overgrown and root bound. If you have a tree with heavy roots and you cannot dig, just surround the tree with potted hostas for a great display. Create interesting patio containers for shade by planting miniature hosta, caladium, coleus, and fern together.

Hostas can be divided and replanted if they become too large for their location or for increase. Mid–October to mid–November is the best time to divide them in our area. Dig up the entire hosta and wash off all soil with a garden hose so you can clearly see how to divide the plant. Some must be cut into sections with a sharp knife while other varieties can be gently pulled apart. Alternatively, you can take a sharp-shooter shovel and cut out a section of the mother plant while still in the ground and move or pot it up. Backfill the hole that was created with good soil.

While hostas can be grown from seed or tissue culture, it is much easier to purchase new plants or divide existing ones.

PESTS AND DISEASES

Slugs and snails are the main pest, feeding on hosta leaves on summer nights, and leaving a distinctive slime trail. Use slug bait, such as Sluggo®, and follow directions; be careful about using slug bait if you have pets. Place pellets around the plants and near paving stones and pots in late October to eliminate slugs before they lay their eggs. Apply again in late February or March, and then only where you see damage. There are many home remedies (beer traps, etc.), all of which have little effect on the majority of the slug population.

If you are very serious about slugs, you can spray your hostas at night with a mixture of 20% household ammonia and 80% water, by volume. Ammonia kills the slugs instantly and keeps them away until watering or rain washes it off the leaves. Ammonia is nitrogen-based and your hostas will love it as long as it is no more than a 20% solution. Slug damage will not kill a plant; it is just unsightly. Remove any damaged leaves.

If you find circular bites taken out of the side of the leaf, this is normally caused by a *caterpillar*. If you have a sun garden with plants that butterflies love, then you will have caterpillars. You can accept the leaf disfiguration and enjoy the butterflies. Alternatively, caterpillars can be hand-picked and added to the bird feeder, or controlled with a regular pesticide.

Hostas are relatively disease-free. The most common problem in the mid-south is *Southern Blight*, a form of crown rot caused by poor air circulation. Heavy rains washing dirt or mulch into the crown adds to the problem. The leaves will drop off, and the crown and leaf stems will have a white, creamy substance on them. Dig the plant up, wash off all soil, and cut away any soft gooey parts. Spray the plant with a fungicide or a mixture of dishwashing soap and antiseptic mouthwash and pot up the plant for replanting in the fall.

Voles, the root-eating relative of the insect-eating *mole,* can decimate a handsome patch of hosta in no time. If there is a quarter-sized hole in the ground near the plant, then you have voles. You can put rat poison down the hole, being

348

careful that your pets can't get to it. But as voles eat plant roots, they are not attracted to most poison baits. Cats are helpful in dealing with voles.

VARIETIES OF HOSTA

There are more than 3,000 varieties of hosta registered with the American Hosta Society. New garden-worthy cultivars, variegated green, blue, yellow, and white, are being introduced every year. All like part shade and good loam.

A few favorites in the Mid-South are 'Sum and Substance', 'Frances Williams', 'Elegans', 'Spilt Milk', 'Royal Standard', 'Patriot', 'Halcyon', 'Krossa Regal', 'Guacamole', 'Stained Glass', 'June', 'Striptease', 'Paul's Glory', and 'Albomarginata'. Many additional species and cultivars are listed in the table below and in catalogs.

TABLE 35. VARIETIES OF HOSTA

KEY: P – Perennial   V – Variegated

SCIENTIFIC NAME/ COMMON NAME	KEY	HEIGHT	FLOWER COLOR/ BLOOM TIME	COMMENTS
Hosta decorata **Blunt Hosta**	P	18" – 24"	Lavender to white/ Aug – Sept	Green leaves with white border. 'Thomas Hogg'.
Hosta fortunei **Fortune's Hosta**	P	12" – 24"	Lavender/ June	'Albopicta', 'Aurea'
Hosta plantaginea **Fragrant Hosta**	P	18" – 30"	White/ August	'Grandiflora': Fragrant larger white flowers, large arching heart-shaped leaves, bright yellow green, not variegated. Likes more sun than most hostas.
Hosta sieboldiana **Siebold Hosta**	P	24" – 36"	White, pale purple/ August	This species has some of the best hostas; Thick bluish leaves are heart shaped or rounded. Flowers are held on shorter stems.
Hosta sieboldiana **'August Moon' Hosta**	P, V	2' x 2' – 3'	Pale lavender/ June	Yellow-green crinkled foliage. An old cultivar, and still reliably good.
Hosta sieboldiana	P, V	3' x	Lavender/	'Elegans' has large steel

349

Scientific Name/ Common Name	Key	Height	Flower Color/ Bloom Time	Comments
'Elegans' Hosta		4' – 5'	July	blue leaves, and lavender flowers.
Hosta sieboldiana 'Frances Williams' Hosta	P, V	2' – 3'	White, Pale purple/ July	Ribbed blue-green leaf rimmed in gold. A favorite.
Hosta sieboldiana 'Kabitan' Hosta	P, V	8"	Blue-violet/ June – July	Yellow with green edge. Narrow leaf; wavy margins. Good edging hosta. Earlier blooming.
Hosta ventricosa Blue Hosta	P, V	18" – 36"	Violet/ July- Aug	'Variegata'. Green and white variegated foliage.
Hosta x 'Diamond Tiara' Hosta	P, V	8"	Blue-violet/ June – July	Good variegated edging or ground cover hosta. Sport of 'Golden Tiara' with white edging.
Hosta x 'Gingko Craig' Hosta	P, V	10"	Blue-violet/ July	Good variegated edging hosta. Green with cream edge.
Hosta x 'Golden Tiara' Hosta	P, V	10"	Blue-violet/ July	Green with yellow edge. Good edging hosta.
Hosta x 'Krossa Regal' Hosta	P	30"	Blue-violet/ July	Large blue-green hosta for the shady background.
Hosta x 'Royal Standard' Hosta	P	24" – 36"	White/ June – July	Solid yellow-green, slightly puckered leaf. Larger hosta for the middle or background. Lovely white flowers. Vigorous and reliable variety; likes more sun than most hostas.
Hosta x 'Sagae' Hosta	P, V	18"	Blue-violet/ June	Blue green with cream edge.

Scientific Name/ Common Name	Key	Height	Flower Color/ Bloom Time	Comments
Hosta x **'Sum and Substance' Hosta**	P	2' x 5'+	White/ July	Huge ribbed leaves. Very handsome. Great bright green color.
Hosta x tardiana **'Halcyon' Hosta**	P	15" – 20"	Blue-violet/ June	Best blue green hosta. Medium sized, use in background.

ORNAMENTAL GRASSES

Ornamental grasses have gained popularity in the last few years because of their architectural presence, low maintenance, pest resistance, and four-season interest.

Shade lovers include **Golden Hakone Grass** (*Hakonechloa macra Aureola*), **Mondo Grass** (*Ophiopogon*), and **Sedge** (*Carex*). Shade-lovers prefer well-drained, moist loam.

For sunny spots consider **Feather Reedgrass** (*Calamagrostis*), **Dwarf Pampas Grass** (*Cortaderia*), **Maiden Grass** (*Miscanthus*), **Switchgrass** (*Panicum*), or **Fountain Grass** (*Pennisetum*). Sun-loving grasses prefer ordinary garden soil and require little fertilizer.

351

FLOWERS – BULBS

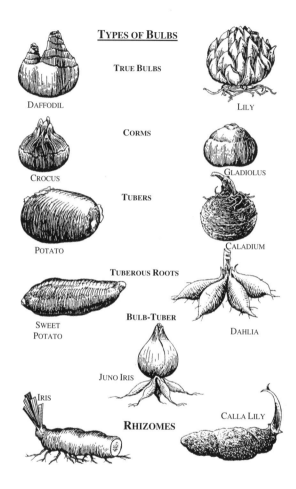

TYPES OF BULBS

TRUE BULBS

DAFFODIL

LILY

CORMS

CROCUS

GLADIOLUS

TUBERS

POTATO

CALADIUM

TUBEROUS ROOTS

SWEET POTATO

BULB-TUBER

DAHLIA

JUNO IRIS

IRIS

CALLA LILY

RHIZOMES

PLANNING THE BULB GARDEN

Flowering bulbs produce beautiful blooms year after year with very little effort on the gardener's part. Bulbs are classified into five categories: *true bulbs* (tulip, daffodils), *corms* (crocus, gladiolus), *tubers* (caladium), *tuberous roots* (dahlias), and *rhizomes* (iris). All have one common characteristic, and that is a food storage system for underground living.

By selecting a variety of bulbs, you can have something flowering from February through November. The season begins with the early spring-flowering

353

crocus, hoop petticoat (miniature daffodil), grape-hyacinth, scilla, and snowdrop. Then daffodil, Jack-in-the-pulpit, Dutch hyacinth, bletilla, lily-of-the-valley, peony, and tulip bloom in mid- to late-spring. Next are allium, arum, wind anemone, daylily, gladiolus, iris, lily, and tuberose in summer, followed by hardy amaryllis, dahlia, hedychium ginger lily, Japanese anemone, and colchicum in early- to late-fall. Hardy cyclamen blooms in late-fall to early-winter.

Color, height, sun requirement, and bloom time are the most important considerations when planning to use bulbs in your garden. Interplant bulbs with perennials and annuals, because even though a selection of bulbs can give you flowers over a long period, a single bulb plant rarely flowers for longer than two or three weeks. There are some exceptions: bletilla and calanthe orchids bloom for six weeks, canna and dahlia even longer.

Most spring-blooming bulbs, including daffodil, hyacinth, scilla, crocus, etc., are hardy and may be left undisturbed for years. Many summer-blooming bulbs such as Asiatic and hybrid lily, daylily, iris, peony, and crocosmia are quite hardy in zones 7 – 8 and may be left in the ground. A few summer-bloomers like gladiolus, dahlia, and caladium, are tender and must be dug up every fall and stored; or treated as annuals and replanted yearly. There are a few tropicals which are surprisingly hardy left in the ground in the Mid-South – certain ginger lily (*Hedychium*), elephant's-ear (*Colocasia, Alocasia*), taro, calla, and canna. It is necessary to leave the dead brown foliage on these tropical bulbs through the winter and remove it in mid-spring after all threat of frost is past. This prevents winter rain from getting into the cut stalk of the underground rhizome or tuber and freezing or rotting the plant.

GENERAL BULB CULTURE

Buy Grade A bulbs without soft spots or bruises. There are many excellent mail order/ internet sources in addition to your local nurseryman. Most bulbs need sun and will not flower well in shade. This is true for daffodil (*Narcissus*), iris, peony, gladiolus, tulip, and daylily (*Hemerocallis*).

However, arum, Jack-in-the-pulpit (*Arisaema*), dog-tooth violet (*Erythronium*), bletilla, calanthe, caladium, lily-of-the-valley (*Convallaria*), and hardy cyclamen thrive in partial shade. Some lilies prefer sun, some partial shade; see the Special Article below.

Good soil preparation is the first step to successful bulb gardening. Make sure the soil is loose and porous. Amend the planting area with one part humus, one part coarse builder's sand, and a half-part peat moss, added to two parts dirt. To encourage root development work a little bulb nutrient (bulb booster, 0–20–20, or bone meal) into the soil. Well-drained soil is a must or bulbs will rot. If possible plant bulbs in raised beds.

1. PREPARE BED	2. CONDITION SOIL	3. PLANT	4. COVER AND MULCH
Dig out the soil to proper depth. A shovel is quicker and easier than a trowel.	Loosen the soil and amend with humus, sand, peat moss and bone meal.	Place bulbs firmly in soil, pointed end up. Plant bulbs in clusters, 12 or more to produce best effect.	Cover the bulbs with soil, water well. Add 1" – 2" of mulch.

The **depth to plant bulbs** depends on their size and category. *True bulbs* are planted twice as deep as the diameter of the bulb; small bulbs should be covered with 1" – 2" of soil while large bulbs should be covered with 4" – 6". *Corms* are planted about 2" – 3" deep. *Tubers, rhizomes,* and *tuberous roots* are planted shallow, just below the surface with their tip visible. Packages will recommend planting depth.

BULB PLANTING DEPTHS

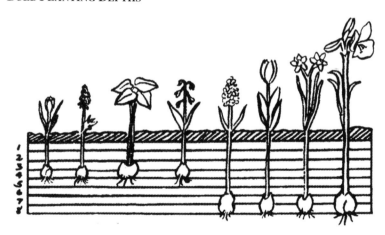

For naturalizing, plant deeper as the bulb will not multiply as quickly, thus precluding frequent division. Most of the small bulbs and many of the larger ones, like daffodil, tulip, hyacinth, and lily, are not lifted for three years or more until they have multiplied sufficiently to be separated and replanted. If your old bulbs are getting enough sun, and still aren't flowering well, they may be overcrowded; try dividing and replanting them.

355

The **spacing of bulbs** depends largely on the effect you are trying to achieve. The most effective planting technique is to plant in groups rather than in straight lines. Place bulbs according to color with the softer colors in the front and the more vibrant in the background. Group bulbs according to height and in sequential bloom pattern for a long-lasting show of color.

As few as 4 or 5 bulbs of the larger plants like crinum lily, Martagon lily, canna, elephant's-ear (*Colocasia, Alocasia*), fritillaria, ginger lily (*Hedychium*), and so on, will make quite a statement. On the other hand you may need to plant 100+ crocus, daffodil, or scilla to create an impressive "naturalized" effect.

After planting, cover bulbs with soil, water well, and mulch with pine needles or shredded pine bark. The mulch helps prevent mud splashing on flowers and conserves soil moisture. In the spring when the first shoots appear, sprinkle lightly with bulb food (a bulb booster or 0–20–20). This will encourage the flowering and also help rebuild the bulb for the next year. If the weather is dry, water the bulbs during their growing period. When the flowers begin to fade and before a seed pod forms, cut the flower head, being careful to leave the foliage to die back naturally. Sprinkle again lightly with 0–20–20 or a bulb booster or wood ashes from the fireplace in the fall.

Growing bulbs is very easy if you follow the few rules below.

ALWAYS plant bulbs in borders or beds that have good drainage.

DO NOT apply any strong commercial fertilizer or fresh manure when planting bulbs.

ALWAYS plant spring blooming bulbs in the fall, and plant summer – fall blooming bulbs in the spring. See the exception under Lilies below.

ALWAYS cut as little foliage as possible when cutting flowers from your bulbous plants. Let foliage die back naturally as that helps the bulb store food for next year's blooming. If you want to divide for increase, do so after the foliage dies back.

DO NOT let the flower go to seed. Cut flowers as they fade and remove any seed pods that form. Leave the foliage to keep the bulb strong.

DO NOT grow tulip bulbs year after year in the same place. Sooner or later they may be attacked with a fungus disease called fire blight, which affects both foliage and flowers. Either replace the old soil with amended, or change the location; in other words, follow the principle of crop rotation.

ALWAYS label the bulbs as you plant them. Label each bulb for show flowers or each clump when naturalizing. Use labels that are big enough so that 2" – 3" of the label is below soil level. Labeling prevents you from accidentally digging up bulbs out of season. If you participate in a flower show, the name of the flower is required, so make a chart of the planting site in case of lost labels.

ALWAYS check in the spring to see if shallow-planted bulbs are adequately covered with soil. Smaller bulbs can get heaved out of the soil during winter freezing and thawing.

RODENTS

If bulbs are attacked by rodents, try moth balls, red pepper, or tobacco mixed in the soil, or enclose bulbs in wire mesh. Voles can be especially troublesome; they dig a quarter-sized hole near the plant and burrow down and devour the bulb. They are vegetarian and are not attracted to many poisons, but rat poison in peanut butter dropped into the hole may be effective. Be sure your pets cannot get to the poison.

Allium bulbs are said to deter voles, chipmunks, and squirrels. Interplant alliums among tulips and hostas, which seem to be special favorites, to discourage rodent attack.

STORAGE

To store tender summer-flowering bulbs, dig the bulbs when the foliage has withered or turned brown by a light frost. Air-dry in a well-ventilated shady area for a week. Then remove all soil from the bulbs. Bulbs must be dried before storing or they will rot. Dust the bulbs with a fungicide and store in dry peat moss or wood shavings in a brown paper bag, open crate, netted bag or even old pantyhose. Store them at 50° – 55° in a dry location until time to replant. Many people prefer to treat tender bulbs as annuals and replant new ones every year.

TABLE OF BULBS

TABLE 36. BULBS FOR THE MID-SOUTH

KEY:	B – Bulb	T – Tuber
	C – Corm	TR – Tuberous Root
	R – Rhizome	e – evergreen
	h – herb	A – annual
	gc – ground cover	

SCIENTIFIC NAME/ COMMON NAME	KEY	HEIGHT	FLOWER COLOR/ BLOOM TIME	SUN NEEDS	COMMENTS
Allium caeruleum **Azure Allium**	B	1½' – 2'	Clear blue/ early summer	Sun to light shade	Azure blue flower clusters 1" across. Plant in masses between other perennials. Naturalizes. Many new varieties of *Allium* in catalogs.

357

Scientific Name/ Common Name	Key	Height	Flower Color/ Bloom Time	Sun Needs	Comments
Allium giganteum **Giant Allium, Giant Onion**	B	3' – 4'	Lavender/ summer	Sun to light shade	Flowers 4" across, excellent cut flowers. Plant in spring or fall. Use any garden fertilizer after growth appears. *Alliums* keep voles away.
Allium moly **Golden Garlic, Leek Lily**	B	6" – 18"	Yellow/ late spring	Sun to light shade	Showy clusters 2" – 3" flowers. Culture same as above.
Allium sativum **Garlic**	B, h	2'	Purple/ summer	Sun	Plant segments 8" apart and 2" deep; do not confuse with wild garlic. When leaves turn yellow, dry in sun, hang in kitchen.
Allium schoenoprasum **Chives**	B, h	10"	Blue purple/ summer	Sun	Onion scented. Plant in flowerbeds to discourage aphids; can be potted indoors for winter use. Dig and divide every 2 to 3 years.
Alstroemeria nurantiaca **Peruvian Lily**	TR	2' – 3'	Orange with red stripes/ summer	Sun to part shade	Many varieties, minimum of 5 peduncles per stem, good cut flower. Can be potted. Good drainage; plant 6" – 9" deep. 'Laura'.
Alstroemeria psittacina **Parrot Lily**	TR	2' – 3'	Green, wine, spotted/ summer	Sun to part shade	Well-drained garden soil. Good for cutting. Tolerates heat better than some Alstro's.

SCIENTIFIC NAME/ COMMON NAME	KEY	HEIGHT	FLOWER COLOR/ BLOOM TIME	SUN NEEDS	COMMENTS
					Spreads.
Amaryllis *Hippeastrum* See *Container Plants.*					
Amorphophallus **Voodoo Lily**	T	1' – 5'	Maroon, green/ spring	Partial shade	One of several interesting Aroids (see *Arisaema*) that are weird and wonderful additions to the shade garden. Bizarre flowers. Hardy. See catalogs.
Anemone blanda **Anemone**	T	3" – 6"	Blue/ spring	Sun or partial shade	Daisy-like 2" diameter flowers. Soak tuber overnight, cover with 2" soil. Bulbs must be replaced each year. Loved by voles.
Anemone. coronaria **Windflower**	T	8" – 12"	White, red, blue/spring	Sun or partial shade	Poppy-like flower, brilliant clear colors with black center, good cut flower. Recommended strains: 'de Caen' and 'St. Brigid', see catalogs. Plant in fall, treat as above.
Arisaema dracontium **Green Dragon**	T	1' – 4'	Pale green/ spring	Partial shade	Flower similar to Jack-in-the pulpit, large spathe with yellow spike spadix, handsome palmate leaf stalk, cluster of red berries in fall;

359

SCIENTIFIC NAME/ COMMON NAME	KEY	HEIGHT	FLOWER COLOR/ BLOOM TIME	SUN NEEDS	COMMENTS
					leaf mold. Native.
Arisaema triphyllum **Jack-in-the-pulpit**	T	12"	Green & brown/ spring	Partial shade	Spathe and spadix flower followed by rich, red berries; damp leaf mold. Native.
Arum italicum **Arum, Cuckoopint, Lords & Ladies, Winter Hosta**	T	10" – 20"	White spathe and spadix/ spring	Partial shade	'Pictum' is great variegated cultivar. Rich, moist woodland; front of shade border. Tuber. Arrow shaped variegated leaves appear in late summer and persist through winter. White flower in spring followed by showy red berry stalks. Wonderful plant.
Belamcanda chinensis **Blackberry Lily**	R	1½' – 4'	Orange/ late spring – summer	Sun	Ornamental black fruit. Rich, sandy soil. Member of *Iris* family. Native.
Bletilla striata *Bletilla striata alba* **Hardy Ground Orchid**	B	10" – 18"	Magenta, white/ spring	Part sun to light shade	Order from catalogs, easy to grow. Leaves have prominent lengthwise pleats; long lasting cut flower and pot plant. Light mulch year around. Plant 3" deep in groups in spring or fall. Blooms for 6-weeks in early summer.

SCIENTIFIC NAME/ COMMON NAME	KEY	HEIGHT	FLOWER COLOR/ BLOOM TIME	SUN NEEDS	COMMENTS
					Dozen 1" flowers on stem. Rich moist soil. Hardy in the ground.
Brodiaea **Brodiaea**	C	6" – 18"	Blue, purple/ late spring	Sun	Many varieties, thrives in any soil that is not wet or heavily manured, use winter mulch. Good cut flower, good for naturalizing. Attracts hummingbirds. Plant 4" – 6" deep in fall.
Caladium hortulanum **Caladium, Caladium hybrids**	T, A	6" – 24"	Variegated foliage, red, pink, white, green/ all summer	Partial to full shade	Grown for decorative heart- or spear-shaped leaves, many varieties. Good for bedding or outdoor pots. Dig and store tubers in fall; replant 1" deep in April when soil is warm. Tubers may be started inside in March or buy new ones yearly.
Calanthe **Hardy Chinese Ground Orchid**	B, e	6" – 18"	Maroon, yellow, cream, green/ spring	Partial shade	Order from catalogs. Rather easy, pest-free. Several species. 'Kozu' hybrids are easy. Also 'Sieboldianii'. Pleated evergreen foliage. Flower spike with many 1" blooms. Clump

361

SCIENTIFIC NAME/ COMMON NAME	KEY	HEIGHT	FLOWER COLOR/ BLOOM TIME	SUN NEEDS	COMMENTS
					increases. Rich moist woodland soil.
Camassia quamash **Camassia, Quamash**	B	12" – 18"	Blue to white/ early spring	Sun to part shade	Spikes of starry 1/4" flowers. Plant early fall, 3" – 4" deep in clumps of 9 or more; tolerates wet areas.
Canna x hybrida **Canna hybrids**	TR	2½' – 7'	Red, orange, yellow, salmon, pink, pastels, variegated foliage/ early summer to frost	Sun to part shade	Tropical-looking foliage green, bronze, purple-black, or variegated. Does best in rich, moist soil, but not fussy. Can be grown in water garden. Fertilize twice a season. Many new varieties. 'Bengal Tiger', 'Phaison', 'Lady Di', 'Pretoria', Pfitzer dwarfs, 'Panache'. Leaf roller can be a problem.
Chionodoxa luciliae **Chionodoxa, Glory-of-the-snow**	B	6"	Blue/ early spring	Sun	White and pink varieties available; naturalize for best effect. Plant in clumps 2" – 3" deep. Keep moist.
Claytonia virginica **Spring-beauty**	B	4"	Pink & white/ spring	Part sun, partial shade	Any soil; bulb that naturalizes in lawns. Native.
Colchicum autumnale **Colchicum,**	C	8"	Pink, lavender,	Sun to partial	Flowers appear before foliage. Plant 2" – 3" deep in

SCIENTIFIC NAME/ COMMON NAME	KEY	HEIGHT	FLOWER COLOR/ BLOOM TIME	SUN NEEDS	COMMENTS
Autumn Crocus			white/ fall	shade	August, leave undisturbed.
Convallaria majalis **Lily-of-the-valley**	R	8"	White, pink/ late spring	Partial shade	Very fragrant, tiny bell-shaped flowers. Colonizes under trees and shrubs where happy. Native. Rich woodland. Divide in fall. Pips can be forced in winter; cover with 1" soil.
Crinum x herbertii **Crinum Lily, Milk and Wine Lily**	B	1' – 3'	White with pink stripes, red, pink, yellow/ mid-summer	Sun to part shade	Heirloom plant, many lovely cultivars. Related to Amaryllis. Long wide strap leaves. Damp leaf mold for some, ordinary garden soil for others, bog gardens for others. Can leave undisturbed for decades. Some new cultivars are inter-genus crosses with Amaryllis and are called *X Amarcrinum*. See catalogs.
Crinum americanum **Crinum Lily, Swamp Lily**	B	1' – 3'	White/ mid-summer	Light shade	At home in swamps and bogs. Dramatic white flower. Native.
Crocosmia **Crocosmia, Montbretia**	C	1' – 3'	Yellow, red, orange/ summer	Sun to light shade	Several varieties. Resembles a relaxed gladiolus, good for cutting. Plant 1"

363

SCIENTIFIC NAME/ COMMON NAME	KEY	HEIGHT	FLOWER COLOR/ BLOOM TIME	SUN NEEDS	COMMENTS
					deep at any time; sun. 'George Davidson', 'Lucifer', 'Emily McKenzie'.
Crocus **Crocus**	C	to 5"	Shades of purple, white, yellow and striped/ late winter – early summer	Sun to partial shade	Many varieties, sizes, and bloom times. Plant 2½" deep. Naturalizes, first splash of spring.
Cyclamen hederifolium **Hardy Cyclamen**	C	3" – 7"	Pink, white/ fall – early winter	Partial shade	Easy in dry shade under maple or crape myrtle trees. Underused. The pink rabbit ears appear in October before the variegated ivy-shaped foliage. Green through winter, summer dormant. Plant large corm on the surface in a slight depression and do not cover with soil; it finds its depth. Do not disturb once planted. Needs good drainage and to be fairly dry in summer. Naturalizes where happy. Also try *Cyclamen coum*.
Daffodil	B	3" – 2'	Yellow,	Sun to	Many beautiful

Scientific Name/ Common Name	Key	Height	Flower Color/ Bloom Time	Sun Needs	Comments
(*Narcissus*) See Special Article below.			white, pink, gold, orange, multi/ early – late spring	light shade	varieties.
Dahlia **Dahlia**	T	1' – 7'	All colors/ fall for most, miniatures bloom all summer	Sun to light shade	Some varieties bloom all summer, most in October. Flower can be 12" across. Must be dug in fall or treated as annuals. Hundreds of varieties.
Eremurus himalaicus **Foxtail Lily, Desert-candle**	TR	3' – 5'	Orange and yellow/ summer	Sun to light shade	3' – 4' spike of tiny flowers; good cut flower lasting to 3 weeks; impressive in garden. Plant September to December in deep rich sandy loam with cow manure; leave undisturbed.
Eremurus robustus **Foxtail Lily, Desert-candle**	TR	4' – 7'	Pink, white/ summer	Sun to light shade	Similar to other Foxtails but taller.
Eremurus x shelford **Shelford hybrid Foxtail Lily**	TR	4' – 6'	Yellow, pink, white, copper, orange/ summer	Sun to light shade	Long foxtail racemes in early summer. Plant goes dormant after blooming, so over-plant with arum, hardy begonia, or annuals. Needs well-drained soil.

365

Scientific Name/ Common Name	Key	Height	Flower Color/ Bloom Time	Sun Needs	Comments
Erythronium albidum **Trout Lily**	B	6" – 9"	White/ early spring	Partial shade	Moist leaf mold. Charming, native.
Erythronium americanum **Dog-Tooth Violet, Yellow Adder's Tongue Yellow Trout Lily**	B	4" – 10"	Yellow/ early spring	Partial shade	Mottled leaf; single lily-trumpet flower; not a violet. Moist leaf mold. Wonderful woodland native. Dies back late spring. Spreads slowly.
Fritillaria imperialis **Fritillaria, Crown Imperial**	B	2½' – 4'	Orange, yellow/ late spring	Sun to light shade	Large clusters of striking flowers on top of 2½' stem. Prefers good rich soil.
Fritillaria mealeagris **Guinea-hen Flower**	B	12" – 15"	Mauve, purple, cream/ late spring	Sun to light shade	Flower is checkered red with veins of purple. Rich soil; plant in fall.
Galanthus nivalis **Snowdrop**	B	4" – 6"	White/ late winter – early spring	Light shade	Sweet scent, nodding blooms. Needs no fertilizer; can be naturalized; hardy. Plant at least 25 – 50 bulbs. 'Flore Pleno' has double flowers.
Galtonia candicans **Galtonia, Summer Hyacinth**	B	1' – 4'	White/ summer	Sun to part shade	20 – 30 fragrant, bell-shaped flowers; culture same as gladiolus but can be left in ground with winter mulch in Zone 5 – 7. Will multiply.
Gladiolus					

Scientific Name/ Common Name	Key	Height	Flower Color/ Bloom Time	Sun Needs	Comments
Gladiolus See Special Article below.					
Hedychium coronarium **Ginger Lily, Butterfly Lily**	TR	4' – 7'	White/ late summer – fall	Part sun, partial shade	Fragrant butterfly-like flower. Rich, moist soil, but tolerates heavy clay. All *Hedychium* need lots of moisture, as in the tropics. Not hardy above Zone 7. Flowers last longer with protection from Western sun. Clumps expand and may be divided in early spring. Plant very shallow. Leave dead foliage on plant in winter for protection.
Hedychium gardnerianum **Hardy Ginger Lily**	TR	3' – 6'	Yellow, salmon, orange/ late summer – fall	Sun to part shade	Large beautiful flower heads. Lush tropical foliage. Leave dead foliage on plant in winter. Many new hardy cultivars. See catalogs.
Hedychium hybrids **Hardy Ginger Lily**	TR	4' – 8'	Orange, yellow, salmon/ late summer – fall	Sun to part shade	Many wonderful, hardy, fragrant cultivars. Plant in masses for best tropical effect; just one plant looks like corn. They grow and spread in time so start with about

367

SCIENTIFIC NAME/ COMMON NAME	KEY	HEIGHT	FLOWER COLOR/ BLOOM TIME	SUN NEEDS	COMMENTS
					5. 'Daniel Weeks', 'Flaming Torch', 'C.P. Raffil', 'Elizabeth', 'Dr. Moy', etc. See catalogs. Moist rich soil preferred; tolerates heavy clay.
Hemerocallis fulva **Daylily**	R	3' – 4'	Copper, orange, pink, white, yellow, red, green, burgundy/ late spring – fall depending on variety	Sun to light shade	Garden soil. Early to come up in spring. Pretty massed. Long strappy foliage. Do not plant near Oriental hybrid lilies. Propagate by root division. Native. Easy and reliable. Hundreds of named cultivars.
Hemerocallis x reblooming hybrids	R	15"	Yellow/ May – Sept.	Sun	'Happy Returns' Good, low-growing, reblooming daylily. 'Stella D'Oro' also has yellow blooms all summer.
Hyacinthoides hispanica (formerly *Endymion hispanicus*) **Spanish Bluebells**	B	12" – 15"	Blue/ spring	Light to medium shade	Bell-shaped flowers on 12" spike. Woodland garden; plant 50+ in fall for naturalized effect.
Hyacinthus orientalis hybrids **Dutch Hyacinth, Common Hyacinth**	B	8" – 12"	White, pink, blue, yellow, orange, lavender/	Sun to light shade	Species is very fragrant but not showy. Dutch hybrids are much improved. Plant 5"

SCIENTIFIC NAME/ COMMON NAME	KEY	HEIGHT	FLOWER COLOR/ BLOOM TIME	SUN NEEDS	COMMENTS
			early spring		deep in fall, water freely. Single or double varieties; can be forced in pots. Plant new bulbs each year; 6 – 12 make a nice display. May naturalize slowly.
Hyacinthus romanus or *Bellevalia romanus* **Roman or French Hyacinth**	B	6" – 12"	White, blue/ early spring	Sun to light shade	Fragrant, good for rock gardens. Plant in fall; not hardy above Zone 6. Plant new bulbs each year. May naturalize slowly.
Hymenocallis caroliniana **Spider Lily**	B	1½'	White/ spring	Partial shade	Fragrant; marsh and bogs, Zone 7 and south. Native.
Hymenocallis narcissiflora **Peruvian Daffodil, Spider Lily**	B	2'	White/ summer	Sun to partial shade	Clusters of very fragrant flowers; blooms a few weeks after planting, must lift bulbs in fall.
Iris **Iris** See Special Article below.	R				
Kniphofia uvaria **Torchlily, Red Hot Poker**	R	2' – 3'	Red, orange, yellow/ late spring	Sun to light shade	Dramatic bloom; if plant looks shabby after blooming cut back by half.
Leucojum aestivum **Snowflake, Summer Snowflake**	B	12"	White with green dot/ spring	Sun to light shade	Green-tipped, white bell-like flowers clustered on stalk. Can be naturalized; long-lived bulb.

369

SCIENTIFIC NAME/ COMMON NAME	KEY	HEIGHT	FLOWER COLOR/ BLOOM TIME	SUN NEEDS	COMMENTS
					Woodland.
Leucojum vernum **Spring Snowflake**	B	12"	White/ early spring	Sun to light shade	Same as above. Woodland conditions.
Liatris elegans **Blazing-star**	C	1' – 3'	Purple to pink and white/ summer – fall	Sun	Ordinary garden soil. Easily transplanted. Native. Z (4–9/ 9–1).
Liatris spicata **Liatris, Gayfeather**	C	1' – 3'	Purple/ summer	Sun	Florescent bloom from top to bottom of spike. 'Kobold'. Native. Z (4–9/ 9–1).
Lilium **Lily** See Special Article below.					
Lycoris africana **Lycoris, Golden Spider Lily**	T	1½'	Yellow/ fall	Sun to light shade	Foliage appears and dies back before flower appears. Leave undisturbed. Plant 3" – 4" deep in garden soil.
Lycoris radiata **Spider Lily**	T	1' – 2'	Coral red	Sun to light shade	Strap-like foliage dies back before flower appears. Same as above.
Lycoris squamigera **Resurrection Lily, Autumn Amaryllis, Magic Lily, Naked Lady**	T	2' – 3'	Rosy purple, pink/ late summer	Sun to part shade	Fragrant, hardy. Very desirable. Plant 5" deep in ordinary soil.

370

Scientific Name/ Common Name	Key	Height	Flower Color/ Bloom Time	Sun Needs	Comments
Montbretia **Montbretia**	C	2'	Coral, yellow, red/ summer	Sun	Very similar to *Crocosmia*
Muscari botryoides **Grape Hyacinth**	B	4" – 7"	Deep blue, white/ early spring	Sun to light shade	Several varieties; can be naturalized. Plant in fall.
Narcissus **Daffodil, Jonquil, Buttercup** See Special Article below.	B	3" – 2'	White, pink, red, yellow, orange/ early – late spring	Sun to light shade	Many varieties.
Ornithogalum umbellatum **Star-of-Bethlehem**	B	4" – 12"	White with green stripe/ spring	Part sun, partial shade	Any soil; bulb that naturalizes well. Do not confuse with Spring-beauty (*Claytonia*). Native.
Oxalis regnellii **Purple Oxalis**	B, e	4" – 8" x 12"	Pink, white/ summer	Sun or shade	Delicate, shamrock-shaped purple leaf. Many varieties. Can spread too freely.
Oxalis violacea **Wood Sorrel**	B, e	6" – 8" x 12"	Pink to white/ spring – summer	Partial shade	Shamrock-shaped foliage is green above and purple beneath. Use in border or rock garden. Will naturalize in partial shade. Cut back to rejuvenate in hot weather. Acid soil. Native.
Paeonia **Peony** See Special Article below.	B	1' – 2½'	White, pink, red, mixed/ late spring	Sun	Long-lived and reliable plant. Blooms are gorgeous but last only a week.

371

Scientific Name/ Common Name	Key	Height	Flower Color/ Bloom Time	Sun Needs	Comments
Peltandra virginica **Arrow Arum**	T	1' – 2'	White/ summer	Partial shade	Looks like *Arum* with arrow-shaped, green leaves. Rich, moist soil. White spathe and spadix flower. Can be grown in woodland garden or pond.
Polianthes tuberosa **Tuberose**	B or T	3' – 4'	White/ summer	Sun to light shade	Very fragrant, good cut flower. Plant in spring after danger of frost; feed monthly with 5–10–5 fertilizer; store in fall.
Scilla sibirica **Scilla, Siberian Squill, Wood Hyacinth**	B	3" – 4"	Deep blue/ spring	Sun to medium shade	Dainty, good for naturalizing. Plant in fall.
Sprekelia formosissima **Aztec Lily, Jacobean Lily**	B	12" – 18"	Red/ spring	Sun to part shade	Flowers are 4" long. Plant in April, dig in fall; store in peat.
Sternbergia lutea **Sternbergia**	B	6" – 12"	Yellow/ fall	Sun to light shade	Glossy flower on 4" stem; crocus-like shape. Good for dry areas; winter mulch; plant in late spring to early summer, do not disturb.
Tulipa **Tulip** See Special Article below.	B	6" – 3'	Various/ early – late spring	Sun to light shade	Many flower forms and colors.

Scientific Name/ Common Name	Key	Height	Flower Color/ Bloom Time	Sun Needs	Comments
Zantedeschia aethiopica **Calla Lily**	R	2' – 3'	White, pink, yellow/ summer	Sun to part shade	Marginally hardy, site carefully. Rich, humusy soil; good drainage; or in water garden. Elegant spathe and spadix flower with variegated tropical foliage. Japanese beetles and root rot may be problems. 'Crowborough' is reliable. See catalogs.
Zephyranthes atamasco **Atamasco Lily, Rain Lily, or Fairy Lily**	B	12"	White, pink/ spring – summer	Partial shade	Grassy leaf, funnel-shaped flower to 3"; leaf mold. Native.

373

SPECIAL ARTICLES ON SELECT BULBS

DAFFODIL

NARCISSUS

Daffodils, indigenous to the northern hemisphere, are members of the amaryllis family, *Amaryllidaceae*. Although they are referred to as jonquil or buttercup, the proper names are daffodil (common) and *Narcissus* (scientific). *Jonquils* are one of the twelve classifications of daffodils, as shown below.

There are thousands of exciting and beautiful daffodils, ranging in color from white, pink, yellow, orange, to red, and combinations of colors. The forms vary greatly – trumpets, large and small cups, doubles, clusters, and miniatures. Some are fragrant, some aren't. The time of bloom extends from March to May among the varieties. Visit local daffodil shows, study the bulb catalogs, and see your local nurseryman to help in choosing.

Daffodils may be planted in a show bed, a flower border, or a natural wooded place, but not in dense shade. For the best effect plant only one variety in each clump. In the border try planting them in the back instead of the front because daffodils bloom early, and later the dying foliage may be hidden by perennials and annuals.

For a large area, a naturalized planting more closely resembles the flower in its wild state. The best effect is created by planting fifty to a hundred bulbs of one variety in each drift. Do not plant in grassy areas as grass cannot be mowed until foliage turns brown.

CULTURE

To some extent, the type of soil regulates the depth at which the bulb should be planted. In a good loamy soil 4" of dirt over the top of the bulb should be sufficient. A shallow planting will require more frequent lifting and division as the bulbs tend to split up more quickly. Plant small and miniature bulbs twice the depth of the bulb length, measuring from tip to root base. Daffodils need watering during the active growing season.

Lifting of daffodils should be done every two years for show flowers, every three or four years for the flower border, and every five or six years when naturalized. Bulbs should be dug with care as soon as foliage browns, separated into smaller clumps, and replanted. Daffodils may also be moved in clumps while in bloom. This is an aid to landscaping, as it is easier to place and find bulbs. When transplanted with a ball of dirt bulbs do not know they have been moved. Replant carefully, leaving all foliage and as much root as can be saved.

374

After blooming, if the flower has not been picked, cut off flower stem below seedpod, as it will draw strength away from the forming bulb. Stem, roots, and foliage should be left intact because they furnish food for next year's flower.

DAFFODIL CLASSIFICATION

1. **Trumpet** – 1 flower to a stem; trumpet or crown as long as or longer than perianth segments.

2. **Large Cup** – 1 flower to a stem; cup or crown more than one-third, but less than equal to length of perianth segments.

3. **Short cup** – 1 flower to a stem, cup or crown not more than one-third length of perianth segments.

4. **Double** – crown double, perianth double, or both.

5. **Triandrus** – usually more than 1 flower to a stem, head drooping, and perianth segments often reflexed.

6. **Cyclamineus** – 1 flower to a stem, perianth segment reflexed, crown straight and narrow.

7. **Jonquil** – usually several flowers to a stem, often fragrant. Usually stem is round, dark green rush-like foliage.

8. **Tazetta** – usually 2 to 6 or more flowers to a stem, generally globular shaped, sweet-scented, very short cup. Perianth segments rounded and somewhat crinkled.

9. **Poeticus** – 1 flower to a stem, very white perianth segment, small, flat crown, edged with red or green throat.

10. **Species – Wild Forms** – all species and wild forms; double forms of these varieties are included.

11. **Split Crown** – crown split for one-third of its length.

12. **Any Others**

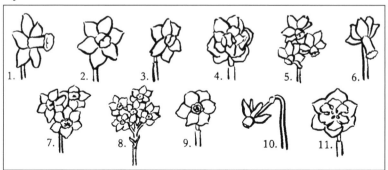

DAYLILY

HEMEROCALLIS

There is no more adaptable flower in the garden than the daylily. It has no insect enemies, will grow in almost any soil, will bloom in either full sun or partial shade, and can be planted anytime the ground is workable.

Colors of new hybrids range from red, mahogany, orange, pink, purple, melon, gold, lemon yellow, greenish yellow, to almost white. Heights range from 1' to over 4'. Flower heads range from 1½" – 9" in diameter.

For help in choosing varieties, daylilies may be seen and purchased in some local gardens while in full bloom, or ordered for later delivery. The local chapter of the American Hemerocallis Association can supply the names of commercial growers in the area. Varieties change frequently and new hybrids are introduced yearly.

Although a single flower lasts only one day, each stalk will produce blooms for 2 to 5 weeks, depending on the variety and weather conditions. Although June is the month when the majority of daylilies are at their flowering peak, there are some varieties that start blooming in late April or May, others during July and some, known as re-bloomers, that will flower continuously until frost.

CULTURE

Daylilies make a good background for lower plants. Remember when placing daylilies, the flower heads turn toward the strongest light. Daylilies multiply vigorously. Allow room for the spreading foliage. *Caution*: Our native roadside orange daylily should not be planted near hybrids because it will crowd them out.

Do not plant too deep. There should be only 1" of soil on the top of the roots. Make a small mound in the center of a generous hole and place 3 to 5 plants on top of the mound with the roots spreading down and around. Fill in the hole with soil. Daylilies prefer a slightly acidic soil, but are not fussy. A good mixture is 2 parts soil: 1 part sand or pine bark chips: 1 part humus, with a little cottonseed meal or 6–12–12.

Although daylilies bloom and multiply in spite of neglect, they do respond to a light fertilizing. When new growth first appears, sprinkle lightly with 6–12–12, or super-phosphate. Do not let fertilizer touch the foliage. If old established plants appear to need a little fertilizer, feed lightly four to six weeks after the peak of bloom with a low-nitrogen fertilizer (4–8–12). A too-rich soil produces foliage at the expense of blooms. Mulch new plants lightly; old plants need no mulch. Daylilies will survive near drought conditions as well as damp areas. To preserve next year's bloom, do not remove yellow foliage in fall until dead. To divide an overgrown clump, dig up with a fork, cut into smaller pieces with a sharp shovel, and replant.

376

GLADIOLUS

GLADIOLUS

Gladiolus has spectacular floral value. Their tall, handsome, flowering spikes in radiant colors will bloom all summer if given sun, room, and care.

CULTURE

Follow bed preparation and planting instructions under *General Bulb Culture*. By setting the corms out at one to three week intervals, after danger of frost is past, there will be an extended succession of bloom. Generally they bloom 90 days after planting. Plant corms 4" – 6" apart and 4" – 6" deep, as described above. Deeply planted corms do not require as much staking. When the plants are a few inches high, begin to spray for thrips, their deadly enemy. Refer to *Garden Care – Pests and Diseases* and *Month by Month*.

Corms should be lifted in the fall. The top part should be cut off closely, the withered old corm removed, and the new corm stored in a frost-free location over the winter. Dust with an insecticide/ fungicide before storing. If bulbs are left in the ground, they will come back for two or three years, but with fewer and smaller blooms. Some people treat glads as annuals and plant new ones every year.

VARIETIES OF GLADIOLUS

Flowers are classified as:

Large-flowered, which have blossoms 4" – 5" across;

Butterfly-flowered, which are half the size of large-flowered types and have striking throat markings or blotches;

Miniatures, which have 1" – 3" wide flowers borne on shorter stems; and

Open-face types, whose flowers are wide open and point more upward than those in the other classes.

While there are 250 species of gladiolus, the commercially available ones are almost all improved hybrids. **Byzantine Gladiolus** and **Abyssinian Gladiolus** species as well as dozens of hybrids can be found in catalogs, if your local nurseryman does not have what you are looking for.

377

TABLE 37. VARIETIES OF GLADIOLUS

SCIENTIFIC NAME/ COMMON NAME	HEIGHT	FLOWER COLOR/ BLOOM TIME	SUN NEEDS	COMMENTS
Gladiolus byzantinus **Byzantine Gladiolus**	2' – 3' x 2'	Maroon/ summer	Part shade	Species gladiolus has narrow foliage, 1" – 3" flowers borne loosely; 6 – 12 per stem.
Gladiolus callianthus (formerly *Acidanthera*) **Abyssinian Gladiolus**	2' – 3' x 1'	White with purple throat/ late summer – fall	Sun to light shade	Narrow foliage; white flowers with purple throats are borne 4 – 6 per stem. While hardy, flowering diminishes if not dug and stored. Or treat as annuals.
Gladiolus x hortulanus **Gladiolus hybrids**	2' – 5'	Many colors/ late spring – summer	Sun	Tall showy stems with flowers opening from the bottom up for several weeks. Tender and should be dug. Flowering diminished when left in the ground.

IRIS

IRIS

Iris constitutes a vast genus with hundreds of species and thousands of hybrids. This hardy rhizome is one of the best perennials for spring and early summer bloom. The often-fragrant flowers are desirable for arrangements and the evergreen, sword-like foliage is attractive all year. Look for the new re-blooming hybrids which flower in spring and again in fall.

All shades of blue, purple, pink, yellow, white, russet, coral, as well as bi-colors and blends are available. A flower lasts in the garden for about 7 days, but several buds on one plant open over a period of about a month.

CULTURE

Plant in full sun and provide good drainage, a raised bed if possible. As irises are widely adapted, they don't all have the same growing requirements. Bearded iris prefers a neutral to alkaline soil. Many other irises prefer acidic loam. A few prefer a bog. Individual preferences for soil and sun are discussed in *Table 38 – Varieties of Iris.*

Plant iris any time in July or August. For best effect, plant three rhizomes of the same variety in a clump. Dig a hole about 5" deep, leaving a mound in the center. Place the rhizomes on the mound with the fans facing outward, spreading the roots on each side. Arrange the soil around the rhizomes leaving the top halves exposed. Firm the soil around the roots. Too-deep planting will prevent bloom.

Iris will not tolerate mulch as sun is needed on rhizome to prevent rot. Water after planting and fairly frequently for two weeks until new root system is established.

Iris will thrive without feeding, but respond well to a light sprinkling of 5–10–10 or bone meal around the rhizome in early spring and again one month after blooms fade. Do not over-fertilize or over-water. Old bloom stalks should be removed after flowers wither.

For largest blooms, clumps should be divided every three or four years. Division may be done from early July through August. Break or cut apart at joints of healthy rhizomes and discard old ones. Wash with a hose and expose newly cut surface to the sun for several hours. Replant 8" – 12" apart with the leaf fan facing the same direction. Cut fan back to about 4".

DISEASES AND PESTS

Irises are quite resistant to diseases and pests.

Crown rot – This attacks the base of the plants, causing the leaf fans to disintegrate and fall over. Use a fungicide.

379

Soft rot (rhizome deterioration) – Scrape out all of the infected tissue and dispose of it carefully. Cut scraped area on a slant, expose to sun, and pour diluted household bleach solution over the wound.

Fungus leaf spot – Brown spots appear on leaf and often cause the entire leaf to turn brown and die. Remove dead and infected leaves and destroy. Spray plants and surrounding ground with a fungicide.

Borer – This is a worm that hatches from eggs laid on old blossom stalks, debris in bed, etc. The borer eats its way through the leaf fan to the heart of the rhizome. Small holes and a wet appearance on the leaf may be an early indication. Kill worm if possible, clean bed, and dispose of debris. Consult local garden centers for specific recommendations.

VARIETIES OF IRIS

The main garden irises are **Aril Iris, Bearded Iris,** and **Beardless Iris.** Each group of rhizomes has its unique qualities, and there is great diversity of form and flower within the genus, as it has been hybridized for over 500 years. Additionally, there are true bulb irises that originated in Europe.

The abbreviations in parentheses under bearded iris are the categories used by judges in iris competitions.

TABLE 38. VARIETIES OF IRIS

SCIENTIFIC NAME/ COMMON NAME	HEIGHT SUN NEEDS	FLOWER COLOR/ BLOOM TIME	COMMENTS
Iris oncocyclus and *Iris regelia* **Aril Iris**	1' – 3' Sun	Various/ spring	Two very different types of irises are grouped together under the term "aril". These are the *oncocyclus* and *regelia* irises of the Near East. Although they have beards, they are not classified as bearded irises because they are so different. Their beards are rather sparse; long and straggly on *regelia*, and just a wide fuzzy patch on *oncocyclus*. Arils show much veining and speckling, in a wide range of colors. Arils are difficult to grow in all but the warmest and driest regions of the United States.
Arilbreds (AB)	2' – 3' Sun	Various/ late March –early May	Hybrids produced by crossing arils with bearded irises. These are called "arilbreds" (AB), and are usually very

SCIENTIFIC NAME/ COMMON NAME	HEIGHT SUN NEEDS	FLOWER COLOR/ BLOOM TIME	COMMENTS
			easy to grow and still display the best features of the arils. Most arilbreds are tall and have large blooms. Crosses of arils with small bearded iris are called "aril-medians".
Iris germanica **Bearded Iris**	3" – 40" x 1' – 2' Sun	Various/ spring – early summer	The bearded irises are the most widely grown and come in many colors. They require well-drained, slightly sweet (alkaline), good loamy soil, and six hours of full sun a day. They do not like to be mulched. Propagate by division of rhizomes. Very popular and beautiful flower with thick bushy "beards" on the lower falls (petals). Six categories for judging purposes. Very hardy; some re-bloom. Z (4–9/ 9–1).
Miniature Dwarf Bearded (MDB)	3" – 8" Sun	Various/ early March	The tiniest of the bearded irises, and earliest to bloom. Plant in drifts in rock garden for carpet of color. 'Bantam' (ruffled deep red-purple), 'Scribe' (white with blue edging), 'Zipper' (golden yellow with blue beards). *Re-bloomers*: 'Ditto' (cream and maroon bicolor)
Standard Dwarf Bearded (SDB)	8" – 16" Sun	Various/ March – April	Profuse bloomers are small replicas of the tall bearded iris. They are ideal for low borders and rock gardens. Bloom after the miniatures in many colors. 'Bay Ruffles' (ruffled light blue), 'Software' (pinkish cream edged in salmon), 'Starlight Waltz' (ruffled cream), 'Violet Lulu' (soft violet), 'Watercolor' (yellow standards with brown falls). *Re-bloomers*: 'Baby Blessed' (light yellow), 'Jewel Baby' (deep purple), 'Plum Wine' (plum red with violet

381

SCIENTIFIC NAME/ COMMON NAME	HEIGHT SUN NEEDS	FLOWER COLOR/ BLOOM TIME	COMMENTS
			shading), 'Refined' (pale yellow), 'Sun Doll' (yellow)
Intermediate Bearded (IB)	16" – 27½" Sun	Various/ April – May	Similar in form to the tall bearded and are prolific bloomers in many colors. They flower slightly later than the dwarf varieties. Plant in clumps or as specimens. 'Baby Blue Marine' (light blue), 'Brighten Up' (orange with coral beards), 'Piece of Cake' (pink with orchid markings), 'Red Zinger' (deep red). *Re-bloomers*: 'Blessed Again' (light yellow), 'I Bless' (cream, flowers nearly all summer), 'Honey Glazed' (pale yellow standards with mustard-yellow falls), 'Low Ho Silver' (silvery white)
Border Bearded (BB)	16" – 27½" Sun	Various/ May – June	Same size as (IB) but blooms later. Often have ruffled petals. 'Just Jennifer' (white), 'Pink Bubbles' (pink), 'Predictions' (pink standards with falls), 'Tulare' (yellow). *Re-bloomers*: 'Double Up' (blue and white bicolor with dark violet borders), 'Ultra Echo' (lavender with violet)
Miniature Tall Bearded (MTB)	16" – 27½" Sun	Various/ May – June	This class is distinguished by daintiness and delicacy. Blooms are smaller than on a BB and the stems are thin and wiry. An MTB clump looks like a cloud of butterflies. Often called "Table Irises" because they are so well suited for arrangements. 'Chickee' (ruffled deep yellow), 'Disco Jewel' (reddish-brown with violet), 'Loreley' (yellow and violet) 'New Wave' (clear white), 'Rosemary's Dream' (white and orchid)

Scientific Name/ Common Name	Height Sun Needs	Flower Color/ Bloom Time	Comments
Tall Bearded (TB)	27½" – 40" Sun	Various/ May – June	Have branching stalks with many buds. Each stalk makes a stately arrangement in the garden or in a vase. TBs have ruffling and lacing and gorgeous color combinations. Their bloom time may be extended by a selection of early-, mid-, and late-season varieties. 'Beverly Sills' (pink), 'Crystal Glitters' (cream and salmon), 'Darkside' (purple), 'Fringe Benefits' (orange), 'Lullaby of Spring' (yellow and lavender), 'Silver Fizz' (orchid), 'Spinning Wheel' (blue standards), 'Venus and Mars' (violet). *Re-bloomers*: 'Bountiful Harvest' (white and purple), 'Champagne Elegance' (white and pink bicolor, ruffled petals), 'Clarence' (white with violet falls), 'Feed Back' (medium blue-violet), 'Eternal Bliss' (violet with tangerine falls), 'Late Lilac' (pale purple), 'Immortality' (white, may re-bloom up to three times), 'Misty Twilight' (pale violet-blue), 'Pink Attraction' (ruffled pale pink), 'Queen Dorothy' (white, stitched with violet edges, nearly an ever-bloomer), 'Silver Dividends' (white), 'Suky' (violet with white zones), 'Summer Olympics' (light yellow), 'Violet Music' (violet), 'Zurich' (white with yellow beards).
Beardless Iris	1½' – 5' Sun to part shade	Various/ May – June	Culture of the beardless irises differs from the bearded irises. They should be transplanted in the fall or in early spring. The roots should never be allowed to dry out while they are out of the ground and they should be watered heavily after transplanting.

383

SCIENTIFIC NAME/ COMMON NAME	HEIGHT SUN NEEDS	FLOWER COLOR/ BLOOM TIME	COMMENTS
			They should be set slightly deeper than the tall bearded. Japanese iris should be planted in a distinct depression in heavy soil to assist in supplying moisture to the plant (or in a water garden).
Iris cristata **Crested Iris**	4" – 8" Part shade	Blue, white/ spring	Their small blue and white flowers with touches of yellow and orange appear in late March or early April. They are very effective in a woodland or rock garden, and grow well in light shade. Will not bloom in dense shade. Garden soil. Native
Iris ensata (formerly *Iris kaempferi*) **Japanese Iris**	2' – 4' x 2' Sun with afternoon shade	Various/ summer	The beautiful, 6" – 10", large flat, ruffled flowers range through shades of blue, pink, purple, lavender, to white. Japanese have hybridized them for 500 years. This iris requires rich, acid soil kept constantly moist from spring through bloom time, or they may be used in a water garden. Thick roots are great water-purifying filters in the water garden. Plant 2" deep in part shade.
Iris fulva **Louisiana Iris**	2' – 3½' Sun	Tawny orange, yellow, etc./ spring	Derived from species native to the marshes of Louisiana, and may be grown in water gardens or in flower beds. (Their roots are good water purifiers.) Their culture is almost opposite to that of bearded. They require fertile acid soil with an abundance of moisture and sun. Rhizomes must be protected from the sun with mulch. Their flat showy flowers offer a broad range of color. Damp location, hardy. Native.
Iris prismatica **Slender Blue**	1' – 3' Sun	Blue/ early summer	Moist, marshy. Water gardens. Native.

SCIENTIFIC NAME/ COMMON NAME	HEIGHT SUN NEEDS	FLOWER COLOR/ BLOOM TIME	COMMENTS
Flag			
Iris pseudacorus **Yellow Flag Iris**	4' Sun	Yellow/ spring	Damp location, or in pond. Large plant. Native.
Iris sibirica **Siberian Iris**	2' – 3½' x 2' Sun to part shade	Blue, white, purple/ late spring	Narrow grass-like foliage, smaller flowers than bearded types. Elegant and desirable. They require a damp, acid soil with plenty of compost, and full sun. Rhizomes should be planted 1" – 2" deep. Do not divide unless bloom production decreases.
Iris spuria **Spuria Iris**	6" – 5' usually 2' Sun	White, blue, wine, yellow/ late spring	Looks like a Siberian and has same culture needs, but the foliage is larger and taller and the flower is more like an orchid; flowers last longer but are less profuse. Spurias should be mulched in late fall with well-rotted manure and the clumps left undisturbed for years.
Iris tectorum **Roof Iris**	12" – 18" x 18" Sun to light shade	Pale purple/ summer	6" wide Pale purple flowers held over 6" – 8" wide evergreen chartreuse foliage. Well-drained.
Iris verna **Vernal Iris**	4" – 6" Part shade	Blue with orange/ spring	Prefers dry well-drained soil; similar to *I. cristata* but not crested. Native.
Iris versicolor **Larger Blue Flag Iris**	2– 3' Sun	Reddish- or bluish-purple/ early summer	Damp soil. Similar to *I. pseudacorus*. Native.
Bulbous Iris	1½' – 2' Part sun	Various/ spring – early summer	These true perennial bulbs should be planted in the fall. They are propagated by natural bulb division.

385

SCIENTIFIC NAME/ COMMON NAME	HEIGHT SUN NEEDS	FLOWER COLOR/ BLOOM TIME	COMMENTS
Dutch Iris	1½' – 2' Part sun	Blue, yellow, lavender, purple, or white/ April	Plant 4" deep in slightly sandy, well-drained soil where they will receive several hours of sun a day. Lovely arch-like flowers.
Spanish Iris	1½' – 2' Part sun	Blue, yellow, orange, bronze/ May	These irises bloom a few weeks after the Dutch irises.
English Iris	1½' – 2' Part sun	Blues, shades of purple, and white/ June – July	They are more difficult to grow than the Dutch and Spanish irises. They require moist, heavier soil, and less sun.

LILY

LILIUM

True lilies (genus *Lilium*) are spectacular, hardy perennial bulbs that will multiply and provide years of bloom with a minimum of care. Daylilies, calla lilies, canna lilies, crinum lilies, ginger lilies, and water lilies are not true lilies in that they do not belong to the genus *Lilium*.

Lilies make excellent, long-lasting cut flowers and most are very fragrant. They are available in a variety of sizes, flower shapes, and all colors except blue. By planting different varieties, bloom time may be extended from May until August or September. Bulbs are labeled early, midseason, or late, according to the time of bloom.

CULTURE

The **Asiatic hybrids** may be planted in full sun or part shade in all regions. Plant other types of lilies where they will be protected from hot afternoon sun. This is especially important with **Oriental hybrids** and most of the species. Avoid low areas where water stands. Lilies prefer their heads in the sun and their feet in the shade. Tall varieties may be staked.

While a few lilies may be planted in the spring, mid-November is the preferred time for most varieties. Good drainage and deep soil preparation are essential. Most lilies prefer a slightly acid soil.

However, **Madonna lilies** need a rather heavy, limey soil and are planted in September through October. Madonna lilies put forth foliage in the fall which persists through winter. They flower in spring, and die back in the heat of summer.

Lilies are heavy feeders. Apply a little 6–12–12 fertilizer as soon as the shoots emerge in the spring, and continue with smaller supplemental feedings every 3 – 4 weeks during the summer. Never allow the fertilizer to touch the stems or leaves as it will burn the plant. Water thoroughly after fertilizing; lilies need moist, not soggy soil.

As for transplanting and dividing, lilies resent disturbance. Transplant in the fall only when they have become overcrowded. Move Madonna lilies in the summer after blooming. Do not try to transplant a **Martagon lily**. When transplanting, dig, divide, and replant at once. Change the bulbs to another location or amend the old soil with bone meal and humus. The small bulblets may be removed and planted. They will produce flowers in two or three years.

Modern hybrid lilies have been bred for disease resistance. Proper planting and sanitation should prevent most problems. Lily bulbs will be weakened if the plants are allowed to go to seed; therefore cut faded flowers promptly before the seed

387

pods form. In cutting flowers, leave one-third of the stem or the bulb will deteriorate.

VARIETIES OF LILIES

Lily classifications are based on origin and flower form. Modern growers have developed vigorous new hybrids far superior to their ancestors. Therefore, except for a few species listed below, the new hybrids are recommended

TABLE 39. VARIETIES OF LILY

SCIENTIFIC NAME/ COMMON NAME	HEIGHT SUN NEEDS	FLOWER COLOR/ BLOOM TIME	COMMENTS
Lilium hybrids **Hybrid Lily**			
American Hybrid Lily	4' – 6½' Part shade	Dark red, yellow, orange, maroon, pastels/ June – early July	Not fragrant; 4" – 6" nodding flower. 'Uchida' and many others.
Asiatic Lily	2' – 4' Sun to part shade	Red, orange, yellow, pink, pastel, bi-colors/ May	Outward facing or pendant, open-cup flowers. Easiest to grow; earliest to bloom. 'Pixie', 'Lollipop', 'Connecticut King', many others. Z (4–8 / 8–1).
Martagon Lily	3' – 6' Part shade	White, yellow, orange, purple/ May – June	Not fragrant; numerous 3" – 4" flowers in Turk's-cap form nodding flower with recurved petal tips. Woodland conditions. Likes alkaline soil. Needs afternoon shade. 'Paisley' hybrids, 'Enchantment'.
Orienpet Lily	3' – 5' Part sun	White, red, pink, yellow, orange, mixed/ July	Lovely crosses of Oriental and trumpet lilies. Dislike hot afternoon sun.
Oriental Lily	2' – 7' Part shade	White, pink, red, streaked, bi-color/ July – August	Taller with larger flowers and blooming later than Asiatic lilies. 6" – 12" across, very fragrant flower with recurved petals. Can be flat-faced or bowl-shaped. A

SCIENTIFIC NAME/ COMMON NAME	HEIGHT SUN NEEDS	FLOWER COLOR/ BLOOM TIME	COMMENTS
			little more difficult to grow, but very showy. Must have afternoon shade. 'Casablanca', 'La Reve', 'Olivia', 'Trance', many others. Z (4–8 / 8–1).
Trumpet Lily	4' – 6' Part sun	White, pink, copper, yellow/ July – early August	Fragrant 6" – l0" flowers. Many named cultivars.
Lilium species **Species Lily**			
Lilium auratum **Gold-Band Lily**	5' – 6' Sun to part shade	White with yellow band/ June	Fragrant. Z (4–8 / 8–1).
Lilium candidum **Madonna Lily**	2' – 4' Part shade	White/ June	Fragrant, trumpet. Plant bulb shallow, and near other ground cover to shade bulb but not foliage. Plant in early fall. Best adapted to well drained, alkaline soils. Moderately difficult to grow but long-lived if happy. 'Nanking Lily', 'Apollo', 'Zeus'.
Lilium formosanum **Philippine Lily**	2' –3' Part shade	White/ July	Fragrant white trumpets. Plant in spring. Easy to grow.
Lilium longiflorum **Easter Lily**	2' – 3' Part shade	White/ May – June	Florist lily at Easter time. Can be planted outside and will bloom following summer. Related to *L. candidum*. White trumpet. Fragrant. Plant in spring. Moderately difficult to grow. Z (4–8 / 8–1).
Lilium michauxii **Carolina Lily**	1' – 4' Part shade	Orange, red/ late summer	Leaf mold. Heat tolerant. Turk's-cap type flower; related to *L. superbum*. Native.

389

SCIENTIFIC NAME/ COMMON NAME	HEIGHT SUN NEEDS	FLOWER COLOR/ BLOOM TIME	COMMENTS
Lilium regale **Regal Lily**	3' – 5' Part shade	White/ July – early August	Fragrant trumpet. Long-lived. Multiplies. Don't disturb once planted.
Lilium speciosum **Species Lily**	4' – 7' Part sun	White, red, pink/ August – Sept.	Old-fashioned. Native.
Lilium superbum **Turk's-cap Lily**	4' – 7' Part sun to part shade	Reddish-orange spotted with purple/ July – August	Damp, rich soil. Nodding flower. Native.
Lilium tigrinum **Tiger Lily**	2' – 5' Sun to part shade	Orange with black spots/ June – July	Easy to grow. Not fussy about soil or sun/shade, but best adapted to acid, sandy soil. Plant in spring or fall. Not fragrant; multiple open-faced, nodding flowers on each stem.

PEONY

PAEONIA

Peonies are long-lived perennials that produce gorgeous, fragrant flowers in May. When cutting for arrangements, leave at least three leaves below the cut for the strength of the plant. For larger blooms, remove all but one bud per stem. Peonies range in color from white, yellow, pink, lavender, red, and bi-colors.

CULTURE

Peonies prefer a cold climate but can be grown very successfully in the Mid-South if given plenty of moisture, good drainage, deeply prepared soil, and a pH of 6.5 – 6.9, a little more alkaline than woodland soil. Late-bloomers sometimes do not open well because of heat. Peonies usually take 3 to 5 years to mature to blooming size.

Peonies should be planted in the fall, late September to November, in full sun to part shade. Plants should be set so the eyes are even with or 1" below the soil; avoid too-deep planting. Do not plant near large trees because of root competition. Correctly planted, they may be left undisturbed for many years.

Peonies are heavy feeders. Put a cupful of bone meal or Milorganite® around each plant in March and August, and a top-dressing of wood ashes or dolomitic lime in February. The size of the bloom may be increased by applying a commercial fertilizer such as 0–20–20 after buds have formed in the spring and also by disbudding in April.

When the leaves turn brown in the fall, cut the stems to the ground and discard. Tree peonies should not be cut back. Do not mulch in winter because peonies should be allowed to freeze. Apply new mulch lightly in the spring.

Peonies may be divided for increase in fall. Discard any soft roots and remove all old dirt. Wash off plant with a hose. With a sharp knife cut through the crown in sections of from 3 to 5 eyes, as new roots come from the eyes. Roots are very brittle. Avoid replanting where disease has occurred.

PESTS AND DISEASES

While peonies are usually pest free, they may be affected by *blight*, characterized by young shoots wilting and dying, or tips turning brown. Remove immediately all infected parts and dispose of. Spray with a fungicide several times in the spring. Cut all tops in the fall and destroy. This sanitation helps control blight and leaf spot. Continually remove all diseased parts. *Crown rot* is best controlled by good drainage. See *Garden Care – Beneficial Insects and Wildlife* for a discussion of ants and peonies.

391

VARIETIES OF PEONY

Chinese (*Paeonia lactiflora*) – single, Chinese (or **anemone-flowered**) peonies are beautiful in the garden because heads do not bend down in the rain. They are also good cut flowers.

Doubles are lovely but need staking because of the weight of the flower heads. Many good named cultivars.

Tree (*Paeonia suffruticosa*) – Single and semi-double, have woody growth above the ground, and do not die back in the fall. Many beautiful cultivars are available.

TULIP

TULIPA

In the Mid-South, tulips bloom April – May with dogwood and azaleas. Many bulb catalogs list the relative time of blooming of different varieties. By planting early, midseason, and late varieties, the blooming sequence can be extended for six to eight weeks.

There are tulips for any desired color scheme. For the best effect, tulip bulbs should always be planted in groups of twelve to twenty-four of one kind instead of in rows, unless a formal look is desired. In planting a border some prefer a rhythmic repetition of the same variety, which gives a dramatic landscape effect. Others enjoy working out transitions from one color to another. A simple but very effective compromise is to choose two varieties, one early and one later blooming. Alternate the two in groups throughout the border, giving two distinct seasons of bloom.

Most tulips do not naturalize well, and will not thrive under deciduous trees, as will daffodils and some other bulbs. Do not plant bulbs before November 15th. Bulbs planted earlier sprout too soon and risk damage by cold weather. In a large garden change location of tulips each year for best results and reduced chance of disease spread. Most people replant tulips yearly and treat as annuals. A few varieties are true perennials and re-bloom faithfully every year.

VARIETIES OF TULIP

EARLY-SEASON VARIETIES

Fosteriana: Very large blossoms that open with the daffodils, and are of dwarf habit.

Kaufmanniana: 4" – 8" tall, produce large flowers with pointed petals that open horizontally, and therefore, are often called the "water lily tulip".

MID-SEASON VARIETIES

Darwin Hybrid: 22" – 30" tall. Large, fragrant, and spectacular, and weather-resistant flowers.

Mendel: 16" – 26" tall. Good growers that survive wind and rain.

Triumph: 16" – 26" tall. Large flowers. They are good to fill the gap between early and late tulips.

393

LATE-SEASON VARIETIES

Cottage: 16" – 24" tall, with long, rather pointed petals. They vary greatly in form and color.

Darwin: 22" – 30" tall; large, deep-cupped flowers on long stems; very showy.

Double Late: 18" – 24" tall, blossoms similar to peonies, good for cutting. Need some protection from hot sun.

Greigii: 8" – 12" tall, have long-lasting blossoms and bloom very late.

Lily-Flowering: 18" – 26" tall, have striking blossoms with long, pointed, curved petals.

Parrot: 20" – 28" tall, produce slightly reflexed flowers with streaked or feathered petals. They often have heavy heads.

Rembrandt: 20" tall; petals are streaked, flushed, striped or veined with contrasting colors, often white.

FORCING SPRING BULBS FOR INDOOR BLOOM

Forcing bulbs is accomplished by artificially controlling light, water, and temperature in order to bring the bulbs into early maturity with a root system sufficiently developed to support the flower.

Tulip and daffodil force in soil while paperwhite narcissus, hyacinth, crocus, snowdrop, scilla and many more of the minor spring bulbs force successfully in rocks and water as well as in soil.

The important thing to understand is that the root system must be well developed before the bulb will produce good flowers. If rooting outdoors has not been successful, leave the pots of bulbs in the soil where they are and let them mature in their normal season. If the roots look weak and thin when planting indoors, discard and replant, or wait until next fall. Order top quality bulbs, as inferior bulbs are often disappointing. If bulbs arrive before the planting season, store them in a refrigerator until time to plant.

PLANTING IN POTS FOR OUTDOOR ROOTING

A 6" clay pot will hold 6 tulip or daffodil bulbs, or 3 hyacinths, or 15 crocuses. A light soil is absolutely essential for good drainage. A mixture of ⅓ garden loam, ⅓ peat moss, and ⅓ sand will insure this. No fertilizer is necessary as bulbs contain their own food. Do not use soil in which bulbs have been grown previously. Pots must be scrubbed clean and soaked overnight before planting. Bulbs like to sit snug. Do not try to re-force bulbs again, but they may be planted in the garden after flowering and they may bloom next year.

Pots must have good drainage holes covered with broken clay, flat stones, or plastic screening to prevent clogging. A handful of sand on top of this will keep slugs out if the clay becomes dislodged.

Fill pots half full of soil mixture and place bulbs firmly but gently with tips 1" below the top of the pot. Place tulip bulbs with their flat sides facing the side of the pot. Cover with ½" soil and top with ½" sand to keep slugs from spoiling the foliage when it appears. Label pots carefully, noting color, variety, and date of planting; then soak thoroughly. The pots are now ready to be buried.

Bury the pots in a convenient place near water in case of a prolonged dry spell. The loose soil of a flowerbed, a vegetable garden, or a cold frame makes digging a trench easy. Trenches must be deep enough for the pots, allowing for a 2" cover of sand, soil, straw, leaves or brush. Good drainage in the trench is essential, as bulbs will rot if left standing in water for the 12 weeks necessary to develop the root system. If the trench holds water, an inch or two of gravel or sand may be necessary in the bottom.

In the Mid-South timing the flowering of bulbs is difficult. A too-warm November, December, and/or January will certainly make a difference, but the rule is

395

that after 12 weeks the pots will have roots coming through the hole in the bottom and the top sprouts will be 1" to 3" tall. Taking a pot out of the trench to examine it does not hurt it at all. If it is not ready, put it back and recover it. When the signs of a mature root system are seen, the pots can be brought into a warm place. For staggered bloom, check labels to select colors desired and note removal dates for the following year.

When brought in, place the pots in a 50°– 65°F area. At this point invert an empty clay pot over the bulb pot. The light coming through the hole in the bottom of this pot will draw the flower out of the soil. Regular watering is necessary during this period. When the flower stem is 4" or 5" tall the covering pot must be removed. The ½" of sand on top of the soil can be brushed off. Too-high temperatures at any time will shorten the life of the flower.

PLANTING IN ROCKS AND WATER

When planting bulbs in rocks and water for forcing many different kinds of containers can be used, but added pleasure comes from selecting those that compliment the color, the size, and the form of the bulbs selected. A notable example of this is the "crocus pot" that is designed very functionally for the successful forcing of crocus, while also showing to perfection the flowers when in full bloom.

The container should be at least three times the depth of the bulb to allow room for good root growth without running the risk of having roots force the flower out of the container into a grotesque shape. Dense planting is best only for small bulbs. Hyacinths grow faster in rocks and water than in soil; they make massive roots and require large containers. The water in the container should cover the rocks and it should touch only the bottom of the bulb. Any kind of rock will do, but smaller rocks are easier to set evenly than are large ones.

ROOTING INDOORS

Place planted containers or pots in a cool, dark cellar, a garage, refrigerator (lights off), shed, or any place where they will not freeze. Check the soil for dampness and do not let dry out. If left in the dark too long, the foliage will grow long and unattractive, but if the bulbs are brought in when sprouts are 2" to 3" high with well-developed roots, the flowers and foliage will develop to a desirable height. At this point place bulbs in a warm room, 65° – 70°, and watch them come into full bloom.

If the bulbs are planted in soil, the best method for forcing the roots is outdoor planting in trenches, but they will also force using the indoor method under optimum conditions.

AMARYLLIS

Plant, preferably in a clay pot, with ⅓ to ½ of the bulb protruding above the soil line. Water thoroughly once and then sparingly until growth starts. Then

396

increase water and fertilizer (giving bottom heat if possible) and place in a sunny spot. Stake if necessary.

Feed and water all summer to prepare bulbs for forcing next winter; they are one of the few bulbs that may be forced year after year. About August or September store cool and dry. A dormant period is necessary to prepare for forcing. In October or November bring into a warm place, fertilize, and water.

LILY-OF-THE-VALLEY

Refrigerate for 2 – 4 weeks. Plant pips straight up and cover tops with 1" of soil. They will bloom about 3 – 4 weeks after potting and will grow at average room temperature.

LENGTH OF TIME FROM PLANTING TO BLOOM

Amaryllis: 6 – 8 weeks in soil

Hyacinth: 8 weeks in water

Crocus: 6 – 7 weeks in water

Lily-of-the-valley: 4 wks in soil

Daffodil and **Tulip:** 8 weeks in soil

Paperwhites: 6 – 7 wks in water

Freesia: 10 – 11 weeks in soil

Scilla: 8 weeks in soil

FLOWERS – ANNUALS AND BIENNIALS

Annuals grow quickly to flowering size and most bloom all summer. The enormous variety in color choice, foliage texture, and so on, make annuals a designer's delight for patio containers, prominent beds, and cutting gardens.

Many are available in nursery flats and others are best grown from seed. See *Garden Care – Planting* for information on setting bedding plants, and *Garden Care – Propagation* for seed planting. Many sun-loving annuals prefer ordinary garden soil, whereas shade-lovers like a richer loam.

Annuals appreciate a light application of a "bloom-builder" fertilizer a couple of times a season. Deadheading promotes continued flowering; refer to the chart in *Garden Care – Deadheading* to see which plants will re-bloom.

TABLE OF ANNUALS

TABLE 40. ANNUALS & BIENNIALS FOR THE MID-SOUTH

Key: **A = Annual** – A plant that lives for one year or season, and dies when freezing weather comes.

B = Biennial – A plant that produces roots and leaves one year and the following year blooms, disperses seed, and dies.

SCIENTIFIC NAME/ COMMON NAME	KEY	HEIGHT	FLOWER COLOR/ BLOOM TIME	SUN NEEDS	COMMENTS
Ageratum **Ageratum**	A	3" – 2'	Blue, pink/ all summer	Sun	Well-drained soil. Good cut flower.
Ageratum houstonianum **Houston's Ageratum**	A	3" – 2'	Blue (pink or white less common)/ all summer	Sun to part shade	Start seeds indoors 6 – 8 weeks before last frost. Also dwarf variety.
Alcea rosea **Hollyhock**	A/B	5' – 9'	White, yellow, pink, red, lavender, maroon/ summer	Sun	Rich soil. Single, double, ruffled, or fringed flowers. Plant seed in open ground in June or July for next year's bloom.

399

Scientific name/ Common name	Key	Height	Flower Color/ Bloom Time	Sun Needs	Comments
					Z (4-7 / 7 – 1).
Anchusa **Bugloss**	B	3' – 4'	Blue/ April	Sun to part shade	Very hardy. Cut back for fall bloom.
Anchusa capensis **Cape Forget-me-not**	B/A	1½'	Blue/ May	Partial shade	Flower clusters; self-sows.
Anethum graveolens **Dill**	A	2' – 4'	Yellowish green/ late summer	Sun	Sow early spring, does not transplant well. Young leaves and seeds for seasoning.
Anthriscus cerefolium **Chervil**	A	1½' – 2'	Herb	Part sun to shade	Thrives in shade, rich soil. Used like parsley; one of the French "fine herbs".
Antirrhinum majus **Snapdragon**	A	6" – 4'	Every color but blue/ summer	Sun	Good soil. Likes cool evenings. Good for cutting. Three heights, tall must be staked. Single and double versions; see catalogs.
Aquilegia x hybrids: **Columbine hybrids**	A	1½' – 3'	Various/ spring	Sun to part shade	'McKana', 'Musik', 'Song Bird', 'Wind-swept'. Lovely spurred flowers; foliage subject to leafminer; relatively short lived and hybrids do not come true from reseeding; ordinary well-drained soil.
Armoracia rusticana **Horseradish**	A	to 15"	Spring	Sun	Plant 4" deep; best treated as annual. Harvest in fall.

Scientific name/ Common name	Key	Height	Flower Color/ Bloom Time	Sun Needs	Comments
Begonia semperflorens **Begonia** See Special Article in *Container Plants*	A	6" – 9"	Pink, white, red/ all summer until frost	Partial shade	Rich moist soil. Buy young plants in spring. Bring in house for winter bloom. Cuttings will root for summer bloom.
Bellis perennis **English Daisy**	B/A	6"	White, pink/ spring	Sun to part shade	Will not tolerate extreme heat. Good for border. Seed in fall for spring bloom.
Borago officinalis **Borage**	A	1½' – 2'	Blue or purple/ summer	Sun	Attracts bees. Young tender leaves used for seasonings, imparts flavor of cucumber.
Browallia **Browallia**	A	12" – 18"	Blue, white/ June to frost	Sun to partial shade	Moderately rich soil. Pinch for compact growth. Easy to grow, self-sows. Bring inside and cut back for winter bloom. Buy young plants or start indoors 6 – 8 weeks before last frost. Prefers cool nights.
Brugmansia **Angel's-trumpet**	A	5' – 8'	White, yellow, pink, coral/ summer	Sun to light shade	Tropical beauty; large plant covered with long trumpets. Heavy feeder. Over-winter indoors.
Calendula officinalis **Calendula or Pot Marigold**	A	12" – 15"	Yellow, orange/ summer	Sun	Fertile soil. Cool growing weather; will not tolerate heat.
Calibrachoa **Million Bells**	A	12" – 15"	Pink, purple,	Sun to part	Prolific bloomer; in petunia family. Good

401

Scientific name/ Common name	Key	Height	Flower Color/ Bloom Time	Sun Needs	Comments
			rose, magenta/ summer	shade	in hanging baskets. Likes moist soil.
Callistephus chinensis **China Aster**	A	8" – 2½'	Lavender, pink, red, purple, white/ Sept – Nov	Sun to part shade.	Moderately rich, alkaline soil. Work wood ashes into soil. Choose wilt-resistant varieties. Start in cold frame or indoors 6 weeks before last frost. Use insecticide for leaf hoppers. Good cut flower.
Carum carvi **Caraway**	A/B	2'	White or pinkish/ spring	Sun	Sow seeds where plants will remain for two seasons; seeds produced second summer. Seeds and tender leaves used for seasoning.
Catharanthus roseus or *Vinca rosea* **Periwinkle, Vinca, Madagascar Periwinkle**	A	8" – 18"	Pink, white/ summer to frost	Sun	Any soil. Good bedding plant. Looks fresh in the hottest weather. May reseed. Not to be confused with vinca minor ground cover, which is also called periwinkle.
Celosia cristata **Cockscomb**	A	1' – 3'	red, yellow, magenta, orange/ summer	Sun	Compact or feathered head. Good for drying; dry by hanging upside down.
Centaurea cineraria **Dusty-miller**	A	1'	Silver foliage/ summer	Sun	Average soil. Grown for attractive foliage. Border plants.
Centaurea cyanus	A	2'	True blue,	Sun	Pick to continue

Scientific name/ Common name	Key	Height	Flower Color/ Bloom Time	Sun Needs	Comments
Cornflower or Bachelor's-button			pink, rose, purple, mauve, white/ summer		bloom; good for cutting. Garden soil.
Cleome spinosa **Spiderflower, Cleome**	A	3' – 5'	White, pink, orchid, purple/ summer and fall	Sun to part shade	Any soil; prolific seeder. Good cut flower. Thorny stem. Attracts butterflies and hummingbirds. Native.
Coleus blumei or *Solenostemon* **Coleus**	A	6" – 24"	Multi-hued leaf/ summer	Partial shade to mostly sun	Plant for foliage; many gorgeous new cultivars. May keep flowers pinched off if you don't like them. Good bedding or container plant.
Consolida **Larkspur**	A	1' – 3'	White, blue, lavender, pink/ early spring to summer	Sun	Prefers cool evenings. Annual species of delphinium. Reseeds.
Coreopsis grandiflora **Coreopsis**	A	1' – 3'	Yellow/ summer	Sun	Rank. Good for cutting. Many varieties, including dwarf. 'Sunray', 'Early Sun Rise'.
Coreopsis tinctoria **Calliopsis**	A	2' – 3'	Yellow, yellow and maroon/ summer	Sun	Very prolific. Native.
Cosmos **Cosmos**	A	3' – 4'	Lavender, pink, white, yellow, orange/	Sun	Poor soil. Good for cutting; keep picked for more blooms. Native.

403

SCIENTIFIC NAME/ COMMON NAME	KEY	HEIGHT	FLOWER COLOR/ BLOOM TIME	SUN NEEDS	COMMENTS
			July – Nov		
Crotalaria **Rattlebox**	A	1½' – 2'	Yellow/ late summer	Sun	Garden soil. Spike flowers resembling lupine; good for cutting. Needs long growing season; plant seeds and do not disturb. Reseeds. Poisonous to cattle. Native.
Cuphea hyssopifolia **Mexican Heather**	A	1' – 2'	Purple/ all summer	Sun to part shade	Tolerant of heat and humidity. Mexican sage has attractive spiky mounding habit and blooms all summer. Good new plant.
Datura inoxia **Angel's-trumpet**	A	2' – 6'	White, pastels/ summer	Sun to part shade; pot	Large trumpet-shaped, fragrant flowers, blooms at night; grow in pot and over-winter indoors. Tropical. Rich, moist potting soil.
Dianthus barbatus **Pink or Sweet William**	B	1½' – 2'	Pink to yellow/ summer	Sun	Well-drained, alkaline soil
Dianthus caryophyllus **Carnation**	A	1½' – 2'	White, pink, yellow, orange, lavender/ early summer – fall	Sun	Good cut flower. Prefers cool nights. Dwarf varieties for bedding plants.

SCIENTIFIC NAME/ COMMON NAME	KEY	HEIGHT	FLOWER COLOR/ BLOOM TIME	SUN NEEDS	COMMENTS
Dianthus chinensis **China Pinks**	A	6" – 12"	Pink, scarlet to white/ summer	Sun	Well-drained, alkaline soil. Clove-scented, single or semi-double flowers.
Digitalis x Hybrids **Foxglove**	B	2' – 3'	White, pink, purple, yellow/ early summer	Part sun to medium shade	Tall spike flowers. Plant seed in July, leave in cold frame until February. Worth the trouble it takes to grow. Or buy in pots from nursery.
Eupatorium perfoliatum **Boneset**	A	2' – 3'	White/ late summer	Sun	Garden soil. Native.
Euphorbia marginata **Snow-on-the-mountain**	A	3'	Pale green/ summer and fall	Sun	Insignificant flower, broad white margins on leafy bract; garden soil. Poisonous milky juice. Reseeds. Native.
Fuchsia hybrids **Fuchsia**	A	1' – 3'	Red, purple, pink, bi-colors/ spring-summer	Part shade	Lovely in hanging baskets. Some heat-tolerant varieties. Loved by hummers. 'Checkerboard', 'Gartenmeister Bonstedt', 'Christmas Elf', 'Cardinal', 'Autumnale'.
Gaillardia lanceolata **Blanket flower**	A	18" (A) 8" – 2'(P)	Yellow, red, orange, bi-colored/ early summer – frost	Sun	Light sandy soil. Tolerates dry conditions. Easy to grow, true perennial. Large daisy-like flowers. Good cut flower.
Gazania rigens	A	1'	White,	Sun	Prairie type, daisy-

405

Scientific name/ Common name	Key	Height	Flower Color/ Bloom Time	Sun Needs	Comments
Gazania, Treasure Flower			yellow, gold/ late summer to fall		like flower for full sun. Ordinary soil, drought tolerant.
Helianthus annuus **Sunflower**	A	12' – 15'	Yellow/ summer	Sun	Common sun flower. Super bird food. Many selections.
Iberis sempervirens **Evergreen Candytuft**	A	9" – 12"	White, lavender, pink/ spring	Sun or partial shade	Evergreen. Cut back to prevent legginess.
Impatiens balsamina **Balsam**	A	6" – 2'	White, salmon, pink, red/ June – October	Part sun to medium shade	Rich, light, moist soil. Often self sows. Sow seeds in garden after last frost.
Impatiens walleriana **Impatiens, Touch-me-not, Busy Lizzy**	A	to 18"	White, pink, red, magenta, salmon/ summer	Shade	Premier annual. Rich, moist soil. New Guinea variety tolerates more sun. May be potted and overwintered indoors.
Lantana camara **Lantana**	A	3" – 6"	Orange, pink, yellow, red, white/ summer	Sun	Colorful creeper for the sunny border. Can take the heat.
Lantana montevidensis **Lantana** or **Polecat Geranium**	A	12" – 15"	Orange, pink, yellow, red, white/ summer	Sun	Rank. Good for border or training into standard in container; bring indoors before frost. Many varieties, some trailing. Subject to whitefly.
Lathyrus odoratus **Sweet Peas**	A	8" – 10"	Pastels/ summer	Sun	Prefers cool evenings. Rich soil.

406

SCIENTIFIC NAME/ COMMON NAME	KEY	HEIGHT	FLOWER COLOR/ BLOOM TIME	SUN NEEDS	COMMENTS
					Dwarf or climbing varieties; climbers must be supported.
Lobelia erinus **Annual Lobelia**	A	3" – 8"	Blue, white, carmine/ all summer	Sun to part shade	Good in hanging baskets. New hybrids bloom all summer and are nice texture in containers or beds.
Lobularia maritima **Sweet Alyssum**	A	2" – 9"	White, pink, yellow, lavender/ summer to late fall	Sun, tolerates partial shade	Any soil. Shear to prolong bloom. Sow seeds in early spring outdoors; inside 6 – 8 weeks before last frost. Rock garden, edging, hanging baskets.
Melampodium divaricatum **Melampodium**	A	1' – 1½'	Golden yellow/ all summer	Sun to light shade	'Derby' is prolific bloomer with clean foliage. Good in baskets.
Mirabilis jalapa **Four-o'clock**	A	2' – 3'	Multi/ summer	Sun	Rich, well-drained soil. Blooms open at same time every afternoon. Re-seeds.
Myosotis scorpioides semperflorens **Forget-me-not**	B	8" – 12"	Blue, pink, white/ late spring to early summer	Partial shade	Woodland conditions. Clusters of tiny flowers. Self-sows where happy. Native.
Myosotis sylvatica **Forget-me-not**	B	8" – 24"	Blue, pink, white/ summer	Partial shade	Same as above.
Nicotiana alata grandiflora **Flowering Tobacco**	A	1' – 1½'	White to scarlet and off shades/ May – June	Sun to part shade	Well-drained soil. Do not divide. Dwarf 'Nicki' series is excellent.

407

Scientific name/ Common name	Key	Height	Flower Color/ Bloom Time	Sun Needs	Comments
Nigella damascena **Love-in-a-mist**	A	1'	Deep to pale blue, white, pink/ summer	Sun	Good for cutting. Feathery foliage.
Ocimum basilicum **Basil**	A	6" – 20"	Herb white/ late summer	Sun	Pinch out tips for a bushy plant. Use leaves green or dried for seasoning. Easily grown from seeds or cuttings. Var. 'Dark Opal', purplish foliage. Many good varieties.
Papaver orientale **Oriental Poppy**	A	2' – 3'	Pink, scarlet, orange/ May	Sun	Stately flower has tissue-paper-like petals. Pods are handsome after flower fades; harvest pods before they spill their seeds. Plant seeds in fall; difficult to transplant. Plant dies back after flowering. Good drainage essential.
Papaver somniferum **Opium Poppy**	A	2' – 3'	Salmon, pink/ May	Sun	Opium poppies have been cultivated for centuries. Prefers cooler climate, but grows here and reseeds. Lovely blooms for two weeks. Cut and save dried seedpods and re-broadcast seeds in late summer or fall.
Pelargonium	A	1' – 1½'	Red,	Sun to	Great window box

SCIENTIFIC NAME/ COMMON NAME	KEY	HEIGHT	FLOWER COLOR/ BLOOM TIME	SUN NEEDS	COMMENTS
Annual Geraniums			orange, salmon, pink, white/ all summer	part shade	plants. Cheerful blooms, pretty round ruffled leaves.
Pentas lanceolata **Pentas**	A	12" – 15"	Red, pink, purple/ all summer	Sun	Good new annual with verbena-like flowers.
Petroselinum **Parsley**	B	6" – 8"	Herb	Sun to part shade	Medium rich soil. Can be easily transplanted; soak seeds before sowing. Curly and fern-leaved varieties. Treat as annual.
Petunia **Petunia**	A	to 1'	All colors/ summer	Sun	Indispensable bedding flower; keep pinched back. 'Wave' series is good. Many great new hybrids.
Physalis alkekengi **Chinese-lantern**	A	1' – 2'	Orange pod/ summer	Sun to part shade	Interesting lantern shaped pod. Good for drying and in arrangements.
Plectranthus amboinicus **Cuban Oregano**	A	1' – 2'	Variegated	Part shade	Variegated cascading plant with fuzzy textured leaves. Good for containers.
Portulaca grandiflora **Portulaca, Purslane, Moss Rose**	A	6"	Red, pink, white, orange/ all summer	Sun	Warm, sunny location. Plant in masses in dry spots where nothing else will grow. Flowers close at night.
Rudbeckia gloriosa	A	2' – 3'	Yellow, gold,	Sun to part	Cut to encourage bloom. Single and

SCIENTIFIC NAME/ COMMON NAME	KEY	HEIGHT	FLOWER COLOR/ BLOOM TIME	SUN NEEDS	COMMENTS
Gloriosa Daisy			orange, mahogany/ July – Sept	shade	double. Many varieties.
Rudbeckia hirta **Black-eyed Susan Daisy**	A	2'	Yellow with black or brown center/ summer	Sun	Many varieties. Long bloom season. Spreads without being invasive. Good cut flower.
Rudbeckia triloba **Three-Lobed Coneflower**	B	2' – 3'	Yellow/ summer	Sun	Yellow petals with raised central black disc. Underused native. Reliable biennial. Reseeds.
Salvia farinacea **Blue Sage, Mealycup Sage, Blue Salvia**	A	2' – 3'	Pale blue/ all summer	Sun to part shade	Garden soil. Native.
Salvia splendens **Annual Salvia**	A	1½'	Red, purple/ summer	Sun	Red attracts hummingbirds.
Sanvitalia procumbens **Creeping Zinnia**	A	4" – 16" x 24"	Orange, yellow/ all summer	Sun to part shade	Not a true zinnia, but has same culture requirements. 'Orange Sprite', 'Irish Eyes'.
Satureja hortensis **Summer Savory**	A	14"	Herb	Sun	Pinch tips for bushier plants. Propagate from cuttings or root division. Aromatic, good for seasoning. Cut and dry branches by hanging upside down.
Scaveola aemula **Fan Flower**	A	1'	Purple/ summer	Sun to light shade	Excellent bloomer, interesting fan-shaped flower. Good in hanging baskets.

410

SCIENTIFIC NAME/ COMMON NAME	KEY	HEIGHT	FLOWER COLOR/ BLOOM TIME	SUN NEEDS	COMMENTS
Strobilanthes dyeriana **Persian Shield**	A	2' – 4'	Purple foliage with silvery sheen/ all summer	Part sun	Lovely foliage plant for purple accent. Lance-shaped leaves with chevron ribs.
Tagetes **Marigold**	A	6" – 3'	Orange, yellow, brown/ summer – frost	Sun	Many varieties. Heat tolerant, dependable. Plant around vegetables or flowers to discourage insects.
Talinum paniculatum **Jewels-of-Opar**	A	2'	Tiny, orange buds. Tiny hot pink flower on spike/ all summer	Partial shade	Any soil. Good filler for arrangements. Self-sows.
Tithonia rotundifolia **Mexican Sunflower**	A	to 6'	Rich orange/ summer to frost	Sun	Good cut flower, var. 'Torch' recommended.
Torenia **Wishbone Flower**	B	8" – 10"	Blue, violet, yellow/ summer	Part shade	Good for bedding; used to replace pansy. Self-sows. Has a tiny wishbone in throat of the flower.
Tropaeolum majus **Nasturtium**	A	8"	Yellow to mahogany/ summer	Sun	Prefers cool evenings. Pick to encourage bloom. Does not like to be transplanted. Soak seeds before planting. Flowers are tasty in a salad.
Verbena x hybrida **Verbena**	A	10"	Pink, red, blue, white,	Sun	Fertile soil. Profuse bloomers; good

411

SCIENTIFIC NAME/ COMMON NAME	KEY	HEIGHT	FLOWER COLOR/ BLOOM TIME	SUN NEEDS	COMMENTS
			lavender, purple/ summer		bedding plant. Many good new varieties.
Viola **Pansy**	B	6" – 8"	Multi, purple, blue, yellow, russet, white/ early spring –– summer	Sun to part shade	If grown from seed, plant in late August. Bedding plants may be set out any time from October – March. Well-drained, humusy soil. Fertilize. Mulch lightly. Deadhead for prolonged bloom.
Zinnia **Zinnia**	A	6" – 3'	Multi, orange, red, magenta, yellow, pink/ summer	Sun	Good cut flowers; many varieties; see catalogs. Broadcast seed in bed once soil is warm in spring. Water at ground level to avoid mildew.

FERNS

OVERVIEW

The word "fern" conjures up images of delicate, lacy greenery luxuriating in a shady spot, but there is great diversity in form and texture in this plant group. They originated about 300 million years ago, and there are about 12,000 species of ferns and fern allies worldwide today.

Ferns are one of a few non-blooming plants, others being mushrooms, club mosses, equisetum, liverworts, and lycopodium. Ferns do, however, have a vascular system, a relatively advanced feature, which is basically a network of veins for the transport of water, nutrients, and food. Their stems are often modified into rhizomes; at times these are very obvious and showy, and at other times they're hidden in the soil.

Ferns reproduce by spores, instead of flowering and setting seed. Spores appear in two forms: 1) a fertile stem of all spores (i.e., sensitive fern), and 2) a frond similar to the fern frond but with spore cases on its underside (as with ostrich and lady ferns). Identification of the family, genus, and species is done by examining the arrangement of the spore cases. Some are along the edges in a row, or in circles, or in other patterns. A magnifying glass reveals that great variety of design of the spore cases. Do not confuse the spore cases with insect scale.

Their leaves vary in size from 1/8 inch to 60 feet, and their colors range through the full spectrum of green and also white, silver, gold, yellow, red, pink, copper, burgundy, and even blue. Fern fronds come in different textures and can be thick and leathery, somewhat succulent, hairy, waxy, or super thin.

Ferns are indigenous to a wide variety of habitats. Those adapted to temperate zones may be grown in the ground in the Mid-South; see *Table 41 – Varieties of Hardy Fern*. Thousands of ferns are native to tropical rainforests, and

413

can only be grown in greenhouses or indoor containers; see *Table 42 – Varieties of Tender Fern*. Other ferns have adapted to bodies of water, and even the desert, but these are not widely cultivated.

From a design perspective, ferns are very versatile, blending equally well into formal or rustic settings. Some people shy away from growing ferns, thinking that they are too difficult. However, with proper selection and care, they are very gratifying plants.

HARDY FERNS

CULTURE

Hardy ferns, as opposed to tender ferns, are a wonderful addition to any shade garden. Do not dig ferns in the woods unless they are threatened by the bulldozer. Refer to *Garden Care* for making woodland or loamy soil.

Try to create the same environment as their native habitat. Some ferns grow in limestone areas and should have lime added annually. Most prefer acid soil, especially in hardwood areas. The need for moisture varies, so consult *Table 41* for individual preferences. Watering should be frequent in drought periods. Ferns are fairly self-sufficient when correctly sited.

Do not rake fallen leaves from the fern bed in spring; the fiddleheads (new growth) force their way through the leaf cover and raking may break them. If cover is too heavy use a blower to remove some leaves. Ferns are fragile and the stems are brittle; keep dogs out of them.

Fertilizing is up to individual choice. Be very cautious of nitrogen fertilizers that will burn the fronds; fish emulsion used at half the recommended strength is a good choice. Ferns do not need super-phosphate because they do not bloom. A little added humus in the spring is probably best.

Usually they are beautiful in the spring and summer. To renew the fern foliage for fall cut back in late July and August. Shear close to the rhizome and cut off all broken stems and scruffy fronds as low as possible, using sharp scissors.

414

TABLE 41. VARIETIES OF HARDY FERNS

KEY   **D** – deciduous   **E** – evergreen

SCIENTIFIC NAME/ COMMON NAME	KEY	HEIGHT	WIDTH OF FROND	COMMENTS
Adiantum capillus-veneris **Southern Maidenhair Fern**	D	to 1'	2"	Delicate and feathery. Slightly pendulous, shiny black stems similar to Northern but without the whorls, fan-shaped leaflets, spore cases wrapped under leaflet. Shade, moist, prefers lime.
Adiantum pedatum **Northern Maidenhair Fern**	D	1½' – 3'	2"	Airy fan-shaped, blue-green fronds held on thin black stipes in tight clumps. Fronds divided into fingers, with overall horseshoe-shape. Prefers moist, limey humus in partial shade. Tolerates some drought.
Adiantum x mariesii **Maidenhair Fern**	D	1½'	2"	Veil-like cascade of little tear shaped leaves. Moist, shady, neutral soil.
Arachniodes simplicior 'Variegata' (syn. *Arachniodes aristata* 'Variegata') **Variegated Holly Fern, Indian Holly Fern**	E	1' – 1½'	5"	Satiny sheen; green with bright yellow stripes. Hardy; likes total shade and moist, not wet, soil.
Asplenium trichomanes **Maidenhair Spleenwort**	E	7"	1"	Evergreen, sterile fronds lie on ground surface year round, fertile fronds bright green and erect. Withers in winter. Good drainage is essential, shade, alkaline soil.
Athyrium filix-femina **Lady Fern**	D	2½'	10"	Delicate, frilly. Grows in circular clusters; spore cases curved or horseshoe-shaped on underside of fertile frond. Moist acid soil, partial shade.

415

SCIENTIFIC NAME/ COMMON NAME	KEY	HEIGHT	WIDTH OF FROND	COMMENTS
				Propagates easily. 'Rubellum' has dark red stems.
Athyrium nipponicum 'Pictum' **Japanese Painted Fern**	D	1' – 1½'	8"	Silver variegation lights up shady spots. One of the most elegant ferns. Can have burgundy accents on silver and green frond. Easy and reliable. Acid soil, leaf mold, shade.
Athyrium pycnocarpon **Narrow-leaved Spleenwort**	D	3'	6"	Tall, slender, pale green fronds. Spore cases under fertile leaflet on fertile frond. Neutral soil, open sunny spots or open woodlands, plenty of moisture.
Athyrium x 'Ghost' **Ghost Fern, Branford Beauty Fern**	D	2½'	10"	Cross between Lady and Japanese Painted ferns. Upright habit, silvery sheen to foliage. Beautiful in shady border.
Botrychium virginianum **Grape Fern, Rattlesnake Fern**	D	10"	12"	Deciduous, lacy, fertile frond rises from juncture of sterile frond. Shade, moist or dry acid soil.
Cyrtomium falcatum **Japanese Holly Fern**	E	2' – 3'	5"	Glossy, leathery foliage. Bold texture. Evergreen. Excellent fern for woodland gardens.
Cystopteris fragilis **Fragile Fern**	D	1'	4"	Delicate, lacy appearance, bright green spring growth, first to appear. Spore cases dotted on underside of fertile frond, wrapped in tip of frond. Damp, rich, acid soil; shade.
Dennstaedtia punctilobula	D	1½'	5"	Delicate foliage; sterile and fertile fronds similar, spores

SCIENTIFIC NAME/ COMMON NAME	KEY	HEIGHT	WIDTH OF FROND	COMMENTS
Hay-scented Fern, Boulder Fern				contained in tiny cups under fertile fronds. When crushed it smells like hay. Partial shade; dry, acidic, humusy soil.
Dryopteris erythrosora **Autumn Fern**	E	2' – 2½'	12"	Hardy evergreen fern. One of the best for shady gardens. New fronds are coppery-pink.
Dryopteris goldiana **Goldie's Fern**	D	3'	12"	Golden-green color; 12 alternating leaflets, spore cases on back of darker frond. Moist, rich, acid soil; cool woods.
Dryopteris marginalis **Woodfern, Leatherleaf Fern**	E	1' – 1½'	6"	Many varieties. Evergreen, blue-green leathery fronds; spore cases on margin of leaflets. Shade, any woodsy soil, good drainage.
Dryopteris spinulosa **Toothed Wood Fern, Florists' Fern**	D	2½'	8"	Many varieties. Variable size fronds; spore cases on margin of leaflets. Shade, damp, acid soil.
Lygodium japonicum **Climbing Fern**	D	climber	4" – 6"	Vine-like growth. Grows well in ground or potted, and trained on a trellis. Moist shade; acid soil. Dies back in winter except in greenhouse. Excellent choice.
Matteuccia struthiopteris **Ostrich Fern**	D	4' – 5'	14"	Brown fertile fronds shorter than graceful green plume-like sterile fronds. Can be grown in cultivation for a large specimen. Shade or partial shade; low wet open woodlands; acid soil.
Onoclea sensibilis **Sensitive Fern**	D	2½'	12" – 14"	Invasive. Fertile frond is a separate stalk containing

417

SCIENTIFIC NAME/ COMMON NAME	KEY	HEIGHT	WIDTH OF FROND	COMMENTS
				small, brown, round beads. Can be used in flower arrangements. Part shade, damp, acid soil.
Osmunda cinnamomea **Cinnamon Fern**	D	3'	6"	Fertile frond is separate with cinnamon-colored spore cases. Hardy. Moist shade; any soil.
Osmunda claytoniana **Interrupted Fern**	D	2½'	5"	Fertile fronds are interrupted in the center by four or more pairs of leaflets bearing spore cases that later turn brown. Rocky, dry, alkaline soil; sun or part shade.
Osmunda regalis **Royal Fern**	D	1' – 5'	12"	Coarse fronds with fertile tips containing spore cases. Partial shade, acid soil, wet-lands; will grow in water.
Polypodium polypodioides **Resurrection Fern**	D	to 7'	2"	Grows like ivy on trees or dead stumps; lives without soil. In dry weather it looks dead, revives with rain. Spore cases under tip of leaflet on fertile frond, fronds short. Partial shade.
Polystichum acrostichoides **Christmas Fern**	E	2'	4"	Hardy evergreen, abundant in most areas, spore cases top third of fertile frond. Shade; alkaline soil.
Polystichum lonchitis **Northern Holly Fern**	D	2'	5"	Shiny, serrated leaflet dies back in winter. Spore cases dotted under fertile sub-leaflet. Moist, alkaline soil; shade.
Polystichum polyblepharum **Korean Tassel Fern**	E	1'	8"	Easy to grow in shade. Tassel fern has glossy evergreen fronds with "eyelashes" along stem.

SCIENTIFIC NAME/ COMMON NAME	KEY	HEIGHT	WIDTH OF FROND	COMMENTS
Pteridium aquilinum **Bracken Fern**	D	to 3'	18"	Leaflets on long coarse stem, spore cases on narrow lines near margin. Crisp brown erect growth after first frost. Invasive. Sun or shade; any soil.
Selaginella braunii **Chinese Lace Fern, Arborvitae Fern**	D	1' – 1½'	6"	Arborvitae-like foliage on a ferny woodland plant. Never invasive, but slowly spreads. Late to emerge in spring. Charming. Ancient plant. Peacock Moss (*Selaginella uncinata*) is similar but smaller.
Thelypteris hexagonoptera **Broad Beech Fern**	D	2'	14"	Triangular frond, spore cases scattered in margin. Semi-moist, open spots in rich woods, acid soil.
Thelypteris kunthii **River Fern**	D	4'	10"	Excellent, hardy, vigorous large fern for shade garden. Will take some sun. Moist, fertile, acid soil.
Thelypteris palustris **Marsh Fern**	D	1½'	6"	Spore cases in curled up leaflets. Grown in open marshy places, often in full sun, woodland soil.
Thelypteris phegopteris **Long Beech Fern**	D	1'	8"	Triangular frond; bottom pair of leaflets turn down, 12 pairs in all. Shaded, moist bank, acid soil.
Woodsia ilvensis **Rusty Fern**	D	6"	1"	Small coarse fronds growing in tufts; leaflets rusty underneath in dry weather; spore cases on underside of fertile leaflet. Moist, neutral soil, partial shade, good drainage.

419

SCIENTIFIC NAME/ COMMON NAME	KEY	HEIGHT	WIDTH OF FROND	COMMENTS
Woodsia obtusa **Woodsia, Blunt-lobed Cliff Fern**	E	1' – 1½'	4"	Evergreen, lacy. Fronds hairy underneath, most common and largest woodsia. Spore cases on underside of fertile leaflet. Part shade, neutral moist soil, needs protected location.

TENDER FERNS

CULTURE

METHODS OF DISPLAY: 1. Conventional potting
2. Baskets of wire with a sphagnum moss or coir lining
3. Plaquing for staghorns

SOIL MIXES: When it comes to potting and soil mixes, it is useful to divide ferns into two categories: *terrestrial* and *epiphytic*. *Terrestrial ferns* grow naturally in the ground and make good potted plants. For these ferns, use a soft, organic soil mix such as 2 parts loam, 2 parts organic matter (leaf mold, compost, or peat moss), 1 part perlite, 1 part vermiculite, 1 part charcoal, and 1 part very fine grade orchid bark. A simpler recipe is a combination of potting soil and perlite or sand. Ferns tend to have small, delicate root systems, so when potting, don't disturb the root ball too much and firm the soil in place, but don't "pack" it in.

Epiphytes naturally grow in trees or on rocks, etc., not in the earth. Most epiphytic ferns have an extensive rhizome system that grows around their support structure. The rhizomes will grow all around your basket or pot, so they should be "planted" on the surface and then allowed to grow "outside" the container. Epiphytes require a different mix: 1 part of the terrestrial mix above combined with ½ part of very fine grade orchid bark and ½ part tree fern fiber. Some ferns grow best in soil-less potting mixes, like Pro-Mix®.

WATERING: The majority of cultivated ferns prefer soil which is consistently moist, not soggy. Less active growing periods require less water. Ferns in small pots, clay pots, or loose, sandy soil will require more frequent watering. Since over-watering can cause root damage, try to water when needed rather than by a set schedule.

Water thoroughly until water drains out of the bottom, remembering a crowded fern will require more time and water for the moisture to be absorbed into the interior of the root ball. Always try to water under the foliage as some of the finer fern foliage can be injured by water standing on their tips. It is best to water early in the day.

HUMIDITY: With many ferns, humidity is the key to success. Most require at least 35 percent humidity; 40 to 50 percent is even better. The typical home has lower humidity than ferns require, especially with central heat and air conditioning.

There are several things you can do to increase the humidity around your plants. Running a humidifier will produce the best results, and it's also good for you, your wood furniture, books, paintings, and so on. Mass or group your plants together, and set them on trays of gravel filled with water, but be certain to raise the bottom of your containers above the water level. Ferns will not tolerate standing in water. Add a few pieces of charcoal to the tray, and clean it thoroughly with a 10% bleach solution or scalding water every two months or so.

You can also mist ferns with larger leaves, but bear in mind that one little spritzing a day won't increase humidity for very long – when the droplets have dried up, the humidity is basically gone. An alternative is to enclose your plants in a terrarium of some kind. Fancy growth chambers date back to Victorian England; and they maintain high humidity, prevent drafts, and provide a little additional warmth.

TEMPERATURE: Ferns vary greatly in their temperature requirements. Inside ferns prefer a 55°F – 70°F temperature range. Do not place a fern too near the ceiling, on top of a TV or refrigerator, or in the flow of air from a heating duct. They need to be protected from hot air and drafts although a small amount of air circulation is desirable.

LIGHT: Contrary to what many people think, ferns do not grow in the dark. Ideally, ferns prefer bright, indirect light for best growth, and many will benefit from a little sun in winter. Many will tolerate lower light, but under these conditions, they merely survive and won't grow very much. If using artificial grow-lights, do not place ferns closer than 12" – 14" from the light source.

FERTILIZING: Light fertilizing is essential for all potted ferns. Container-grown ferns require frequent feedings as plant food is flushed out of containers. Choose a fertilizer that indicates it is "low burn". It is advisable to use half-strength and fertilize more frequently. Fish emulsion is good for ferns.

PESTS: Carefully check ferns periodically, looking on the underneath side of the fronds. Do not confuse the spore cases with insect scale. The most common pests on ferns are scale and mealybug. Picking mealybug off by hand or with a Q-tip dipped in alcohol or soapy water is very effective, although tedious. Scale is even more difficult to remove manually.

The best control method is prevention by keeping clean containers and plants. Old fronds should be cut back to soil level for, if left intact, they harbor insects

421

and disease and interfere with the development of new fronds. New ferns should be isolated for several weeks to make certain they are disease free. If insect infestation appears, isolate the plant and use a mild insecticide, such as dipping in a 5% Sevin® solution, since ferns are very sensitive to chemicals. *Adiantums* are easily burned. Mildew fungus is prevalent on some ferns. Always read labels carefully and follow directions. If possible, reduce dosage.

REPRODUCING AND DIVIDING: Ferns most commonly reproduce by spores, but parts of the root, rhizome, or frond may also produce new plants. Some ferns produce bulblets, others can be multiplied by dividing, while still others produce runners that start new plants. For more detailed information consult a fern grower's manual.

Multiple crowns: Some ferns produce an abundance of crowns as they get older. Becoming heavily massed, they crowd and rise above the growing medium. When these ferns reach this stage and when good, strong, new growth is noted in the spring, they should be divided. In the event that an unusual spell of early warm weather encourages new growth, do not divide. Be certain the spring warmth is going to be consistent. When the proper period arrives, an abundance of new fiddle heads will be noted about ready to uncurl. Dividing at the wrong time will result in loss of plants unless they are in a heated greenhouse to provide warmth for constant growth.

Ferns without crowns (those having a creeping, spreading root system), and *epiphytes* can be propagated from rhizome (stem) cuttings. These take best if the pieces have at least one leaf and preferably roots. Some types become so matted that dead areas will be noted. Sections without good new growth should be removed. This is true of types grown in the ground also.

Some ferns, commonly called "mother ferns", make baby plantlets along their leaves, and these can easily be separated and grown in a separate pot. Most ferns can also be grown from *spores*, and is not as difficult as it may sound, but takes much longer.

VARIETIES OF TENDER FERNS

The following table lists ferns according to their use and type, and all can be grown in containers. A few of the ferns are ground-hardy, but eminently suited to container culture, so they are listed in both the *Hardy* and *Tender Fern Tables*.

The great majority of ferns in *Table 42* are tender houseplants or epiphytes from tropical regions. Some are suitable for mixed container plantings; some are bold and unusual and should be grown as specimens. Many potted ferns thrive outdoors in the shade in summer; others are strictly house/greenhouse plants. The notation "pro-mix pot" refers to growing in a container in a soil-less mixture, or in one of the above-described soil mixes. The notation "woodland" indicates the fern is hardy in the ground in sandy loam and partial shade.

TABLE 42. VARIETIES OF TENDER FERNS

FERN TYPE	SCIENTIFIC NAME/ COMMON NAME	SUN/ SHADE	SOIL	CULTURE
1. Adiantum Ferns (Maidenhair)	*Adiantum aethiopicum* **Common Maidenhair**	Light shade	Neutral to limey wood-land/ moist soil	Spreads nicely, smaller than Southern maidenhair.
	A. anceps **Double-Edge Maidenhair**	Shade	Pro-mix pot/ lime/ moist soil, dry foliage	Difficult; even temp, high humidity. New fronds come all year; cut off old.
	A. bellum **Bermuda Maidenhair**	Shade	Pro-mix pot/lime/ moist soil	Finicky, no drafts, high humidity, new fronds all year, cut off old.
	A. capillus-veneris **Southern Maidenhair**	Light shade	Woodland/ pro-mix pot/ lime/ moist soil, dry foliage	Easy. Native. Damp in winter, water well in spring and summer. Runner roots, spreads slowly in moist limey loam. 'Imbricatum' and 'Green Petticoats' are good.
	A. caudatum **Walking Maidenhair**	Part shade	Woodland/ pro-mix pot/ lime/ moist	3" tall deciduous fern. Walks by sprouting where frond touches the ground. Moist.
	A. hispidulum **Rough Maidenhair**	Part shade	Woodland/ lime/ moist	Rather easy. Cut old fronds off as new ones emerge in spring.
	A. macrophyllum **Bigleaf Maidenhair**	Part shade	Pro-mix pot/ lime/ moist soil	Rather easy, high humidity. New foliage is pink. New fronds come all year; cut off old.

423

Fern Type	Scientific Name/ Common Name	Sun/ Shade	Soil	Culture
				Almost hardy in the ground.
	A. raddianum **Delta Maidenhair Fern**	Part shade	Woodland/ pro-mix pot/lime/ moist	Finicky, no drafts, high humidity. New fronds all year, cut off old. Cultivars include 'Pacotti', 'Grandiceps', 'Lady Geneva', 'Fritz Luthii', & 'Pacific Maid'.
	A. tenerum **Brittle Maidenhair, Black-stick Maidenhair**	Part shade	Pro-mix pot/ lime/ moist soil/ dry foliage	Difficult, high humidity, even temp. New fronds come all year; cut off old. 'Farleyense'
	A. trapeziforme **Giant Maidenhair**	Part shade	Pro-mix pot/ lime/ moist soil/ dry foliage	Difficult, high humidity, even temp. New fronds come all year; cut off old.
	A. venustum **Evergreen Maidenhair**	Part shade	Pro-mix pot/ lime/ moist	Rather easy, large triangular fronds.
2. Basket or Hanging Ferns	*Nephrolepis biserata* **Giant Sword Fern**	Shade	Pro-mix pot/ dryish soil but humid air	Finicky, high humidity, even temp. New fronds come all year; cut off old. 'Furcans'
	Nephrolepis exaltata **Boston Fern**	Part shade	Pro-mix pot/ dryish soil/ dry foliage	Rather easy, no drafts, high humidity, new fronds all year, cut off old. Cultivars 'Anna Foster', 'Rooseveltii',

FERN TYPE	SCIENTIFIC NAME/ COMMON NAME	SUN/ SHADE	SOIL	CULTURE
				'Norwoodii', 'Smithii', 'Verona', 'Whitmanii'
	Nephrolepis obliterata **Australian Sword Fern**	Part shade	Pro-mix pot/ dryish soil/ dry foliage	Rather easy, high humidity, new fronds all year, cut off old. 'Kimberly Queen'
	Polypodium angustifolium or *Campyloneurum angustifolium* **Narrow-leaved Strap Fern**	Part shade	Pro-mix pot/ moist	Finicky, no drafts, high humidity, new fronds all year, cut off old.
	Polypodium polycarpon **Crested Bird's Nest Fern**	Part shade	Pro-mix pot/ moist	New fronds come all year, cut off old fronds. Houseplant. 'Cristatum'
	Polypodium polycarpon **Bird's Nest Fern, Brazilian Form**	Part shade	Pro-mix pot/ moist	Finicky, no drafts, high humidity, new fronds all year, cut off old. 'Grandiceps'
	Polypodium polycarpon integrifolium **Climbing Bird's Nest**	Shade	Pro-mix pot/ moist	Difficult, high humidity, even temp. New fronds come all year; cut off old.
	Polypodium subauriculatum 'Knightiae' **Knight's Polypody**	Part shade	Pro-mix pot/ moist	Rather easy, keep damp in winter, water well in growing season. Cut off old fronds in spring.
	Woodwardia orientalis **Oriental Chain Fern**	Part shade	Pro-mix pot/ moist	Easy; new fronds all year, cut off old fronds. Grows new fronds at leaf tips,

425

FERN TYPE	SCIENTIFIC NAME/ COMMON NAME	SUN/ SHADE	SOIL	CULTURE
				forming a chain.
3. Footed Basket Ferns (Rabbit's Foot Fern)	*Aglaomorpha meyeniana* **Bear's Paw Fern**	Part shade	Pro-mix pot/ moist	Finicky, no drafts, high humidity, new fronds all year, cut off old.
	Davallia fejeensis **Rabbit's Foot Fern**	Part shade	Pro-mix pot/ moist	Epiphytic. Needs humidity. House-plant. 'Plumosa', 'Major' and 'Dwarf Ripple' are good.
	Davallia solida **Squirrel's Foot Fern**	Part shade	Pro-mix pot/ moist	Epiphytic. Needs humidity. Houseplant. Cultivars 'Ornata' and 'Ruffled Ornata'.
	Davallia trichomanoides **Rabbit's Foot or Squirrel's Foot Fern**	Part shade	Pro-mix pot/ moist	Easy. Cut off old fronds in spring as new ones emerge.
	Humata tyermannii **Bear's Foot Fern**	Part shade	Pro-mix pot/ moist	Easy. Cut off old fronds in spring as new ones emerge.
	Phlebodium aureum **Cabbage Palm Fern, Golden Polypody, Golden Serpent Fern**	Part shade	Pro-mix pot/ moist	Easy. Cut off old fronds in spring as new ones emerge.
	Polypodium aureum **Bear's Paw Fern**	Part shade	Acidic woodland/ pro-mix pot/ moist	Easy. Cut off old fronds in spring as new ones emerge. 'Mandaianum'

426

FERN TYPE	SCIENTIFIC NAME/ COMMON NAME	SUN/ SHADE	SOIL	CULTURE
	Polypodium scolopendria or *Microsorum scolopendria* or *Phymatodes scolopendria* **Wart Fern**	Part shade	Pro-mix pot/ moist	Very easy. Spreads by runners. Will climb if given something to cling to. Cut old fronds off as new ones emerge in spring.
	Polypodium vacciniifolium **Brazilian Polypody**	Shade	Pro-mix pot/ moist to wet	Difficult, high humidity, even temp. New fronds come all year; cut off old. Brazilian epiphyte.
	Pyrrosia lingua **Leatherleaf**	Part shade	Acid woodland/ pro-mix pot/ moist	Rather easy. Cut old fronds off as new ones emerge in spring.
4. Low-Growing Ferns	*Asplenium daucifolium* **Mother Fern**	Part shade	Acid woodland/ pro-mix pot/ moist	Rather easy. Cut off old fronds in spring as new ones emerge.
	Athyrium goeringianum pictum or *Athyrium nipponicum pictum* **Japanese Painted Fern**	Part shade	Acid woodland/ pro-mix pot/ moist	Easy. One of the finest garden ferns. Many good cultivars with red and silver variegation. Keep moist in winter. Deciduous. Pot or woodland.
	Doryopteris pedata **Hand Fern**	Shade	Pro-mix pot/lime/ moist	Finicky, no drafts, high humidity, new fronds all year, cut off old.

427

FERN TYPE	SCIENTIFIC NAME/ COMMON NAME	SUN/ SHADE	SOIL	CULTURE
	Dryopteris erythrosora **Autumn Fern**	Dappled sun	Acid woodland/ moist	Easy; new fronds all year, cut off old fronds. One of the best evergreen garden ferns.
	Dryopteris filix-mas **Male Fern**	Part shade	Pro-mix pot/ rich acid woodland/ moist to wet	Easy in moist rich soil. Runner roots. Hardy in ground or potted. Deciduous. 'Cristata'
	Nephrolepis cordifolia **Sword Fern, Boston Fern**	Shade	Pro-mix pot/ dryish	Difficult, high humidity, even temp. New fronds come all year; cut off old. Runner roots. 'Duffi'
	Nephrolepis exaltata **Boston Fern**	Part shade	Pro-mix pot/ dryish to moist	Easy. Runner roots. Houseplant. Likes humidity. 'Fluffy Ruffles'
	Pellaea falcata **Sickle Fern**	Part shade	Pro-mix pot/ moist	Rather easy. Cut old fronds off as new ones emerge in spring.
	Pellaea rotundifolia **Button Fern**	Part shade	Acid woodland/ pro-mix pot/ moist	Rather easy. Cut old fronds off as new ones emerge in spring.
	Phyllitis scolopendrium or *Asplenium scolopendrium* **Hart's Tongue Fern**	Shade	Woodland/ pro-mix pot/ lime/ moist	Evergreen, rather easy. Prefers limey woodland or pot culture. Moist, humid. Hardy. 'Cristata'
	Pityrogramma calomelanos **Silverback**	Part shade	Pro-mix pot/ moist	Finicky, no drafts, high humidity, new fronds all year, cut

428

FERN TYPE	SCIENTIFIC NAME/ COMMON NAME	SUN/ SHADE	SOIL	CULTURE
				off old.
	Pityrogramma chrysophylla **Goldback Fern**	Part shade	Pro-mix pot/ moist	Finicky, no drafts, high humidity, new fronds all year, cut off old.
	Pityrogramma triangularis **Goldback Fern**	Part shade	Woodland/ pot/ dryish to moist	Easy. Hardy in the ground, good in containers. Well-drained damp soil is preferred.
	Polystichum polyblepharum **Korean Tassel Fern**	Part shade	Acid woodland/ pro-mix/ moist	Easy; new fronds all year, cut off old fronds. Dark, glossy evergreen fronds on low clump. Divide in spring. Even moisture. Good choice for pot or ground.
	Polystichum setosum **Japanese Lace Fern, Japanese Tassel Fern**	Dappled sun	Acid woodland/ moist	Easy. Cut old fronds off as new ones emerge in spring. Hardy evergreen. Pot or ground.
	Polystichum tsus-simense **Tsu-sima Holly Fern**	Dappled sun	Acid woodland/ moist	Rather easy. Cut old fronds off as new ones emerge in spring.
	Pteris cretica **Cretan Brake Fern, Table Fern**	Dappled sun	Acid woodland/ pro-mix pot/ moist	Easy. Cut old fronds off as new ones emerge in spring. 'Rivertoniana', 'Wilsonii', 'Wimsetti',

429

FERN TYPE	SCIENTIFIC NAME/ COMMON NAME	SUN/ SHADE	SOIL	CULTURE
				'Albolineata'
	Pteris ensiformis **Slender Brake Fern**	Shade	Pro-mix pot/ moist	Difficult, high humidity, even temp. New fronds come all year; cut off old. 'Victoriae'
5. Medium-Tall Ferns	*Asplenium bulbiferum* **Mother Fern**	Part shade	Pro-mix pot/ wet soil	Easy; new fronds all year, cut off old fronds
	Athyrium filix-femina **Lady Fern**	Dappled sun	Acid woodland/ wet soil	Easy. Multiple crowns. Deciduous. Keep moist, not soggy, in winter.
	Cyrtomium falcatum **Holly Fern**	Dappled sun	Acid woodland/ moist	Easy. Adds beautiful texture to shade garden. Cut old fronds off as new ones emerge in spring.
	Dryopteris filix-mas **Male Fern**	Dappled sun	Acid woodland/ pro-mix pot/ moist	Rather easy. Cut off old fronds in spring as new ones emerge. Multiple crowns.
	Nephrolepis cordifolia **Sword Fern, Fishbone Fern**	Dappled sun	Acid woodland/ pro-mix pot/ moist	Easy; new fronds all year, cut off old fronds
	Osmunda regalis **Royal Fern**	Part shade	Acid woodland/ pro-mix pot/ moist	Easy. Cut off old fronds in spring as new ones emerge. Hardy, deciduous
	Pellaea viridis **Green Brake Fern**	Part shade	Pro-mix pot/ moist	Rather easy. New fronds all year; cut off old ones.

430

FERN TYPE	SCIENTIFIC NAME/ COMMON NAME	SUN/ SHADE	SOIL	CULTURE
	Polystichum munitum **Western Sword Fern**	Dappled sun	Acid woodland/ moist	Easy. Cut old fronds off as new ones emerge in spring.
	Pteris cretica **Cretan Brake Fern**	Dappled sun	Acid woodland/ pro-mix pot/ moist	Easy. Cut old fronds off as new ones emerge in spring. 'Parkeri'
6. Tall Ferns	*Asplenium nidus* **Bird's Nest Fern**	Shade	Acid woodland/ pro-mix pot/ wet soil	Rather easy. New fronds all year. Cut off old fronds.
	Matteuccia struthiopteris **Ostrich Fern**	Part shade	Acid woodland/ pot/ moist to wet	4' tall deciduous fern for partial shade and constant moisture. Potting soil.
	Pteris quadriaurita **Silver Fern**	Shade	Acid woodland/ moist	Rather easy. Multiple crowns, new fronds all year, cut off old ones. 'Argyrea'
	Pteris vittata **Chinese Ladder Brake Fern**	Dappled sun	Acid woodland/ pro-mix pot/ moist	Easy. Multiple crowns, new fronds all year, cut off old ones.
	Tectaria gemmifera **Snail Fern**	Shade	Acid woodland/ moist	Easy; new fronds all year, cut off old fronds. Large 8' – 9' fern, hardy, likes humidity
7. Tree Ferns, Low-Growing	*Todea barbara* **Austral King Fern**	Dappled sun	Acid woodland/ pro-mix pot/ moist	Easy; new fronds all year, cut off old fronds

431

FERN TYPE	SCIENTIFIC NAME/ COMMON NAME	SUN/ SHADE	SOIL	CULTURE
	Blechnum brasiliense **Brazilian Tree Fern**	Part shade	Acid woodland/ moist	Finicky, no draft, high humidity. Multiple crowns, new fronds all year, cut off old ones.
	Blechnum gibbum **Dwarf Tree Fern**	Shade	Pro-mix pot/ moist	Finicky, no draft, high humidity. Multiple crowns, new fronds all year, cut off old ones. Must be kept moist.
8. Tree Ferns, Tall-Growing	*Cibotium glaucum* **Hawaiian Tree Fern**	Dappled sun	Climbing/ pot/ woodland/ moist	Easy; new fronds all year, cut off old fronds. Keep moist
	Alsophila australis **Australian Tree Fern**	Dappled sun	Climbing/ pot/ moist	Easy; new fronds all year, cut off old fronds
	Dicksonia antartica **Soft Tree Fern**	Dappled sun	Climbing/ pot/ woodland/ moist	Easy; new fronds all year, cut off old fronds
9. Climbing Ferns	*Lygodium japonicum* **Japanese Climbing Fern**	Dappled sun	Climbing/ pot/ woodland/ moist	Easy. Cut old fronds off as new ones emerge in spring.
	Stenochlaena palustris **Vine Fern**	Part shade	Climbing/ pot/ woodland/ moist	Easy; new fronds all year, cut off old fronds
10. Platyceriums (Staghorn)	*Platycerium bifurcatum* **Staghorn Fern, Elkhorn Fern**	Part shade	Pro-mix pot/ moist	Easy, epiphyte. Hang on board and mist.
	Platycerium grande **Staghorn Fern**	Shade	Pro-mix pot/ dryish	Rather easy, many staghorn varieties.

CONTAINER PLANTS

DESIGN CONSIDERATIONS

Container plantings, for both indoors and out, have come into their own as design elements in recent years. Flank your entryway with a pair of urns, soften garden steps and pathways, add color and form to the patio, pool area, porch, or sunroom with potted plants. From a design perspective, architectural strengths can be accentuated and weaknesses can be camouflaged with the artful use of containers.

There is one major down-side to container gardening, however, and that is *the need for continual watering.* While moisture-control potting soil helps, in hot weather and full sun pots may need watering twice a day. If it is feasible, hook up drip irrigation tubing and a timer to automatically water containers.

Almost any sort of container with a drainage hole can be used for planting, whether terra cotta, plastic, fiberglass, ceramic, metal, etc. Choose plants that will be in scale with the container when they are mature. Decorative cachepots, baskets, and so on, can be used to disguise a plain pot. Be sure the decorative container will accommodate both the pot and the waterproof saucer it sits in. Florists' moss or mulch can be used to fill in around the top of the container.

Classic outdoor containers include strawberry pots, window boxes, hanging baskets, and urns. Small, peaceful water gardens can be created in galvanized tubs, wooden barrels with liners, wall-hung water basins, and the like. Wooden planter boxes, lined with plastic and equipped with drain holes, may be integrated into deck handrails or built-in seating in a number of attractive ways.

If you are grouping several containers, you may want to plant all-one-thing in a couple of the pots so the final effect is not too busy. Outdoor pots of all-one-thing work best if the plant either *flowers all season* like impatiens and fibrous

433

begonia, or has *great foliage with or without showy flowers* like fern, caladium, heuchera, croton, and agapanthus.

MIXED PLANTINGS have become very popular and provide endless possibilities. Houseplants, annuals, bulbs, small vines, ferns, certain perennials, small shrubs, standards, and small trees can be used in your creations.

As a rule of thumb in mixed planting design, use *trailers* to drape gracefully over the edge of the pot; use *uprights* to give the planting stature and form; and use *fillers* for fullness and texture. Many gardeners like to plant "three-of-a-kind", if the container size permits. There's also the question of symmetry and balance. It is important that you combine plants with the same sun and water requirements in any container.

Choose a variety of flower forms (clusters, trumpets, panicles, singles, doubles, etc.) to create aesthetically pleasing combinations. Foliage plants, especially variegated or trailing ones, are great additions. There are wonderful new plants, variegated or solid, with silver, purple, red, amber, yellow, chartreuse, and blue leaves, so the design palette is extensive.

Consider the size, form, and color of the foliage and flowers you are combining; create bold contrast or subtle harmony, as you like. Echo the reddish-pink stripe in a 'Pink Sunburst' canna leaf (*upright*) with the same pink in a wave petunia (*trailer*), a hybrid pink verbena (*filler & trailer*), and pink and green sun-tolerant coleus (*filler*), for example, for a gay and colorful patio urn in a sunny spot. Or you could put the pink striped canna (*upright*) with silver dusty-miller (*filler*), a white-with-rose-eye periwinkle (*filler*), and 'Blackie' *Ipomoea* (*trailer*) for a completely different look, still choosing colors from the canna leaf and planning for sun. With the second urn, you might have a companion pot of 'Gin' begonias, with pink flowers and maroon-bronze foliage. The black-purple of the sweet potato vine 'Blackie' should harmonize with the begonia leaves and with the dark stripe in the canna leaf. The silver dusty-miller and white vinca add lightness and good texture without being flashy or competitive.

Mixed plantings offer an easy way to change looks with the season. If you are growing a viburnum standard, crape myrtle, oleander, or dwarf pear, for example, in a large diameter pot, create holes for 4" or 6" pots to be evenly spaced around the trunk of the main plant. Seasonally, insert pots of annuals, bulbs, small vines, or perennials into the pre-dug holes; whatever suits you and your sun situation. Hydrangeas, azaleas, and gardenias grow well in pots and can be under-planted with any number of low-growing annuals or perennials.

RECOMMENDATIONS: While there are endless beautiful mixtures, below are listed a few plants and combinations to start with.

LONG-FLOWERING PLANTS FOR CONTAINERS

alyssum	lantana	portulaca
begonia	lobelia	salvia

browallia	marigold	sanvitalia
canna	million bells	snapdragon
coleus	nasturtium	thunbergia
fan flower	pansy	verbena
geranium	pentas	zinnia
impatiens	periwinkle	

FOLIAGE PLANTS FOR CONTAINERS

aspidistra	ferns	Persian shield
aucuba	heuchera	pittosporum
caladium	hosta	sedum, stonecrop
coleus	ipomoea	variegated ivy
dusty-miller	pachysandra	vinca minor

EXAMPLE CONTAINER COMBINATIONS

SHADE

1. 'Dragon Wings' Begonia (*Begonia x hybrida* 'Dragon Wings'),
   White-Variegated Flax Lily (*Dianella tasmanica* 'Variegata'),
   Variegated Creeping-charley (*Glechoma hederacea* 'Variegata').

2. 'Aaron' Caladium (*Caladium x* 'Aaron'),
   'Kimberly Queen' Fern (*Nephrolepis obliterata* 'Kimberly Queen'),
   'Marble Queen' Pothos (*Epipremnum aureum* 'Marble Queen'),
   Cuban Oregano (*Plectranthus amboinicus*).

SUN

3. 'Tropicana' Canna (*Canna x* 'Tropicana')
   Yellow Lantana (*Lantana camara*),
   Goldfish Plant (*Columnea*),
   'Line' Coleus (*Coleus x* 'Line')
   Golden Creeping Jenny (*Lysimachia nummularia*).

4. 'Purple Homestead' Verbena (*Verbena x* 'Homestead Purple'),
   'Marguerite' Sweet Potato Vine (*Ipomoea batatas*),
   Blue Superbells (*Calibrachoa* hybrids),
   'Oriental Limelight' Artemisia (*Artemisia vulgaris* hybrid),
   'Inky Fingers' Coleus (*Coleus x* 'Inky Fingers').

435

CONTAINER PLANT CULTURE

PURCHASING

- Familiarize yourself with the houseplants' growing requirements; choose those suited to your natural indoor light levels.

- When purchasing, find the strongest and healthiest young plant. Avoid ones that are root bound or have brown edges on the leaves. A younger plant acclimates itself to house conditions better than an old one.

- It is advisable to isolate the new purchase from other plants for several weeks as disease or insects might appear.

POTTING

- Never use dirty pots. Soak in bleach or ammonia water and scrub. Use sterile potting soil.

- It is imperative to have good drainage and a light soil mixture. Always place a piece of potshard, crumpled newspaper, pebbles, or nylon screening over the drainage hole before filling container to within 2" – 4" from the top with potting mix. Place plant at the depth it has been growing and press potting soil gently but firmly around the roots.

- New "moisture-control" potting soils are available that contain a gel polymer which regulates the amount of water released to the plant roots. Most also contain time-released fertilizers. These new lightweight potting mixes are ready-to-use, economical, and suitable for most container plants. Alternatively, you can put a household sponge above the drainage rocks but under the potting soil to help with continual, slow delivery of water to the roots.

- If desired, use 1" of shredded pine bark mulch or moss on the surface to help retain moisture.

- Never use garden soil for container plants as it compacts too much and doesn't allow air to reach the roots.

- Provide all containers with a waterproof dish or saucer to retain water for the plant to absorb over several hours, and to protect floors and tables from water damage.

- Be sure all plants in the container have the same sun and water requirements.

- Never place a houseplant in a draft, such as in front of heat ducts or doorways, or on top of the TV or refrigerator because of bottom heat.

- Houseplants may be repotted any time they need it. Repot if new leaves come out smaller than average, plants wilt between waterings, lower leaves turn yellow, roots appear on surface or through hole in the bottom. Most outdoor containers are planted or revised in spring.

- Soak all terra cotta pots overnight before using because dry pots will absorb water from the soil. Plants in clay pots need water more frequently than those in plastic, fiberglass, resin, or metal pots.

- While unglazed terra cotta pots are handsome, they "spall" (layers of terra cotta crack off) if left out in freezing wet weather, and they are very heavy to move. It will help to paint the pot inside and out with a transparent, matte masonry sealer [available at brickyards, paint stores, or tile stores]. It doesn't add a shine, but seals against water penetration. Thompson's Water Seal® is not the same as masonry sealer and will not protect terra cotta pots as well.

- Look for the attractive resin and fiberglass pots which are weatherproof, lightweight, and easily painted or antiqued to suit your taste.

  Hint: *To "moss" your terracotta, stone, resin, or fiberglass pot*, take a clump of moss (from under a tree or scraped off a brick walk, for example) and equal parts water and buttermilk and puree it in the blender. Paint the slurry on the container and place in the garden in a shady spot and keep misted with water daily for a few days. Some people recommend painting the container with beer before applying the moss slurry. Moss should start growing and give a stately "been there for years" effect.

  To create *the effect of aged bronze, lead, or wrought iron*, spray paint the container with a dark raw umber, a warm gray, or flat black and let dry. For the patina, "wipe on – wipe off" a matte, bluish-pea green or pale gray acrylic paint thinned with water to the consistency of ½ & ½ cream. Wipe on and off with a piece of old t-shirt or cheesecloth, and allow the glaze to accumulate slightly in the cracks and crevices as natural tarnish would. There are many other ways to faux-finish your pots, but this is easy.

- Putting large houseplants on rolling caddies prevents water damage to floors and makes it easier to move them outside in spring.

- If the pot will be moved frequently and you want to keep weight down, add your drainage rocks or screen, and then add several inches of Styrofoam packing peanuts before adding the potting mix and the plants.

- Conversely, if the container will be planted with a top-heavy small tree, prevent tipping in the wind by adding a few bricks in the bottom of the pot to make it heavier.

- For a hanging basket, use a wire frame lined with coir or sphagnum moss, then fill it 2/3 full with potting mix and add the plants. Add more soil if needed to fill in between plants, and water well. If you keep the moss basket misted it will stay green. If you need to revive the moss basket, spray it with a 1:1 buttermilk and water solution (with or without beer added) and keep misted so it will green-up.

437

WATERING

- Proper watering is one of the most important considerations. **If pots are outdoors in the summer, be prepared to water every day.** Watering should be done early in the morning to minimize fungus diseases on foliage.

- To check for moistness, stick a finger ½" into the pot. Let houseplants dry out slightly before watering. Outdoors, however, don't let soil in pots dry out completely as plants are subject to hotter temperatures and higher evaporation rates. That being said, it is generally safer to under-water than to over-water.

- Insufficient water results in the edges of the leaves turning brown and wilting. Edges can be trimmed with scissors. Smear egg white with finger on trimmed strap leaves to prevent brown edges as it seals leaf tips.

- Too much watering usually results in leaves yellowing and dropping off at the base of the plant, and root rot. Let the plant dry out and see if it recovers, or repot it providing better drainage when you first notice the waterlogged state.

- Improper drainage should be corrected and watering schedules adjusted. Never let the roots stay submerged and waterlogged, as when the saucer is full of standing water. You cannot easily see if there is water standing in the bottom of most decorative containers, and it won't be easy to feel the soil if the planting is lush. It is easier than you might think to drown houseplants. You can add a few inches of turkey grit or pebbles at the bottom of the pot, and then add the potting soil to insure sharp drainage for plants that are finicky about wet feet.

- If the plant needs humidity, mist it with water in a spray bottle, and/or place a tray with pebbles and water under the pot. The pebbles raise the pot and roots out of the water and the plant gets humidity as the water evaporates. In winter, use a humidifier or place containers of water near heating vents for additional humidity. Mist plants more often in winter.

- Water houseplants with tepid water. Cold water can damage fine root hairs. Never use ice cubes.

- When watering dracaena, let water stand overnight so chlorine will evaporate, or use rainwater, to keep leaf tips from turning brown.

- African violets do not like water on their foliage. Place the pot in a shallow saucer and pour the water and/or fertilizer solution into the saucer. The water will wick up into the dry potting soil through the drainage hole and encourage roots to grow deep while keeping foliage dry. If desired, a wick can be rigged through the drainage hole at planting time to aid in this water uptake; a piece of cotton shoelace is all you need.

- Drip irrigation works well for outdoor containers. A do-it-yourself kit includes plastic tubing (available in several diameters) to discretely run to each pot, various delivery heads, a water pressure regulator, an adapter, and timer which can be hooked to your hose bib or outdoor faucet. Drip irrigation can also be controlled by an automatic sprinkler system.

438

- If planning a trip, water plants thoroughly, enclose entire pot and plant in a clear plastic bag, secure at the top and under pot. It will conserve moisture for 2 weeks or more. Do not place in the sun. This isn't necessary if you have drip irrigation or if containers are watered by automatic sprinklers.

LIGHT

- Light needs of plants vary, but a general rule is the closer to the window the better. If it is a good sunny window, the plant will have to be turned to keep from growing lopsided.

- Artificial light can be used to grow any plant. Incandescent 60–watt bulbs, Gro-lux grow lights, fluorescent grow lights (one tube of warm white and one of cool white) or a combination of cool white fluorescent with incandescent bulbs are satisfactory. Artificial lights should be kept on 12 – 16 hours a day; consider automatic timers. For average size houseplants, the lights should be 1' – 2' away. For a tray of seedlings, you may have the light as close as 6".

FERTILIZER

- Container plants need more water and fertilizer when they are in active growth or are flowering, less water and no fertilizer when they are resting (dormant). A light application every two or three weeks during the growing season is advised.

- Use time-released all-purpose plant food pellets like Osmocote®, or a dilute solution of Miracle-Gro®, Peter's® or Schultz's® houseplant food. Occasional applications of fish emulsion, cottonseed meal, Milorganite®, or dehydrated manure are also recommended. Bloom builders (high phosphorus content) can be used on flowering plants and high-nitrogen fertilizers are good for foliage plants. Special formulas are available for orchids and African violets. Use according to directions and alternate using several different fertilizers so all nutritional requirements will be met.

- If a plant is fertilized too much, it will quickly outgrow space allotted for it and the tips of the foliage will look burned. You stand less chance of burning plants if you use time-released fertilizer or mild fertilizers like fish emulsion or cottonseed meal.

- Since most commercially grown plants have a slow-release fertilizer in the soil, do not fertilize immediately after buying.

- Never fertilize when the soil is dry or the plant is in bad shape.

- When moving or repotting a plant, avoid feeding until plant has adjusted to new environment.

MAINTENANCE

- Clean the foliage of plants regularly. If there is a dust build-up, light will not penetrate. Some people "shine" their leaves with furniture polish or other oil, but

439

this can make it difficult for the plant to respire. Washing with water is better. Spray the plants outside with a hose or in a tub in the house.

- Deadhead spent blossoms to keep containers looking tidy and to encourage re-bloom.

- Plants like to be moved outside in the summer. Move them slowly, leaving on a porch or covered area for several weeks to acclimate. Then, always situate them in part shade and never direct sun.

- When bringing plants back inside before first frost, wash the foliage and container and check that there are no insects on the plant. If insects appear, use an insecticide intended for houseplants. Read the directions before using as the spray can burn some plants.

Cyclamen houseplants arrive loaded with flowers and beautiful large green leaves but, after the flowers fade, leaves often get leggy and turn yellow. At this point they are often discarded. Cyclamen can be kept, but their requirements are a little different than most houseplants.

Winter care: Place in an east-facing window with bright, indirect light. Cyclamen crowns and foliage are susceptible to fungal rot if too wet, so water only from the bottom (setting the pot in a bowl of water for a few minutes works well). For best flowering, keep humidity high and temperatures cool (60°F). You might try fertilizing with an all-purpose fertilizer at half-strength.

Spring care: After flowers fade, gradually withhold water until foliage withers. Store pots in a cool, dry location or remove corms from soil and store at 40° to 50°F in a perforated plastic bag filled with dry peat moss.

Summer care: In July, repot the corms in soil-less potting mix, leaving half of each corm above the soil surface. Place the pot outdoors in a shaded location; when new growth begins, fertilize the cyclamen with all-purpose houseplant food and keep the soil evenly moist.

Fall care: Bring the pot indoors before first frost. To induce flowering by Christmas, place in an east-facing window with 55°F temperatures.

Table 43, lists many good, tender foliage and flowering houseplants. It should be noted that several plants included in *Table 43* are covered in other chapters and are ground hardy; they are included here because of their adaptability to pot culture. Following the main table are Special Articles on Begonias, Bonsai, Orchids, and Palms.

TABLE OF CONTAINER PLANTS

TABLE 43. CONTAINER PLANTS

KEY	**B** – Blooming
	F – Foliage
	G – Greenhouse

SCIENTIFIC NAME/ COMMON NAME	KEY	HEIGHT	COMMENTS
Aeschynanthus radicans **Lipstick plant**	B	to 16"	Many varieties. Hanging baskets. Dark green waxy leaves; cut back stems to 6" after flowering for new growth. Sunny window, warm, humid. *Color*: orange-red.
Agapanthus africanus **Agapanthus, Lily-of-the-Nile**	B	1½' – 2'	Half day sun, cool, keep moist and fertilize only during growing season; likes to be pot-bound. Ground hardy varieties are available. *Color*: blue, white.
Aglaonema **Chinese Evergreen**	F	1' – 2'	Several varieties; slow growing. Will tolerate little light and dry conditions, prefers light and moisture; will grow in water.
Aloe **Aloe**	F	to 1'	Succulent; best in half day sun or bright indirect light; allow to become dry then water thoroughly; fertilize once a year. Many varieties. First aid plant. Spread jelly-like liquid from broken stem on burns and insect bites.
Amaryllis belladonna **Amaryllis, Belladonna Lily**	B	2'	*Color*: White, pink, red. Follow directions in *Bulbs* for *Forcing Bulbs for Indoor Bloom.*
Ananas comosus **Pineapple**	F	3'	Spiny-edged leaves of grayish to bronze-green, gracefully arching. Half day sun, moist. Top of a pineapple with 2" of pith may be rooted in water, changed frequently. When roots appear, plant in potting soil.

441

SCIENTIFIC NAME/ COMMON NAME	KEY	HEIGHT	COMMENTS
Anthurium andraeanum **Anthurium**	B, G	2' – 3'	Bright, indirect sunlight, warm, moist; fertilize every two weeks. *Color*: orange- red, rose or white spathe and spadix flower; arrow shaped foliage.
Anthurium scherzeranum **Anthurium**	B	12"	Same as above. Some grown for leaves with insignificant flower. *Color*: red, rose, white.
Aphelandra squarrosa **Zebra plant**	B	1' – 1½'	Large flower cluster of bracts, ovate leaves with veins marked with white. Sun, moist. Fall bloom, occasionally other seasons. *Color*: yellow.
Aralia **Aralia**	F	to 4'	Many varieties, many heights; interesting growth pattern; good for bonsai; noted for feathery foliage. Warm, moist soil, tolerates poor light.
Araucaria heterophylla **Norfolk Island Pine**	F	to 12', but usually much smaller	Pyramidal, very symmetrically branched ornamental. Bright light, barely moist; repot at 3 – 4 year intervals.
Asparagus setaceus **Asparagus Fern**	F	Trailing stems to 4'	Many varieties and leaf forms. Older plants bloom white followed by red berry. Moist, warm, filtered light. Not a true fern. Hardy in the ground.
Aspidistra elatior **Aspidistra, Cast Iron Plant**	F	1' – 3'	Noted for foliage; good for floral arrangements. Will tolerate heat, cold, wet soil or drought, neglect, and dim light; grows best with good care. Hardy in the ground. Great upright evergreen for shade.
Azalea - Rhododendron **Azalea**	B	1'	Belgian hybrids are popular florist gift plant. Hardy in the ground. *Color*: shades of pink, lavender, coral, and white.
Begonia **Begonia**			

442

SCIENTIFIC NAME/ COMMON NAME	KEY	HEIGHT	COMMENTS
See Special Article below.			
Beloperone guttata **Shrimp plant, Mexican Shrimp Plant**	B	1½'	Flowers white, bracts colored in drooping terminal spikes. Sun; rich, well-drained soil; keep trimmed. *Color*: yellow or coral.
Brassaia actinophylla **Schefflera, Umbrella tree**	F	to 6'	Palmate leaf. Half day sun to partial shade, warm, semi-dry between waterings; cut back to keep bushy. Also dwarf variety.
Bromeliad **Bromeliad**	F, B		Large genus of many species and hybrids. Leaves long and stiff forming a rosette; decorative foliage and long-lasting brilliant blossoms. Warm, filtered light; water in rosette cup. To force bloom, place a piece of cut apple in rosette and cover entire plant with plastic bag until bud appears. Methane gas given off by apple stimulates flowering. *Color*: many showy colors.
Brunfelsia australis **Yesterday-today-and-tomorrow**	B	2'	Fragrant flowers change from purple to white over three-day period. Half-day direct sun, moist, bloom best when pot bound. *Color*: purple, lavender, white.
Cactus **Cactus**	B, F	6" – 24"	Hundreds of varieties, interesting shapes; check specialty cactus books. Succulent, keep barely moist. *Color*: various pink, red, white, purple.
Caladium **Caladium**	F	1½'	Noted for foliage; effective all summer in high to partial shade. Water freely, feed lightly. Leave in pots and store in fall. Do not water until spring. Or treat as annuals. Many wonderful cultivars; also dwarf varieties. *Color*: pink, red,

443

SCIENTIFIC NAME/ COMMON NAME	KEY	HEIGHT	COMMENTS
			white, green variegated leaves.
Calathea makoyana **Peacock plant**	F	to 2'	Red stalks, green leaves with purple and red underneath. High humidity, bright indirect sun; best in terrarium.
Calceolarza crenatiflora **Pocketbook plant**	B	6" – 12"	Richly colored pouch-like flowers, often spotted; profuse bloomer in spring. Cool, part sun, dies back after blooming. *Color*: yellow, red, orange, bronze.
Carissa grandiflora **Carissa**	F, B	3' – 5'	Fragrant star-shaped flowers, glossy leathery leaves, scarlet plum-like fruit. *Color*: white.
Carissa macrocarpa compacta **Carissa,** **Natal plum**	F, B	1½' – 2'	Dwarf variety. *Color*: white.
Cattleya See Special Article on Orchids below.			
Ceropegia woodii **Rosary vine,** **Hearts-entangled**	F	Vine to 3'	Purple stems bearing heart-shaped, silver speckled leaves with purplish undersides. Bright indirect light, water after moderately dry, feed every two or three weeks from spring to mid-summer only.
Chlorophytum comosum **Spider plant**	F	to 2'	Grass-like arching leaves, small flowers in graceful sprays. Plant produces long wiry stems that terminate in small plantlets, which may be rooted easily. Also variegated varieties. Filtered sun, moist; best in hanging basket, tolerant of house conditions. *Color*: white.
Chrysanthemum frutescens **Marguerite**	B	to 3'	Half-day sun, moist. Keep pinched for desired height; blooms winter and spring. Hardy in the ground. *Color*: white, yellow.

444

SCIENTIFIC NAME/ COMMON NAME	KEY	HEIGHT	COMMENTS
Cissus rhombifolia **Grape Ivy**	F	vine	Shiny green leaves; good for hanging baskets. Bright indirect light; let dry before watering thoroughly.
Citrofortunella mitis **Calamondin Orange**	B, F	to 3'	Ornamental form and foliage; fragrant bloom; small, orange, acidic fruit; blooms and fruits in cycles. Full sun; let soil dry slightly between waterings; fertilize early spring, early summer, and fall. *Color*: white.
Citrus limonia **Lemon**	B, G	to 4'	'Ponderosa'. Fragrant flowers followed by extra large lemons. Half-day sun, semi-dry between watering, fertilize early spring, early summer, and fall. To control size pinch off new growth any time. *Color*: white.
Clivia miniata **Clivia, Kaffir Lily**	B, G	2'	Lily-like flowers, thick evergreen strap-shaped leaves. Likes to be pot bound; fertilize lightly every two weeks during growing season; let rest in fall without fertilizing; indirect light. Keep evenly moist. *Color*: coral, orange, yellow.
Codiaeum variegatum **Croton**	F	3' – 5'	Many varieties; foliage in shades of green, yellow, orange, pink, red, and crimson; requires sun to retain color. Fast grower, should be kept pruned. Milky sap poisonous.
Coleus x hybrids **Coleus**	F	to 2½'	Great new varieties for shade and sun. Grown for foliage of maroon, green, crimson, yellow, pink, cream, chartreuse or combination of these colors. Keep pinched back, insignificant flowers should be removed.
Columnea **Columnea**	G, B, F	vine to 4'	Vine-like plant, use in hanging containers; velvety foliage, flowers

445

SCIENTIFIC NAME/ COMMON NAME	KEY	HEIGHT	COMMENTS
			spring into fall. Keep evenly moist; bright indirect light. *Color*: red, yellow, or orange.
Cordyline terminalis **Ti Plant**	F	2½'	Long drooping leathery leaves grow palm-like at top of stems. Very humid, sun. Used for roof thatching and hula skirts.
Crassula argentea **Jade plant**	F	to 3'	Succulent. Fat, thick, oval green leaves, inconspicuous white flower. Slow grower. Half-day sun; let soil dry out before watering.
Crossandra **Crossandra**	B	to 12"	Gardenia-like leaf; blooms year round. Direct sun. Keep evenly moist; fertilize once a month. *Color*: pastel, salmon orange.
Cyclamen persicum **Cyclamen**	B	12"	Florist cyclamen. Petals are reflexed and elegant. Cool night temperatures, good drainage, and bright indirect light. Also dwarf varieties. See note in **Maintenance** for tips on growing cyclamen houseplants. Hardy cyclamen (*C. coum* & *C. hederifolium*) grows in dry shade very easily; see *Flowers – Bulbs. Color*: white, pink, red.
Cymbalaria muralis **Kenilworth Ivy**	F	vine	Hanging basket, decorative trailer. Bright indirect light, moist. Keep pinched.
Cyperus papyrus **Paper plant**	F	2½' – 4'	Umbrella-like foliage at top of stalk. Water copiously. Pots can be submerged in water garden in summer. To propagate: cut stem and clip foliage to 2" long. Insert foliage-end (upside down) in narrow vase of water. Roots grow down from center of leaves and new stem emerges upward. When enough roots have formed, pot up.
Dieffenbachia	F	to 10'	Many varieties; handsome leaves,

446

SCIENTIFIC NAME/ COMMON NAME	KEY	HEIGHT	COMMENTS
Dieffenbachia, Dumb Cane			spotted with white, cream or yellow markings. Moderate light, do not over-water; needs to be cut back when leggy. Poisonous.
Dizygotheca elegantissima **False Aralia**	F	3' – 5'	Jagged, dark green leaflets. Bright indirect light, keep barely moist.
Dracaena **Dracaena, Corn plant**	F	3' – 15'+	Many varieties, many different shapes and sizes of leaves. Light, rich soil, will thrive in sunless rooms. To water let tap water stand overnight so chlorine can evaporate, or use rain water, to keep leaf tips from turning brown. *Color*: White berries on coral stem.
Epipremnum aureum **Pothos**	F	vine	Variegated leaves resemble philodendron and culture is same.
Euphorbia pulcherrima **Poinsettia**	B	to 4'	Prized for colorful bracts produced around Christmas. Sunny, moist, no drafts. Difficult to bring into bloom the following year due to demanding light requirements. *Color*: red, pink, white; also variegated.
Fatsia japonica **Fatsia**	F	4' +	Bold shiny leaves, can be pruned to desired height; variegated varieties. Half day direct light, barely moist. Hardy in the ground.
Ferns See *Ferns* chapter for hardy and tender ferns.			
Ficus benjamina **Fig, Weeping fig**	F	6' +	Small glossy light green leaves; may lose leaves when moved. Prefers bright light; keep moist.
Ficus elastica **Rubber Plant**	F	to 12'	Large shiny dark green oval leaves, will branch when cut back. Semi-moist, tolerates much neglect. Also variegated form.

447

SCIENTIFIC NAME/ COMMON NAME	KEY	HEIGHT	COMMENTS
Ficus lyrata **Fiddle-leaf Fig**	F	to 12'	Shiny large fiddle-shaped dark green leathery leaves. Filtered to bright light; heavy, semi-moist soil, good drainage; do not over-water.
Ficus pumila **Creeping Fig**	F	vine	Semi-hardy outdoors. Small leaf, clinging vine; excellent for training on courtyard walls, topiaries and hanging baskets. Humidity, direct light; susceptible to red spider. See *Vines* chapter.
Fuchsia **Fuchsia, Lady's Eardrops**	B, G	1' – 4'	Many varieties, good for hanging basket. Protect from hot sun, prefers cooler weather. Needs light. Water well while blooming then reduce water for resting period. Prune Jan. to Feb. Subject to whitefly. *Color*: red, purple, white, pink.
Gardenia jasminoides **Gardenia, Cape Jasmine**	B, G	1' – 3'	Very fragrant, dark glossy green leaves. Half-day sun, moist soil, high humidity, good drainage, fertilize monthly. Subject to whitefly. Hardy in the ground. See Article in *Shrubs. Color*: white.
Gerbera jamesonii **African Daisy**	B, G	to 1½'	Sun, moist; attractive cut flower. *Color*: shades of scarlet to orange, yellow, white.
Hedera helix **Ivy**	F	vine	Many varieties. Leaf sizes ½" – 6"; shapes: lobed, rounded, wavy, or smooth. Good for topiary and hanging baskets. Half-day sun. Will root in water. See Article in *Vines. Color*: leaves green, variegated with cream, yellow, pink, or white.
Heliotropium **Heliotrope**	B	6" – 12"	Fragrant, several hybrids. Half-day sun, moist. Can be treated as tender annual outdoors. *Color*: purple, yellow.

448

SCIENTIFIC NAME/ COMMON NAME	KEY	HEIGHT	COMMENTS
Hibiscus **Hibiscus**	B, G	to 4'	Many varieties; prune to keep desired height. Full sun, keep moist. Flower lasts only one day but blooms all summer. Move outside in summer. *Color*: white, yellow, red, salmon, orange.
Hippeastrum hybrids **Amaryllis**	B	1' – 2'	Bright indirect light, moist. Fertilize monthly until Sept., and then dry off until a month before desired bloom. Then move into light and water again. Blooms: winter – spring. *Color*: pink, white, red, salmon and mixed colors.
Hoya **Hoya, Wax plant**	B	vine	Fragrant; some basket varieties. Half-day sun, moist. *Color*: many colors.
Hydrangea macrophylla **Hydrangea**	B	1½' – 2'	Florists' flower; plant outside when bloom is finished. Part shade, moist. Lime for pink flowers, aluminum sulfate for blue. *H. serrata* and 'Pee Gee' are also suitable for containers. See Special Article in *Shrubs*.
Hylocereus undatus **Night-blooming Cereus**	B, G	to 15'	Climber; fragrant flower opens slowly at night, then dies by dawn. *Color*: white.
Impatiens walleriana **Impatiens**	B	1½' – 2'	A favorite that blooms nonstop from spring to frost. Partial shade, keep pinched for fullness, requires little care. For blight, spray with a fungicide. Some varieties with variegated leaves. *Color*: white, pink, salmon, magenta, orange, purple.
Ipomoea batatas **Sweet Potato Vine**	F	15'	Vine with lovely glossy foliage; edible tuber. Best new varieties are 'Blackie' with dark purple foliage and 'Marguerite' with bright chartreuse leaves. Good in

449

Scientific Name/ Common Name	Key	Height	Comments
			containers and hanging baskets.
Ixora coccinea **Ixora**	B	to 4'	Half-day sun, moist; can be kept below 2' by pruning. *Color*: red, yellow
Jasminum **Jasmine**	B	to 2'	Fragrant; many varieties. Half-day sun, moist. Some are ground hardy. *Color*: white.
Justica carnea **Jacobinia**	B	1' – 3'	Half-day sun. Late spring bloom in greenhouse, summer bloom when pots are put outdoors in partial shade. Requires much fertilizer and water. Similar to shrimp plant but maybe better. *Color*: rosy-pink.
Kalanchoe blossfeldiana **Kalanchoe**	B	1½'	Many varieties; succulent. Bright light, heavy soil, good drainage, cool nights. Drench and then let dry. *Color*: pink, red, salmon, yellow. Discard after blooming.
Maranta leuconeura **Prayer Plant**	F	6" – 8"	Dark green leaves with red veins in fishbone pattern, purple undersides; leaves close at night. Bright indirect light; moist, dry side in winter; feed every 2 months from spring to fall.
Maranta leuconeura var. *kerchoviana* **Rabbit's Tracks**	F	6" – 8"	Leaves have dark spots resembling rabbit's tracks. Culture same as above.
Monstera deliciosa **Monstera, Split-leaf Philodendron**	F, B	vine	Very large plant; old plants have spathe-like flower to 1', large leathery perforated leaves, long cordlike aerial roots. Tolerates any condition except freeze, soil barely moist. Climber and needs support.
Nerium oleander **Oleander**	B, G	to 8'	Dark dull green lance-shaped leaf; cut back after flowering. Bright light; subject to scale and mealy bugs; set outside in summer. All parts very poisonous if eaten.

SCIENTIFIC NAME/ COMMON NAME	KEY	HEIGHT	COMMENTS
			Color: salmon, pink, red to white.
Orchid See Special Article below.			
Oxalis acetosella **Shamrock**	B	to 1'	3 leaflets. Sun, moist. Symbol of Ireland. *Color*: white, pink.
Palm See Special Article below.			
Pandanus veitchii **Pandanus, Screw Pine**	F	3' – 5'	Slow grower. Bright indirect sun, semi-dry between waterings, use charcoal in soil. Do not let water stand in axils as leaf will rot and fall off.
Pelargonium **Geranium**	B	1' – 1½'	Many varieties, including variegated. Direct sun; let dry out between waterings; do not over-fertilize; high clay content in soil. Do not let water touch leaves. Pinch back for a bushier plant. Outside, keep in indirect light. *Color*: white, pink, red, coral.
Peperomia **Peperomia, Radiator Plant**	F	to 1'	Many varieties, leaves smooth or wrinkled, striped or variegated. Warm; bright indirect light; keep moderately dry between thorough watering.
Persea americana **Avocado**	F	to 10'	Large seed can be sprouted in water. Coarse leaf. Easy for children to grow. Pinch back to 1 ft.
Philodendron **Philodendron**	F	vine	Many varieties, green and variegated; will climb or trail; most popular and dependable. Keep cut to desired size. Medium light, moderately dry. Grows in water or soil.
Pilea cadierei	F	to 10"	Dark green and silver quilted

451

Scientific Name/ Common Name	Key	Height	Comments
Aluminum Plant			leaves, other varieties have different color combinations. Bright indirect light, moist, good for terrariums. Propagate by stem cuttings in early spring.
Pilea microphylla **Artillery Plant**	F	10"	Warm, moist, filtered light; small succulent leaf, slow growing.
Plectranthus australis **Swedish Ivy**	F	vine	Waxy light green leaves on square stems. Bright indirect light, barely moist; pinch for bushiness. Good in hanging baskets. *Color*: insignificant white flower.
Primula **Primula, Primrose**	B	6"	Pastel to strong colors; winter to spring bloom. Must have very cool conditions, part shade, moist. Some are ground hardy. *Color*: All colors.
Punica granatum 'nana' **Dwarf Pomegranate**	B	2'	Spring and summer flowers followed by reddish fruit. Cool, moist, half-day sun, fertilize every 4 months. Attractive as bonsai. *Color*: flame.
Rhoeo spathacea **Moses-in-the-cradle**	F	8" – 15"	Dark green sword-like leaves with purple beneath. Bright indirect light, barely moist.
Rosa chinensis 'minima' **Miniature Rose**	B	6" – 12"	Fragrant. Half-day sun, moist; fertilize every two weeks; subject to red spider. Blooms year round. Hardy in ground. *Color*: white, pink, red, yellow.
Saintpaulia **African Violet**	B	6"	Many varieties of this easy-to-grow *Gesneriad*. Bright indirect sun, barely moist. Once a week, add water to the saucer for absorption through the drain hole. Once a month add dilute violet fertilizer solution to saucer. Do not wet foliage. Cut off old blooms. Many gorgeous new hybrids. *Color*:

SCIENTIFIC NAME/ COMMON NAME	KEY	HEIGHT	COMMENTS
			white, blue, pink, red, purple, etc.
Sansevieria trifasciata **Mother-in-law's-tongue, Snake Plant**	F	1½' – 2½'	Toughest houseplant; stiff thick leaves often mottled with white; keep washed or dusted.
Selaginella kraussiana **Club Moss**	F	to 6"	Emerald green, overlapping scale-like leaves; good for hanging baskets, ground cover for bonsai and terrariums. Moderately moist, warm, indirect light.
Senecio **Cineraria**	B	10"	Daisy-like flowers, discard after blooming. Moist; cool. Many varieties. *Color*: every color except yellow.
Sinningia speciosa **Gloxinia**	B	to 12"	Velvety bell-shaped blooms. Warm, moist; high humidity. Water with tepid water only; do not get water on leaves. *Color*: white, red, pink, purple.
Solanum pseudocapsicum **Jerusalem Cherry**	B	1' – 1½'	Flowers followed by cherry-sized poisonous scarlet fruit. Half-day sun, let dry before good watering, keep out of drafts. *Color*: white.
Soleirolia soleirolii **Baby's Tears, Mind-your-own-business**	F	¼" – 1"	Moss-like creeper grown for delicate foliage; ground cover for bonsai and greenhouse floor. Cool, partial shade.
Spathiphyllum clevelandii **Spathiphyllum**	F	1' – 1½'	Lance-shaped dark green leaves, long-lasting flower. Filtered sunlight, moist; tolerates low light. Also dwarf variety. *Color*: white, light green.
Strelitzia reginae **Bird-of-Paradise**	B, G	2' – 3'	Large, striking flower resembling a bird's head. Rich soil, good light. *Color*: orange, blue.
Streptocarpus rexii **Streptocarpus, Cape Primrose**	B	to 10"	Open-faced flower, long narrow quilted basal leaves. Moist, 14 – 16 hours of light a day for continuous

453

SCIENTIFIC NAME/ COMMON NAME	KEY	HEIGHT	COMMENTS
			bloom. Some varieties have dormant period. Also dwarf and variegated varieties. *Color*: white, pink, red, purple.
Tolmiea menziesii **Pickaback Plant, Piggyback Plant**	F	1'	Furry leaves bear tiny plantlets at their bases. Easily propagated at any time from leaves bearing plantlets. Moist, fertilize every two months, bright indirect light.
Trachelospermum jasminoides **Star Jasmine**	B	vine	Fragrant star-shaped flowers, dark green leathery leaves. Sun, semi-dry between waterings. *Color*: white.
Tradescantia fluminensis **Wandering Jew Small-leaf Spiderwort**	F	trailer	Smooth leaves and stems; insignificant lavender flowers. Sun, moist. Good for hanging baskets; easy to grow. *Color*: green, red and green, green and purple foliage.
Tropaeolum majus **Nasturtium**	B, G	1' – 6'	Bush or trailing. Several varieties, some double; check label on seed package. Sun, moist, cool greenhouse. Will not tolerate high heat. *Color*: all colors except blue.
Zygocactus truncate **Christmas Cactus**	B	1'	Flower borne on succulent stem, blooms Oct. – Feb. Good light, do not over water. *Color*: white, orange-pink to magenta.

BEGONIA

BEGONIA

Begonias are an enormous family of plants that are grouped by the type of root – bulbous, fibrous, tuberous, or rhizomatous. Some have showy flowers while others are grown for foliage alone. Begonia leaves may be tiny and delicate or large and bold; most are larger on one side of the main vein. Begonia flowers grow in clusters and their colors range widely. Each flower is male or female but not both.

CULTURE

SOIL – All begonias require a rich, humusy, slightly acid soil with enough coarse sand to drain well. Good potting mixtures are commercially available or you can mix your own with 3 parts loam, 2 parts well-rotted manure, 1 part peat, and 1 part vermiculite.

WATER – Begonias require lots of humidity. With more delicate varieties, this may mean a daily misting. If the houseplant is very dry, submerge it carefully upside down in a pail of water. This also cleans the leaves and allows them to breathe. Never let the sun shine on begonia foliage when wet. Do not over-water begonias, as the roots will quickly rot. Good drainage is important.

LOCATION – Begonias do not do well in deep shade (although, a hardy begonia can take a lot of shade). They need light to bloom indoors, so in winter a south window is best. In summer, move outside to an eastern exposure because begonias do not like hot direct summer sun. Begonias thrive under artificial light and some will pass up their dormancy period in the house. Outdoors, good air circulation is necessary to prevent fungus problems from high humidity.

DORMANCY – As dormancy approaches, double male flowers may become single. Leaves turn yellow and dry. Rex begonias, especially, may lose all of their leaves and stop growing. Stop fertilizing and give just enough water to keep the plant from completely drying out. Remove it from direct light while resting. Dig and store tubers and rhizomes if planted outdoors. Hardy begonia is left in the ground.

FERTILIZING – Feed with 4–12–4 when the plant begins to produce new growth after its dormant period, and every few weeks while in bloom.

PRUNING – Most begonias need some pruning after flowering. *B. semperflorens*, especially, should be cut back at this time for maximum bloom and a more bushy plant. Severely prune all straggly, middle-aged begonias.

PROPAGATION – Propagation is easy. New plants can be grown by rooting stems, rhizomes, or leaves; by seeds; by layering; and by dividing old plants or tubers. See *Garden Care–Propagation* for details on these techniques.

455

HYGIENE – Dust tubers and rhizomes with a good fungicide before planting or storing. If insects are a problem, wash leaves in soapy water, and, if necessary, spray with an insecticide. Removing all dead leaves and flowers can prevent many problems. Allowing the soil to dry out before watering prevents rot. Check for slugs.

There are many species and varieties of begonia of which only a few can be mentioned.

TABLE 44. VARIETIES OF BEGONIA (*BEGONIA*)

SCIENTIFIC NAME	COMMON NAME / COMMENTS
Begonia coccinia **Angel Wing Begonia**	These begonias range in size from 1' – 6'. They have bamboo-like stems and distinct joints. They are grown both for foliage, which may be green, pink, or splotched in a great variety of textures, as well as attractive flower clusters. Houseplant.
Begonia feastii **Beefsteak Begonia**	They have thick, round leaves, green on their upper surface and rusty beneath. It has pale pink blossoms. Place the beefsteak begonia in a north window.
Begonia grandis or B. evansiana **Hardy Begonia**	A fine, tall ground cover for wooded areas and an over-planting for crocus, daffodils, and other spring bulbs, as it is late to emerge in the spring. The richly veined leaves are red underneath and are stunning when backlit. The lovely panicles of pink and white flowers appear in late July and bloom until frost.
Begonia heracleifolia **Star Begonia**	This is a very hardy houseplant. It has pink or white flowers and a star-shaped leaf.
Begonia hiemalis **Rieger Begonia**	The Rieger is a tuberous-rooted hybrid. Glossy leaves in many shades of green; flowers white, pink, yellow, orange, red, single and double. Keep slightly dry between waterings. Feed once a month; 4 hours of sun. Houseplant.
Begonia rex **Rex Begonia**	This is a fibrous type which is used primarily in the house or greenhouse. It bears small pink and white flowers every spring, but is usually grown for its foliage, which runs the gamut of color, texture, and size. *Culture* – Rex Begonias tend to be delicate but are worth the effort. They need protection from direct sunlight, but plenty of indirect light. They prefer a night temperature of 60° – 65°F, and a daytime temperature of 68° – 72°F. They like moist soil and

SCIENTIFIC NAME	COMMON NAME / COMMENTS
	high humidity, but do not mist hairy-leaved varieties as this breeds disease. Remove flower buds to promote strong leaf growth.
Begonia scharffi **Scharff Begonia**	This one has large clusters of white flowers with pink beards. It is a profuse bloomer, and has large white hairy leaves which point downward. It is tall and shrubby. Houseplant.
Begonia semperflorens **Wax Begonia**	This is the best known of all fibrous begonias. It is popular as a houseplant, an outdoor container plant, or an annual bedding plant in the flower border. *B. semperflorens* has glossy heart-shaped foliage which may be green, bronze, or mahogany. This begonia blooms all summer until frost outdoors and off and on throughout the year in the house. Many new varieties have semi-double or double flowers in all shades of pink, red, and white. *Culture* – *B. semperflorens* needs more light and less humidity than other begonias. However, during the heat of summer, frequent misting of outdoor plants is necessary; allow soil to dry slightly between watering. Some new varieties are more heat resistant. Part shade.
Begonia tuberhybrida **Tuberous-rooted Begonia**	Summer-flowering tuberous-rooted Begonia has large, showy blossoms, which resemble camellias or roses. Flowers range from white to salmon, pink, red, yellow, and orange. *B. tuberhybrida* are among the most effective plants for hanging baskets in the house or greenhouse. They are also easy to force with florescent lights for indoor bloom during the winter. *Culture* – Outdoor planting is not recommended in the South as these prefer cool nights (50° – 55°F) and 75° – 80°F during the day. If planted outdoors, water and mist often to reduce temperature. Find a shady spot, with no more than 2 hours of morning sun. Start tubers or seeds in early spring, 2 months before 50°F nights are expected. Put plants in the potting garden outside when the night temperature reaches 50° and bring back in the house when it is 75°F.

BONSAI

JAPANESE ART OF DWARFING TREES

Bonsai (pronounced bone-sigh), literally translated, means "tray planting". Simply, it is the Japanese art of keeping a tree or shrub dwarfed by confining it to a small pot. Horticulturally speaking, it is the highest art form of all, blending artistic ability and horticultural expertise. Controlling the size of any bonsai is done by pruning the roots and branches at the time of planting. During its lifetime, it will periodically be unpotted, root-pruned, and repotted with new soil so as to retain its size and shape. It will also demand constant pruning and pinching of new growth.

These are basically outdoor plants, although bonsai can be tropical indoor plants. They must have protection when temperatures drop below 28°F and be protected from wind and continuous freezing and thawing. Water is an important factor in growing bonsai. They must never be allowed to dry out as it will kill them instantly. In most places, this means watering them every day in the summer. If the drainage is correct, they can never be over-watered.

There are five basic styles of bonsai: *formal upright, informal upright, slanting, cascade*, and *semi-cascade*. There are variations to these basic styles including *forest* and *clump* style.

CULTURE

Here are some brief guidelines to follow for making a bonsai. First, in the spring before the leaf buds begin to swell, find a hardy conifer such as a juniper or any plant with an interesting trunk and small foliage. Look at the root and trunk structure and decide which side is the most interesting. That becomes the front of the plant. The *formal upright* style, for instance, requires that the bottom third of the branches be removed in most cases. This not only reveals the trunk, but gives the look of age. The lowest, longest, and thickest remaining branch should be the first branch. Wire it to reach slightly forward and lean either to the left or right of the trunk. Now, a back branch should be wired either to the left or right to give depth. The third branch should be slightly higher on the opposite side of the first branch.

458

Continue this alternating of branches, pruning to make them smaller, and then wire the apex of the tree. Each branch should form a triangle and the finished tree will be a triangle with the trunk tapering from bottom to top.

Use aluminum wire as it is easier to manipulate. Since it comes in various gauges, use a size that is one-third the size of the branch being wired. Always wrap the wire toward the front and keep a constant distance between each wrap, bending the branch to the desired curve. As the tree grows, watch for wire damage and remove when damage shows, as the tree can be rewired at any time.

Bonsai pots come in all sizes and shapes. Each tree is styled and shaped and a bonsai pot is selected for that individual tree. The pots are unglazed inside and have large drainage holes which should be covered with one-eighth inch hardware cloth cut slightly larger than the holes and wired down. This keeps the slugs from coming into the pot and the soil from coming out. Unglazed pots in brown, gray, or terracotta are generally used for evergreens, while glazed pots are used for deciduous trees. The length or breadth of the pot should be approximately two-thirds the height of the tree. Straight trunks are better in a rectangular pot while curved trunks look better in round or oval pots. Cascade pots are deep and usually tall.

Always use new clean soil. A good average mix is equal parts commercial potting soil, peat moss, and a large- to medium-sized aggregate. A rule of thumb is that equal amounts of root and foliage should be removed. Leave the small hair-like surface roots on the ball. Loosen the root ball and rake away most of the soil, then cut away one-fourth, one-third or one-half the root system, depending on how much has been cut off the top of the tree. If it has a tap root, cut it out and also remove old clumps of dirt under the root. Place soil in the bottom of the container and fit the tree into the container, cutting the roots to the size and shape of the pot. Straighten all roots and finish potting making certain soil is in, under, and around all roots with no air pockets remaining. Use a chop stick or a pencil to achieve this. The plant should be tied down with a length of wire going through the bottom holes and around the plant to secure it.

Place the bonsai in a tub of water. Water should come to brim of bonsai container. When soil is entirely wet, remove and place in a semi-shaded area for a week to ten days. Do not fertilize for a month or two. If new growth appears, pinch back continuously. The plant should eventually be placed in full sun and watered daily. If the sun gets too hot, filtered sun is favored. Fertilize with bonsai fertilizer or any organic fertilizer. Water and protect it in the winter from 28°F or colder. Bonsai can be wintered by burying the pots in the compost bin to keep pots from cracking.

Bonsai is a living art form that is constantly evolving because of growth and change. Make one or buy one, but enjoy one. Some classic plants used for bonsai are listed in Table 45.

TABLE 45. PLANTS FOR BONSAI

EVERGREEN		
Boxwood	Five-needle Pine	Podocarpus
Camellia	Japanese Black Pine	Pyracantha
Cedar	Japanese Holly	San Jose Juniper
Chamaecyparis Cypress	Japanese Juniper	Satsuki Azalea
Dwarf Alberta Spruce	Norway Spruce	Shimpaku Juniper
DECIDUOUS		
Bald Cypress	Flowering Apricot	Japanese Maple
Barberry	Flowering Quince	Red Maple
Beech	Ginkgo	Sweet Gum
Cotoneaster	Hackberry	Trident Maple
Crabapple	Hawthorn	Wisteria
Elm	Hornbeam	Zelkova Elm
INDOOR BONSAI		
Aralia	Ficus	Myrtle
Camellia	Gardenia	Natal Palm
Citrus	Jade Plant	Olive

ORCHIDS

The orchid family is the most extraordinary, exotic, and vast group of all plant life. It is the largest family in the world with 25,000 known species. They come in dazzling colors, fanciful shapes, and many fragrances. They grow from the equator to Greenland; from sea level to 14,000 feet; in swamps, forests, deserts, and meadows.

The texture and substance of the orchid tissue is remarkable. It is fleshy, thick, and waxy which explains the lasting quality of the blooms. Some look as though they have been lacquered. Their shapes are unlike any other flower, both spectacular and unique. In some, their foliage and roots are not attractive, but others are grown for their interesting foliage alone. The flowers range in size from less than 1" to 8" across.

There are two types of orchids: 1) *Epiphytic* – which means that they grow on trees in nature, their roots clinging to the bark. They get nourishment from the air, debris, and rain. Their thickened leaves and stems store water and they can tolerate periods of dryness; and 2) *Terrestrial* – which means that they grow in the ground and must have water supplied. Several Chinese ground orchids are hardy in the Mid-South, and are surprisingly easy to grow in dappled woodlands. Calanthe, bletilla, and pleione are the most widely available; many cultivars can be found in catalogs.

The best place to obtain orchids is from a professional grower. Choose a plant while it is in bloom to see the color and type.

CULTURE

All orchids have virtually the same cultural requirements: the correct potting mix, perfect drainage, proper amount of water, frequent fertilizing, correct amount of light, correct temperature, and proper ventilation. Special pots for orchids have larger drainage holes.

POTTING MIX FOR EPIPHYTES – tree fern fiber, which does not disintegrate, and/or fir bark. Add 3 or 4 pieces of potshard for drainage and nylon screen over draining hole to prevent slugs.

461

POTTING MIX FOR TERRESTRIALS – 1 part gravel, 1 part leaf mold or compost, 1 part tree fern fiber or fir bark (available at garden centers). The Chinese ground orchids require rich, well-drained, neutral, loamy soil.

FERTILIZING – As buds appear and during blooming period use an 18–18–18 orchid fertilizer, such as Peter's®, every two weeks. After blooming use a 30–10–10 orchid fertilizer every two weeks. These are the general rules for fertilizing. For more details, check with a grower. Plants require less fertilizer when light intensity is low and when they are not actively making new growth during winter.

GREENHOUSE AIDS – *Cool* water and mister for summer, evaporative cooler with thermostatic control. Fan is not necessary, but helpful. Automatic opening and closing control for vents.

TEMPERATURE – *Cool*: 50°F nights; 60° – 70°F days.

Intermediate: 50° – 55°F nights; 65° – 70°F days.

Warm: 60° – 65°F nights; 70° – 85°F days.

PESTS – Orchids are surprisingly pest and disease free. Most pests can be removed with soap and water.

Aphids – Leave a black fungus called sooty mold. Wash off with water and detergent or spray with a dilute insecticidal soap.

Mealy Bugs – Produce a cottony mass. Remove with cotton swabs dipped in alcohol. Rinse with water.

Scale – Appears as hard-shelled bumps. Pick or scrape off or swab with rubbing alcohol. Spray with oil-based insecticide.

Slugs and Snails – You will see chewed holes in leaves and flower, and damaged roots. Put cotton wool around stem to protect flowers. Trap with commercial slug bait or saucer of beer at night.

Spider Mites – Cause stippled leaves or white webbing on underside of leaf. Scrub and rinse with warm water. Spray heavy infestation with a dilute insecticidal soap.

DISEASES – A combination fungicide/bactericide (available from orchid growers) will control most diseases.

Black Rot – Brown blotches with yellow edges on leaves caused by fungus and too much water or humidity. Destroy badly diseased plants.

Petal Blight – Small brown dots on the flowers (a fungus). Cut off and destroy infected flowers.

Virus – Yellow-brown streaking and malformation in leaves and flowers. No cure. Destroy infected plants. Avoid by sterilizing pots and tools. Dip potting sticks in household bleach.

462

Orchids give great pleasure and are not difficult to grow, provided their cultural needs are met; they even tolerate some neglect. They can survive if watered once a week, given occasional fertilizer, and repotted every few years. Orchids like being slightly pot-bound and the epiphytes are really using the potting mix as a structural anchor. One orchid grower said, "It takes a genius to kill them!"

TABLE 46. VARIETIES OF ORCHIDS

Key: E – Epiphyte
      T – Terrestrial
      *DGS – During Growing Season

ORCHID GENERA	E / T	a. LIGHT b. TEMPERA-TURE	a. HUMIDITY b. WATER	a. COLOR b. BLOOM TIME	DESCRIPTION
Bletilla striata **Hardy Ground Orchid**	T	a. Part sun, dappled, part shade b. Hardy in ground	a. Does fine in humid summers b. Moist, well-drained loam	a. Magenta, white b. Spring for 6 weeks	Expanding clump of herbaceous pleated upright foliage. Stems have dozen tiny Cattleya-like flowers. Easy and charming. Pest-free.
Brassavola nodosa **Lady-of-the-night Orchid**	E	a. 4 hrs sun daily *DGS b. Intermediate	a. Medium b. Keep moist, not wet	a. White & greenish-white b. Spring, summer, & winter	Easy to grow. Tough leathery green leaves from pseudo-bulbs and shiny oval pointed leaves. Large spider-like flowers. Fringed lips. Reduce water for two weeks when new pseudo-bulbs appear.

ORCHID GENERA	E / T	a. LIGHT b. TEMPERA-TURE	a. HUMIDITY b. WATER	a. COLOR b. BLOOM TIME	DESCRIPTION
Calanthe **Hardy Chinese Ground Orchid**	T	a. Dappled or part shade b. Hardy in ground	a. Does fine in humid summers b. Moist, well-drained loam	a. Yellow & maroon, green & red, many bi-colors b. Late March – mid-May	Easy to grow in loamy soil. Slowly expanding clump of evergreen leaves. Flower spike with dozens of 1" flowers up the stem. 'Kozu' hybrids and *C. sieboldianii* are good. Catalogs.
Cattleya	E	a. Bright b. Intermediate	a. High b. Once a week, nearly dry between waterings	a. Clear purple, pink, yellow, orange, white b. All 12 months depending on species	Flower stalks, 2" – 8" across of 2 to 6 flowers each. All are fragrant. Important commercially; good for beginners. Do not fertilize in winter.
Cymbidium	T	a. Bright b. Difficult in hot climates. Should have cool nights in Aug. (50°F) to set blooms	a. High b. Keep damp at all times	a. Solid and combinations of green, yellow, rose, maroon, bronze, and white b. Late fall to spring. Blooms last 6 wks to 2 mos.	Use ice cubes on roots in August. Flowers borne on spikes; 2 – 40 flowers per stem. Narrow grass-like foliage. Likes to be pot-bound.

464

ORCHID GENERA	E / T	a. LIGHT b. TEMPERATURE	a. HUMIDITY b. WATER	a. COLOR b. BLOOM TIME	DESCRIPTION
Cypripedium or *Paphicipedilum* **Lady's Slipper Orchid**	T	a. Bright filtered b. Intermediate	a. Medium humidity b. Medium water. Moist not soggy	a. White, green, pink, yellow, orange, maroon, multi-colors b. Spring, summer. Blooms last 1 – 2 months	Mottled leaf varieties are good house plants. Some are ground hardy in Z 7. Name is from ballet-shoe shape of lip. Several other "slipper orchid" genera. Native.
Dendrobium	E	a. Bright filtered b. Intermediate	a. Medium humidity b. Needs cool, dry period from Nov. 1 – Jan. 15	a. Golden-yellow, white, pink, violet, purple, magenta b. Early spring. Lasts 2 – 3 wks	Can be grown like a Cattleya. 1" to 2" flowers borne on drooping spikes. Good for home growing. Direct sunlight will burn leaves.
Epidendrum **Dancing Ladies Orchid**	E	a. Bright b. Intermediate	a. Medium b. *DGS allow to become almost dry between waterings	a. White, green, yellow, pink & multi-colors b. Spring, summer. Long-lasting flowers	Three wide, leathery leaves and reed-like stems. Waxy single or clusters of blooms. Tiny to 3" on long spike. Fragrant.
Laelia	E	a. Sun 4 – 8 hrs/day b. Intermediate to warm	a. Medium b. *DGS allow to become moderately	a. Vivid and fiery yellows, and red-orange, rich violets	1 or 2 evergreen, blade-like leaves. Flowers 1½" to 4" on various length sprays from

ORCHID GENERA	E / T	a. LIGHT b. TEMPERATURE	a. HUMIDITY b. WATER	a. COLOR b. BLOOM TIME	DESCRIPTION
			dry	b. All seasons. Flowers last more than 2 mos.	pseudobulbs. Similar to *Cattleya*, but with narrower petals. Genus used to produce brilliant hybrid colors.
Oncidium **Yellow Bee Orchid, Dancing Ladies Orchid**	E	a. Bright sun except at noon b. Intermediate	a. 40% to 60% b. Adjust to growing cycle. More water while growing	a. White, green, yellow, orange, pink, red, multi-colored b. Flowers last 2 – 6 wks.	Tips look like flaring skirt. Generally grown like *Cattleya*. Most have showers of up to 100 bright yellow blooms on long, arching stalks. Other varieties have large flowers.
Phalaenopsis **Butterfly Orchid, Moth Orchid** Also miniatures	E	a. Filtered b. Warm	a. 50% – 70% b. They do not have pseudo-bulbs for water storage. Must be kept moist, not soggy	a. White, soft pink, brown, lavender, purple, green, yellow, b. Bloom once a year. Jan – Mar. Bloom spray lasts 2 mos. After bloom cut back to third node for another bloom spike	Good house plant. Flowers resemble tropical moths on long, flat, sprays of 6 – 15 3" blooms. Some have wide, flat, leathery yellow-green leaves, long roots. Should be protected from excessive heat.
Pleione **Hardy**	T	a. Part shade	a. Likes humidity	a. White, pink, violet	Grows on decaying tree

ORCHID GENERA	E / T	a. LIGHT b. TEMPERA- TURE	a. HUMIDITY b. WATER	a. COLOR b. BLOOM TIME	DESCRIPTION
Ground Orchid		b. Hardy in ground; grows on old logs	b. Moist shade	b. Spring	logs in moist, temperate forests in the wild. Plant outdoors in soil amended with hardwood bark.
Vanda	E	a. 6 hrs. bright sun. Shield from noon sun b. Warm	a. 40% to 60% b. Keep constantly moist but not soggy. Water less *DGS	a. Blue, red, salmon, pink, purple, & bi-colors. Used in many hybrid crosses b. May & June. Flowers last 3 – 6 wks.	Erect plant with opposite leaves. Open-faced flowers on long fluttering stalks that emerge from evergreen leaves, either cylindrical, strap, or V-shape. Stem may need support. 5 to 80 blooms. Repot as little as possible. Easy to grow.

467

PALMS

There are 3,000 species of palms worldwide and most are from either moist-tropical or dry, arid, sub-tropical regions, but a few are adapted to temperate deciduous forest conditions. The four that are ground-hardy in Zone 7 are:

Needle Palm (*Rhapidophyllum hystrix*) is hardy to about -10°F and is a trunk-less variety that forms a wide multi-stemmed clump about 5'h by 8'w.

Chinese Windmill Palm (*Trachycarpus fortunei*) is a sizeable 40' tree! It's ground-hardy in the Mid-South, and adds a great tropical effect.

Dwarf Palmetto (*Sabal minor*) and **Saw Palmetto** (*Serenoa repens*) are more reliable in zone 8, but can be successfully grown in zone 7, and are similar in form to Needle Palm.

All like heat and "sun" to "light or high shade". Foliage can look sunburned in full sun if there is not enough moisture. For the first few years all these palms will need extra winter protection; add a deep layer of leaves around the base.

CULTURE

The great majority of commercially available palms, like the ones listed in *Table 45*, are for the house or greenhouse. They are slow growers, so purchase the desired size. Palm leaves should be deep green in a healthy plant. Do not purchase a plant with yellow fronds.

Bright indirect light is best; near an east- or north-facing window. Some varieties tolerate low light. Some palms can be put outdoors in the shade for summer; others do not like sweltering humidity and temperature fluctuations so leave those indoors.

They should be kept moist, not wet, to avoid root rot. Good drainage is essential; set the pot on a bed of pebbles in the saucer. Water the whole surface of the soil to wet all the roots, rather than pouring the water in one spot. Though tolerant of neglect, they appreciate a little high-nitrogen fertilizer. For cosmetic reasons, remove dead fronds with scissors.

Palms like to be pot bound. If re-potting is necessary, be very careful of the fragile roots and do not remove old soil. Be sure the consistency of the new soil is similar to the old soil or the roots will not spread.

TABLE 47. VARIETIES OF PALMS

SCIENTIFIC NAME/ COMMON NAME	COMMENTS
Beaucarnea recurvata **Pony Tail**	Not a true palm; bulbous at base of trunk for water storage; wrinkled ball of bark, leaves form a tuft at top of trunk. Let dry between waterings, do not over-water; fertilize in spring only.
Caryota mitis **Fishtail Palm**	Leaves shaped like fish tail; tolerates being pot-bound. Culture same as Butterfly Palm likes humidity, place well away from air conditioner.
Chamaedorea elegans **Parlor Palm**	Feather-like arching fronds; to 18'; dwarf variety often used in terrariums. Does best in north exposure; tolerant of neglect, low light, and air conditioning.
Chamaerops humilis **European Fan Palm**	Stiff, 5' fan-shaped, dark green leaves. Needs good light, cooler room than most houseplants.
Chrysalidocarpus lutescens **Areca Palm or Butterfly Palm**	Arching feather-like fronds, yellowish stalks. Bright indirect light; moist, do not let stand in water. Suckers can be rooted.
Cycas revolute **Sago Palm**	Not a true palm but a *Cycad*; shiny, dark green, leathery leaves resembling fern fronds; slow grower. Semi-dry between thorough watering; fertilize every two months, spring to mid-summer only.
Howea forsterana **Sentry Palm**	Feathery, arching leaves with many slender leaflets; slow grower. Barely moist, use several plants in container. Tolerates cooler temperature than other palms.
Livistona chinensis **Chinese Fan Palm**	Open, fan-shaped leaves on long thin stalks; a tough plant. Keep moist; slow grower.
Phoenix roebelenii **Miniature Date Palm**	Graceful, arching leaves consisting of many leaflets, rarely exceeds 2 feet; culture same as Butterfly Palm.
Rhapis excelsa **Lady Palm**	Shiny, fan-shaped leaves grow intermittently along fibrous trunk. Tolerates cool or warm conditions; keep soil drier than other palms. Heavy feeder.
Rhapis excelsa **Miniature Japanese Palm**	Many varieties. Dark green, pleated leaf. Tolerates low light; requires little water.

VEGETABLES

PLANNING THE GARDEN

It is gratifying to grow your own vegetables because in addition to the old favorites, you can plant varieties not always available in groceries and have plenty to share with friends. Whether grown in containers, on a small plot, or on several acres, good gardening fundamentals must be observed.

Choose a slightly sloping, well-drained spot with a minimum of six hours of sunlight (full sun preferred). Leafy vegetables tolerate more shade than root crops. Raised beds are also desirable.

Plant cool and warm season crops in different sections. The cool crops should be harvested by mid-summer and can be replanted for a fall garden. Rotate crops each year to reduce disease. Arrange rows so taller plants will not shade shorter ones.

CULTURE

Refer to *Garden Care* for detailed information on these topics.

SOIL PREPARATION

Soil should be tilled to a depth of 6" – 7". Never work soil when too wet. To test soil, roll a handful into a ball. If it doesn't crumble easily, it is too wet to work.

Vegetables require a slightly acidic, fairly rich, loose-textured soil. Add enough compost or other organic matter to comprise ½ of soil mixture.

LIMING AND FERTILIZING

The soil pH should be 6.0 – 6.8. Check the pH every 3 years. It is best to add ground dolomitic lime in the fall and mix it into the soil so it can have time to work its magic over winter. Pelletized dolomitic lime may be applied in the spring as well, since it does not burn plants like the fine powdered lime can.

Vegetables require a complete fertilizer, such as 6–12–12 or 13–13–13. It should be applied in the spring and worked into the soil before planting. Do not over-fertilize vegetables. Well-rotted, dehydrated manure, which adds organic material and beneficial micro-organisms, can be used to supplement chemical fertilizer. Green manure will burn.

471

PLANTING

Seeds – Consult package for proper spacing and planting depth. Do not sow too deeply or too thickly. Keep soil moist until seedlings emerge. Let plants reach 1½" – 2" before thinning to the recommended spacing. Crowded plants will not produce well.

Transplants – Broccoli, cabbage, cauliflower, eggplant, pepper, tomato, and a few others are usually transplanted rather than direct seeded. Select small, stocky healthy plants. Plant on a cool day or in late afternoon. Water in with ½ – 1 pint of starter solution per plant (1 tablespoon 10–50–10 per gallon of water). Set plants at the depth they grew or slightly deeper.

WATER AND MULCH

Vegetables require 1" – 1½" of water per week. Soak thoroughly, as shallow watering causes shallow root growth. Water early in the day so foliage will dry before night.

Mulch to conserve moisture and reduce weeds. Apply 2" – 3" of organic mulch, such as straw, ground bark, or compost, around the established plants but keep away from the stem a few inches. Do not use grass clippings to which herbicides and heavy metal chemicals have been applied. The best inorganic mulch is black plastic which is discussed below.

STAKING AND TRAINING

English peas, sugar snap peas, tomatoes, cucumbers, and pole beans may be trained on a stake, wire cage, or fence.

WEEDS

Shallow hoe cultivating is the only safe method of weed control. Do not use herbicides in the home garden. Use mulch to reduce weeds.

INSECTS AND DISEASES

Select disease-resistant varieties. Check local garden center or local extension service center for suitable spray or dusts. Many sprays are unsafe for vegetable gardens. Follow directions carefully.

HARVESTING

Frequent picking increases yield.

BLACK PLASTIC GARDENING FOR VEGETABLES

ADVANTAGES:

• Little soil preparation is required.

- Hastens soil warming in spring by 10°. Promotes earliness in warm season crops.
- Planting unhindered by spring rains.
- Less insect damage.
- Clean vegetables.

DISADVANTAGE:

- Because of increased soil temperature, not well suited for cool-season crops.
- Lack of air in the soil can destroy beneficial micro-organisms.

METHOD:

Six weeks before spring planting, sprinkle 15 pounds of 6–12–12 fertilizer per 1,000 square feet. Lime if necessary. Loosen soil with a hoe or garden claw if it is compacted.

Spread 6 mil 20' x 40' black plastic. Secure plastic with boards, bricks, or earth.

At planting time cut X-shaped holes large enough to accommodate the small starts or sets. As the vegetables grow, you may need to enlarge the hole in the plastic for ease of watering. Root crops not recommended. Beans, cabbage, corn, eggplants, melons, squash, and strawberries do especially well. Leafy vegetables are also recommended.

For aesthetic appearance and to help insulate roots from the heat absorbed by the black plastic, you can mulch on top of the plastic.

After growing season, discard and use new next year.

HELPFUL HINTS:

- If rabbits or squirrels are eating vegetables, dust with red pepper or blood meal. *Dogs, however, are attracted to blood meal.*
- To ripen green tomatoes, place tomatoes in a plastic bag with a cut ripe apple. Tie securely. They will turn red soon.
- Strawberries like a pine needle or straw mulch.
- Do not plant cucumbers near melons. The melons will taste of cucumber.
- To prevent cutworm damage to seedlings, surround each plant with a plastic cup from which the bottom has been removed.
- See *Garden Care – Pests and Diseases – Companion Gardening* for natural insect control suggestions.

TABLE OF VEGETABLES

TABLE 48. VEGETABLES

COMMON NAME	PLANTING DATES	INCHES BETWEEN PLANTS	COMMENTS
Asparagus Plants	February	18"	Plant 2 year old roots in a separate bed. Remove and set aside top 6" of soil. Work in 2" of rotted manure and a sprinkling of 5–10–5 to a depth of 6" or more. Spread roots, cover with reserved soil. Mulch. Feed with 5–10–5 in spring before growth starts. Harvest for only 1 week the first year, 2 weeks the second. Do not cut back foliage until frost.
Beans, Lima Bush	May 1 – June 15	3" – 4"	Require warmer growing conditions than snap beans. *Planting to harvest*: 65 – 75 days.
Beans, Lima Pole	May 1 – June 15	3" – 4"	Require support. *Planting to harvest*: 80 – 90 days.
Beans, Snap Bush	April 15 – June 20	3" – 4"	More tender than pole beans but not as much yield. Make successive plantings for longer season. *Planting to harvest*: 60 – 65 days.
Beans, Snap Pole	April 15 – June 20	3" – 4"	Provide support. *Planting to harvest*: 60 – 65 days.
Beets	Early March	3" – 4"	Thin to improve size. Alkaline soil. *Planting to harvest*: 55 – 65 days.
Broccoli Plants	March 1 – April 1	18"	Begin insect control soon after transplanting. Harvest before flower develops. Hot weather reduces yield. *Planting to harvest*: 60 – 70 days.
Brussels Sprouts Plants	Feb. – March	12" – 18"	Hot weather reduces yield. To reduce disease, do not plant in the same spot each year. *Planting to harvest*: 90 – 100 days.

COMMON NAME	PLANTING DATES	INCHES BETWEEN PLANTS	COMMENTS
Cabbage, Spring (Plants)	Late Feb. – March	18"	Begin insect control early. Do not plant in the same spot each year. Reduce moisture near maturity to prevent splitting heads. Cabbage prefers cool weather. *Planting to harvest*: 62 – 75 days.
Cabbage, Fall (Plants)	July 5 – Aug. 15	24"	Begin insect control soon after planting. *Planting to harvest*: 80 – 90 days.
Cantaloupe	May 1 – 15	24"	Requires bee pollination. Spray only in late afternoon. Do not plant near cucumbers as they assimilate the taste. Late plantings subject to mildew. *Planting to harvest*: 80 – 100 days.
Carrots	March 1 – April 1	3" – 4"	Avoid heavy soil. Thin to improve size. *Planting to harvest*: 75 – 85 days.
Cauliflower Plants	March 1 – April 1	18" – 24"	Begin insect control early. Too much heat prevents proper maturation. Tie leaves overhead to blanch when curd is visible. *Planting to harvest*: 60 – 70 days.
Collards	March or July	12"	Begin insect control early. *Planting to harvest*: 65 – 75 days.
Corn, Sweet	April 1 – June 1	8" – 12"	For pollination, plant 3 rows or more in blocks. Successive planting for continued harvest. *Planting to harvest*: 80 – 95 days.
Cucumber	May or June	12" if trellised	Requires bee pollination. Spray only in late afternoon. Trellising increases quality and yield. Do not plant near melons. Burp-less varieties available. *Planting to harvest*: 50 – 55 days.
Eggplant Plants	May or June	24"	Requires high temperatures. *Planting to harvest*: 75 – 80 days.
Kale	Feb. or Aug.	12"	Begin insect control early.

475

COMMON NAME	PLANTING DATES	INCHES BETWEEN PLANTS	COMMENTS
			Planting to harvest: 60 – 90 days.
Lettuce, Leaf (Loose-leaf)	Feb. – April	4" – 6"	Plant shallow. Requires moist soil to germinate. Becomes bitter and bolts in hot weather. Fall crops possible. *Planting to harvest*: 40 – 50 days.
Lettuce, Head (Bibb, Boston)	Feb. or Sept.	12" – 15"	Plant shallow. Requires moist soil and light to germinate. *Planting to harvest*: 60 – 70 days.
Okra	May 5 – May 20	18"	Soak seed overnight before planting. Plant only after soil warms to 70°F. Dwarf varieties available. *Planting to harvest*: 50 – 60 days.
Onions	Feb. 1 – Mar. 31	3" – 4"	Withstands heavy frost. Soil should be loosened to produce larger bulbs. For storage, harvest when stalk falls over. *Planting to harvest*: 30 days for bunch, 90 days for storage.
Parsley (Biennial)	May or July	2"	Soak seeds overnight before planting. Do not let go to seed. *Planting to harvest*: 90 – 100 days.
Peas, English	Feb. 1 – Mar. 20	3" – 4"	Staking and early planting increases yield. Very cold-resistant. Do not tolerate heat. *Planting to harvest*: 80 – 90 days.
Peas, Sugar Snap	Feb. 1 – Mar. 20	3" – 4"	May exceed 6' in height. Plant early. Edible pods require stringing. Very cold-resistant. Do not tolerate heat. *Planting to harvest*: 70 – 80 days.
Pepper, Bell (Plants)	May or June	18"	Temperatures above 90°F cause blossom drop. Do not plant near hot peppers. *Planting to harvest*: 70 – 80 days.
Pepper, Hot	May or June	18"	Temperatures above 90°F cause

COMMON NAME	PLANTING DATES	INCHES BETWEEN PLANTS	COMMENTS
(Plants)			blossom drop. *Planting to harvest*: 60 – 70 days.
Potatoes, Irish	Mar. 5 – Mar. 20	8" – 12"	Cut potato into pieces 3 – 7 days before planting. Seed pieces must have an eye. *Planting to harvest*: 90 – 120 days.
Radish	Feb. 15 – Apr. 15	1" – 2"	Fall crops possible. High temperatures and dry soil reduce quality. Good plant for children to grow. *Planting to harvest*: 21 – 30 days.
Spinach, Spring	Feb. 5 – Feb. 15	3" – 4"	Very cold-resistant. Climbing variety available. *Planting to harvest*: 45 – 50 days.
Spinach, Fall	Sept. 10 – Sept. 20	6" – 8"	*Planting to harvest*: 40 – 50 days.
Squash, Summer (yellow, zucchini)	May – June	12" – 24"	Requires bee pollination. Spray only in late afternoon. Later plantings possible with rigid insect control. Plant 5 seeds in hills of soil, thin to three plants, or plant in row. First flowers generally drop. *Planting to harvest*: 45 – 55 days.
Squash, Winter	May or June	24" – 36"	Spray only in late afternoon. First flowers generally drop. Let mature on vines until skins are extremely hard. *Planting to harvest*: 90 – 110 days.
Tomato Plants	April 15 – June 15	24"	Mulching aids disease control. Lime soil to reduce blossom end rot. Leggy plants will root along stem if buried 2" – 3" below soil surface. Provide support. Feed once a month with 6–12–12 fertilizer scattered in a circle well away from stem. Water copiously. Cutworms can be a problem. Remove suckers between stem

COMMON NAME	PLANTING DATES	INCHES BETWEEN PLANTS	COMMENTS
			and stalk. *Planting to harvest*: 70-80 days.
Turnip Greens	March or Aug. – Sept.	3" – 4"	Scatter seeds. *Planting to harvest*: 30 – 40 days.
Watermelon	May 1 – May 31	48"	Spray as for cucumbers and cantaloupe. For large gardens. *Planting to harvest*: 80 – 90 days.

PREPARING FLOWERS FOR ARRANGEMENTS

FRESH FLOWERS

To prolong the life of cut flowers and foliage, three steps should be followed. *Cutting* is the first step. Next, *conditioning* is the process of soaking flowers or foliage in solutions for about two hours or burning the stem ends. *Hardening* is the process of soaking flowers or foliage overnight in deep tepid water. Most flowers are conditioned and then hardened.

CUTTING

DO'S

- Use garden flowers if possible. However, these suggestions also apply to florists' flowers.
- Cut flowers very early in the morning or late afternoon on the day before arranging (not in sun), then condition and harden.
- Use sharp clippers or a florist's knife, and cut at a 45° angle to maximize exposed surface area of the stem.
- Place cut flowers immediately in a bucket of tepid water.
- Remove leaves to the water level of bucket.
- Always clip off about 2 inches of stem under water. If the cut is made under water, air cannot get into the stem; an air bubble could prevent further water uptake through the stem and shorten the life of the flower.

479

DON'TS

- Avoid cutting flowers in the sun.
- Don't beat woody stems with a hammer. This used to be the preferred method, but now one is advised to split the woody stems a few inches up with a sharp knife to expose more vascular tissue to water. Crushing with a hammer will destroy the plant tissue's ability to draw up water.
- Never leave cut flowers in the sun or in a breeze.
- Don't spray flowers after conditioning.
- Don't use more than one chemical when conditioning flowers. See below for treatment of specific flowers.
- Never soak white-stemmed flowers (bulbs) in water over four inches deep.
- Don't change the water in an arrangement if foliage has been removed below the water line. Just add fresh water.

CONDITIONING

Refer to *Table 49* for instructions on conditioning various flowers. All ingredients are obtainable from grocery, florist, or pharmacy.

FLOWER CONDITIONING INGREDIENTS

Alcohol (rubbing)	Florist's Preservative	Salt (table)
Alum	Glycerin	Seven-Up or Sprite colas
Ammonia (household)	Oil of Peppermint	Sugar
Boric Acid	Paraffin	Vinegar
Camphor (liquid)	Salt (rock)	Washing Soda (sodium carbonate)

HARDENING

Soak the flowers "neck high" in tepid water overnight. (Delicate leaves, wildflowers, and ferns should be completely submerged.) This is known as *hardening*.

While hardening, a long leaf may be shaped by taping a wire on the back in the desired position. After hardening, remove the wire and the tape. Shape lupine, stock, and snapdragon by placing at an angle while hardening.

TABLE 49. FLOWER & PREPARATION METHOD

African Violet – Burn ends – Harden

Ageratum – Dip the tip of the stem in boiling water – Harden

Almond – Split woody end with several vertical cuts – Dip in boiling water – Harden

Alyssum – Condition in ½ tbsp. sugar to 1 quart water – Harden

Amaryllis – Condition in 1 tsp. peppermint oil in 1 quart water – Harden

Anemone – Scrape lower 2 inches of stem – Condition in 1 pint of water to ½ cup vinegar – Harden

Apple Blossoms – Cut while in bud; split woody end with several vertical cuts – Condition in 1 tbsp. household ammonia to 1 quart water – Harden

Aster – Condition in 1 tsp. sugar per quart of water – Harden

Azalea – Burn stem – Condition in 1 tbsp. alcohol per gallon of water – Harden

Baby's Breath – Condition in 1 tsp. alcohol to 1 pint water – Harden

Bamboo – Remove foliage and use stalk only.

Begonia (tuberous) – Condition in 2 tbsp. salt to 2 quarts water – Do not harden

Bells-of-Ireland – Split stem end with several vertical cuts – Harden

Bird-of-Paradise – Condition in ½ cup vinegar to 1 quart of water – Harden

Bittersweet – Split stems – Harden

Bougainvillea – Dip tip of stems in peppermint oil 2 seconds – Harden

Broom – Dip tips of stems in boiling water – Harden

Caladium – Put salt on end of stems – Harden

Calla Lily and Leaves – Condition in ½ cup vinegar to 1 quart water – Harden for 24 hours

Camellia – Place flower between layers of cool damp cotton for an hour. If stems are short, float flower in bowl of water; if stems are longer, put in a vase

Canna – Condition in 2 tbsp. vinegar to 2 quarts of water – Harden

Canterbury Bells – Burn ends – Condition in 2 quarts of water plus 2 tbsp. soda – Harden

Carnation – Cut below node – Condition in ⅛ tsp. boric acid to 1 quart water – Harden

Cherry Blossoms – Break stems – Plunge in boiling water – Harden

Chrysanthemum – Burn stems – Condition in 2 quarts of water with 8 drops of oil of peppermint – Harden 24 hours

Clematis – Burn ends – Condition in 3 tbsp. of alcohol to 2 quarts of water – Harden

Coleus – Dip stem in alcohol for 2 minutes – Harden

Cosmos – Harden overnight

Cyclamen – Put salt on end of the stem before hardening

Daffodil – Cut blooms with a sharp knife on an angle above the white part of the stem – Put in shallow warm water for 12 hours – Re-cut stems and immerse in tepid water – They can be refrigerated for several days; mist blooms often

Dahlia – Burn ends – Condition in ½ cup of vinegar per gallon of water – Harden

Daisy (all) – Condition in water containing 8 drops of oil of peppermint per quart – Harden

Delphinium – Split stem end with several vertical cuts – Condition in 1 tbsp. of alcohol per pint of water – Harden

Dogwood – Split ends – Plunge in hot tap water – Harden

English Ivy – Split stems 3" – Harden completely covered by cool water

Eucalyptus – Split ends – Plunge in hot tap water – Harden

Evergreens – Split woody end with several vertical cuts – Condition in 1 quart water and 1 tsp. glycerin – Harden

Fall Foliage – Burn tips of stems immediately – Condition in deep water with 1 cup of vinegar – Harden

Ferns – Harden completely covered with cold water; hardy ferns are difficult

Flax – Dip in peppermint oil about a second – Harden

Freesia – Condition in ½ tsp. alcohol in 1 quart water – Harden

Fuchsia – Burn stem tips – Harden

Galax – Wrap leaf in damp paper.

Gaillardia – Condition in 1 pint of water with 2 tbsp. salt – Harden

Gardenia – Spray lightly with water. Float in a bowl of water

Geranium – Condition with 1 tsp. alum to 1 quart water – Harden

Gladiolus – Break stems – Condition in water containing 1 tbsp. alcohol per quart – Harden

Grape Hyacinth – Dip ends in hot tap water – Condition in 1 tsp. alcohol to 1 pint of cold water – Harden

Heliotrope – Split the stem, plunge in hot tap water – Harden – This can be repeated if need be

Helleborus, Christmas Rose, Lenten Rose – Do not cut leaves but split blooming stems – Harden. The stem may be cut short and the flower floated in a bowl of water, or the stem may be left long and put in a vase.

Hollyhock – Remove all leaves, split the stems, and burn the tips – Condition in 2 quarts water with one handful of rock salt – Harden

Hosta, Funkia – Condition in 1 pint of cold water and ½ cup vinegar – Harden

Hyacinth – Squeeze fluid from stem – Harden in cold water

Hydrangea – Cut flower heads when a majority of the florets have opened. Cut and split stems and immerse in boiling or hot water (or vinegar) for 30 seconds. Then immerse stems in deep, cold water adjusted to pH of 4.0 by adding 2 tbsp. of vinegar and 2 tbsp. sugar to quart of water. Harden overnight.

Alternatively harden hydrangea by splitting stem about 1" and submerging entire flower head and stem in bucket of cold water overnight. See Special Article in *Shrubs – Hydrangea* for more on this.

Iris, Rhizomatous – Burn the tip of the stem – Harden

Iris, Bulbous – Condition in 3 tbsp. of salt to 1 quart of water – Harden

Lantana – Dip in hot water – Harden

Larkspur – Condition in 2 quarts of cold water with ½ tsp. of alcohol – Harden

Lilac – Leave only the leaves near the head – Split the stems – Spray the flower heads with tepid water – Harden in tepid water

Lily (all garden lilies) – Turn them upside down and allow cool water to flow over them – Harden

Lily-of-the-valley – Plunge the tips of stems into boiling water – Harden in cold water

Lily (Water) – Pump water into the stems with a syringe – A drop of paraffin in the center will keep flowers open – Harden

Lupine – Harden

Magnolia – Split the stems – Dip in boiling water – Harden

Maple – Split the stems – Dip in boiling water – Harden

Marguerite – Condition 2 hours in 1 quart of water and 1 tsp. of oil of peppermint – Harden

Marigold – Condition in water containing 8 drops of oil of peppermint per quart – Harden

Nasturtium – Condition in 3 tsp. of sugar to 1 quart of cold water – Harden

Pansy – Harden

Peach Blossoms – Dip the stem tips in boiling water – Harden in cold water overnight

Peony – Split the ends – Condition in 1 quart of water with 3 tsp. of sugar – Harden

Petunia – Condition in cold water with 1 tbsp. of alcohol per pint – Harden

Pine – Condition in 1 part water and 1 part alcohol for 10 minutes – Harden

Pinks – Condition in 3 tbsp. of table salt to 1 quart of water – Harden

Poinsettia – Burn the stem – Rub salt into the burned end – Harden in cold water

Poppy – Burn the stem – Rub salt into the burned end – Harden in cold water

Primrose – Dip the stems in boiling water – Harden

Rose – Cut when in bud into a container of warm water. Remove the lower leaves and thorns. Then place the cut end of the stem into boiling water (heat turned off), with the flower heads protected by a piece of aluminum foil, for about a minute (or count to 60). After that, put the stem ends into cold water for at least a few hours.
Some say rose stems should be cut underwater. Some say they should be cut at a slant. Some also say that it doesn't matter how you cut them. Put roses in warm water after the lower leaves and thorns have been removed and keep them in a cool place until they are ready to be used.

Shasta Daisy – Burn the ends – Harden

Snapdragon – Scrape the ends – Condition in 3 tbsp. of salt to 1 pint water – Harden overnight

Spirea – Split the ends – Condition in hot water – Harden

Statice – Condition in 3 tbsp. of sugar to 1 pint of water – Harden

Stock – Split the stems – Condition overnight in cold water with 1 tbsp. sugar and 2 tbsp. of white vinegar per quart of water

Sunflower – Burn the ends – Harden overnight

Sweet Peas – Condition in 1 tbsp. of alcohol per quart of water – Harden in water with 1 tbsp. of sugar to each quart of water

Sweet William – Condition in 1 tbsp. of alcohol to 1 pint of water – Harden

Thistle – Condition in 3 tsp. of alcohol to 1 quart of water – Harden overnight
Tulip – Wrap petals with wet tissue. Harden in cold water overnight
Verbena – Split the stems – Harden
Violet – Let stand in ice water up to neck
Wildflowers – Condition in water with ¼ cup of sugar to 1 gallon of water – Harden
Willow – Dip split stems in boiling water – Harden
Wisteria – Cut after sundown – Split the stems – Condition in ¼ cup of vinegar to 1 quart of water – Harden
Zinnia – Condition in 2 tbsp. of alcohol to 1 quart of water – Harden

HELPFUL HINTS

- To force blooms to open on cut flowers, put a little ammonia in the water. Cover container tightly with a plastic bag. Alternatively, put in very hot water up to the neck. Flowers will open the next day.

- To force a spray of flowers to open slowly, such as gladiolus or *Dendrobium* orchid, pinch off the very top tiny buds. Do not mist orchid flowers as they will spot.

- To make gladiolus show more color in a flower arrangement, strip off green sheath on all upper flowerets.

- To keep blooms open longer, add a small amount of a colorless, sugared soft drink (7-Up or Sprite) or buy commercial powder from florist called Florist's Preservative.

PRESERVING FLOWERS AND LEAVES

The peak of maturity is the best time to collect and dry flowers and foliage. Do not gather material when damp because it will mold. One of the four methods below should be selected depending upon the general character of the plant.

PRESSING

Flowers, leaves, and small branches can be pressed between layers of newspaper. Open and lay out a section of newspaper, placing the material on the lower half of the inside sheet. Fold a loose sheet of newspaper in half horizontally and place on top of material. Next, fold over the upper half of the first section of newspaper. Place on top of the whole stack any substantial weight such as board, bricks, or heavy books. Twenty-four hours later, remove the horizontally folded sheet from the top of the flowers. Removing the absorbed moisture will lessen the chance of discoloring or molding. Replace the weight and leave for ten days or longer until thoroughly crisp and dry.

Any number of flowers can be pressed this way by stacking layers of paper under increased weights. Clean leaves or small branches with a cloth dampened with mineral oil and proceed as above. Clean ferns gently with a light brush. Fall leaves retain their color when pressed between two sheets of waxed paper with an iron at low heat. Then press between newspapers under weight for two days.

NON-FLORAL MATERIALS FOR PRESSING

Autumn foliage	Oak foliage
Beech foliage	Rose foliage
Chestnut or Buckeye foliage	Scotch broom
Forsythia foliage	

HANGING

Flowers and leaves which do not contain a great deal of moisture can be hung in the air to dry. Tie several cuttings together loosely for good air circulation. Hang in a warm, dry place but out of sunlight to preserve color. Fine textured grasses, feathery weeds, and flowers with small blossoms along the stem dry well this way. They should be crisp in less than a month.

PLANTS WHICH CAN BE DRIED BY HANGING

Ageratum	Herbs	Pepper pods
Bittersweet	Hickory	Pomegranate
Blue Grass	Honey Locust pods	Poppy pods
Bramble	Hydrangea	Princess-feather
Buckeye	Iris seed pods	Pussy Willow
Catalpa pods	Japanese Iris	Pyracantha
Chinese-lantern	Lavender	Redbud
Cockscomb	Magnolia cones	Sage
Dock	Milkweed pods	Strawflower
Dollar plant (Honesty)	Mimosa pods	Summer Seed Pods
Feather grass	Oats	Wheat
Goldenrod	Onion bloom	Yarrow
Gourds	Palm	Yucca

COVERING

When a flower is heavy with moisture and less delicate it must be covered with one of the following drying substances.

Sand and Borax – Mix one part fine dry sand with two parts borax; add one tablespoon of table salt to each quart of this mixture.

Yellow Corn Meal and Borax – Half and half mixture.

Commercial products containing silica gel – An effective but expensive method. The chemical keeps indefinitely and can be reactivated by warming in the oven.

Method: To dry by *covering*, line flat containers with waxed paper and fill with at least 1" of the drying mixture. Individually place flowers with 2" stems on the mixture. Sift more drying mixture gently through and around petals until each bloom is completely covered. Place flowers with curved petals, like lilies, stem down to preserve their shape; place flat flowers, like daisies, face down. Do not make two layers. Do not put a cover on top. Let flowers remain in the mixture until crisp and dry but not long enough to crumble. Varying lengths of time are required for drying depending on flower texture. Remove flowers gingerly. Remove small clinging particles with a soft brush. The foliage must be dried separately according to its type. Later attach the dried flowers to their stems with florist wire.

MATERIALS WHICH CAN BE DRIED BY COVERING

Apple blossom	Daisy	Narcissus
Aster	Dogwood	Pansy
Bachelor's-button	Forsythia	Peony
Bells-of-Ireland	Hollyhock	Queen-Anne's-lace
Black-eyed Susan	Lantana	Rose
Calendula	Larkspur	Snapdragon
Carnation	Lilac	Sunflower
Chrysanthemum	Lily	Tulip
Daffodil	Marguerite	Thistle
Dahlia	Marigold	Zinnia

GLYCERIN TREATMENT

Glycerin treatment works well for plants with smooth leaves like the Southern magnolia. Late summer is the best time for harvesting magnolia and beech for preservation. Split stems vertically 2" – 3" with a sharp knife. Clean leaves with cold water. Immerse in hot water for a short while then place in a solution of two parts water and one part glycerin. Stem should extend at least 6" into the solution. Leaves turn golden, bronze, or dark brown depending on the type of foliage. Make sure there is enough solution in the container at all times. To hasten absorption, re-cut stems by another ½" once a week. The process takes 2 – 3 weeks, a little longer for thick leathery leaves. When desired color is reached, remove material and store in a dust free place until used.

Submerge galax and English ivy completely in a solution of half water and half glycerin. Late spring to mid-summer is the best time to treat these plants. Glycerin-treated foliage will last for years. It can be used dry or combined with fresh flowers. Water does not injure treated stems.

489

MATERIALS FOR GLYCERIN TREATMENT

Beech foliage	Forsythia foliage	Oak foliage
Chestnut foliage	Galax foliage	Periwinkle foliage
Cleyera foliage	Ivy foliage	Photinia foliage
Dogwood foliage	Magnolia foliage	Rhododendron

POISONOUS PLANTS

Castor Bean

Plants make many interesting substances (alkaloids, esters, ketones, and so on) that are medicinal and/or toxic. The Chinese have relied on herbal medicine for thousands of years. Medical researchers are hopeful that tropical rain forest plants will provide a cure for cancer and many other diseases. Foxglove produces digitalis which is given for heart problems, aloe soothes burns, poppies are the source of opium and morphine, and valerian root produces the sedative in Valium®. These and other plants are both medicinal and toxic, depending on how they are processed and the quantity ingested.

Some plants, however, are considered primarily poisonous and we should learn to recognize and avoid them. Fortunately, relatively large amounts of most plants are necessary to produce serious or fatal poisoning in adults. However, much less of the toxin can cause very severe or fatal reactions in children. One or two seeds could cause death in some instances. A few plants cause extreme skin irritation, or dermatitis, when touched.

HOW TO AVOID PLANT POISONING

- Become familiar with dangerous plants in the home and garden and know them by name. Be pro-active. If unsure of whether or not a plant around your facility is poisonous, check with your nurseryman, the agricultural extension service, or local botanic gardens.

- Teach young children to keep plants and plant parts out of their mouths. Keep all plants, seeds, fruits, and bulbs away from infants.

- Teach children to recognize poison ivy and other dermatitis-causing plants.

- Do not allow children to make "tea" from leaves or suck nectar from flowers.

- Do not rely on pets, birds, squirrels, or other animals to indicate non-poisonous plants.

- Do not eat wild plants, including mushrooms, unless positive of identification.

491

- Label garden seeds and bulbs and store out of reach of children.
- Be careful of jewelry made from seeds or beans.
- As a general precaution, avoid plants with milky or colored juices, all unknown red or white berries, all bulbs lacking the smell of onion or garlic.
- If plant poisoning occurs, or is suspected, immediately call a poison control center, physician, or hospital.

IN CASE OF EMERGENCY

EMERGENCY POISON CONTROL CENTER PHONE NUMBER

(800) 222-1222

Be prepared to provide the following information:

1. Name of the plant, if known?
2. What parts and how much were eaten?
3. How long ago was it eaten?
4. Age of individual?
5. Symptoms observed?
6. A good description of the plant. Save the specimen for identification by a plant taxonomist at a local university.

Additional emergency phone numbers are given in *Garden Care – Pests and Diseases.*

PLANTS WITH TOXIC PROPERTIES

PLANTS CAUSING SKIN IRRITATION OR DERMATITIS

Bull nettle, buffalobur nightshade (*Solanum rostratum*)

Spurge Nettle, Finger Rot, Tread Softly (*Cnidoscolus stimulosus*)

Poison ivy (*Toxicondendron radicans* or *Rhus radicans*)

Poison oak (*Toxicondendron diversilobum* or *Rhus diversiloba*)

Poison sumac (*Toxicondendron vernix* or *Rhus vernix*)

Spotted spurge (*Euphorbia maculata*)

Trumpet creeper (*Campsis radicans*)

Wood nettle (*Laportea canadensis*)

PLANTS CAUSING INTERNAL POISONING TO VARIOUS DEGREES UPON INGESTION

House Plants

All bulbs lacking the smell of onion or garlic

Castor Bean

Dumb cane (*Dieffenbachia*) leaves

Elephant's-ear

Jerusalem Cherry

Lantana

Mistletoe berries

Monstera leaves

Oleander roots, leaves, berries

Philodendron leaves

Poinsettia milky sap

Vegetable Garden

Potato (all parts except tuber)

Rhubarb

Tomato (*Lycopersicon esculentum*) stems and leaves

Flower Garden

Angel's-trumpet (*Brugmansia* and *Datura*)

Cardinal flower (*Lobelia cardinalis*) all parts

Foxglove

Lantana (*Lantana camara*) unripe fruits

Larkspur

Lobelia (*Lobelia* spp.) all parts

Madagascar periwinkle (*Catharanthus roseus*) all parts

Bulbs

All bulbs lacking the smell of onion or garlic

Caladium (*Caladium* spp.) all parts

Field Plants and Wildflowers

Buttercup

Castor bean (*Ricinus communis*) seeds

Death Cap (Mushroom or Toadstool)

Jimsonweed (*Datura stramonium*) all parts

Mayapple

Poison Ivy

493

Poison Oak

Poison Sumac

Pokeweed (*Phytolacca americana*) all mature parts

Snow-on-the-mountain

Vines

English ivy (*Hedera helix*) all parts

Hyacinth bean (*Dolichos lablab*) pods and seeds

Morning-glory

Peppervine (*Ampelopsis arborea*) caution with berries

Porcelain berry vine (*Ampelopsis brevipedunculata*) caution with berries

Sweet Peas (*Lathyrus* spp.) seeds

Trumpet creeper, Trumpet Vine (*Campsis radicans*)

Vetchling (*Lathyrus* spp.) seeds

Virginia creeper (*Parthenocissus quinquefolia*) berries

Wisteria (*Wisteria* spp.) seeds

Yellow Allamanda, Yellow Trumpet Vine (*Allamanda cathartica*) all parts

Yellow Jessamine (*Gelsemium sempervirens*) all parts

Shrubs

Azalea (*Rhododendron* spp.) all parts

Boxwood (*Buxus* spp.) Leaves

Buckeye

Elderberry, Black Elder

Heavenly bamboo (*Nandina domestica*) berries, potentially

Hollies (*Ilex* spp.) berries, when eaten in quantity

Hydrangea (*Hydrangea* spp.) bark, leaves, flower buds

Mountain laurel, Sheep-laurel, Lamb-kill (*Kalmia latifolia*) all parts

Oleander (*Nerium*) all parts

Privet

Rhododendron (*Rhododendron* spp.) all parts

Trees

Black locust (*Robinia pseudoacacia*) inner bark, twigs, young leaves, seeds

Dogwood

Golden-chain tree

Fruit Trees (seeds)

Apple

494

Apricot

Black cherry (*Prunus serotina*) all parts, except ripe fruit flesh

Cherry

Mulberry (*Morus* spp.) unripe fruits and milky sap

Peach

Plum

GLOSSARY OF BOTANICAL TERMS

acanth (a-*kanth*): spiny, spiky or thorny

-aceae (ay-*se*-ee): family; suffix indicates botanical family

acu (ak-*yew*): sharply pointed

aden (*aid*-en): sticky

adsurgens (ad-*ser*-jens): pushing straight upward

aeneus (*ee*-neus): of a bronze color

aggregatus (ag-gre-*ga*-tus): clustered

alatus (a-*lay*-tus): winged

alb-, albi-, albo-, albus (*al*-bo): white

albiplenus (al-bee-*plee*-nus): double white flowered

alpinus (al-*pi*-nus): above timberline

alternifolius (al-ter-ni-*foe*-lius): with alternate leaves

altus (*al*-tus): tall

americanus (am-er-*ikon*-us): American

amurensis (am-oor-*en*-sis): of Amur River area in eastern Asia

angustifolius (an-*gus*-ti-*fo*-lius): narrow-leaved

anosmus (a-*nos*-mus): lacking scent

apodus (a-*pod*-us): having flowers without a stalk

aquaticus (ak-*wa*-ti-kus): growing in or near water

arenarius (a-ren-*arr*-ius): growing in sandy places

argenteus (ar-*jen*-ti-us): silvery

ater-, atra-, atrum- (*ay*-ter): dead, black

atlanticus (at-*lan*-ti-kus): of Atlantic regions

atro- (*at*-ro): dark

aurantiacus (aw-*ran*-ty-*ak*-us): orange colored

aureo- (*aw*-reo): golden

australis (aw-*stral*-is): southern

baccatus (*bak*-ay-tus): fleshy, berried

bellus (*bell*-us): handsome

biennis (by-*enn*-is): biennial, living two years

botryoides (bot-*ri*-oy-deez): resembling a bunch of grapes

brachy (*brack*-i): short
bullatus (bul-*ay*-tus): puckered

caeruleus (see-*rool*-eus): dark blue
calcicola (kal-*kik*-o-la): growing in limey soil
calla (*kal*-la): beautiful
callicarpus (kal-i-*karp*-us): with beautiful fruit
camellia (kam-*ell*-ia): pronunciation preferred
campanulatus (kam-*pan*-ew-*lay*-tus): bell-shaped
canadensis (kan-a-*den*-sis): of North America or Canada
canescens (kan-*ess*-ens): downy, gray
cardiopetalus (kar-dio-*pet*-a-lus): with heart-shaped petals
cernuus (ser-*new*-us): nodding, drooping
chinensis (chy-*nen*-sis): Chinese
chrysanthus (kris-*anth*-us): golden-flowered
ciliatus (sil-i-*ay*-tus): hairy-fringed or -margined
coccineus (kok-*sin*-eus): scarlet
columnaris (kol-um-*nar*-is): columnar
compactus (kom-*pak*-tus): compact
coniferous (ko-*nif*-er-us): cone-bearing
contortus (kon-*tort*-us): twisted
cornutus (kor-*newt*-tus): horned
crenatus (kree-*nay*-tus): scalloped

dasy- (*das*-i-): thick
deciduous (de-*szed*-yew-us): with parts falling such as leaves
dentatus (den-*tay*-tus): toothed
dioecious (dy-*oi*-kus): having male and female flowers on separate plants
diurnus (dy-*urn*-us): day-flowering
divaricatus (dy-var-i-*ka*-tus): straggling or spreading

echinatus (ek-in-*ay*-tus): covered with prickles
elatus (el-*lay*-tus): tall
erythro (er-*rith*-ro): red
exoticus (ex-*ot*-i-kus): foreign, not native

498

fastigiatus (fas-tij-i-*ay*-tus): growing like a column

fili (filly): thread-like

flavus (*flay*-vus): yellow

flore-pleno (*flor*-e-*plee*-no): with double flowers

floribundus (*flor*-i-*bund*-us): flowering profusely

florida (*flor*-i-da): flowering

foetidus (*fe*-tid-us): bad smelling

formosus (for-*mo*-sus): handsome, beautiful

Forsythia popularly (for-*sith*-ia), preferably (for-*sigh*-thia): early-blooming shrub
 with bright yellow flowers and loose, arching habit.

fragrans (*fray*-grans): fragrant

fructescens (fruk-*tess*-ens): fruit-bearing

frutescens (frew-*tess*-ens): shrubby or bushy

fulvus (*ful*-vus): tawny orange

glaber, glabra, glabrum (*glay*-ber, *glab*-ra): smooth

glaucus, glauca (*glaw*-kus): covered with grayish, powdery coating

gloriosus (glor-i-*o*-sus): superb

gracilis (gra-*sill*-is): slender, graceful

grandis (*grand*-is): big, showy

guttatus (gu-*tay*-tus): spotted, speckled

gypsophila (jip-*soff*-ila): baby's breath

haemanthus (heem-*an*-thus): with blood red flowers

helix, properly (*hell*-ix), often (*he*-lix): twining

herbaceous (her-*bay*-shus): not woody

heter-, hetero- (*het*-er-o): diverse

hirsutus, hirsute (her-*su*-tus): hairy

humilis (*hew*-mil-is) or (hew-*mil*-is): low-growing, dwarf

hyacinthus (hy-a-*sin*-thus): dark, purplish blue

ibericus (eye-*ber*-i-kus): Spanish, Portuguese

ilicifolius (ill-*liss*-i-*fo*-lius): holly-leaved

imperialis (im-*peer*-i-*ay*-lis): fine or showy

indicus (*in*-di-kus): of India

insignis (in-*sig*-nis): remarkable, outstanding

japonicus (ja-*pon*-i-kus): Japanese

kaempferi (kamp-*fer*-eye): varietal name of azalea

Kalanchoe (ka-*lan*-cho-ee): Chinese succulent

kousa (*koo*-sa): Japanese dogwood species, *Cornus kousa*

labiautus (lab-i-*ah*-utus): lipped

lactatus (lak-*ta*-tus): milky

lancifolius (lan-see-*fo*-lius): lance-leaved

latifolius (lat-i-*fo*-lius): broad-leaved

leuco- (*lew*-ko): signifies white

longifolius (lon-ji-*fo*-lius): long-leaved

luteus (lew-*te*-us): yellow

macro- (*mak*-ro): large or long

maculatus (*mak*-yew-*lat*-tus): spotted

majalis (ma-*ja*-lis): May flowering

mega- (*meg*-ga): big

micro- (*mike*-row): small

mollis (*moll*-is): soft or with soft hairs

nanus, nana (*na*-nus): small, dwarf

Narcissus (nar-*sis*-us): daffodil

niger (ny-*jer*): black

nivalis (niv-*ay*-lis): snow white or growing near snow

nudus (*new*-dus): naked, bare

obtusus (ob-tuz-sus): blunt

occidentalis (oxi-dent-*tah*-lis): of the Western world, as opposed to orientalis.

odoratus (o-do-*ray*-tus): fragrant

officinalis (o-*fiss*-in-ay-lis): medicinal or useful

ortho- (*or*-thow): upright, straight

500

pallens (*pal*-ens): pale

palustris (pal-*us*-tris): marsh-loving

paniculatus (pan-ik-yew-*la*-tus): with flowers arranged in panicles

parvus (*par*-vus): small

patens (*pay*-tens): spreading

pedatus (pee-*day*-tus): like a bird's foot

pennatus (pen-*nay*-tus): feathered

penta- (*pen*-tah): five

phlogiflorus (flog-i-*flo*-rus): flame-colored flowers or phlox-like flowers

pilosus (py-*lo*-sus): covered with long soft hairs

platy- (*plat*-ee): flat or broad

plenus (*plee*-nus): full, double

poly- (*poll*-ee): many

praecox (*pree*-cocks): very early

Pteris (*teer*-is): feathery fronds

pubens (*pew*-bens): downy

pungens (*pun*-jens): sharp-pointed

quercifolius, quercifolia (kwer-si-*fo*-lius): with leaves like an oak

racemosus, racemosa (ras-see-*mo*-sus): bearing flowers on a short stem connected to a longer stem

radicans (rad-i-*kans*): having rooted stem

recurvus, recurva (ree-*kur*-vus): curved backward

repens, reptans (*rep*-pens, *rep*-tanz): creeping

reticulates, reticulata (ree-tik-yew-*lay*-tus): netted, net-veined

rotundus (ro-*tun*-dus): rounded

rubens (*roo*-bens): red or ruddy

sanguineus (sang-*win*-eus): blood red

sativus, sativa (sat-*ty*-vus): cultivated

scandens (*skan*-dens): climbing

sempervirens (*sem*-per-*vir*-rens): evergreen

sept-, septo- (*sept*): seven

serratus, serrata (ser-*ray*-tus): saw-toothed

sessilis, sessile (*sess*-il-is): stalkless

501

sylvestris, sylvestris (sil-*vest*-tris): growing in woods

sinensis (sin-*nen*-sis): of China

speciosus (*spess*-i-*o*-sus): showy

spectabilis (spek-ta-*bil*-is): spectacular

splendens (*splen*-dens): splendid

stellaris (stel-*lar*-ris): starry

standard – a: a shrub or herb grown with an erect main stem so that it forms or resembles a tree, or
   b: a fruit tree grafted on a stock that does not induce dwarfing.

steno- (*sten*-no): narrow

strepto-(*strep*-toe): twisted

striatus, striatum (stry-*ay*-tus): striped

suffrutescens (suf-froo-*tess*-ens): somewhat shrubby

sylvaticus (sil-*vat*-i-kus): of woods and forests

tenuis (*ten*-yew-is): slender, thin

tetra- (*tet*-tra): four

tinctorius, tinctoria (tink-*tor*-ius): pigment or tincture used in dying

tomentosus, tomentosum, tomentosa (to-men-*to*-sus): densely wooly

tri-(*try*): three

tuberosus (tew-ber-*o*-sus): having a thick, fleshy rootstock; tuberous

umbellatus, umbellate, umbellatum (um-bell-*ay*-tus): umbrella-like

variegatus, variegatum, variegata (vair-re-*gah*-tus): irregularly colored

vegetatus (vej-et-*tah*-tus): vigorous

vernus, vernum (*ver*-nus): of spring

versicolor (*verz*-si-kolor): variously colored

virens (*vy*-rens): green

vulgaris (vul-*gar*-ris): common

xanthinus, xantho- (zan-*thin*-nus): yellow

REFERENCES

American Daffodil Society: *Daffodils to Show and Grow.* Tyner, NC: The American Daffodil Society, 1980.

American Hydrangea Society. "New Hydrangeas in the News". <http://www.americanhydrangeasociety.org/new_hydrangeas.html>, December, 15, 2005.

American Iris Society. *What Every Iris Grower Should Know,* n. p.: The American Iris Society, 1969.

Antique Rose Emporium catalog. 9300 Lueckemeyer Road, Brenham, Texas 77833. Phone: (800-441-0002). <http://www.weAREroses.com).

Answers.com. "Chrysanthemum". <http://www.answers.com/topic/chrysanthemum>, June 22, 2006.

Armitage, Allan M. *Herbaceous Perennial Plants.* Illinois: Stipes Publishing, L.L.C., 1997.

Asiatica Nursery: International Rare Plant Resource catalog. P. O. Box 270, Lewisberry, Pennsylvania 17339. Phone: (717-938-8677). <http://www.asiaticanursery.com>.

Bailey, H. L., Hortorium, Cornell University. *Hortus Third.* New York: Macmillan, 1976.

Baumgardt, J. P. *How to Prune Almost Everything.* New York: Wm. Morrow, 1968.

Beatty, V. *Consumer Guide Rating and Raising Indoor Plants.* Skokie, IL: Consumer Guide/Publications, 1975.

Bender, Steve and Rushing, Felder. *Passalong Plants.* University of North Carolina Press, Chapel Hill, 1993.

Bluestone Perennials Nursery catalog. 7211 Middle Ridge Road, Madison, Ohio 44057. Phone: (800-852-5243). <http://www.bluestoneperennials.com>.

Brent and Becky's Bulbs catalog. 7900 Daffodil Lane, Gloucester, Virginia 23061. Phone: (toll-free 877-661-2852). <http://www.brentandbeckysbulbs.com>.

Brooklyn Botanic Gardens. *Handbook on Dwarfed Potted Trees.* Brooklyn: Brooklyn Botanic Gardens, 1959.

Bush-Brown, L. and Bush-Brown, J. *America's Garden Book.* New York: Scribners, 1955.

Chaplin, Lois Trigg. *The Southern Gardener's Book of Lists The best plants for all your needs, wants, and whims.* Lanham, Maryland: Taylor Trade Publishing, 1994.

Childs, Jim. "The Secret to Long-Lasting Color – Deadheading." *Garden Gate Magazine.* August 2005: 26–29.

Cobb, Broughton. *The Field Guide to the Fern.* Boston: Houghton Mifflin, 1956.

503

Crockett, J. U. *The Time-Life Encyclopedia of Gardening*. New York: Time-Life Books, 1978.

Dave's Garden reference website, <http://www.davesgarden.com>.

Dean, B. E. *Trees and Shrubs in the Heart of Dixie*. Birmingham: Southern University Press, 1968.

De Long, Eric, compiler. Chemung County, 11.01, rev. 3.04, S. Reiners. Cornell Cooperative Extension, Chemung County. "Fertilizing Garden Soils." n. d. <http: //www.gardening.cornell.edu/factsheets/soil/fertilizing.PDF.>, December 27, 2005.

Dirr, Michael A. *Dirr's Hardy Trees and Shrubs*. Portland, Oregon: Timber Press, Inc., 1997.

Dirr, Michael A. *Manual of Landscape Woody Plants*. Champaign, Illinois: Stipes Publishing, L.L.C., 1998.

DiSabato-Aust, Tracy. *The Well-designed Mixed Garden: Building Beds and Borders with Trees, Shrubs, Perennials, Annuals, and Bulbs*. Portland: Timber Press, 2003.

DiSabato-Aust, Tracy. *The Well-tended Perennial Garden: Planting and Pruning Techniques*. Portland: Timber Press, 2006.

Dutch Gardens catalog. 144 Intervale Road, Burlington, Vermont 05401. Phone: (800-944-2250). <http://www.dutchgardens.com>.

Evans, Erv. "Bearded Iris for the Home Landscape". North Carolina State University Horticulture Information Leaflets; revised 7/98 HIL-8506. <http://www.ces.ncsu.edu/depts./hort/hil/hil-8506.html>, May 15, 2006.

Evans, Erv. "Trees: Selecting Plants". North Carolina State University Consumer Horticulture, 2000. <http://www.ces.ncsu.edu/depts./hort/consumer/factsheets/trees-new/text/selecting_plants.html> January 7, 2006.

Fell. Derek. *Annuals: How to Select, Grow and Enjoy*. Tucson, Arizona: H P Books, 1983.

Free, Montague. *Plant Pruning in Pictures*. New York: Doubleday, 1961.

Great Plant Company catalog. P. O. Box 1041, New Hartford, Connecticut 06057. Phone: (800-441-9788). <http://www.greatplants.com>.

Hales, Mick. *Gardens Around the World: 365 Days*. Harry N. Abrams, Inc. Publisher, New York, 2004

Harper, Pamela J. *Time-Tested Plants: Thirty Years in a Four Season Garden*. Portland, Oregon: Timber Press, Inc., 2000.

Hawkes, A. D. *Orchids*. New York: Harper & Row, 1961.

Heronswood Nursery catalog, 300 Park Ave., Warminster, PA 18974. Phone (877-674-4714). < http://www.heronswood.com>.

Jackson & Perkins Company catalog. 81 Rose Lane, Medford, Oregon 97501. Phone: (800-292-4769). <http://www.jacksonandperkins.com>.

Johnson, H. *The International Book of Trees.* New York: Bonanza Books, 1973.

Julien, Don. "Much Ado About pH". American Rose Society. First published in *Rose Petals,* October, 1998, newsletter of the Seattle Rose Society. <http://www.ars.org/ About_Roses/soil-ph.htm>.

Lacy, Allen. *In a Green Shade – Writings From Homeground.* Houghton Mifflin Co. New York, 2000.

Lannotti, Marie. "Amending Your Garden Soil – Making Good Soil Out of Bad." About.com: Gardening, n.d., <http://gardening.about.com/od/gardenprimer/a/ Amending_Soil_2.htm> June 22, 2005.

Lannotti, Marie. "Viburnums: Flowering Shrubs for the Landscape and the Birds." About.com: Gardening, n.d., <http://gardening.about.com/od/treesshrubs/d/ Viburnums.htm> August 1, 2005.

Lazy SS Farm Nursery catalog. 2360 Spottswood Trail, Barboursville, Virginia 22923. Phone: (contact by e-mail). <http://www.lazyssfarm.com>.

Lee, F. P. *The Azalea Book.* New York: Van Nostrand, 1965.

Lenden, Joanne. *Flowers for Bouquets–Conditioning Plant Material for Flower Arranging.* 223 Westchester Drive, Delmar, NY 12054. FAX: 518–439–2889 or email: Joanne@Lenden.com to order copies.

Logee's Greenhouses, Ltd. catalog. 141 North Street, Danielson, Connecticut 06239-1939. Phone: (888-330-8038). <http://www.logees.com>.

LilyBLOOMS Aquatic Garden's website. North Canton, Ohio. Phone: (800-921-0005). <http://www.lilyblooms.com>.

Long, Elizabeth, A. "Identifying Problems of Garden Flowers". University of Tennessee Agricultural Extension Service Publication SP 370-K, May 2002. <http://www.utextension.utk.edu/publications/spfiles/SP370K.pdf> June 5, 2005.

Monrovia Nursery Company website. Several wholesale-to-the-trade and propagation nurseries, but company is based in Asuza, California. <http://www.monrovia.com>.

Naka, J. K. vol. I, 1975; vol. II, *Bonsai Techniques I and II.* Santa Monica: Dennis-Landman, 1982.

Peterson, Roger Tory, and McKenny, M. *A Field Guide to Wildflowers.* Boston: Houghton Mifflin, 1968.

Petrides, G. A. *A Field Guide to Trees and Shrubs.* Boston: Houghton Mifflin, 1958.

Plant Delights Nursery, Inc. catalog. Juniper Level Botanic Garden, 9241 Sauls Road, Raleigh, North Carolina 27603. Phone: (919-772-4794). <http://www.plantdelights.com>.

Powell, M. A. "Residential Landscaping". Publication AG-248. North Carolina Cooperative Extension Service, NorthCarolina State University. <http://ipm.ncsu.edu/urban/horticulture/res_landscaping.html>.

Probst, Darrell. "The Epimedium Page". <http://home.earthlink.net/~darrellpro/>.

Reader's Digest. *Complete Book of the Garden.* Pleasantville, NY: Reader's Digest Association, 1979.

Rickett, Harold William. *Wildflowers of the United States.* New York: McGraw-Hill, n.d.

Rockwell, FF. and Grayson, Esther C. *The Complete Book of Bulbs.* Doubleday, New York. Copyright – Joanne Lenden 2004. To order contact joanne@lenden.com.

Seymour, E. L. D. *The Wise Garden Encyclopedia.* Union City, NJ: W. H. Wise & Co., 1970.

Shaver, J. M. *Ferns of Tennessee.* Nashville: George Peabody College, 1954.

Smith, A. W. *A Gardener's Book of Plant Names.* New York: Harper & Row, 1963.

Smith, Arlo I. *A Guide to Wildflowers of the Mid-South.* Memphis: The Press of Mid-America, 1979.

Smith, Kevin E., compiler. "Physiography of Tennessee". Tennessee Archaeology Net. <http://www.mtsu.edu/~kesmith/TNARCHNET/physio.html>.

Smith, P. Allen. *Container Gardens.* New York, NY: Clarkson Potter/ Publishers, 2005.

Spring Hill Nursery catalog. 110 West Elm Street, Tipp City, Ohio 45371-1699. Order Processing Center: P. O. Box 330, Harrison, Ohio 45030-0330. Phone: (513-354-1509). <http://www.springhillnursery.com>.

Stebbins, Robert L., and MacCaskey, Michael. *Pruning: How-To Guide for Gardeners.* Tucson, Arizona: H P Books, 1983.

Steffek, E. M. *Complete Book of Houseplants and Indoor Gardening.* New York: Crown Publishers, n.d.

Stokes Tropicals website. 4806 E. Old Spanish Trail, Jeanerette, LA 70544. Phone (337-365-6998). <http://www.stokestropicals.com>.

Sunset Books. *How to Grow Orchids.* Menlo Park, CA: Lane Publishing, 1979.

Sunshine Farm & Gardens: Rare and Exceptional Plants for the Discriminating Gardener and Collector website. Barry Glick, HC 67 Box 539B, Renick, West Virginia 24966. Phone: (304-497-2208). <http://www.sunfarm.com>.

Taylor, N. *Taylor's Encyclopedia of Gardening.* Boston: Houghton Mifflin, 1948.

Terra Nova Nurseries, Inc. website. Wholesale-to-the-trade and hybridization nursery. <http://www.terranovanurseries.com>.

William Tricker, Inc. website. America's oldest water garden and aquarium specialist. 7125 Tanglewood Drive, Independence, Ohio 44131. Phone: (800-524-3492). <http://www.trickeri.com>.

Tyson, R. *Growing Home Orchids.* New York: Van Nostrand, 1962.

United States National Arboretum. "Hydrangea Questions and Answers". Updated 9/28/2005. <http://www.usna.usda.gov/Gardens/faqs/hydrangeafaq2.html>, July 17, 2006.

Van Bourgondien Nursery catalog. P. O. Box 2000, Virginia Beach, Virginia 23450-2000. Phone: (800-622-9959). <http://www.bulblady.com>.

Van Engelen Inc. bulb catalog. Also known as John Scheepers, Inc. 23 Tulip Drive, P. O. Box 638, Bantam, Connecticut 06750-0638. Phone: (860-567-8734 or 860-567-0838). <http://www.vanengelen.com>.

Wasowski, Sally. *Gardening With Native Plants of the South.* Dallas: Taylor Publishing Co., 1994.

Wayside Gardens catalog. 1 Garden Lane, Hodges, South Carolina 29695-0001. Phone: (800-845-1124). <http://www.waysidegardens.com>.

Weinstein, Mobee. "At Home With Ferns". Brooklyn Botanic Garden. <http://www.bbg.org/gar2/topics/indoor/handbooks/landscaping/ferns.html> January 20, 2006.

Welsh, Douglas F. and Janne, Everett. "Follow Proper Pruning Techniques". <http //aggie-horticulture.tama.edu/extension/pruning/pruning.html.> March 22, 2006.

Wigginton, B. E. *Trees and Shrubs for the Southeast.* Athens: University of Georgia Press, 1963.

White Flower Farm catalog. P. O. Box 50, Litchfield, Connecticut 06759-0050. Phone: (800-503-9624). <http://www.whiteflowerfarm.com>.

Wilkerson Mill Gardens catalog. 9595 Wilkerson Mill Road, Palmetto, Georgia 30268. Phone: (770-463-2400). <http://www.hydrangea.com).

Wilson, Jim. *Bulletproof Flowers for the South.* Dallas: Taylor Publishing Company, 1999.

Yucca Do Nursery, Inc. catalog/website. Specializing in drought- and heat-tolerant plants. FM 359 @ FM 3346, P.O. Box 907, Hempstead, Texas 77445. Phone: (979-826-4580). <http://www.yuccado.com>.

The AMERICAN HORTICULTURAL SOCIETY is the headquarters for all plant societies. For further information see <http://www.ahs.org.>

INDEX OF SCIENTIFIC NAMES

509

513

517

520

521

INDEX OF COMMON NAMES AND GENERAL SUBJECTS

529

531

534

537

542

543

547

NOTES

NOTES

NOTES

NOTES

NOTES

NOTES

NOTES

NOTES

NOTES

hydrangeas - all exc. oak leaf - white & colors
lily vally
peonies
box
holly like box
hollyhocks - single
foxglove
gardenia 2 in back
hosta
viburnum - snowball
rose - ? no tea only shrub
butterfly bush
vitex

NO
  azalea, nandina, crepe myrtle?
  magndia